Keyboard Shortcuts for QuickBooks

To produce dates...	Press
Increase date by one day	+
Decrease date by one day	-
Today	t
First day of week	w
Last day of week	k
First day of month	m
Last day of month	h
First day of year	y
Last day of year	r
Display date calendar	Alt+down arrow

To edit text...	Press these keys...
Copy selected characters	Ctrl+c
Cut selected characters	Ctrl+x
Decrease check or form number by one	-
Delete character to left of insertion point	Bksp
Delete character to right of insertion point	Del
Delete line	Ctrl+Del
Edit current transaction in register	Ctrl+E
Increase check or form number by one	+
Insert line	Ctrl+Ins
Paste cut or copied characters	Ctrl+v
Undo changes made	Ctrl+z

While using dialog boxes or forms...	Press these keys...
Close window	Esc
Display help	F1
Move across one word at a time in field	Ctrl+right arrow
Move across report columns to left	Left arrow
Move across report columns to right	Right arrow
Move back to previous word in field	Ctrl+left arrow
Move down one line on form or report	Down arrow

continues...

...continued

While using dialog boxes or forms...	Press these keys...
Move down one screen in report	Page down
Move to beginning of current field or row	Home
Move to end of current field or row	End
Move to first item on list or previous month in register	Ctrl+page up
Move to last item on list or next month in register	Ctrl+page down
Move to next option or topic	Tab
Move to previous option or topic	Shift+Tab
Move up one line on form or report	Up arrow
Move up one screen in report	Page up

To perform QuickBooks activities...	Press these keys...
Quickfill and Recall (type first few letters of name and press Tab – rest of name fills in)	*abc* + Tab
Display account list	Ctrl+a
Delete current check, invoice, transaction, or item from list	Ctrl+d
Edit list or register	Ctrl+e
Find transaction	Ctrl+f
Hide/show Qcards	Ctrl+F1
Go to register of transfer account	Ctrl+g
Show history of accounts receivable or accounts payable transaction	Ctrl+h
Create invoice	Ctrl+I
Display Customer:Job list	Ctrl+j
Display list for current field	Ctrl+l
Memorize transaction or report	Ctrl+m
Create new invoice, bill, check, or list item	Ctrl+n
Copy transaction in register	Ctrl+o
Print	Ctrl+p
QuickReport of transaction or list item	Ctrl+q
Display memorized transaction list	Ctrl+t
Display register	Ctrl+u
Display transaction journal	Ctrl+v
Write check	Ctrl+w
QuickZoom on report	Enter
Display QuickBooks overview	F2

Using
QuickBooks®
&
QuickBooks®
Pro Version
6.0

Gail Perry

que®

A Division of Macmillan Computer Publishing, USA
201 W. 103rd Street
Indianapolis, Indiana 46290

Contents at a Glance

Using QuickBooks & QuickBooks Pro Version 6.0

Library of Congress Catalog No.:98-84560

ISBN: 0-7897-1660-7

99 98   6 5 4 3 2 1

Interpretation of the printing code: The rightmost double-digit number is the year of the book's printing; the rightmost single-digit number, the number of the book's printing. For example, a printing code of 98-1 shows that the first printing of the book occurred in 1998.

Composed in Janson Text by Macmillan Computer Publishing.

Printed in the United States of America.

Trademarks

Executive Editor
Karen Reinisch

Acquisitions Editor
Renee Wilmeth

Development Editor
Nancy Warner

Technical Editor
David Garrett

Managing Editor
Thomas F. Hayes

Project Editor
Sossity Smith

Copy Editors
Kelli Brooks
Barbara Hacha
Shannon Martin
Malinda McCain
Tom Stevens

Indexer
Becky Hornyak

Book Designers
Nathan Clement
Ruth Harvey

Cover Designers
Dan Armstrong
Ruth Harvey

Production Team
Betsy Deeter
Lisa England
Becky Stutzman

Contents

About the Authors

Gail Perry is a CPA and is a graduate of Indiana University. She has worked in public accounting for over 20 years and has spent that time helping her clients make the best use of the tax laws and accounting rules that benefit them. Gail is a former senior tax consultant with the international CPA firm of Deloitte and Touche, where she specialized in providing tax planning services and advice to small businesses.

Gail is the author of over a dozen books including *The Complete Idiot's Guide to Doing Your Income Taxes*, and *Using Quicken 5 for Windows*. She is a columnist for *The Indianapolis Star* where she fields tax questions on a weekly basis.

In addition, Gail has been an instructor of computer education since 1985 and currently teaches classes in QuickBooks for the Indiana CPA Society.

Dedication

To Katherine and Georgia, who constantly remind me that I have a life beyond the computer keyboard.

Acknowledgments

Special thanks to the great crew at Macmillan Computer Publishing who worked long hours, including weekends and nights (did any of us actually sleep?) to get this book out on time. I particularly want to thank Renee Wilmeth, Nancy Warner, and David Garrett who worked so hard to make sure this book would be the excellent resource that it is. Thanks also to Winston Steward for his contributions to the original manuscript. I also want to thank Rick Pranitis, who continuously made sure my computer could keep pace with my flying fingers, and whose constant encouragement keeps me going.

We'd Like to Hear from You!

Que Corporation has a long-standing reputation for high-quality books and products. To ensure your continued satisfaction, we also understand the importance of customer service and support.

Tech Support

If you need assistance with the information in this book or you have feedback for us about the book, please contact Macmillan Technical Support by phone at 317-581-3833 or via email at support@mcp.com.

Orders, Catalogs, and Customer Service

To order other Que or Macmillan Computer Publishing books, catalogs, or products, please contact our Customer Service Department:

Phone: 1-800-858-7674

Fax: 1-800-835-3202

International Fax: 1-317-228-4400

Or visit our online bookstore: http://www.mcp.com/.

Introduction

Welcome to *Using QuickBooks 6.0 and QuickBooks Pro 6.0*

This book is the most comprehensive and useful reference available for QuickBooks 6, an Intuit program. With this book you will learn how to put the nation's number one selling business accounting software program to work for you, how to keep track of all the financial activity of your business, and how to produce useful information that will help you with budgeting, planning for the future, and meeting important deadlines such as tax return filing dates, financial statement reporting dates, and so on.

Having learned to do bookkeeping on a manual system—using large ledger pages and lots of erasers—I have a vast appreciation for many of the important timesaving elements of this program.

With QuickBooks you can:

- Produce professional-looking financial statements and reports and be assured of their accuracy
- Quickly customize and revise reports to include just the information you need
- Produce reports for any time period you like
- Easily compare data from one year to the next
- Prepare tax forms
- Create a budget and monitor your performance
- Cross-reference numbers on reports to the documents where the original numbers were entered

This is just a short list of the major changes you will see when moving to a computerized program. The section below presents you with a sample of all of the day-to-day transactions you will be able to perform, effortlessly, with QuickBooks.

Using QuickBooks Every Day

Whether you enter your business transactions daily, or catch up on a weekly or less-frequent basis, depends on many factors. Some of these factors are how many transactions you have, how organized you are, how much time you have to devote to computer data entry, and how important it is to you to have up-to-the-minute reports at your fingertips.

Just look what you will be able to do, as frequently as you like, with QuickBooks at your side:

- *Create and maintain a Customer list.* You can keep an up-to-date list of all your customers: name, address, shipping address, phone, email, fax, contact name, favorite color (Really! You can save any type of information you like!), not to mention accounting type information like the terms you usually apply to a particular customer's order, and whether or not the customer is subject to sales tax.

- *Create and maintain a Vendor list.* Keep information handy on all of your vendors: name, address, phone, fax, email, contact name, your account number, hours of business, items you normally order from each vendor.

- *Write and print checks.* Enter checks on an onscreen form that look just like your own checks, then print the checks on actual check forms. All you have to do is sign the check! Check amounts are automatically deducted from your bank account balance and charged to the appropriate expense account.

- *Write and print invoices.* Prepare invoices for your customers on an onscreen form that looks just like a real invoice. If you prepare estimates in QuickBooks Pro, you can generate invoices right from the estimates. Print the invoice on a form you design yourself—one that conforms to your own business needs.

- *Write and print purchase orders.* Fill out a purchase order onscreen, entering the items you want to purchase. Choose a vendor name and the address fills in automatically. Print the purchase order on a form you design yourself (or use one of the standard forms that come with QuickBooks).

- *Reconcile your checking account.* All right, so you probably won't do this one every day—but when you're ready to reconcile, the process is easier than you can imagine. Just check off every check and deposit that appear on your bank statement, and you're finished!

- *Record payments from your customers.* Enter amounts received from your customers by simply checking off items from a list of amounts owed to you. Your accounts receivable balance is updated automatically.

- *Enter and pay bills from vendors.* Update your accounts payable immediately as you enter each bill you receive. Cross-check bills against purchase orders and records of merchandise received. Then make bill payments by checking off which bills you wish to pay. Checks are prepared automatically.

- *Create and print numerous reports.* Use the standard reports that come with QuickBooks—reports for nearly every situation—or customize your own reports to reflect just the activity you want to show. Prepare Quick Reports with a simple mouse click, displaying the detail behind the numbers on your reports or showing all the activity for any one of your customers or vendors.

- *Create a budget.* Use QuickBooks to style a budget that will help you stay in touch with your company's potential. Know how to plan the future performance of your company.

- *Generate payroll tax forms.* Prepare all your federal payroll tax forms in QuickBooks: Form 941, Form 940, W-2, W-3, and W-4.

- *Prepare income tax reports.* Create quarterly and annual reports to help you in the preparation of your business income tax returns. Export tax information to TurboTax software for computerized tax return preparation.

- *Use QuickBooks for more than one company.* You can keep records for as many companies as you like with a single copy of QuickBooks software.

- *Record separate financial activity for different locations of your business.* Use the Class feature of QuickBooks to identify separate divisions or locations of the same business. Then you can generate reports for each class individually or for the company as a whole.

- *Produce sales tax reports.* Always know how much you owe in sales tax by preparing a sales tax payable report.

- *Generate aging reports.* Find out how much is owed by your customers, and find out how much of that is overdue, by producing an aging report.

Conventions Used in This Book

With over a decade of experience writing and developing the most successful computer books available, Que has learned what special features help users the most. Look for these special features throughout *Using QuickBooks and QuickBooks Pro 6.0.*

Chapter Roadmaps

Each chapter begins with a roadmap, a list of topics that are covered in the chapter. This way, you can tell at a glance what you will find in each chapter.

Step-By-Steps

Step-By-Steps walk you through a process with numbered steps that don't leave out any instructions. Follow along with Step-By-Steps as you perform tasks at your own keyboard. Here's an example of a Step-By-Step:

Setting up a new income account

1. Make sure **Yes** is selected, then click on **Next**. The Adding an Income Account screen appears.

2. Enter the name of an income account you want to add (for example, Catering or Lumber Sales or Machine Rental).

3. Choose a tax line for the account if you plan to use QuickBooks to help you summarize information for your income tax return (as discussed in Chapter 31).

4. Click **Next** and you will see that your new income account has been added to the list of income accounts for the company.

SideNotes

SideNotes point out key features, warnings, real-world examples, technical, and non-essential, interesting information that you might not otherwise pick up from using the program. You can learn the program without reading the notes, but you'll find they will greatly enhance your experience with QuickBooks. The following are a few examples of SideNotes:

Can I open my QuickBooks report in another program?

You can print a report to a file instead of a printer. By doing so, you have the ability to open the file in another program (such as a spreadsheet program) and further manipulate the numbers. Choose **File, Print**, then click on **File**. Enter the name you want to give the file, then click **Print**.

Tip for setting up tax lines

Keep a copy of last year's tax return nearby to use as a reference for assigning tax lines. If this is the first year your company will file a tax return, use a blank tax form as a reference.

Warning: credit card statement date must fall on or before start date

You will get an error message if you try to enter a credit card statement date that falls after your start date. The implication is that there was a balance due on your start date that is not being properly reflected. If there was no balance due on your start date, go ahead and set up the credit card, entering zero in the Statement Ending Balance area. If you can't find the credit card statement from just prior to your start date, you can back into the amount that was on that statement by looking at the beginning balance on the first statement from after the start date.

See Alsos

Throughout the book you will find See Alsos, which are cross-references designed to take you to other places in the book that include information that may be helpful to the topic at hand. A See Also looks like this:

SEE ALSO

➢ *To memorize a report, see page 411*

In addition to the features listed above, there are several other conventions designed to help you find your way through the program.

Underlined Hot Keys, or Mnemonics

Just like an onscreen menu that contains underlined letters as keyboard alternatives to the mouse, the menu and screen references in this book contain underlined letters. To activate a feature using an underlined letter, press the **Alt** key, then press the underlined letter. You do not need to (and often should not) hold down the **Alt** key while pressing the underlined letter. For instance, to choose the **Next** button, press **Alt**, then press the letter **N**. The **N** does not need to be capitalized.

Shortcut Key Combinations

Shortcut key combinations are presented with plus signs joining the keys. For example, Ctrl+Z means hold down the Ctrl key, while you press the Z key.

Menu Commands

Instructions for choosing menu commands are presented like this:

Choose **Activities, Lists**

This example means open the **Activities** menu and select **Lists,** which in this case opens the box displaying all the types of lists for your company.

This book also has the following typeface enhancements to indicate special text, as indicated in the following table:

Typeface	Description
Italics	Italics are used to indicate new terminology.
Boldface	Bold is used to indicate the text you type or instructions you choose.
MYFILE.DOC	File names and directories are set in all capital letters to distinguish them from regular text.

Getting Started in QuickBooks

QuickBooks Overview

QuickBooks has many accounting capabilities for tracking the comings and goings of your business transactions

There are many changes in Version 6, the latest version of QuickBooks

Don't forget to back up your data—often!

Use QuickBooks Reminders to help you stay organized and on top of all your obligations

Welcome to Intuit's QuickBooks, a program designed for you and your business. QuickBooks is an accounting program that has been especially created for people who don't have a background in accounting. There is very little accounting jargon in the program, and the data entry screens have been created with actual business forms in mind. You'll find you don't have to learn new accounting or data entry techniques to take advantage of this program.

There are many aspects of operating a business that can be simplified and better understood with the help of QuickBooks and your computer. For example, QuickBooks will help you do all of these tasks:

- Keep records for your business
- Track sales activity
- Pay the people who work for you
- Produce reports about financial aspects of your business
- Learn more about your business
- Prepare and use budgets
- Plan for the future
- Prepare payroll tax forms
- Prepare job costing and estimates
- Prepare income tax forms
- Keep lists of customers and vendors
- Prepare form letters and mailing labels
- Keep track of separate locations and departments of the same company
- Bank and pay bills online

With this book, you will learn how to make all of the preceding tasks part of your regular routine.

QuickBooks and QuickBooks Pro

Which program should you purchase: QuickBooks or QuickBooks Pro? Both programs offer nearly the same features. Here are the features that are unique to QuickBooks Pro:

- **Time Tracking.** Use timesheets right on your computer to enter employee time and have it automatically flow to the payroll features. You can also associate time with jobs automatically and bill that time on your invoices. Create reports to help analyze how employees use their time by displaying employee time organized by job and type of activity.

- **Estimates and Bids.** Use QuickBooks Pro to keep track of bids you make on jobs, compare actual job costs to your estimates, revise estimates as the job progresses, and prepare various reports incorporating job estimates. Create invoices from your estimates, either billing for the entire estimate, particular items from the estimate, or a percentage of completion.

- **Advanced Job Costing.** Produce reports that display job progress and profitability, and classify the information on these reports by job, by type of service you provide, or by type of item you sell.

- **Multi-User Environment.** Up to five users can work with your QuickBooks Pro company file at one time. Levels of password protection are available so each user can have rights to different parts of the file.

If you don't keep track of separate jobs in your business, or if the time tracking features aren't important to you, then QuickBooks is the program you need. If the preceding features will be of use to you, you should consider QuickBooks Pro.

Network considerations

If you are running QuickBooks on a network, see Appendix B for special network considerations.

Changes in Version 6

The latest version of QuickBooks/QuickBooks Pro has several new features to offer:

- **Simultaneous multi-users.** Multiple users can access information at the same time in QuickBooks Pro version 6.0.

- **General and specific preferences.** You can have master preferences (see Chapter 22, "Setting Preferences") for all users of the program and individual preferences at the same time.

- **Greater restrictions.** Options for protecting sensitive data from prying eyes have been improved in this latest version (see Chapter 28, "Security").

- **Setup Wizard** for adding users. Adding new users is easier than before (see Appendix B, "Sharing QuickBooks on a Network").

- **Follow the trail.** You can keep track of who is making what changes to the company data (see Chapter 28).

- **Entering dates** is easier and faster (see Chapter 11, "Invoicing, Monthly Statements, and Accounts Receivable").

- **Improved sorting options** in the registers (see Chapter 15, "Purchase Orders, Accounts Payable, and Paying Bills").

- **Pop-up menus** with a right-mouse click (mentioned throughout the book).

- **More Web services** available, such as online banking and bill-paying (see Part V).

- **Set up online direct deposit** for employees (see Chapter 18, "Paying Employees and Contractors").

- **Improved handling of state and local payroll taxes** (see Chapter 19, "QuickBooks and Taxes").

- **Track withholding** for Advance Earned Income Credit (see Chapter 19).

- **Various new reports** throughout the program (see Chapter 21, "QuickBooks Reports and Graphs").

As you can see, there are plenty of changes and improvements in the program. If you are already a user of QuickBooks, you will surely find something of interest in the preceding list. If you are new to QuickBooks, then everything you see here will just seem like the most natural thing to you, because you don't need to know how the program ran before these features were added.

Turning On Your QuickBooks Program

If this is the first time you have used QuickBooks, you need to know how to get things started. After installing your program (see Appendix A for information about installation), you have the choice of running QuickBooks from the CD-ROM or from your hard drive.

Running QuickBooks from the CD-ROM

Starting your program when you have a QuickBooks CD-ROM is as simple as turning on the computer and placing the CD-ROM in the appropriate drive. The program starts automatically, and you should see the screen in Figure 1.1.

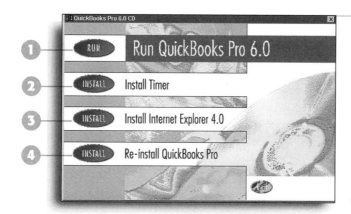

Running QuickBooks from Your Hard Drive

CD-ROM not available? You can still run your QuickBooks program. When you installed the program, a QuickBooks icon probably appeared on your desktop. Double-click the **QuickBooks** icon to start the program.

Enabling/disabling AutoPlay

If your computer does not automatically recognize a CD-ROM when it is inserted in the drive, it might be that the CD-ROM notification feature has been turned off. To turn on CD-ROM notification (or turn it off), click the **Start** button on your Windows 95 taskbar, then choose **Settings**, **Control Panel**, and double-click the **System** icon. Choose the **Device Manager** tab and click the plus sign next to CD-ROM. Click your CD-ROM, then click the **Properties** button. Click the **Settings** tab, then check (or uncheck, if turning this feature off) the box labeled: **Auto insert notification**. Click **OK** to save your settings and exit the box. Click **OK** again to close the System Properties box.

FIGURE 1.1

Inserting your QuickBooks CD-ROM in its drive produces this introductory screen.

1. Click here to start the QuickBooks program.

2. Click here if you are ready to install the QuickBooks Timer (available with QuickBooks Pro only).

3. Click here if you would like to install the Internet Explorer.

4. Click here if you need to install your program again.

Alternatively, click the **Start** button on the Windows 95 taskbar and choose **Programs, QuickBooks Pro**. The QuickBooks program group appears, where you can choose QuickBooks to start the QuickBooks program (see Figure 1.2), QuickBooks Help, or the QuickBooks Timer (if you have that installed).

FIGURE 1.2

Use the **Start** menu to get to your QuickBooks program.

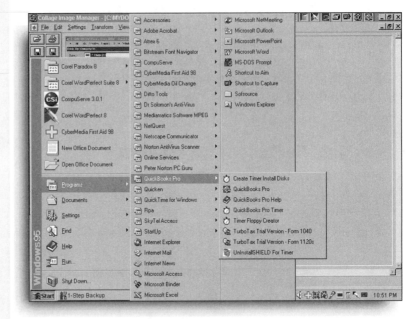

Backing Up Your Data

No doubt, you are anxious to get started with QuickBooks—setting up your company, entering your data, and taking advantage of all the useful forms and reports that QuickBooks will produce for you.

Before you begin, plan a backup schedule. When it comes to entering your company's precious financial data in a computer program, there is nothing more important than keeping backups of the information.

A wise person once said, "A computer that hasn't crashed is a computer that hasn't crashed *yet*." Computers break down, lightning sends its messengers into electrical circuitry, employees betray employers, viruses send ripples through your system, magnets erase or corrupt data stored on disks, and even unexplainable events occur that can cause computer or software failure. The advent of the paperless office may have eased up on our storage needs, but it has caused a new array of problems in the form of vulnerability of data.

Use some sort of backup device and use it frequently—at least every week. After all of your data is entered in QuickBooks, store a backup of your complete data file somewhere away from your business in a safe place in case there is a fire or some other serious damage to your place of business.

There are many ways you can back up your data. Choose the one that is easiest for you to use so that backing up won't be a burden. Here are just a few of the various backup techniques you might want to consider:

- Tape backup system
- Floppy disks
- External hard drive
- Zip drive

How to Back Up

To back up your data on to a disk, zip drive, or another hard drive, choose **File**, **Back Up**. The Back Up Company to... box appears, expecting you to choose a filename and disk drive to receive the backed up data (see Figure 1.3).

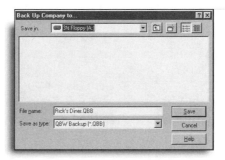

FIGURE 1.3

Not backing up at all is the only wrong method for backing up. Use this window if you want to choose a drive location and filename for your backup.

The backup feature is dim on the menu if you try to back up without any company file open.

Note that only one company file can be backed up at a time using the QuickBooks backup feature. If you are using QuickBooks to keep records for more than one company, you must open each company individually, then perform the backup steps.

The first time you use the File, Back Up feature, you will see a notice about Online-Backup. You can click **Yes** in the box that appears onscreen and be taken to the QuickBooks Web site where you can read more information about backing up to remote locations.

To back up your data using a tape backup system, follow the instructions that accompany the tape system. You do not need to use the backup command found in QuickBooks.

How to Restore

To restore your data from a disk, use the File, Restore command. The Restore From dialog box appears (see Figure 1.4). Choose the filename (the backup file ends in a .QBB extension) and click **OK**. A second dialog box, Restore To, opens which defaults to the QuickBooks directory on your hard drive. Click the **Save** button, and your data will be restored.

FIGURE 1.4

Restoring your data returns you to the last data you backed up. Transactions entered since the last back up will need to be reentered.

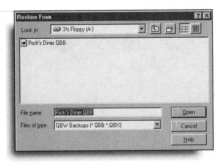

To restore your data from a tape backup system, follow the instructions that accompany the tape system. You do not need to use the restore command found in QuickBooks.

QuickBooks Reminders

Forget about keeping lists and slips of paper all over your desk. QuickBooks Reminders feature keeps the lists for you and tells you what you need to do each day by starting your sessions with a Reminders dialog box (see Figure 1.5).

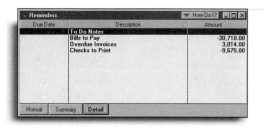

FIGURE 1.5

Let QuickBooks do your thinking for you. Double-click on any item to see the related detail, or click the **Detail** button to see the details of all items.

QuickBooks can remind you of almost anything, including:

- Invoices that are past due for which you haven't received payment
- Bills that you need to pay
- Checks and other forms that you have completed in QuickBooks but have yet to print
- Purchase orders that have yet to be filled
- Money waiting to be deposited
- Memorized transactions that need to be entered
- Whatever else you ask the program to tell you about on your personal To Do list

Setting a reminder

Tell QuickBooks what items you want to be reminded about by following these steps:

1. Choose **File**, **Preferences**. The Preferences window appears.

2. Scroll down through the icons that appear on the left side of the screen and click on the **Reminders** icon when it appears. The Reminders window appears.

3. On the **My Preferences** tab, check the box to have QuickBooks show you the Reminders window each time you start the program.

4. Click the **Company Preferences** tab to view the screen shown in Figure 1.6.

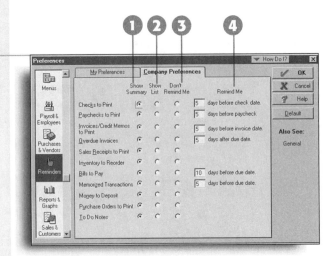

5. Choose one of these three options for each task:

- **Show Summary**. Display the item in the Reminders window when something comes due, but do not display the related detail unless the user requests it.

- **Show List**. Show the detail about tasks and other items that have come due; don't wait to be asked. You might want all the items on your To Do list to show automatically whenever the Reminders window opens, so you won't forget an important engagement.

- **Don't remind me**. Don't include this type of item on the Reminders list. For example, perhaps you don't want to include the Money to Deposit item on your Reminders list. There might be people using the program who don't need to know that undeposited funds are hiding in your desk drawer.

6. Examine the Remind Me section of the screen and choose how close to the deadline you want to have these items appear in your reminder list. If your electric bill isn't due until next Tuesday, do you want to wait to be reminded on

Tuesday, or would you like a few days notice so that you can write the check and get it in the mail before the due date?

7. Click **OK** when you are finished making your choices.

If you choose not to display your Reminders list each time you start QuickBooks, or if you have closed the list and want to view it again, click on the Reminders button on your iconbar, or choose **Lists**, **Reminders**.

Getting Help

This book provides you with illustrations and step-by-step instructions to get you up and running and keep you there

Turn to the program itself for assistance when you're stuck

The Internet offers help on every topic under the sun, and help with QuickBooks is no exception

Intuit helps you use your phone, use your fax, and call the program's makers for expert assistance

One of the greatest frustrations about using any computer program occurs when you have a question and can't find the answer. You've set aside time for computer tasks and you get stuck, unable to proceed without a solution to a problem. Not only does your admiration for the computer program, its manufacturer, and the computer itself decline, but you find yourself wasting valuable time trying to solve what you're certain is a simple problem. Then you have to reschedule time to get back on the computer while other jobs get pushed aside, and you find yourself behind schedule, missing deadlines, and wishing you had stuck to pencil and paper and never messed with the computer.

Use this book, and the other options presented in this chapter, to aid you in putting an end to those frustrations, so you can enjoy using QuickBooks and get back to work.

Using This Book for Help

Before you turn to other resources, spend some time familiarizing yourself with the layout of *Using QuickBooks and QuickBooks Pro Version 6.0*. Read through the table of contents and you will see that the book is broken into seven useful parts:

- **Part I: "Getting Started in QuickBooks."** In Part I, new users learn how to set up a company in QuickBooks and how to enter transactions that have already occurred. You learn how to organize your data to produce the reports and other information that will help your business operate efficiently.

- **Part II: "Taking Care of Business."** This section covers the ongoing accounting tasks that you will perform in QuickBooks on a regular basis. Learn how to record revenue and expense transactions, how to report sales tax, and how to manage your inventory and fixed assets.

- **Part III: "Paying Employees and Contractors."** Most businesses rely on the help of others to get the job done. Learn the difference between an employee and a contractor, set up payroll records for employees, learn which tax forms you are responsible for filing, and generate those tax forms.

- **Part IV: "Making QuickBooks Work for You."** Make QuickBooks change to meet your needs, rather than you having to change to accommodate the program. In this part, you learn how to change the input screens so that they look the way you want them to look, to create the reports that will give you the results you need, and to customize the program so that it performs in ways that make sense to you.

- **Part V: "QuickBooks Meets the 21st Century."** If you are interested in the online features of QuickBooks, online banking and online bill-paying, this part of the book provides you with all the information you need to get up and running with your modem. You also get an introduction to Web services that are available to you.

- **Part VI: "Getting the Most from QuickBooks."** Learn budgeting and forecasting techniques that really work, learn how to protect your QuickBooks data, find out how QuickBooks's Time Tracking feature can help you, and learn what you need to prepare your income tax return using QuickBooks.

- **Part VII: "Appendixes"**

General topics are listed in the Table of Contents. For more detailed digging, try finding the topic you need in the index that comes at the end of this book. Still over a barrel regarding an answer you can't find? Try some of the other sources listed in the remaining sections of this chapter.

Using QuickBooks Help Index

The Help index that accompanies your QuickBooks program provides you with a lengthy, alphabetical listing of all topics covered in the onscreen help file. You can access the QuickBooks Help Index by choosing **Help**, **Help Index**, or clicking the **Index** button whenever a Help window is displayed.

When the Help index appears (see Figure 2.1), you can enter the first few letters of any subject for which you want help. As you type, QuickBooks finds its way to the subject. Double-click on the subject in the list of help index subjects and you will see a list of additional subjects that provide detail about the general subject you chose.

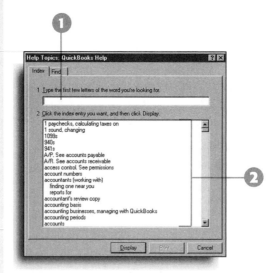

FIGURE 2.1

The QuickBooks Help Index gives you onscreen instructions and descriptions of all facets of the program.

1 Enter the name of the subject for which you want additional information here.

2 Double-click on a subject to get help from QuickBooks.

After the help information is displayed, you have several directions in which you can proceed:

- Choose **Options**, **Print Topic** if you want a printed copy of this help screen.

- The green help topics are hyperlinks and only require a single click to get you to further information.

- Keep the help information on the top of your screen while you work by choosing **Options, Keep Help on Top, On Top**.

- Add your own notations to the help screen as a reminder to you when you open this screen again, or to provide useful comments for the next user, by choosing **Options, Annotate**. A window opens in which you can enter information. Click **Save** when you are finished. A paper clip appears on the help screen indicating annotations are available (see Figure 2.2). Clicking the paper clip displays the annotations.

FIGURE 2.2
Personalize the Help screens with your own comments as you get to know QuickBooks.

1 Click this paper clip to see the annotation.

- Close the help window by clicking the **x** in the upper-right corner of the window.

Using the Help Find Feature

The Find part of QuickBooks Help system goes a step farther than the Help Index. With the Find feature, you can search the text of all QuickBooks help screens for a particular word. QuickBooks displays a list of all help screens that contain the word for which you search. In this way, you can discover help screens that contain references to your topic, even when your topic isn't the main topic on the help screen.

For example, perhaps you want to find out how to record the sale of an asset you are depreciating. If you look up "depreciation" in the Help Index, you won't find any information about selling assets. If you enter "depreciation" using the Find feature, you will discover that several help topics include a discussion of depreciation, including one called "Selling a Fixed Asset."

Using Find

To use the Find feature in QuickBooks, follow these steps:

1. Choose **Help**, **Help Index**. The Help Topics window appears.

2. Click the **Find** tab at the top of the Help Topics window. If you have not used this feature previously, QuickBooks will lead you through two setup screens, at which you can click **Next** and **Finish**, respectively, to set up Find for first time use.

3. In the box labeled **1 (Type the Words You Want to Find)**, enter a word describing the topic you want to find (for my example, I entered "depreciation"). Variations on the word you entered (plural, past tense, and so on) will appear in the area labeled **2 (Select Some Matching Words to Narrow Your Search.)**. By default, all of the choices in area 2 are selected. If you want, you can click on one or more choices instead of leaving them all selected.

4. Area 3, **Click a Topic, Then Click Display**, shows all the help topics that include the word you entered in area 1. Double-click on any topic to see a help screen about that topic.

Using Qcards

Qcards are pop-up boxes that appear onscreen as you move from task to task in QuickBooks. The cards provide descriptive information about the specific place in the program on which you are working.

For example, when you prepare an invoice in QuickBooks, the first area, or field, in which you enter information on the form is the Customer:Job area in the upper-left corner. When you are ready to enter a customer name in this field, a Qcard appears onscreen describing exactly how to enter information in this field and what to do when you're finished (see Figure 2.3). As you move from one field to the next on this form, a new Qcard appears for each field.

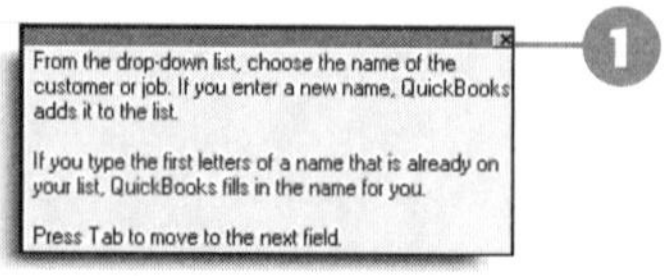

FIGURE 2.3

Qcards provide explanations and instructions as you use QuickBooks.

From the drop-down list, choose the name of the customer or job. If you enter a new name, QuickBooks adds it to the list.

If you type the first letters of a name that is already on your list, QuickBooks fills in the name for you.

Press Tab to move to the next field.

① Click the **x** close box to turn off the Qcards display.

If Qcards do not appear on your screen and you want to see them, choose **Help**, **Hide/ShowQCards**. If Qcards were previously turned off, they will be turned on. If they were on (even if you had temporarily turned off the display by clicking the X close box in the corner of a Qcard box), they will be turned off.

If the QuickBooks iconbar is displayed on your screen, you can click the Qcard icon button off [icon] and on [icon] to quickly turn off and on the view of Qcards.

SEE ALSO

➤ *For more information about the iconbar, including information about how to view the iconbar if it is not visible, see page 430*

To move a Qcard out of the way but keep it visible, drag the colored bar on top of the Qcard box.

Using the How Do I? Button

Every window in QuickBooks includes a How Do I? button at the upper right, which provides you with a quick list of the questions you are most likely to ask while using that particular window. Click once on the button and a drop-down list appears (see Figure 2.4). Click on any question on the list and a help screen opens, displaying information relating to the question.

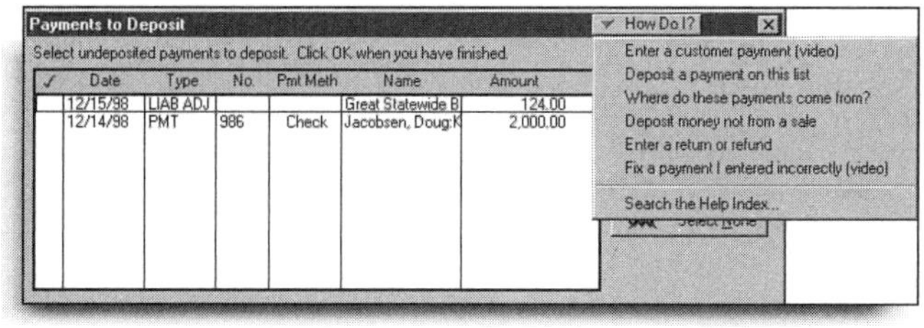

FIGURE 2.4

Click the **How Do I?** button for fast answers to common questions. Click on any question to see the answer, or click anywhere off of the list to remove the list from your screen.

The last item on each How Do I? list is Search the Help Index. Clicking on this opens the main Help Index where you can enter a topic for which you want help (see the earlier section on "Using QuickBooks Help Index").

Getting Help on the CD-ROM

Use your QuickBooks CD-ROM to familiarize yourself with the operation of the program. You can view video presentations that show you how many of the QuickBooks features operate, providing you with a visual display of the QuickBooks program at work.

When you open the QuickBooks program, you see a box in which you are asked if you want to create a new company or open an existing one. Unless you have already set up a company file, you must indicate that you want to create a new company.

If you have opened QuickBooks previously and examined the sample company file, then return to QuickBooks; you will see the screen shown in Figure 2.5. (Note: This screen disappears after you have set up your own file in QuickBooks.)

Choose **See the Introduction to QuickBooks (or QuickBooks Pro)** from the opening screen, click **OK**, then sit back (pop some popcorn if you like) and watch the videos tell you all about your program.

FIGURE 2.5

View the video display when you click **See the Introduction to QuickBooks**.

1 Click here, then click **OK** to see the show.

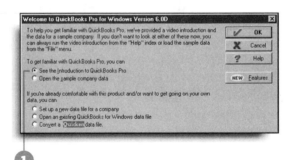

There are four videos from which to choose, each displaying a different part of QuickBooks. The videos are not interactive in that you can't make choices to control screen display, but they are educational, graphically interesting (see Figure 2.6), and provide you with a good introduction to the way the software works.

FIGURE 2.6

The graphic artists at Intuit make QuickBooks approachable and easy to understand.

Using Online Help

Head for the Internet if you want to connect with Intuit and the people who brought you QuickBooks. The QuickBooks Web site is www.quickbooks.com (see Figure 2.7). There you can find answers to frequently asked questions (FAQs). Just click on Frequently Asked Questions under the Technical Support Heading.

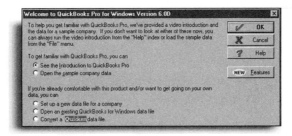

FIGURE 2.7

There's plenty of interesting help, guidance, new product information, and advice at the QuickBooks Web site. Because this site is being constantly upgraded, your screen might not look exactly like this.

In addition, you can visit the User-to-User forums—a place where QuickBooks users post and answer questions. If you're having a problem, you might find that others share your situation and have either posted a question about that problem or comments on how to solve it. You can post your own question and receive answers from experienced QuickBooks users who might have worked through a similar problem.

Click **User-to-User Forums** under the Technical Support heading on the QuickBooks Web site. You are asked to register by giving your name, address, and some other basic information (none of which appear when you post your inquiry); then you can enter the forums.

Even if you're not having a problem with QuickBooks, you will find valuable information in the FAQs and User-to-User forums, including shortcuts and techniques for using the program that you might not have considered. And, if you have figured out a clever way to perform a task or save time in QuickBooks, you can share your expertise with other users in the forums.

Intuit Technical Support

You may find the answers to the questions you have by placing a phone call to Intuit's technical support group.

Using the Automated Expert

You can call Intuit for recorded answers to questions about the way QuickBooks works. The answers are thorough and easy to understand. There are many categories of information from which you can choose by pressing buttons, as directed, on your touch-tone phone.

The topics covered are standard topics, such as printing concerns, installation problems, and information about entering basic transactions.

Call 888-322-7276 to use the Automated Expert. This service is available 24 hours a day.

Telephone Technical Support

If you are still having difficulty, you can try to reach a real person at Intuit who will help you work through your problem. Intuit offers free telephone technical support for problems related to installation, data conversion, and product defects.

To deal with the other problems, you can purchase technical support from Intuit at a rate of $35 per incident. There are also support plans that you can purchase. The "Gold" plan costs $129 and provides you with the right to call with five problems in a 12-month period (additional problems are charged at the $35 per incident rate). The "Platinum" plan costs $249 and you can call with ten problems. You also get a discount on purchasing forms and supplies from Intuit with the Platinum plan. Both plans provide you with a secret phone number that will enable you to bump ahead of other callers who are patiently waiting in the phone-hold limbo.

The number for contacting Intuit's technical support service is 888-320-7276. The hours of operation are Monday through Friday, 5 a.m. to 5 p.m., Pacific time, although extended hours are available if you purchase one of the plans described above.

QuickFax System

Request by fax documents that provide answers to the top 30 common questions about performing various QuickBooks tasks. The questions available by fax are very similar to the Frequently Asked Questions on the QuickBooks Web site.

Call 800-858-6090 to request an index of available documents that will provide you with the documents' numbers for the individual answers to questions. Then you can call back and request specific documents. This service is available 24 hours a day.

QuickBooks and Your Industry

The people at Intuit have compiled useful information about 22 industries. Many familiar business types and industries are included, such as law firms, manufacturing companies, construction contractors, real estate brokers, and so on. This information is designed to help you understand how other people in your line of business keep accounting records. The information is presented in an easy-to-understand format and is extremely informative.

View the information for your industry by choosing **Help**, **QuickBooks and your industry**. A help screen appears showing a variety of topics relating to aspects of record-keeping for your industry. Clicking on any individual topic provides you with detailed information about that topic.

There's a lot of reading here, so you might want to take the time to print the topics that interest you and read them on paper rather than onscreen. Print a topic by choosing **Options**, **Print topic** when the information you want to print is onscreen.

Periodic QuickBooks Activities

Daily Activities keep your records completely up-to-date

Weekly Activities include entering all the paperwork that has piled up during the week

Monthly Activities, such as paying payroll taxes and preparing progress reports, keep you on top of how your business is doing

Quarterly Activities include keeping the tax man happy, and we all know how important that can be!

Annual Activities wrap up the year in QuickBooks with reports and tax returns, budget analysis, and a count of your inventory

Information might not apply to your company

Some of the tasks mentioned in this chapter might not apply to you. For example, if you are a business owner with no employees, the information about due dates of payroll tax forms (mentioned in the Monthly, Quarterly, and Annual sections) might be of little interest to you. When you make your checklists, just leave off the items that don't pertain to you or your business.

Any kind of accounting system works best when you are organized and you stay on top of the record-keeping process. If you fall behind at entering data, all the quick reports that QuickBooks can produce will be wasted because the information they contain will be dated. In fact, one of the greatest benefits of using QuickBooks is being able to produce, at a moment's notice, up-to-the-minute reports giving the status of important balances such as:

- Accounts receivable
- Accounts payable
- Inventory on hand
- Money in the bank
- Orders pending
- Year-to-date earnings
- Amount due on loans

To stay abreast of how your business is doing, there are activities that must be performed on a regular basis. In this chapter, you learn which QuickBooks tasks need to be accomplished regularly and with what frequency. You learn how to create checklists that will help remind you when to perform certain tasks.

Each time you have a question about how a certain aspect of the business is doing, you'll be grateful you read this chapter because all the information you need will be right at your fingertips.

Performing Daily Activities

The easiest way to stay on top of the day-to-day transactions of your business is to enter those transactions each day. The more you let data entry pile up, the more time you will have to set aside to enter transactions, the more difficult it will be to find that time, and the more out-of-date the information in your QuickBooks reports will become.

If your business has very few transactions on a daily basis, or if perhaps there are days when there aren't any transactions at all, you might find it more convenient to skip a few days before performing the tasks listed in this part of the chapter. I strongly recommend, however, that you not let more than a week go by without doing what I call the *daily activities*.

Understanding Types of Activities

These are the activities that should be done on a daily basis and the chapters in this book that discuss how these activities are performed:

- Enter all cash sales transactions (Chapter 11, "Invoicing, Monthly Statements, and Accounts Receivable"). Include all cash sales, if your business allows cash sales, and all charge transactions, if you accept credit card sales.

- Enter all bills and shipments received (Chapter 14, "Keeping Track of Your Inventory"). Keeping on top of bills and shipments means your accounts payable will always be current, and your inventory records will be up-to-date.

- Enter any checks you write by hand and all cash payments. Enter all payments made (Chapter 15, "Purchase Orders, Accounts Payable, and Paying Bills").

- Enter all bank deposits made (Chapter 12, "Recording Income").

- Enter name, address, phone number, and other pertinent information for all new customers and vendors (Chapter 8, "Setting Up Services, Customers, and Suppliers").

- Enter all estimates issued (Chapter 10, "Job-Cost Estimating and Tracking"). (Some companies don't use this feature.) Enter estimates as you create them. They can be revised later if changes in the project occur.

- Record all hourly time in the Time Tracking feature (Chapter 25, "QuickBooks and Time Tracking"). If you use time tracking, your payroll records and related jobs should be updated daily.

Creating a Checklist

Prepare a checklist that can be copied and made available to whomever is entering data. The checklist should have a place for today's date and the name of the person entering data. List each of the preceding items that apply to your business (and any others you can think of that might not be included on this list but that you want to have performed each day in QuickBooks). There should be a check box next to each item and a place to enter additional information, such as the following:

- Quantity of each item entered (such as 12 checks or 2 estimates)

- Reference numbers of the items entered (such as check numbers 2165-2176)

- Comments (such as, "Did not enter estimate #263 because this is for a new customer who is not yet in the system—need customer information such as address, contact name, and so on.")

Your checklist might look something like the one pictured in Figure 3.1.

FIGURE 3.1

A daily checklist helps you remember what should be entered into QuickBooks each day. It also provides a record of who did the data entry and what was entered.

Rick's Construction Co-op

Daily Checklist of QuickBooks Activities

Date: _____   Name: _____

✓	Item	Quantity Entered	Reference Numbers	Comments
	Payments received			
	Cash sales			
	Bills received			
	Shipments received			
	Purchase orders issued			
	Payments made			
	Estimates issued			
	Time on jobs			
	New customers			
	New vendors			
	Other (describe below)			

File your completed checklists in a file drawer or a three-ring binder in case you ever need to trace some information that was entered. It might seem like extra work to prepare and save checklists, especially in an office where only one or two people work. You will find, however, that this is an excellent way of providing a trail that will help you verify if, when, and by whom certain jobs were accomplished. There will be no doubts if you have the checklists.

Performing Weekly Activities

As mentioned previously, some of the items in the Daily Activities section might find their way onto a weekly checklist if their daily occurrence is minimal. In fact, you might find that it is easier to issue all of your payments or invoices on one day of the week instead of performing those tasks on a daily basis.

Here are some additional tasks that should be completed weekly:

- Enter all invoices issued (Chapter 11).
- Enter purchase orders for all items you need to purchase (Chapter 15).
- Perform a full backup of your QuickBooks data files (Chapter 1, " QuickBooks Overview").

Working with Payroll

Every company is different when it comes to payroll. Your company might issue paychecks weekly, every two weeks, semi-monthly, or monthly. Or you might issue weekly paychecks to hourly employees and semi-monthly paychecks to salaried employees. Or you might issue daily paychecks if you have employees who perform piecemeal work for you.

QuickBooks can accommodate any combination of pay periods that fits your needs. No matter when you issue paychecks, you want to do it in an organized fashion. Choose the same time each

Frequency of invoices and purchase orders vary by company

Your company might issue invoices and purchase orders more or less frequently than weekly. These are just general guidelines.

week (or every two weeks, or however often you issue checks), and enter your payroll in the same order each time. Not only does a regular payroll entry schedule make the process go more smoothly for you, it also serves to build expectations in employees so they don't nag anyone for checks ahead of schedule.

Your payroll checklist should include the following steps. These steps should be performed each time the payroll is entered:

- Determine which employees to pay
- Enter hours for hourly employees, verify salaries for salaried employees
- Verify sick time and vacation time usage, if you use these features
- Verify that all benefits are correct
- Print payroll

Information about entering your payroll can be found in Chapter 18, "Paying Employees and Contractors."

Performing Monthly Activities

Once a month, you need to spend more time than usual with QuickBooks because there are many activities that are only performed monthly. In addition, many of the reports you generate that tell you how your business is doing are based on monthly totals, so it is very important to keep on top of the monthly record-keeping requirements.

Activities that you will want to perform monthly include:

- Pay monthly bills (Chapter 15). Some bills come due every month like clockwork—the rent, utilities, loan payments, and so on.
- Payroll tax deposits (Chapter 19, "QuickBooks and Taxes").
- Checkbook reconciliation (Chapter 15). Your bank statement should arrive monthly, but the bank might not necessarily issue the statement on the last day of each month. For individuals, this is often not a problem, but when you're

trying to run a business, you want to confirm your bank balance as of the last day of each month. If your bank statement is issued on some day other than the last day of each month, contact your bank and ask them to change the closing date of your statement.

- Credit card reconciliation (Chapter 17, "Entering Cash Transactions"). Checkbooks aren't the only thing you need to reconcile monthly.

- Funding of retirement plan (Chapter 29, "Income Taxes"). You can wait until year-end to make contributions to your retirement plan, or you might find that it's easier on your cash flow to make regular, monthly payments.

- Produce monthly reports (Chapter 21, "QuickBooks' Reports and Graphs"). The reports you need to produce and examine each month include the following:

  - Profit and Loss statement for the month

  - Monthly Profit and Loss statement for the year-to-date, comparing current year to prior year

  - Balance sheet

  - Monthly payroll summary

  - Accounts receivable aging summary

  - Accounts payable detail

  - Monthly budget report

  - Inventory stock status report

There might be other reports besides these that you find useful for the operation and understanding of your company. The discussion of reports in Chapters 20, "Customizing QuickBook Forms," and 21 will help you decipher the reports and determine what they tell you about how your company is doing.

Performing Quarterly Activities

A few QuickBooks activities need be done at the end of each quarter. Their infrequency, however, does nothing to diminish their importance. Quarterly tax deposits, for example, must be paid. Your company's lenders and investors might require quarterly reports of your business progress. Overall business performance can often be judged more easily when examining a quarter than a month at a time. You can spot trends, for example, which may become evident during a quarter and might not show up on monthly reports.

The following list includes many of the quarterly activities you should perform. Your own business may dictate that other activities be added to this list:

- Pay quarterly deposits of income taxes (Chapter 29).
- Pay quarterly deposits of payroll taxes, especially unemployment tax (Chapter 19).
- Prepare quarterly reports including the following (Chapter 21):
  - Profit and Loss statement for the quarter
  - Profit and Loss statement for the year-to-date, comparing current year to prior year
  - Quarterly Payroll summary
  - Quarterly budget report
  - Income tax summary report for the quarter
  - Income tax detail report for the quarter

Completing Annual Activities

The end of the year is the time to finalize your records for the year, make any necessary corrections, assemble year-end statements, and assess the performance of your business. In addition to the end-of-month and end-of-quarter activities that must be completed at the end of the year, there are some jobs that you only need to accomplish once a year.

The year-end tasks include:

- Prepare W-2 forms for your employees (Chapter 18).
- Prepare 1099 forms for contractors and others with whom you do business (Chapter 18).
- Prepare end-of-year payroll tax reports (Chapter 18). These reports include:

- W-3 form (submitted to the Social Security Administration with your W-2 forms) (Chapter 18)
- State equivalent of federal W-3 form (actual form number and name varies by state) (Chapter 18)
- 1096 form (submitted to the IRS as the cover sheet with 1099 forms) (Chapter 18)
- State equivalent of federal 1096 form (actual form number and name varies by state) (Chapter 18)
- Federal form 940 (Chapter 19)
- State unemployment compensation report (Chapter 19)

- Prepare federal and state income tax returns (Chapter 29).
- Take a physical inventory count (Chapter 14).
- Prepare and print hard copies of the following reports:
  - Income statement for the year (Chapter 21)
  - Comparative income statement for the year (Chapter 21)
  - Income tax summary report for the year (Chapter 29)
  - Income tax detail report for the year (Chapter 29)
  - Review and adjust depreciation expense for the year (Chapter 16, "Managing Fixed Assets")
  - Safeguard your QuickBooks information so that no one can make unauthorized adjustments to your year-end numbers (Chapter 28, "Security")

These year-end tasks cannot all be performed at midnight, December 31 (in fact, you might have much more fun things to do at midnight, December 31!), and they cannot all be performed at once. Your income tax returns, for example, would not be prepared until later in the spring when the filing date approaches.

Nevertheless, these are all considered to be year-end activities and therefore must be planned for on an annual basis. That planning includes preparation of the reports that you will use when you actually check off all of these tasks.

Setting Up a Company in QuickBooks

The Start Date is the starting point at which you begin entering information into QuickBooks

Use the EasyStep Interview to walk you through the setup of your company

General company information includes the name and address of your company and the type of business or service you perform

Answers you give to questions about inventory, sales tax, and payroll put QuickBooks on the right track for setting up your company file

Before you can use QuickBooks, you must set aside time to get some basic company information into the program. You have to tell QuickBooks a few things about your company so that the program will be ready for you to enter transactions and prepare reports.

The Start Date

When you're ready to start entering information into QuickBooks, you need to take a few minutes to consider your company's *start date*. The start date is not necessarily today's date, but the date on which you want to begin tracking information in QuickBooks. When you set up a company in QuickBooks, you need to enter all transactions that have occurred in the company from the start date to today.

If possible, your start date should be the first day of the current year (usually January 1, but see the following note about fiscal years). Or, if the business you are setting up is a new business that didn't get started until sometime after January 1, your start date should be the first day you started doing business.

By starting on the first day of the year (or the first day the company had any activity), the reports and financial statements you produce will include information for the entire year. This is particularly important when gathering information at the end of the year for tax return preparation.

Fiscal year

Most companies begin their *fiscal year* on January 1, just like the calendar year. The fiscal year is one complete 12-month cycle, and sometimes companies have a fiscal year that is different than a calendar year, if it is more appropriate for reporting the activity of the business. For example, the company's fiscal year might go from October 1 to September 30. If you want to change your fiscal year from the calendar year to something else, you must request permission from the IRS.

If your business was in operation all year, but you choose a start date other than the first day of the year, the statements you produce will cover only part of this year. Next year and in future years, of course, your statements will cover the entire year. The advantage to choosing a start date sometime during the year rather than going back to the first day of the year is that you won't have as many transactions to enter at setup.

If it's close to the end of the year (November or December, for example) and you don't have a lot of spare time on your hands for tediously entering checks and deposits for the entire year, you might want to sit tight and wait until January 1 to start fresh with a new year. It really depends on how many transactions you have and how much time you have.

This initial setup procedure might take one or two hours, or several hours, depending on how organized your information is before you start and how much information you have to enter.

Use the accompanying checklist as a guide to help you assemble the information you need to have by your side before you begin setting up your company. Some of the items on the checklist might not be applicable to your company.

Checklist for Setting Up New Business

Have the following items on hand before starting the New Company Interview:

- Company name, address, type of business
- Federal Identification Number
- Bank statements and canceled checks, from the start date forward, including your bank balances as of the start date
- Chart of accounts, if you have one
- Customer list of all the people and companies you sell to regularly, including name, address, telephone number, fax number, personal contact, ship to address, sales tax status, terms you typically apply to this customer, current jobs you are working on for this customer
- Inventory list of all the items you sell, including description of inventory items, cost of items, standard sales price of items, preferred supplier of items, quantity of items on hand, number of items at which a reorder request should be issued
- Detail of all amounts you owe as of the start date
- Detail of all amounts owed to you as of the start date
- The rate at which you charge sales tax; the name and address of the taxing agency, amount of sales tax owed as of the start date
- Vendor list of all your regular suppliers and creditors, including name, address, telephone and fax numbers, personal contact, your account number with each vendor, whether or not the vendors will require a 1099 form
- Any existing budget information
- List of employees, including names and addresses, social security numbers, rates of pay, withholding allowances and other deductions, year to date information (if setting up company after January 1)

Going back an extra year

If you feel truly ambitious, and if your business has been around this long, you might want to designate January 1 of last year as your start date. Naturally, you will have to spend more time entering information into QuickBooks if you plan to enter all of last year's transactions as well as the current year's information, but the result will be the opportunity to produce reports that compare your business activity from one year to the next–an extremely useful tool for planning and projecting.

- Payroll tax information including state unemployment compensation rate, local tax rates, information regarding payroll taxes due as of the start date
- Current value of all assets including original cost, date purchased, methods used for calculating depreciation, accumulated depreciation to date
- Credit card statements you have received since the start date
- Details of all transactions since the start date, including checks written, amounts deposited, credit card transactions, and so on

The EasyStep Interview

The QuickBooks interview is called EasyStep because it leads you through the setup process in a step-by-step fashion, and it is relatively easy. Easy, that is, if you have gathered all the information you were told to get earlier in this chapter. If you skipped over the setup checklist thinking you'd just plow ahead and see what QuickBooks asks you for in the interview, go back and try it again. You'll thank me when the setup process is finished.

When you start the QuickBooks program, you are faced with a screen that gives you an option to set up a new data file for a company (see Figure 4.1). Choose that option and click OK, and you'll be off and running.

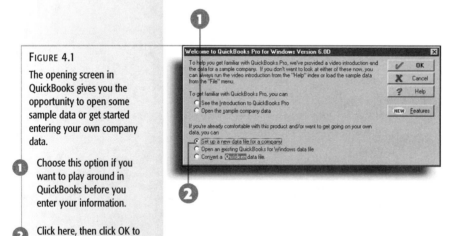

FIGURE 4.1

The opening screen in QuickBooks gives you the opportunity to open some sample data or get started entering your own company data.

1 Choose this option if you want to play around in QuickBooks before you enter your information.

2 Click here, then click OK to begin your own QuickBooks experience.

If you've experimented with the sample data, or used QuickBooks in another way, and you don't want to see the welcome screen, you can get to the EasyStep Interview by choosing the **File** menu, then choosing **New Company**.

The first screen of the EasyStep interview appears telling you to click **Next** to begin. The interview features seven tabs along the right side:

- **General**. In this section, you are asked for your company name, address, federal identification number, what tax form your company files, the type of business, whether you want to use the QuickBooks standard chart of accounts, the start date for when your company will begin using QuickBooks, and some general information about your anticipated usage of some of the QuickBooks features.

- **Income & Expenses**. Create names of accounts that will help you classify your income and expenses.

- **Income Details**. Set up a list of the services that your company offers and the goods it sells. If you plan to keep track of your inventory in QuickBooks, you list the types of inventory items that your company sells here.

- **Opening Balances**. Enter all the bills you owe and all the amounts that customers owe you as of the start date (see "The Start Date" section earlier in this chapter for more information).

- **Payroll**. If you plan to use QuickBooks to keep track of your payroll, you enter your employees' names and vital statistics here, as well as all the payroll taxes you owe and what types of things you pay and withhold from pay for your employees. You can skip this section if you don't have a payroll or if you have another way of paying employees.

- **Menu Items**. Just a few questions about the way your menus will be arranged.

- **What's Next**. This section includes general recommendations for how you should proceed after the interview is completed, information about setting up passwords to protect your data, advice on setting up tracking for vendors who will need 1099 forms at the end of the year, and a general advertisement for the QuickBooks Web site.

You should answer all the questions that are presented to you in the General tab first. After the general questions have been completed, it is possible to proceed haphazardly through the interview, clicking the tabs at the right out of order instead of from top to bottom. Most people, though, move through the entire interview in order, and that is how the interview is explained in this chapter.

Stopping and Restarting the Interview

At any time (dinner time, fingers getting tired…), you can leave the interview. When you return, QuickBooks remembers just where you left off and takes you right back. (However, be sure you've gotten at least as far as the screen in the General section that asks you to save your QuickBooks file and give it a file-name.)

To leave the QuickBooks interview before you have finished answering all the questions, click on the **L**eave button.

To get back to work in the interview, choose **F**ile, **EasyStep Interview**.

Moving Around in the Interview

You can click your way through the interview, or you can use the following keyboard shortcuts for getting from screen to screen:

- Pressing **Enter** generally activates the **Next** button at the bottom of the interview screen.
- Alt+N also activates **Next**.
- Alt+V activates the **Previous** button (Prev).
- The Tab key moves you from one field to another on each screen.
- After you tab to a particular check box or selection circle, pressing the space bar places an x in a check box (or removes one if there's one already there) or makes a selection in a selection circle.
- After you tab to a scroll list, the up and down arrow keys move you through the list. Move to the item you want to select, then press **Tab** or **Enter** to make the selection.

The General Section

Use this section to enter preliminary information about your company—the actual numbers come later.

The first screen you encounter in the General section of the EasyStep interview asks if you want to upgrade from another Intuit product (see Figure 4.2). In other words, have you been using Quicken or QuickBooks to record your data previously? You can upgrade from any prior version of QuickBooks for Windows or Macintosh as well as nearly all versions of Quicken.

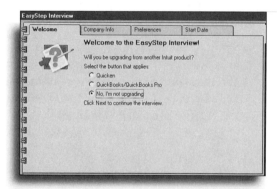

FIGURE 4.2

This screen is for prior Quicken/QuickBooks users. If that's not you, click **Next** and move on.

Upgrading from Earlier Versions of QuickBooks and Quicken

If you have been using an earlier version of QuickBooks, you really don't need to go through the interview process. Click the **Leave** button to leave the interview and choose **File**, **Open**. Request that QuickBooks open your data file from the earlier version and then you are asked if you want to convert that data to the new version of QuickBooks.

When you agree to convert your old data to the new version, QuickBooks makes your old data inaccessible to the earlier version of QuickBooks. To be safe, you should back up your old data before converting, in case something should go wrong with the conversion or if you should want to view the old data in the earlier version (if you have the earlier version of QuickBooks on another computer, for example). You will not be able to go back and forth between the two versions with the same data.

If you plan to use QuickBooks for data that was previously tracked in Quicken, follow the onscreen instructions that advise you about how to separate any personal items from business items that might be in your Quicken file. Then, you are prompted to back up your Quicken file before proceeding with the upgrade.

New Users of QuickBooks

If you have not been using Quicken or QuickBooks to track your company's financial information, or if you are ready to begin tracking information for a new company, choose **No, I'm Not Upgrading** on the first interview screen, then click **Next**.

Skipping the interview is not recommended (see Figure 4.3)—it's kind of like buying a piece of equipment that you have to put together yourself and throwing out the step-by-step instructions before you begin. The **Skip Interview** button looms at you like a dare; this is one dare you shouldn't take. There are many parts to setting up a company in QuickBooks and the interview covers nearly all of them. Unless you are familiar with the software from a previous life, click the **Next** button and pass on the dare.

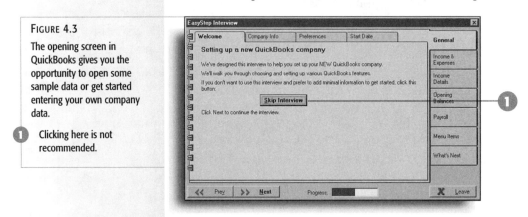

FIGURE 4.3

The opening screen in QuickBooks gives you the opportunity to open some sample data or get started entering your own company data.

1 Clicking here is not recommended.

The next interview screen simply gives you some basic information about how the interview works: The **Next** button moves you forward, **Prev** puts you in reverse, and **Leave** closes shop for the day.

A couple of clicks on **Next** and you see a cheerful reminder that you can always go back and change answers in the interview (see Figure 4.4). Don't believe this! Although there are many times during the interview when you can back up, revisit a screen, and make some changes, there are also plenty of places where you can't make changes until the interview is through with you. The moral of this story: take the interview slowly and answer all interview questions carefully, checking spelling as you type.

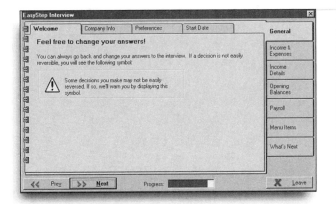

FIGURE 4.4

Keep a laundry list nearby of items you forgot to enter or want to change.

When you complete a section of the interview, the related tab is checked off (see Figure 4.5).

Entering Company Information

It's finally time to limber up your fingers and tell QuickBooks all about your company.

On the first input screen of the company information section, shown in Figure 4.5, you are asked for your company name and the legal name of your company. "What's the difference?" you ask?

Make a list of changes to make later

If you make mistakes (spelling an inventory item incorrectly, for example) during the EasyStep interview, and clicking the **Prev** button doesn't take you to a screen where you can correct your mistakes, keep a list of all the things you want to do when the interview is finished. That way you won't forget the chores that need to be completed later.

FIGURE 4.5

Enter your company name (for example, Rick's Diner), followed by your legal business name (for example, Olive Another Restaurant, Inc.)

1 This check mark means you've graduated to the next section.

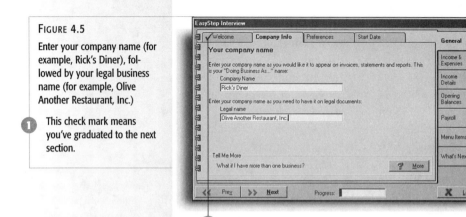

The company name is the name by which your customers know and love you. Your legal name is the name under which your company is registered with the state authorities. The company name is the name that will appear on nearly every statement and report that QuickBooks produces (notable exceptions include tax reports—the IRS wants to know who you really are).

If your company is just you and you don't have any fancy names, legal or otherwise, just enter your own name in both sections of the screen.

More Than One Company

If you are trying to enter information for more than one company into QuickBooks, stop trying. You should enter all the information for one company at once, completing the entire interview. Then, if you have another company to set up, go to **File**, **New Company**, and start all over for the other company.

One Company: Many Locations

If you have multiple locations of the same company (for example, a restaurant company might operate two or more restaurants, or a store owner might have stores in several locations), you can enter all the information for all your company locations into one QuickBooks file.

Using classes

I recommend setting up Classes (see an introductory section on classes later in this chapter and read all about classes in Chapter 9). Classes let you keep different parts of your business separate, while still enabling you to create reports about the entire business.

Setting Up Your Company Address

Enter your company address on the screen shown in Figure 4.6. Entering the address probably seems like a simple matter, unless, of course, you have more than one address.

FIGURE 4.6
The address you enter will appear on statements and reports.

For companies with more than one address (such as a company with a store in one location and an office in another), enter the address that you want to appear most often on the forms you will use most often, such as invoices and purchase orders.

You always have the opportunity to override the address when preparing forms and reports in QuickBooks.

Federal Identification Number

Sounds serious, doesn't it? The Federal Identification Number, or FEIN, is the number the IRS and other state and federal authorities know you by. For regular people, the FEIN is your Social Security number; if your business is not a corporation, this might be the only number you have.

Corporations always have a separate FEIN, and many individuals who own a business sign up for a business FEIN just to keep records separate with the government.

Enter the number you use to identify your business, and this number will appear on all tax forms you prepare in QuickBooks.

First Month of the Year

Usually, a business's fiscal year and tax year are the same.

The QuickBooks interview requests that you enter the first month of both your fiscal year and your tax year (see Figure 4.7). The fiscal year is the 12-month period you use for reporting your business activity on yearly financial statements. If you are like most businesses, you track your financial activity on a calendar-year basis (January to December), so January is the first month of your fiscal year.

FIGURE 4.7

The setup continues with identification number, and fiscal and tax years.

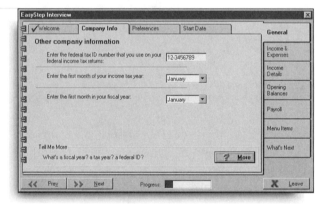

You might find, however, that a different 12-month period more naturally expresses the way in which you do business. For example, imagine a gift store that does a lot of business in late December each year. Revenue is always very high in December, but come January, many people bring in gifts to return or exchange. A better reflection of year-end sales can be accomplished by waiting until the end of January to prepare annual financial statements. This company would benefit from having a fiscal year that goes from February to January.

Corporations choose their fiscal year easily

Corporations (other than S Corporations and personal service corporations, described later in this chapter) do not have to beg the IRS to let them use a tax year that is different from the calendar year. Corporations simply file their first tax return for the year they want to use as a tax year.

Usually, businesses report their income tax based on a calendar year, even if the fiscal year used for financial statements is not the calendar year. In fact, if you want to choose a fiscal year rather than a calendar year for tax purposes, you must make a request of the IRS. Internal Revenue Service Form 8716 (which is available from the IRS) is used for making such a request.

Choose a Tax Return

The QuickBooks' request for you to choose a tax return (see Figure 4.8) is a not-so-subtle way of asking what kind of business you have. The type of business determines the type of tax return you file. Choose from the following forms:

- Form 1120 if you are a corporation. Corporations are entities unto themselves, taxed at their own rates, and liable for their own debts.

- Form 1120S if you are an S corporation. An S corporation is a business that behaves like a corporation except that it is not taxed like a corporation. Income of the business is passed through to the corporation's owners and taxed on their personal tax returns at their personal rates of income tax.

- Form 1065 if you are a partnership. Partnerships are a lot like S corporations. Income is passed through to the partners and taxed on their tax returns.

- Form 1040 for *sole proprietors*, people who haven't turned their business into a corporation or a partnership. The 1040 is the tax return that individuals file, and your business income will most likely show up on Schedule C of your 1040.

- Form 990 if you are an exempt organization. Exempt organizations are usually organizations that are in the business of helping others. The IRS must give your exempt status approval; then the only income that is taxed is income not related to your reason for exempt status.

- Form 990-PF if you are a private foundation. A private foundation is usually a tax exempt organization, but one that must meet stricter rules than your average tax exempt organization.

- Form 990-T is the form you use if you are a tax exempt organization with a little profitable business on the side, a business that is not related to your exempt purpose. Only the activity of this unrelated business is shown on form 990-T.

If you know which tax return is the right one for you, make your choice and move on. If you are just now trying to decide how you should report your business income and just what type of entity you want to become, you should spend a little time with a lawyer or an accountant and talk through all the advantages and disadvantages to the different business types.

FIGURE 4.8

Indicate the form your company uses (or will use) to file its tax return with the IRS.

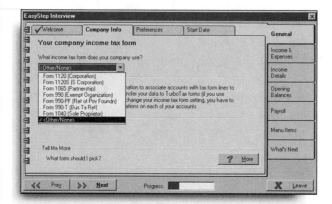

Find a professional who has experience in helping people set up new businesses. You can ask other business owners for a referral, check the yellow pages, or try calling your state CPA society and bar association to ask for referrals. A little time spent up front discussing your business goals and your business financing options with an experienced professional will help you structure the business in the way that best suits your long range needs.

Type of Business

QuickBooks provides you with a listing of many business types (see Figure 4.9) and hopes you will find one that matches, or is similar to, your own.

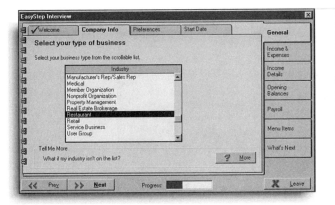

FIGURE 4.9
Clicking on a business type that
is similar but not identical to
your business won't cause any
problems for you.

Your choice of one of the business types from this list aids
QuickBooks in setting up your business by enabling it to determine some standard account names that are appropriate to your
business. Also, QuickBooks gears some of its questions to your
type of business. Choose **Other** if you don't see anything that
comes close to describing your business.

Save Your Work

By now, you might be wondering why you've never been asked
to name the file that contains the data for your company. What
if your computer suddenly loses its supper and shuts down on
you? Nothing you have entered up to this point has been saved,
so you're back to the drawing board.

At this point in the interview, QuickBooks gets around to asking
for a filename (see Figure 4.10). Think of an appropriate name
for your data. If you are working on only one business in
QuickBooks, the name isn't terribly significant. If you plan to
enter more than one business, you have to start giving a name to
each file so it is readily obvious which company's data the file
contains.

FIGURE 4.10

It's official! Your QuickBooks company file has been established!

QuickBooks' Standard (Customized) Chart of Accounts

A *chart of accounts* is a group of categories into which you categorize your company's income, expenses, debts, and assets, so that you can make some sense out of all of your business transactions in the form of professional-looking financial statements.

Without a chart of accounts, your company's financial statements might look like this:

Revenue	$xx,xxx.xx
- Expense	xx,xxx.xx
= Income (Loss)	$xx,xxx.xx

Some say the bottom line is everything, but without the detail that accounts provide, you won't know what kind of expenses you spent money on, and you might not know the source of your income. Without knowing any detailed information about how the money comes in and where it goes, intelligent decisions about how your business should be run cannot be made.

When you chose a type of business, QuickBooks decided on a list of account names that might be useful to you (see Figure 4.11). The accounts are divided into categories and the first accounts you see listed are *income accounts* and *expense accounts*.

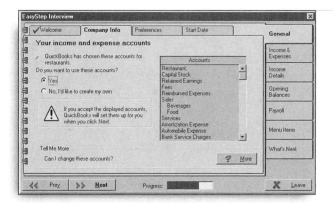

FIGURE 4.11

You can choose not to use the standard accounts, but you'll have a lot more work ahead of you.

Income accounts are accounts that reflect the earnings of your company. You might only have one type of income, such as fees for your services, or you might have many types of income, such as sales of inventory, equipment rental, and service fees. By separating your income into different accounts, you can produce reports that show more clearly the source of your income.

Expense accounts are accounts into which you categorize the expenses paid that keep your business running. Examples of expenses might include purchases of inventory, utilities, rent, supplies, repairs, office expense, telephone, and so on. Just as with income, a detailed breakdown of where your money goes helps you analyze your business performance.

If yours is a new business, I highly recommend that you use the accounts that QuickBooks has chosen for you. You can add accounts to this list during the interview and, after the interview has ended, you can delete accounts that you don't intend to use.

Who Has Access to the Company File?

The QuickBooks interview asks you how many people have access to your QuickBooks company. This is a security question. You do not have an opportunity in the interview to establish levels of security for yourself and others; but when the interview has ended, you can add some password protection to the program to prevent non-authorized people from viewing the company data (see Figure 4.12).

Chapter 28, "Security," discusses security issues in detail.

Use your own account names

An established business might already have a chart of accounts in place. It doesn't make sense to abandon an existing chart of accounts in favor of the accounts that QuickBooks has chosen for you. You might end up having some additional data entry, but if your company is already using a group of account names, you probably should reject the QuickBooks chart of accounts and enter all your own account names.

Adding account numbers

You might find it useful to use account numbers in addition to naming your accounts. Although there is no provision in the interview for numbering accounts, you can see Chapter 7 for instructions for adding account numbers after the interview is finished.

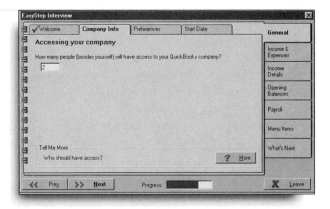

FIGURE 4.12

You can change the numbers of authorized users after the interview has ended.

Do You Have Inventory?

Inventory is the items you sell to earn money in your business. You might sell machine parts, books, or groceries that you purchase somewhere and offer for sale to others. Or, you might produce your own inventory, such as clothing that you make, ships that you build, or pottery that you throw.

These items in total make up your inventory, and you might have a variety of inventory accounts to describe all the items you keep in stock.

Some businesses don't have inventory at all. A business that provides a service, such as a law firm or a doctor's office, might not have anything tangible to sell, making inventory accounts unnecessary.

When QuickBooks asks if you maintain an inventory (see Figure 4.13), it is getting ready to set up inventory and related cost of sales accounts for you.

FIGURE 4.13

Choosing **Yes** here triggers some additional inventory questions in the interview.

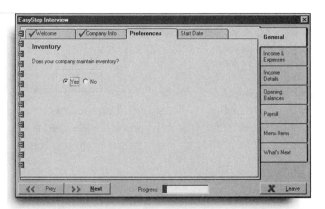

Do You Want to Keep Track of Inventory in QuickBooks?

You might think that because you have inventory you naturally want to keep track of your inventory in QuickBooks. I would say this depends on how complicated a process you use (or plan to use) for valuing your inventory.

QuickBooks is a great program when it comes to keeping track of how many inventory items you have in stock and giving you reminders about when it is time to reorder (see Figure 4.14, which only appears if you selected Yes at the screen shown in Figure 4.13). However, QuickBooks has limited skills when it comes to helping you value your inventory and report on your inventory to the IRS.

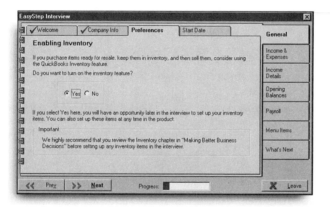

FIGURE 4.14
Let QuickBooks help you keep track of how many items you have in stock.

Chapter 14, "Keeping Track of Your Inventory," provides you with insight into using the QuickBooks inventory features and valuation expectations of the IRS. It also provides you with alternatives to QuickBooks for calculating the value of your inventory.

I recommend that, if you maintain an inventory, you use QuickBooks as a means of keeping track of all of your inventory items. I also strongly recommend that you read Chapter 14 to find out how various IRS rules apply to your situation and what you can do about accommodating those rules.

Do You Collect Sales Tax from Customers?

Chapter 13, "Reporting Sales Tax," provides you with detailed information about who is responsible for collecting and paying sales tax and how the process works in QuickBooks.

If you have determined that you are responsible for collecting sales tax from your customers, choose **Yes** when asked about sales tax in the interview (see Figure 4.15).

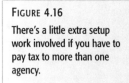

FIGURE 4.15

It might not be fun to collect sales tax, but somebody's got to do it.

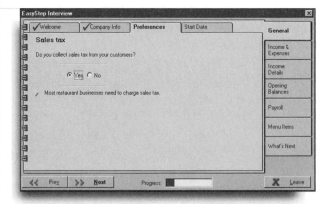

Do You Pay Sales Tax to More Than One Agency?

Your company might have to pay sales tax to multiple taxing agencies if, for example, you have more than one location and each location is situated in a different sales tax jurisdiction.

If you must pay sales tax to more than one agency, choose the multiple tax agencies option in the interview. (See Figure 4.16, which only appears if you selected Yes at the screen shown in Figure 4.15.) You then need to enter information for each agency to whom you pay tax.

FIGURE 4.16

There's a little extra setup work involved if you have to pay tax to more than one agency.

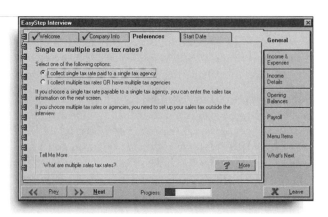

Setting Up a Sales Tax Item

As you use QuickBooks more, you'll get used to hearing about *items*. An item is the QuickBooks way of describing any piece of information that has an amount associated with it and that can appear on a form (an invoice, a purchase order, a paycheck, and so on).

Sales tax is an item because there is an amount associated with the sales tax you charge, and the sales tax amount can appear on invoices that you prepare for your customers.

In the interview, you are asked to set up your sales tax item by describing how you want the item to appear on your forms, the rate at which tax is charged, and the name of the agency to whom you ultimately pay the tax (see Figure 4.17), which only appears if you indicated that you collect sales tax.

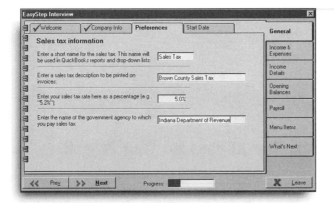

FIGURE 4.17
If you don't know all this information during the interview, you can set up your sales tax item later (see Chapter 13).

Selecting a Stylish Invoice

There are three standard invoice formats, or styles, available in QuickBooks. You can choose the one that you think will work best in your business, the one that most closely resembles forms you have used previously in your business, or you can choose to create your own form.

During the interview (see Figure 4.18), QuickBooks asks if you would like one of the following styles of invoice:

- *Product*. The product invoice is the most detailed, with sections for product description, purchase order number, shipping terms, ship to address, project name, sales representative code, and more. Use this invoice if you sell and track inventory.

- *Professional.* There are places on the invoice for a description and an amount. Use this invoice if you charge for professional fees and plan to enter a description of what your fees cover.

- *Service.* You can enter a quantity, a description, a rate, and an amount on this invoice. If you charge by the hour and plan to break out those charges on the invoice (3 hours for radiator repair, 2 hours to repaint the hood...), choose this invoice.

- *Custom.* Making this choice tells QuickBooks that you plan to create your own invoice, after the interview is finished.

FIGURE 4.18

Choose the invoice style that best fits your business. You have the option of changing your mind later.

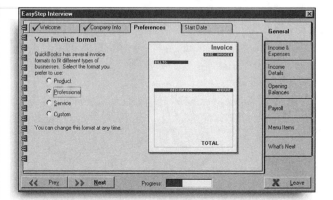

Using QuickBooks for Your Payroll

The QuickBooks interview asks you how many employees you have on your payroll (see Figure 4.19). This is just a general, nosy question, that has nothing to do with whether or not you use QuickBooks for preparing paychecks.

FIGURE 4.19

Enter the number of employees your company has. This number can change later.

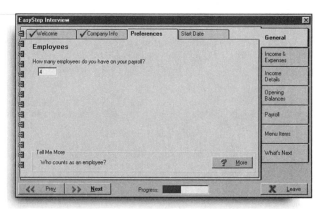

Unless you have a giant payroll and would rather not be bothered doing it yourself, you will probably use the QuickBooks Payroll feature (see Figure 4.20). It is a thorough payroll program that anticipates the payroll needs for nearly every type of business.

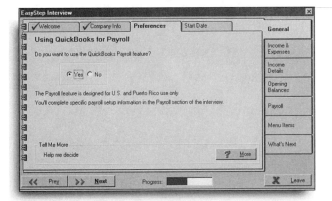

FIGURE 4.20

If you plan to use the QuickBooks Payroll feature, choose Yes here. You actually set up payroll later in the interview.

If you indicate that you plan to use QuickBooks to calculate your payroll, you might be interested to know that QuickBooks tries its best to stay on top of the latest tax withholding tables.

The screen that appears in Figure 4.21 (which only appears if you chose to activate the Payroll feature as shown in Figure 4.20) tells you the version of the payroll tables you have installed with your program. There is a phone number on this screen you can call to verify that your version is the most current. You don't have to call now, but it's a good idea to call every few months to make sure all the tax tales you use are up-to-date.

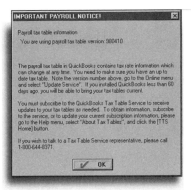

FIGURE 4.21

You don't have to call right this minute, nor should you memorize this phone number. Chapter 18 discusses the process for checking on and obtaining payroll tax updates.

Making Estimates on Jobs

If your company typically prepares estimates for jobs that you perform, you have the option of recording those estimates in QuickBooks (see Figure 4.22).

FIGURE 4.22

Choose **Yes** if you want to track estimates in QuickBooks.

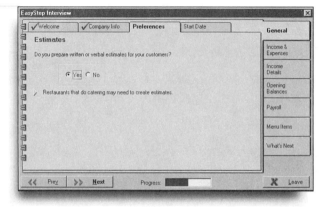

Estimate tracking for your jobs

Estimate Tracking is a feature of QuickBooks Pro.

When you track estimates in QuickBooks, you can bill from those estimates, you can prepare progress reports showing how much of the estimates have been completed, and you can prepare comparative reports that show estimates versus actual costs on jobs.

If you choose to use QuickBooks for creating and monitoring estimates, you have an option to bill for portions of your estimates instead of waiting for a job to be completed (see Figure 4.23). For example, you can prepare an invoice for 30 percent of the estimated price of a job. Or, you can charge your customer for the cost of materials as indicated on the estimate, holding off on billing for labor until later.

FIGURE 4.23

Choose **Yes** if you think you might want to use the QuickBooks partial billing feature.

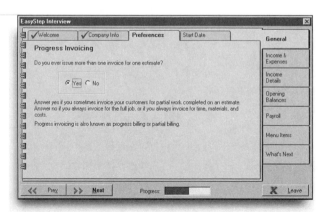

Chapter 10, "Job-Cost Estimating and Tracking," provides detailed information about preparing and using estimates for pricing your jobs.

Tracking Time in QuickBooks Pro

QuickBooks Pro offers a Time Tracking feature that enables you and your coworkers to fill out timesheets that feed directly onto jobs for easy invoicing (see Figure 4.24).

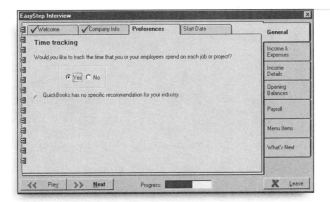

FIGURE 4.24

You can always change your mind later, but check Yes if you think you want to use the Time Tracking feature available in QuickBooks Pro.

See Chapter 25, "QuickBooks and Time Tracking," for more information on the Time Tracking feature.

Using Classes to Separate Your Business

Chapter 9, "Separating Your Company into Logical Divisions," provides detailed information about the QuickBooks Classes feature and how you can report on different segments of the same business as if they were separate businesses.

If you think you want to use this feature, choose **Yes** on the screen shown in Figure 4.25.

FIGURE **4.25**

Classes enable you to prepare reports on different sections of the same company.

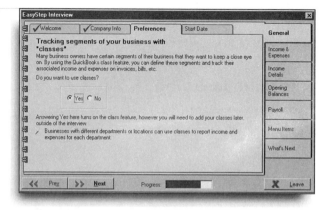

Bill Paying: Now or Later

In Figure 4.26, you are asked if your company plans to pay its bills at the same time they are entered in the computer (in other words, not enter the bills until they are paid), or if you will enter the bills when they arrive and plan on paying them later.

This is a non-technical way of asking if you want to establish an account for your payables, an account that keeps track of how much your company owes at any given time.

FIGURE **4.26**

If you enter bills when you receive them rather than waiting until they are due, QuickBooks gives you nice little reminders so you won't forget to pay your bills on time.

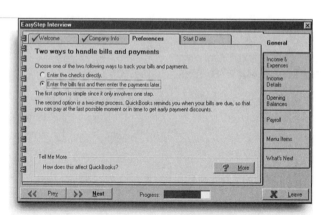

If you choose to enter bills before paying them, the QuickBooks menus are set up in a way that makes this process more intuitive.

Displaying the Reminders List

If you plan to use the QuickBooks Reminders list to keep yourself on top of important due dates and to do's that must be done,
choose At Start Up from the screen shown in Figure 4.27. This
way, you will see the Reminders list each time you start the
program.

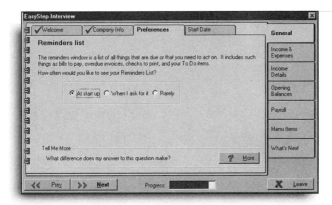

FIGURE 4.27

View reminders at startup and
you have no one to blame but
yourself if your tasks don't get
done!

And that wraps up the General section of your interview. The
other sections aren't nearly so daunting. You've made all the
decisions in the General section, now just sit back and fill in the
blanks when asked questions about those decisions.

Setting Up Accounts, Inventory, Fixed Assets, and Payroll

Income accounts are used to keep track of various sources of revenue

Expense accounts keep track of all types of disbursements of your business

Income items include the items your company sells, the services you provide, discounts you give to customers—anything that you might list on an invoice or sales slip

After you've gotten through the General section of the EasyStep Interview, it's time to set up the actual accounts that you plan to use to keep track of income and expenses for your company. In this chapter, you will also set up your inventory items, fixed assets, loans, and your payroll.

By the time you finish this chapter, you'll be ready to start using QuickBooks on a regular basis.

Setting Up Income Accounts

The next section of the QuickBooks setup procedure is for identifying income accounts. Income accounts are the categories you use to keep track of your various forms of income. If all of your revenue comes from only one source, you might have only one income account (Rent, for example, or Contracting).

Alternatively, you might want more detailed income records that provide more specific sources of income (Apartment Rent, Commercial Rent, or Home Repair, Room Additions, House Painting).

In the setup process of Chapter 4, "Setting Up a Company in QuickBooks," you chose whether to accept a standard chart of accounts for your company. The standard chart of accounts includes some income and expense accounts for tracking your business activity.

If you chose the standard accounts assigned by QuickBooks, you will want to examine all the standard income accounts and set up additional accounts to describe each type of income you want to track.

Setting up a new income account

1. Make sure **Yes** is selected (see Figure 5.1), then click **Next**. The Adding an Income Account screen appears.

2. Enter the name of an income account you want to add, for example, Catering or Lumber Sales or Machine Rental (see Figure 5.2).

3. Choose a tax line for the account if you plan to use QuickBooks to help you summarize information for your income tax return (as discussed in Chapter 29, "Income Taxes").

Typo warning

Type carefully when you enter account name information in the EasyStep Interview. This is one area where you can't go back and make corrections. If you misspell an account name, or decide you want to call the account by another name, you have to wait until the interview is over, then edit the account name (see Chapter 8, "Setting Up Services, Customers, and Suppliers").

Let your tax form be your guide

Keep a copy of last year's tax return nearby to use as a reference for assigning tax lines. If this is the first year your company will file a tax return, use a blank tax form as a reference.

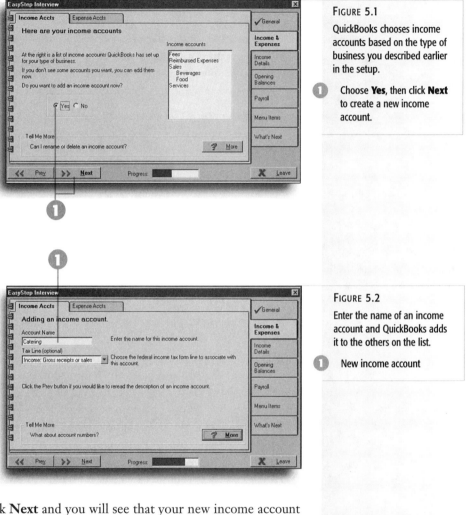

FIGURE 5.1

QuickBooks chooses income accounts based on the type of business you described earlier in the setup.

1. Choose **Yes**, then click **Next** to create a new income account.

FIGURE 5.2

Enter the name of an income account and QuickBooks adds it to the others on the list.

1. New income account

4. Click **Next** and you will see that your new income account has been added to the list of income accounts for the company.

Repeat steps 1–4 until you have added all the income accounts you plan to use. Choose **No** for step 1 when you have finished entering income accounts.

You can add income accounts at any time after you have finished the EasyStep Interview. See Chapter 8, "Setting Up Services, Customers, and Suppliers," for more information about adding accounts.

Setting Up Expense Accounts

The process for setting up expense accounts is nearly identical to that of setting up income accounts. The main difference is that you have an opportunity to designate whether an account is a *parent* or a *subaccount* for your expense accounts.

A parent account is a major category of an expense account. You can provide more detail of the components of a parent account by creating subaccounts. The total value of all the subaccounts of one parent make up the total amount in the parent account.

When presented on financial statements, the subaccounts are indented beneath their parent account (see Figure 5.3).

FIGURE 5.3

A partial chart of accounts with subaccounts indented beneath their parents.

Subaccounts can be broken down into additional subaccounts, thus making the first-level subaccount the parent of lower-level subaccounts. You can have up to five levels of parent/subaccounts. For example, under a parent account of Remodeling you might include subaccounts of Painting, Drywall, and Hardware. The Hardware subaccount might be broken down further into such subaccounts as Lighting Fixtures, Electrical Supplies, and Window/Door Hardware.

Setting up a new expense account

1. Choose **Yes** when asked if you want to set up a new expense account. The Adding an Expense Account screen appears.

2. Enter the name you want to give your new expense account in the box indicated.

3. Choose a tax line for the account if you plan to use QuickBooks to help you summarize information for your income tax return (as discussed in Chapter 29).

4. Check the Subaccount of box if this account is to be a subaccount of another expense account.

5. Choose the parent account of which this account is to be a subaccount, if applicable.

6. Click **Next** and notice that this expense account has been added to your list of other expense accounts.

Repeat steps 1–6 for as many expense accounts as you want to add at this time. When you have finished entering expense accounts, choose **No** for step 1.

General Information About Your Company's Income

The Income Details section of the EasyStep Interview asks for information about the way your company reports its income. Your answers in this section will help QuickBooks further customize your company setup.

The next screen asks if you receive full payment at the time you provide a service or sell a product. A business such as a retail store would probably answer Always to this question, unless the store provides an opportunity for favored customers to open store charge accounts, in which case the appropriate choice would be Sometimes. A manufacturing company that ships its finished goods, then bills for the product, would probably answer Never when asked if full payment is received at the time of sale. The answer you give depends on your own circumstances.

Without overloading you with accounting jargon, QuickBooks is trying to find out if you need to keep track of *accounts receivable*. An accounts receivable account is an account that keeps a running balance of everything that your customers owe you.

If you answer Sometimes or Never to the question about receiving full payment at the time of sale, you are then asked if you charge a fee to your customers for late payments.

Setting Up Items

The word *item* is used extensively throughout the QuickBooks program. The term refers to any amount that you list on an invoice or other sales form. Each item you set up takes one of these forms:

- *Service Item.* A service you perform, such as teaching, writing, manual labor, carpet laying, or child care.

- *Inventory Part Item.* Something that you keep in stock and subsequently sell, such as lumber, T-shirts, or seeds.

- *Non-Inventory Part Item.* Something that you sell but do not hold in inventory. A contractor, for example, might purchase some hardware items specifically for the home improvement job he is performing, then resell those items to his customer. These hardware items are not considered part of his inventory. A farmer raises livestock for resale or grows crops—the livestock and crops that he raises are considered non-inventory items.

- *Other Charge Item.* Other amounts that you charge your customers, such as delivery or packaging fees, go into this category.

In the next section of the EasyStep Interview, you establish the items for which you bill customers in your business.

Creating a Service Item

The first type of item you are asked to create is a service item. If your company doesn't have any service items (if, for example, you sell merchandise, but don't charge for your time), choose **No** and continue to the next section.

Creating a new service item

1. Choose **Yes** on the screen provided, then click **Next**. The Service Item: Name screen appears.

2. Enter a short name for the service (see Figure 5.4). You are limited to 13 characters and spaces. This name is for your reference and is the name you will use to request this item on a sales form.

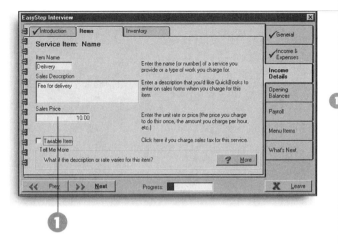

FIGURE 5.4

The sales description is the description that will appear on forms you give to your customers.

① Enter the standard price for which you will sell this item.

3. Enter a description for the service. This is the description that will appear on the sales forms you give to your customers.

4. Enter the normal price you will charge for this service. This can be entered as a flat fee or an hourly rate. If you anticipate the price will change from one customer to the next, you might want to leave the amount blank.

5. Indicate if this service is normally subject to sales tax. Most personal services are not subject to sales tax. To be certain, however, check the sales tax laws applicable in your state.

6. Click **Next** to proceed to the Service Item: Income Account screen.

7. Indicate the income account that relates to this service item (see Figure 5.5). For example, the items Flooring Installation, Drywall Repair, and Finishing might be associated with the income account Remodeling.

Is it taxable?

It's easy to find out if a service is subject to sales tax in your state. Check your phone book in the state government listings and look for Sales Tax. Call the number listed, explain what service your company performs, and ask if that service is subject to sales tax in the state.

FIGURE 5.5

When you record a sale of this service, the revenue is added to the income account you choose.

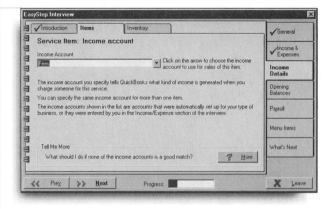

Missing interview screens

Some of the screens described throughout this chapter might not appear when you work your way through the interview. Depending on the choices you make, screens are triggered to either appear or not. Also, some screens (such as any screens relating to preparing estimates) appear only in the Pro version of the QuickBooks software.

8. Click **Next**. The Subcontracted Expenses screen appears. If you ever expect to hire someone else to perform this job and then bill your client for the subcontracted work, choose **Yes**. Otherwise, choose **No**.

9. Click **Next**. The Service Items: Purchase Information screen appears. On this screen, you should indicate a description of the item (see Figure 5.6). This description is for your purposes. It appears on your company check stubs and the bills that you enter in your system when you pay for the item.

FIGURE 5.6

The purchase description appears on your purchase orders, check stubs, and bills.

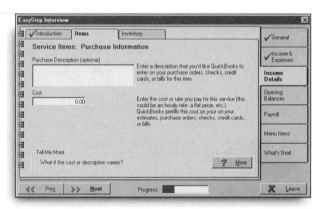

10. Enter your normal cost for this item and click **Next**.

11. On the Service Item: Expense Account screen that appears, indicate the expense account in which you will normally categorize the cost of this item when you purchase it. An account such as Contract Labor, Fees, or Commissions is a typical account to charge for service for which you are sub-contracting and subsequently charging to your customers.

Repeat steps 1–11 for each service item you want to add.

Creating a Non-Inventory Part Item

The next type of item you are asked to create is a non-inventory part item. If your company doesn't have any of these items, choose **No** and continue to the next section.

Creating a new non-inventory part item in the EasyStep Interview

1. Choose **Yes** on the screen provided, then click **Next**. The Non-Inventory Parts: Sales Information screen appears.

2. Enter a short name for the item. You are limited to 13 characters and spaces. This name is for your reference and is the name you will use to request this item on a sales form.

3. Enter a description for the item. This is the description that will appear on the sales forms you give to your customers.

4. Enter the normal price you will charge for this item.

5. Indicate if this item is normally subject to sales tax.

6. Click **Next** to proceed to the Non-Inventory Parts: Income Account screen.

7. Click the **down arrow** to drop down a list of choices for the income account that relates to this item. For example, the item Lumber might be associated with the income account Building Materials. If the income account you want to use is not listed, you can add it quickly by clicking on **Add New**. You are prompted to give a name and description to the new account and note if it is a subaccount of some other income account.

8. Click **Next**. You are asked if this is an item you purchase for a specific customer. If this is a product you raise (like crops) or produce yourself, answer **No** to this question, click **Next**. (Don't worry if you don't see this screen, or those that follow in steps 9 and 10—the appearance of these screens depends on answers you gave to questions earlier in the interview.)

   9. If you select Yes, the next screen asks you for a purchase description and a cost. The purchase description is a specific description of the item that will appear on your purchase orders and other documents. If the cost of the item varies each time you make a purchase, leave the cost section blank. Click **Next** when you have finished entering this information.

   10. Indicate the expense account in which you will normally categorize the cost of this item when you purchase it. A Cost of Sales account is a typical account to charge for items you are purchasing and reselling to your customers.

   Repeat steps 1–10 for each non-inventory part item you want to add.

Creating an Other Charge Item

   Other charge items include such things as delivery charges, shipping and postage costs, packaging, photocopying, and reimbursable expenses that you incur on behalf of your customer.

Creating an other charge item in the EasyStep Interview

   1. Choose **Yes** on the screen provided, then click **Next**. The Other Charges: Name and Sales Information screen appears.

   2. Enter a short name for the item. You are limited to 13 characters and spaces. This name is for your reference and is the name you will use to request this item on a sales form.

   3. Enter a description for the item. This is the description that will appear on the sales forms you give to your customers.

   4. Enter the normal price you will charge for this item. If the price varies from one occurrence of this charge to another, leave the amount blank.

   5. Indicate if this item is normally subject to sales tax.

   6. Click **Next** to proceed to the Other Charges: Income Account screen.

   7. Click the **down arrow** to drop down a list of choices for the income account that relates to this item (see Figure 5.7). Choose the account in which you will record income received for this item, or select **Add New** if you need to create a new account.

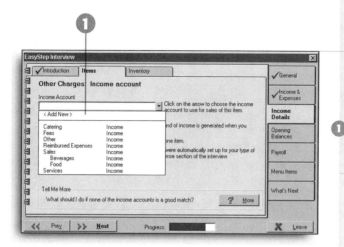

FIGURE 5.7

The drop-down list gives you a choice of all existing income accounts.

1   Click here if the income account you want to use does not appear on the list.

8. Click **Next**. You are asked if this is an item you pay for and for which you seek reimbursement. Sometimes you might acquire supplies or job parts on behalf of your customers, then pass the cost of these items through to your customer. If you choose **Yes**, you are asked for information relating to your purchase of the items. (Don't worry if you don't see this screen, or those that follow in steps 9 and 10—the appearance of these screens depends on answers you gave to questions earlier in the interview.)

9. If you select **Yes** in step 8, the next screen asks you for a purchase description and a cost. The purchase description is a specific description of the item that will appear on your purchase orders and other documents. If the cost of the item varies each time you make a purchase, leave the cost section blank. Click **Next** when you have finished entering this information.

10. Indicate the expense account in which you will normally categorize the cost of this item when you purchase it. A Cost of Sales account is a typical account to charge for items you are purchasing and reselling to your customers.

Repeat steps 1–10 for each other charge item you want to add.

Creating Inventory Items

In this next section, you are to set up your inventory items—the items you regularly keep on hand to sell to your customers and replenish when necessary.

QuickBooks does an excellent job of tracking the quantities of inventory items on hand and reminding you of when to reorder if quantities get low. See Chapter 14, "Keeping Track of Your Inventory," for a complete analysis of the ways in which QuickBooks treats inventory.

Creating a new inventory item in the EasyStep Interview

1. Choose **Yes** on the screen provided, then click **Next**. The Inventory Item: Sales Information screen appears.

2. Enter a short name for the item. You are limited to 13 characters and spaces. This name is for your reference and is the name you will use to request this item on a sales form.

3. Enter a description for the item. This is the description that will appear on the sales forms you give to your customers.

4. Enter the normal price you will charge for this item.

5. Indicate if this item is normally subject to sales tax.

6. Click **Next** to proceed to the Inventory Item: Income Account screen.

7. Click the **down arrow** to drop down a list of choices for the income account that relates to this item. Choose the account in which you will record income received for this item, or select **Add New** if you need to create a new account.

8. The next screen asks you for a purchase description and a cost. The purchase description is a specific description of the item that will appear on your purchase orders and other documents. If the cost of the item varies each time you make a purchase, leave the cost section blank. Click **Next** when you have finished entering this information.

9. You are next asked for information regarding reorder point (see Figure 5.8). Enter the number of items your inventory should drop to in order to trigger a reminder that it is time to reorder. Also, enter the number of items you have on

Inventory tracking for your tax return

QuickBooks tracks inventory using an Average Cost method, which is to say that the value of individual items in your inventory is constantly being revised as you purchase and sell inventory items. This method of inventory valuation does not conform to IRS regulations. See Chapter 14, "Keeping Track of Your Inventory," for information regarding rules and alternative methods for valuing inventory.

hand as of the start date. QuickBooks calculates the average value of these items based on the cost information you entered in step 8.

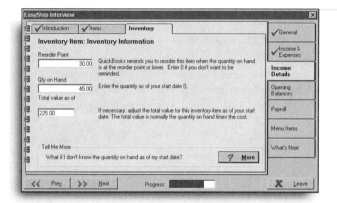

FIGURE 5.8

Enter a reorder point for this inventory item and QuickBooks reminds you when your supplies are running low.

Repeat steps 1–9 for each inventory item you want to add.

Entering Opening Balances

In the Opening Balances section of the EasyStep interview, you are asked to enter information, as of the start date, about which customers owe you money (your *accounts receivable*) and which vendors you owe money to (your *accounts payable*). In addition, you enter opening balances of loan accounts, fixed assets, and other assets and liabilities of your business. If these terms are new to you, don't worry. The process of entering this information is explained in a straightforward way that is easy to understand.

The Opening Balances section of the EasyStep Interview is the place where you enter the balances of all balance sheet accounts as of the start date.

Table 5.1 provides you with the information you need to determine opening balances for many typical balance sheet accounts.

Set up accounts with zero balances

If you don't have all the appropriate balances at your fingertips when you get ready to set up asset and liability accounts, go ahead and set up the accounts anyway, entering zero as the balance. You can go back later and change the opening balance for any account (as discussed in Chapter 6, "Entering Historical Information").

TABLE 5.1   Determine opening balances

Type of Account	Opening Balance
Bank account	Exact amount you had in the bank on the start date.
Current asset (such as deposits, short-term investments, and prepaid items)	Value of the asset as of the start date.
Accounts receivable (amounts owed to you by your customers)	Amount owed by each customer as of the start date.
Fixed asset (such as equipment, vehicles, office furniture, and computers)	Cost of the asset. You should also note the amount of depreciation recorded against the asset from the date of purchase to the start date.
Other asset (such as securities, long-term deposits, and prepaid expenses)	Value of the asset as of the start date.
Current liability (such as down payments on future delivery of goods, loans expected to be paid off within one year, bank overdrafts, and income taxes)	Amount due as of the start date.
Accounts payable (amounts you owe to vendors, utility companies, and so on)	Amount owed to each supplier as of the start date.
Long-term liability (such as mortgages and long-term notes payable)	Amount due as of the start date.
Credit card	Amount due to the credit card company as of the start date.
Owner's equity	Amount invested by owners of date. the business as of the start

Entering Customers

You should plan on entering each customer who owes you money as of the QuickBooks start date. If you feel ambitious, you can also enter other customers while you are in the EasyStep Interview, even if they didn't owe you anything as of the start date. It's really not necessary to do this, however, because entering customers later is an easy process.

When entering customers, you need the following information:

- Customer name
- List of individual jobs for the customer (if you plan to track jobs separately)
- Amount due from customer either in total or for each individual job

Choose **Yes** when you are asked to add a customer, then enter the name of the customer. Be careful when typing the name—if you spell it incorrectly you can't go back and correct it in the EasyStep Interview; you have to wait until later.

Enter the name of the first job for which this customer owes you money and the amount owed, or enter the total amount owed by the customer (see Figure 5.9). Continue entering other jobs until you have finished with this customer.

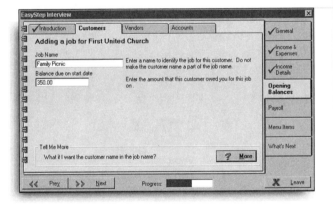

FIGURE 5.9

Entering jobs helps you separate the work you do for a client.

Follow the same procedure for all customers you want to enter at this time.

Note that in the EasyStep Interview, you are not given an opportunity to enter addresses and phone numbers of customers or any other pertinent information, such as whether the customer is subject to sales tax or what payment terms are normally applied to amounts due by this customer. This information must be added outside of the interview, in the customer list. See Chapter 8 for information about entering details regarding your customers.

Entering Vendors

Have ready a list of every person and company to whom you owe money and the amount you owe.

Choose **Yes** when you are asked to add a vendor, then enter the name of the vendor. Be careful when typing the name—if you spell it incorrectly you can't go back and correct it in the EasyStep Interview; you have to wait until later.

Enter the amount you owe this vendor as of the QuickBooks start date (see Figure 5.10).

FIGURE 5.10

Enter the amount owed to this vendor. This amount will be combined with all other amounts owed to form your Accounts Payable balance.

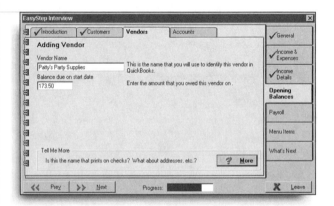

Follow the same procedure for all vendors you want to enter at this time.

Again, note that you are unable to enter detailed information about the vendor, such as the address, phone, and fax number. See Chapter 8 for the steps to enter complete vendor information.

Credit Card Accounts

Does your company have a credit card? Or do you use your personal credit card for company business? You can set up a credit card as a separate liability account in QuickBooks, and the credit card will show up on your financial statements with the amount due on the account.

When you enter credit card information into QuickBooks, you set up the credit card in a manner very similar to setting up a bank account. The opening balance due is the opening balance in the credit card account, with subsequent purchases and payments entered either as they are made or at the end of each month when you get your statement.

To enter a credit card in QuickBooks, you first enter the name of the credit card (MasterCard, Discover, for example). You are then asked to enter the date of the last credit card statement received prior to your start date (see Figure 5.11) and the amount owed on that statement.

Lines of Credit

A *line of credit* is a type of loan, usually a bank loan, from which you can draw money when needed and pay it back on a predetermined schedule. I used to work for a company that received its revenue seasonally. When it wasn't the season for revenue to come in, there were still bills to pay, so the company maintained a line of credit with its bank, a short-term loan account on which the company could draw in the non-revenue season.

To set up a line of credit in QuickBooks, you need the name of the bank or institution issuing the line of credit, the date of the last statement received just prior to your start date, and the amount owed as of the start date. If you don't owe anything on your line of credit as of the start date, enter zero as the statement ending balance (see Figure 5.11).

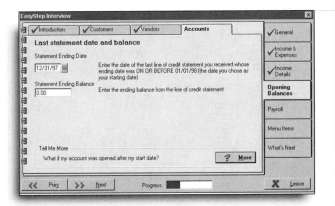

Use your start date as your credit card statement date

You get an error message if you try to enter a credit card statement date that falls after your start date. The implication is that there was a balance due on your start date that is not being properly reflected. If there was no balance due on your start date, go ahead and set up the credit card, entering zero in the Statement Ending Balance area. If you can't find the credit card statement from just prior to your start date, you can back into the amount that was on that statement by looking at the beginning balance on the first statement after the start date.

FIGURE 5.11

Enter the date of your last statement prior to your start date. If you begin doing business on your start date, enter your start date here.

Setting Up Loans and Other Liabilities

When setting up a loan in the EasyStep Interview, you are expected to enter a name for the loan, the unpaid balance as of the start date, and whether this is a long-term loan (see Figure 5.12).

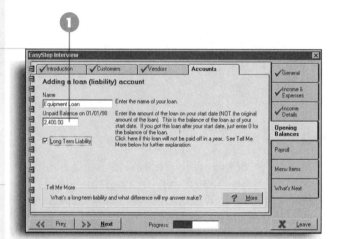

FIGURE 5.12

The name of the loan is the name that will appear on your financial statements.

① The amount due is the amount of principal—not the total payments including interest.

The name of the loan can be tied to what the loan is for (such as Truck Loan or Equipment Loan) or to the name of the lender (Bank of America Loan or First Finance Loan). The name you choose will appear on the financial statements and reports for your company.

To determine the unpaid balance of the loan as of the start date, you might need to examine a loan *amortization schedule*, a report that shows the balance of the loan after each payment is made. If your lender didn't provide you with such a schedule, you can contact your lender and ask for the *principal* amount due on the loan as of a specific date. While you're contacting your lender, you should ask for an amortization schedule so you always know how much of each payment goes toward interest and how much toward principal.

A long-term loan is one that is not expected to be paid off within the current year, or, in this case, within the 12-month period starting with the start date.

Large companies split their loans into two pieces on their financial statements, showing a short-term loan (or current liability) for the amount that will be paid within 12 months of the financial statement, and a long-term liability for the amount that will carry over beyond 12 months. Most small companies report each loan as a single loan and, in this case, would check the Long-Term Liability box if any part of the loan will be unpaid after 12 months.

Set Up Your Bank Account

Most of your day-to-day transactions ultimately flow through your company bank account. Amounts received from sales get deposited into the bank account. Checks you write result in withdrawals from your account. Until you set up a bank account, the tasks you perform in QuickBooks have nowhere to go.

Setting up a bank account

1. Choose **Yes** when asked if you want to set up a bank account, then click **Next**.

2. Enter the name of the bank account. You can either use the actual name of the bank or a descriptive name for the account (such as Checking Account or Savings Account). Then click **Next**.

3. Enter the date of the last bank statement you received prior to your start date. If you are setting up a new bank account where your first bank statement was issued at the end of your first month of business (or sometime thereafter), use the start date as the bank statement date.

4. Enter the ending balance amount from the last bank statement prior to your start date. If you are setting up a new bank account, enter zero as the balance at the start date.

Repeat the preceding steps for each new bank account you want to set up. You can also follow these steps to set up a petty cash account.

Setting Up Asset Accounts

The setup procedures for all types of asset accounts (current assets, fixed assets, and other assets) are essentially the same from one type of account to the next.

Setting up an asset account

1. Indicate that you want to set up an asset account by choosing **Yes** when asked, then click on **Next**.

2. Enter the name of the asset. This is the name that will appear on your financial statements and reports.

3. Indicate if the asset is current, fixed, or other (see Figure 5.13).

FIGURE 5.13

Click the arrow to see a drop-down list of asset types.

4. If you chose Fixed Asset in step 3, you are asked if you keep track of *depreciation* for this asset. Answer **Yes** if you plan to enter depreciation for this asset within QuickBooks.

Although you can enter depreciation in QuickBooks, the program does not have the capability for calculating depreciation expense. When setting up assets in QuickBooks, you have two options with regard to depreciation:

- **Track depreciation** in QuickBooks by calculating depreciation yourself (see Chapter 16, "Managing Fixed Assets," for information on how and when to calculate depreciation) and entering the depreciation adjustments into the program in the form of general journal entries (as discussed in Chapter 6).

- **Do not track depreciation expense** in QuickBooks. Enter your fixed assets at their full value and do not offset that value with depreciation adjustments. This method provides you with statements that accurately reflect the cost of your fixed assets, but does not give you useful information for preparation of your income tax return or for statements to shareholders or lenders. If you choose not to track depreciation in QuickBooks at all, plan on making depreciation adjustments by hand on your tax return and on published financial statements.

One way or another, you must find a way to keep track of depreciation expense so that your tax returns and financial statements provide an accurate reflection of your business. You might want to consult with an accounting professional for help in calculating depreciation or in setting up a system that enables you to make the calculations yourself.

Your Equity Accounts

QuickBooks establishes a set of *equity* accounts for you, based on the type of business entity you chose when you began setting up your company. An equity account is one that equates to the net worth of the company, or the accumulated earnings reduced by accumulated expenses.

An account such as Retained Earnings or Owner's Equity summarizes the net profit of the company, year after year. Corporations have a capital stock account. Partnerships and proprietorships have a draw account for the partner or owner.

A strange account placed in with the other equity accounts is called Opening Balance Equity. This account is created during the EasyStep Interview and is used to offset each entry you make. So, for example, when you enter a new asset valued at $10,000, the Opening Balance Equity account is charged with $10,000 as well as the asset account. In the end, when the interview is finished, you will see how to close out this opening balance account so that it doesn't clutter your financial reports.

There's nothing you need to do during the EasyStep Interview with regard to the setup of equity accounts. Later, if you want to add an equity account (say your business takes on a new owner and you want to create a new draw account) or change the name of an equity account, you can do so. This process is described in Chapter 8.

Setting Up Payroll

The single most time-consuming part of the EasyStep Interview is the payroll setup. You set up payroll for each of your company's employees, indicating such items as:

- Frequency of pay periods
- Regular rate of pay
- Overtime rate of pay
- The state in which your company pays payroll taxes
- Your company's state and federal unemployment tax rates
- The types of deductions withheld from employee paychecks (such as medical insurance, union dues, and local taxes)
- The types of items typically added to employee paychecks (such as mileage and travel reimbursements and reimbursements for other business-related expenditures)
- The name, address, and Social Security number of each employee you plan to enter, as well as the date on which each was hired

When asked if you want to set up or skip payroll, and you have a payroll that you plan to set up in QuickBooks, consider whether you want to set up payroll through the EasyStep Interview or wait until a later time.

If you choose to wait until later to set up your payroll, I recommend that you at least go through the EasyStep payroll screens and set up the elements of your payroll. Indicate whether your paychecks are issued weekly, biweekly, or semi-monthly; indicate which types of withholding apply to your company's employees and which types of benefits are paid on behalf of the employees. Set up your unemployment tax rates and any local income taxes that might be applicable.

Then, when asked if you want to set up the individual employees, you can choose to do this later (see the section on setting up employees in Chapter 18, "Paying Employees and Contractors"), but all of your payroll items will be in place and ready to use.

Setting Up Payroll Items

Setting up the payroll items

1. Answer **Yes** when asked if you want to set up payroll.

2. Indicate the frequency of paychecks issued by your company. You can choose more than one frequency. Some companies pay their hourly employees more frequently (weekly or every two weeks) than their salaried employees. Check each box that applies.

3. Check off each state for which you withhold income taxes (see Figure 5.14). Several screens separate this step from step 4. Just click **Next** at the bottom of each screen to progress to the next screen that asks you for input.

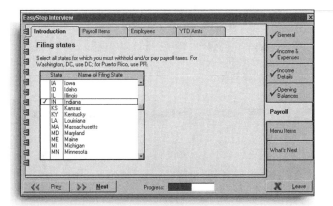

FIGURE 5.14

You might have employees in more than one state. Check each state that applies.

4. Enter the state withholding ID number for each state listed. If you don't know this information, you can enter it later.

5. Enter the state unemployment ID number for each state listed and the rate at which unemployment tax is calculated for each state. Some states require withholding for unemployment taxes (although most states do not). If you pay taxes in such a state, enter a rate in the Emp. Rate column.

6. Indicate if your company qualifies for a FUTA credit. The FUTA credit is the result of offsetting federal unemployment compensation taxes by amounts paid to state unemployment agencies.

Employer's unemployment compensation experience rate

State unemployment tax rates change from year to year as states determine your *experience rate*. The experience rate is determined by looking at a profile of your past employees and claims they have made for unemployment compensation. In the first years of doing business, an employer pays a high unemployment rate. After you have established that your employees do not make claims for unemployment compensation (usually after three years), this rate decreases.

7. Indicate if your employees are paid hourly, salaried, or on commission. Check each box that applies.

8. If your company pays different rates for different types of hourly work (such as higher rates for overtime or holiday hours), indicate that there are multiple rates available by checking the various options. You can check as many options as you need. It's wise to check each item that you think might apply, because then the payroll item has been set up for you and is ready to use when you need it.

9. Just as your company might pay different rates for hourly workers, there might be different rates for types of salaried work as well. Check all items that apply.

10. Place a check next to each payroll deduction that applies to your company's employees. These items (shown in Figure 5.15) are items that would be paid by employees through payroll withholding. If you want to include a deduction that is not on this list (child care, for example), choose Other Net Deduction.

FIGURE 5.15

Check each item that applies to your employees. Check an item even if it applies to only one employee.

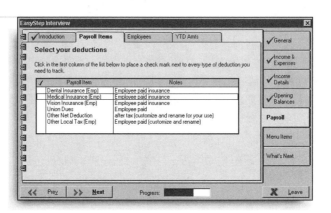

11. Check Mileage Reimbursement if your company has a practice of paying employees for vehicle usage in the form of an addition to their paycheck. If there are other payments that are made to employees in their paychecks (such as moving expense reimbursements), check the Other Taxable Addition item (see Figure 5.16). If you check the Other Taxable Addition item, a series of setup screens appears. On these screens, you are asked the following information:

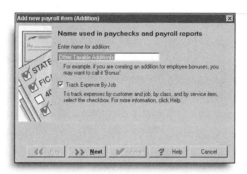

FIGURE 5.16
Enter the name of the item you want to add.

- Name of the new item (Moving Expense Reimbursement, for example).

- Indicate an expense account (such as Moving Expenses) for this item.

- As an item that is taxable to the employee, it should be included in the employee's compensation, and you will be asked to indicate the name of the account you use for compensation (it might be an account called Compensation, or something similar like Salaries and Wages).

- Indicate which withholding taxes apply to this item.

- Indicate if this item is based on quantity. In other words, if the item is a form of compensation that is based on a number of units sold or a number of phone calls made, you check this box.

- If the compensation is based on quantity, you are asked to enter a rate or an amount. A rate is the value per unit, so if each unit sold is worth $5, enter 5. If the rate is a percent, enter the amount with the percent symbol (2%). If the rate varies from one employee to the next, leave this part blank.

- If there is a maximum annual amount that can be earned for this payroll item ($5 per unit, but no more than $500 total), enter that amount.

12. Check off all company-paid benefits (such as medical insurance). Check Other Comp. Contribution if there is a company-paid benefit not listed, and you are asked to set up the benefit by answering questions such as the ones for setting up a compensation item in step 11.

13. Now that all the payroll items are set up, you are asked, on a series of screens, to check off the items that apply to all or most employees. By checking off these items, they automatically appear when you are issuing paychecks. You don't have to use the items that appear on a paycheck entry form, but they will be there, waiting for you to fill in amounts, and you won't have to search for the items in drop-down lists. For more detailed information about all the questions covered on these screens, see Chapter 18.

After you have checked all items that you want to appear on paychecks, you are ready to either set up actual employees or finish payroll setup. If you plan to set up your actual employees at this point, see Chapter 18.

Entering Starting Balances for Payroll

The final few screens of the payroll setup ask you to enter starting balances for employees and payroll taxes. If you chose to set up employees in the interview and your start date is sometime after the first day of the year, you need to enter the year-to-date payroll and withholding totals for each employee. This is so that your payroll tax forms at the end of the year (such as employee W-2 forms) reflect payroll for the entire year and not just part of the year.

If your start date is January 1 (or the first day your company did business), that should be the date on which you begin tracking payroll and payroll tax liabilities. If your start date is later in the year, I strongly recommend that you enter January 1 of the current year as the date on which you start tracking payroll and payroll tax liabilities.

You are asked for a date on which your accounts should be affected by payroll transactions. This should also be January 1 of the current year or the first day on which you began doing business.

Finally, you are asked to enter a date on which you plan to start using QuickBooks to pay your payroll. This is the actual date on which you will begin processing paychecks through QuickBooks.

If you entered employees earlier in the payroll setup, you are now presented with a screen listing all of your employees. Select each employee listed one at a time and enter any year-to-date payroll information for that employee (see Figure 5.17). If you start using QuickBooks to generate a payroll as of January 1 of the current year, you don't have to enter anything here. This is just to catch up the year-to-date numbers from the first of the year to the time when you start issuing paychecks from QuickBooks.

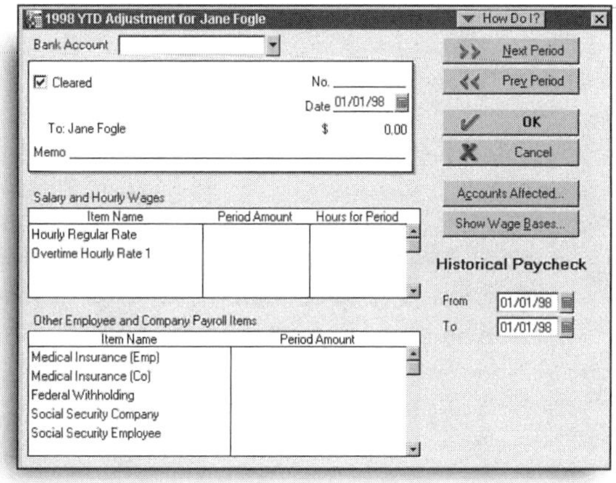

FIGURE 5.17

Enter all the year-to-date information for the selected employee on this screen. Entering this information is extremely important if you want to use QuickBooks to produce W-2 forms at the end of the year.

If your start date is not January 1 and you had payroll during the year prior to your start date, you need to enter the year-to-date tax payments that you have made. When the screen shown in Figure 5.18 appears, click in the area under Item Name. An arrow appears and you can click it to display a drop-down list of all the payroll items you created previously. Choose the items one at a time and enter the related year-to-date amount in the Amount column.

FIGURE 5.18

Click in the Item Name column to get a drop-down arrow. Then choose each tax and liability for which you have made payments during the year.

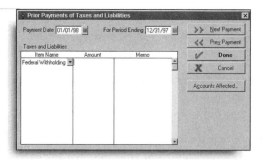

When you have finished entering year-to-date tax and other payroll liability amounts, click **Done**. A box appears asking if you want to use these amounts as your liability account balances. If you don't want the payments reflected in your financial statements for the year, you answer **Do Not Affect Accounts**. If you have paid the amounts and you want the payments to come through on your financial statements, but don't want to include the payments as reductions of your cash account, choose the second option.

To include the tax payments in your financial statements and to reflect the payments in your cash account as well, choose the third option.

Nearly every company will have starting balances for payroll tax liabilities. Unless your first payroll checks are issued at the same time you begin using QuickBooks, you probably owed some payroll taxes as of the end of the prior year. Taxes that were withheld last December wouldn't be due to the government until January, so that withholding is considered a liability as of January 1. If your start date is sometime later in the year, the amount of payroll tax you owe as of the start date is the amount you should enter as your liability.

Entering Historical Information

Enter bills so that all the expenditures made by your company since the start date will be recorded

Enter invoices that reflect all the business your company has had since the start date

Enter the money that your company has spent and received since the start date

Enter year-to-date payroll information so that you will be able to prepare complete and accurate payroll tax forms and so that your payroll will be up-to-date

You can change the start date

You are not required to keep the start date you designated when you set up your company in the EasyStep Interview. If you chose June 1 as your start date (and now you decide you really want to go back to the beginning of the year to enter a full year of transactions), you can change the start date by adjusting the beginning balance and date in your registers, as described in this chapter.

If the start date you choose for your company is a date from the past, you need to go back to that start date and begin entering the individual transactions that will make your company's QuickBooks file complete. Usually, the first day of the year is chosen as a start date. If it's May and you are beginning to enter information for the year in QuickBooks, you need to enter the transactions from January through May.

Use the handy checklist in the chapter to help you gather the documents you need to enter your historical transactions.

Checklist of Items Before You Begin

Continue entering current transactions

Business doesn't have to come to a standstill while you are entering historical transactions. You can continue entering your current transactions on the schedule you normally follow. That way, you won't get behind.

When you enter historical transactions, there is a certain order in which you must make your entries. If, for example, you entered the checks you wrote before you entered the bills you were paying, there would be no way to tie the checks to the bills. Also, if you entered your deposits before entering the customer invoices that were paid, there wouldn't be a clear record of what the deposited funds represent.

Therefore, the transactions that you enter in your bank account will actually be the last transactions you enter.

The list of documents and information you need for entering historical transactions is presented in the order in which you enter those transactions (see the following checklist). By using this convenient checklist, you can gather the appropriate data and perform one task at a time. Check off the task as you do it, then when you come back to enter more historical transactions you will easily see where you left off.

Marking documents as you enter them

Use a special check mark, a rubber stamp, or some noticeable means of marking each document that you enter into QuickBooks. This way, you don't run the risk of entering the same document twice.

After you've collected the documents you use to make entries of historical information, and you've set aside some time to make these entries, you can follow the rest of the instructions in this chapter for getting the historical information into your records, in the proper order.

Checklist for Entering Historical Transactions

- All bills you have received since your start date. Enter one at a time, in the order in which they were received, just as you would a bill that comes in the mail today. Now is a good time to consider getting a date stamp, if you don't already have one, so you can date bills when you receive them. Any bills that were outstanding at the time of your start date should already have been entered when you went through the steps of the EasyStep Interview. Any bills that you have paid recently may have already been entered as well. Make sure you don't enter the same bill twice.

- All invoices from your start date to the present. Enter these first, one at a time, in the order in which they were issued. Enter the invoices in the same way as you would enter an invoice you are issuing today, but make sure you check the date on the invoice. Note that any invoices that were outstanding at the time of your start date should already have been entered when you went through the steps of the EasyStep Interview.

- All money you have received since your start date. This will include cash, checks, and credit card payments, as well as proceeds from loans and money from any other sources. Because you have already entered all of your invoices, noting the payments made by customers is a matter of checking off which invoices have been paid.

- All bills you have paid since your start date. Had you not completed the earlier step of entering the bills you received, you would not be able to do this step now. Simply check off the bills that you paid as you normally would, noting any changes in the amounts paid versus the amounts on the bills as you enter the payments. QuickBooks will offset your cash account by the amounts of the bills that you paid.

- All deposits you have made to your bank accounts since the start date. Since you have already entered the amount of money you have received since the start date, entering the deposits should be a simple matter of checking off the payments to form each deposit. QuickBooks will increase the balance in your cash account by the amount of deposits you indicate.

- Payroll transactions from the start date to the present. Note that you will not be able to use the QuickBooks payroll feature until all historical payroll information has been entered. By entering historical payroll information, you will be able to produce accurate payroll tax reports and year-to-date payroll statements for the company employees.

- All other checks written since the start date, aside from the checks written to pay bills.

Entering Historical Bills Received

The first pieces of historical information you enter are the bills that you received from the start date to the time when you began entering current information in QuickBooks. These are the bills from your vendors, suppliers, and contractors for items and services you purchased.

To make sure you haven't already entered some of these bills in QuickBooks, you can print a list of all bills that you have received, including those that have been recorded as paid, organized by vendor. With this list at your side, you can quickly check to see if a bill has been entered previously. To generate such a report, choose **Reports**, **A/P Reports**, **Vendor Balance Detail**.

As you enter each bill, QuickBooks adds the amount to your accounts payable balance and shows the amount as an expense in the account you indicate on the bill.

Entering a bill

1. Choose **Activities**, **Enter Bills**. (If **Enter Bills** does not appear on your main Activities menu, you can find it under **Activities**, **Other Activities**.) The Enter Bills window opens.

2. Choose a vendor from the drop-down list (see Figure 6.1). If the vendor you want to use does not appear in the list, select **<Add New>** from the top of the drop-down list and enter new vendor information.

3. Make sure the correct date appears in the date area. The date should match the date on the bill.

4. Enter an optional memo.

5. If this bill is for the purchase of inventory items, on the tab marked Items (see Figure 6.2), enter the rest of the information

---

Enter historical invoices and bills

You can enter historical invoices before bill payments if you do not pass through billed amounts to customers. If you pay for items for which you expect reimbursement from your customers, it is necessary that you enter historical bills before invoices, so the billed information will all be available when you get ready to enter the invoices.

Finding menu choices

Depending on how you answered some of the questions in the EasyStep Interview, some menu choices might be hidden. The **Lists** menu has a side menu called **Other Lists** and the **Activities** menu has a side menu called **Other Activities**. You can control which features appear (and don't appear) on these other menus by choosing **File**, **Preferences**, then clicking on the **Menus** icon on the left side of the Preferences window (you might have to scroll down to find it). Check items that you want to hide on the other menus, or uncheck items that you want to move to the main part of the **Lists** and **Activities** menus.

right from the bill: item(s) ordered, description, quantity, and rate. If this bill relates to a particular job (if you use the Job Costing feature), enter the job name in the space provided.

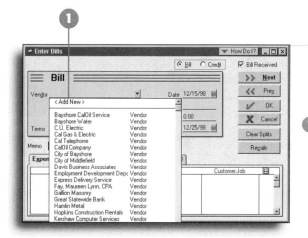

FIGURE 6.1

Scroll through the drop-down list to find the vendor you are looking for.

❶ Click here to add a new vendor.

FIGURE 6.2

Enter detailed information right from your bill at the bottom of the Enter Bills window.

❶ Use the Items tab to reflect inventory items purchased.

❷ Click the Expenses tab to show expenses such as supplies or utilities.

6. If this bill is for expenses (such as repairs or supplies), use the tab marked Expenses and enter the type of expense, an optional memo, and the amount of the bill.

7. Click **Next** to proceed to the next bill, or click **OK** if this is the last bill you intend to enter.

Continue the preceding process until all your bills have been entered.

After you've entered all bills from your start date to the present, the following areas of QuickBooks have been brought up-to-date:

- Records of all inventory purchases since your start date
- Vendor history of all bills received since the start date from each vendor

Entering Historical Invoices

When you have collected all the invoices that you issued between the start date and today, you are ready to enter historical invoices into your QuickBooks company file. Stack the invoices in the order in which they were issued, with the earliest on top.

Before you begin, you might want to see a list of all the invoices you have previously entered into QuickBooks. To generate such a report, choose **Reports**, **A/R Reports**, **Customer Balance Detail**. A detailed list showing all invoices as well as payments received, such as the list shown in Figure 6.3, can be printed by clicking the **Print** button at the top of the report.

FIGURE 6.3

Keep this report by your side when entering historical invoices so that you don't enter the same invoice twice.

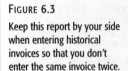

Click here to print a hard copy of the report.

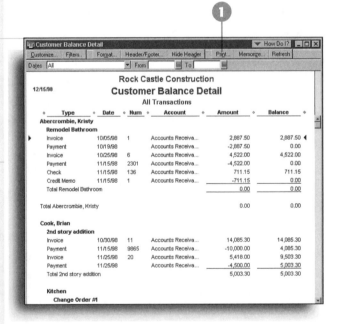

Entering an invoice

1. Choose **Activities**, **Create Invoices**. The Create Invoices window appears.

2. Choose a customer from the drop-down list. If the customer name does not appear, select **<Add New>** and enter new customer information.

3. Make sure the date of the invoice is correct.

4. Enter details of the invoice, following right along from the actual invoice you issued: item, quantity, description, and rate (see Figure 6.4).

5. If an expense was entered from your historical bills that relates to this invoice, click the **Time/Costs** button in the Create Invoices window to pop up the Choose Billable Time and Costs window. Any items charged to the customer through the bills appear here (see Figure 6.5). Check any item that should pass through to this invoice, then click **OK** when finished.

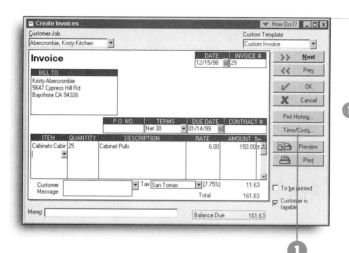

FIGURE 6.4

In the bottom area of the window, enter the detail of each item for which you are billing a customer.

1 Click here to review costs that have been passed through to this customer from the bills you entered.

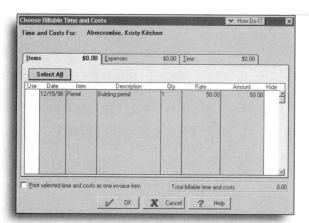

FIGURE 6.5

Check off each item you want to include on this invoice by clicking in the Use column next to the item.

6. Click **Next** to proceed to the next invoice, or click **OK** if this is the last invoice you intend to enter.

Continue the preceding process until all your invoices have been entered.

After you've entered all invoices from your start date to the present, the following area of QuickBooks have been brought up-to-date:

- Complete record of every item and service you have sold since the start date

- Detailed customer history of all business done with each customer since the start date

Entering Money Received

After all of your invoices have been entered, it's time to start recording payments for those invoices. If, in the past, you recorded payments with a receipt book or some form of paper voucher, you can use those receipts or vouchers for entering payments. If you have no such paper trail, you will probably refer to whatever documentation accompanies your bank deposits. Collect all the documents for payments received since the start date.

Entering Payments Against Invoices

Entering historical payments

1. Choose **Activities**, **Receive Payments**. The Receive Payments window appears. This window is for recording payments against invoices only. If you want to record payments for sales without linking the sale to an invoice, see the later section "Entering Cash Payments."

2. Choose a customer name by clicking the drop-down arrow, then clicking on a customer name from the resulting list. Because the payments will be for invoices, and you have already entered all of your invoices, the customer names will already be in the list.

3. Make sure the date of the payment is correct.

4. Enter the total amount of payment received in the Amount area on the receive payments form.

5. All invoices that have been created for this customer will appear in the Outstanding Invoices/Statement Charges list at the bottom of the Receive Payments window (see Figure 6.6). Check each invoice to which this payment relates by clicking in the left-most column across from the invoice.

6. If the amount of payment was not for the entire invoice, reflect the actual payment by entering the correct amount in the payment column across from the invoice. Any remaining balance due stays with this customer and appears the next time you enter a payment for this customer.

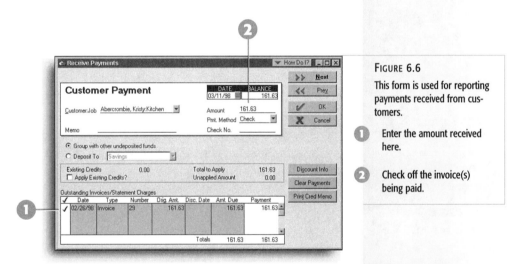

FIGURE 6.6

This form is used for reporting payments received from customers.

① Enter the amount received here.

② Check off the invoice(s) being paid.

7. Click the **Next** button to enter another payment, or click **OK** when you have finished entering payments.

Repeat the preceding steps for each payment you want to record.

Reflecting Credits and Discounts

After entering an invoice in your QuickBooks file, strange things can happen. Between the time the invoice was issued and the payment was made, there might have been a return of merchandise resulting in a credit. Or, there might be a discount that the

Warning: Reflecting payments

Before changing the amount of an invoice to reflect the actual payment due, find out why only part of the payment due was received. If the customer was entitled to a credit or a discount, this should be reflected properly instead of merely changing the amount in the Payment column. See the section "Reflecting Credits and Discounts" for the proper treatment of these items.

customer received for a timely payment. When this happens, the amount of the invoice disagrees with the amount of the payment received.

You can simply change the amount reflected in the invoice summary at the bottom of the Receive Payments screen, but then you forever carry an amount due on the invoice that changed.

Instead, you need to accurately record the credit or discount, so the payment for the invoice appears to be correct, the invoice doesn't remain on your books with an amount due (that really isn't due), and your company's income records are correct.

Reflecting a discount

1. With the Receive Payments window still onscreen, click the **Discount Info** button.

2. The Discount Information window appears (see Figure 6.7). Select an account for the discount (there should already be a discount account in your account list).

3. The discount amount that appears is a result of the terms assigned to the related invoice. You have the option of changing the discount amount. After you're satisfied with the amount, click **OK**. The discount reduces the amount due on the invoice.

FIGURE 6.7

Click **Discount Info** to display this window.

1 Change the discount amount here if necessary.

2 Choose the correct account for recording the discount.

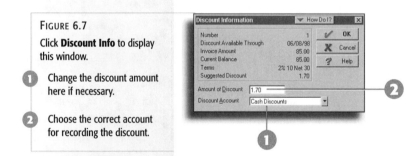

Reflecting a credit

1. Choose **Activities, Create Credit Memos/Refunds**. The Create Credit Memos/Refunds window appears.

2. Select the customer name at the top of the credit form and enter the correct date.

3. In the Item column, indicate the item(s) for which a credit is being issued (see Figure 6.8). Generally, the item you choose will be the same as an item which appeared on an earlier invoice.

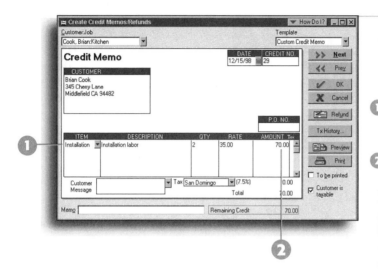

FIGURE 6.8

Enter credits and refunds on this separate form; then the amounts will flow through to the customer invoice.

① Click here to enter the item for which the credit is being issued.

② QuickBooks calculates the amount of the credit based on the quantity and rate you enter.

4. Enter the quantity and rate for the item(s) being credited. Verify whether or not the Customer Is Taxable box should be checked.

5. Click **OK** to issue the credit and record it on your books.

6. Complete steps 1-5 in the earlier section "Entering Payments Against Invoices." When you select <u>A</u>ctivities, Receive Pa<u>y</u>ments and choose a customer job, the amount of credits existing for this customer appears in the middle of the screen (see Figure 6.9).

7. To apply credits, check the **Apply Existing Credits?** box. The credit(s) available for this customer appears in the Payment column at the bottom of the form.

8. Complete the Receive Payments form by clicking **Next** or **OK.**

FIGURE 6.9

Credits appear in the middle of this form, ready for you to apply.

① Check this box to apply credits.

② Credits appear as payments.

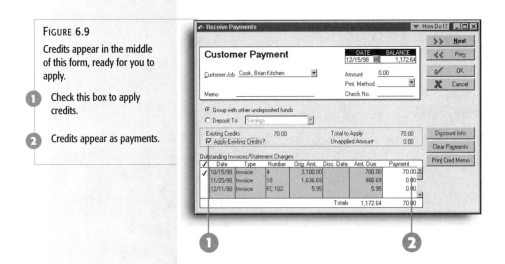

Entering Cash Payments

There are some circumstances in which you will have payments to enter, but no related invoice. For example, your business might conduct cash sales—sales to customers who make purchases on a one-time, walk-in basis, who are not expected to give you their names. You might have customers who make purchases from you regularly but who do not have an open account with you, so they pay cash at the time of the purchase.

Or, you might have decided to streamline your entry of historical information, bypass entering invoices altogether, and just enter cash payments.

Whatever the reason, there might be cash sales lurking among the payments you received that must be recorded to bring your income and cash records into balance.

Entering cash payments received

1. Choose **Activities**, **Enter Cash Sales**. (If the **Enter Cash Sales** menu choice does not appear, look under **Activities**, **Other Activities**. Also, see the note, "Finding Menu Choices," earlier in this chapter.) The Enter Cash Sales window appears.

2. Choose a customer from the drop-down list at the top of the window. If the customer who made the sale is not on the list, you can add a customer by clicking **<Add New>** at the top of the list. If you have a lot of cash sales to enter, particularly sales to strangers or one-time-only customers, you might want to create a new customer called Cash Sales or something similar, and use that customer name each time you have a cash sale to record.

3. Make sure the date of the payment is correct.

4. On the bottom section of the Enter Cash Sales form, enter a description of the item(s) for which the payment was received (see Figure 6.10). By choosing an item or items, QuickBooks knows to which income account the cash should be directed.

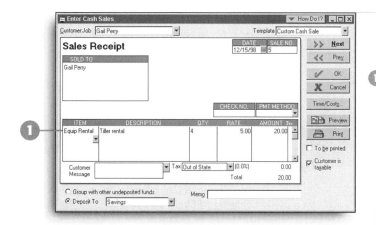

FIGURE 6.10

Enter a cash payment on this screen.

① Click in this column to select the item that was sold or the service that was provided.

5. Enter a quantity and rate, if this information is available. Alternatively, you can enter a total amount in the Amount column at the bottom of the form.

6. Click the **Next** button to enter another payment, or click **OK** if you have finished entering cash payments.

Repeat the preceding steps for each cash payment you want to record.

When all payments have been entered into QuickBooks, the following areas of your QuickBooks file have been brought up-to-date:

- Records of all payments received as of your start date
- Complete customer records showing all sales to customers and payments by customers made since the start date
- Complete records of all unpaid invoices as of the current date
- Accurate reflection of income to date in your company accounts

Entering Bills Paid

All the bills you have paid from the start date to today must now be entered. Otherwise, your records will show that you owe an awful lot of money! Gather all the bills you have paid since your start date. The date and amount paid should be marked on each bill. If you haven't been marking bills paid, now is a good time to start.

Entering bills paid

1. Choose **Activities**, **Pay Bills**. (If you can't find **Pay Bills** on the **Activities** main menu, look under **Activities**, **Other Activities** and you should find it. Also see the note, "Finding Menu Choices," which appeared earlier in this chapter.) The Pay Bills window appears.

2. For the first bill you paid, enter the payment date.

3. Click the **Show All Bills** option in the center of the screen. All outstanding bills appear on the list at the bottom of the screen.

4. Check the bill(s) that corresponds to the payment. If this payment was for only part of a bill, indicate the amount that was paid in the Amt Paid column.

5. Click **Next** to enter the next payment, or click **OK** if you are finished entering payments.

Follow the preceding steps until you have entered all of your bill payments.

When all bill payments have been entered into QuickBooks, the following areas of your QuickBooks file have been brought up-to-date:

- Records of all bill payments made since your start date
- Complete vendor records showing all acquisitions made by your company and payments made by your company since the start date
- Complete records of all outstanding bills (accounts payable) as of the current date
- Accurate reflection of expenses to date in your company accounts

Entering Deposits Made

You've recorded all the cash you received since the start date and have updated your income and receivables records in the process. But so far, your bank account hasn't been affected by these entries. You need to reflect the actual bank deposits so that your cash balance will be accurate.

Gather your deposit slips or other records of the amounts deposited with each bank deposit.

Entering cash deposits

1. Choose **Activities**, **Make Deposits**. The Payments to Deposit window appears.
2. Click on each payment that makes up this deposit. If an amount included in this deposit does not appear on the Payment to Deposit list, don't worry. That is covered in step 5. Click **OK**. The Make Deposits window appears.
3. Indicate the bank account to which you are making this deposit.
4. Verify the date of the deposit.

5. If this deposit included amounts that were not on the Payment to Deposit list, enter the additional deposit amounts on this screen. This might include money from sources other than customers, such as a bank loan or a cash rebate. In the From Account column, indicate the account to which the amount relates.

6. Click **Next** to finish recording this deposit and enter a new deposit, or **OK** to record the deposit and exit this screen.

When all deposits have been entered into QuickBooks, the following area of your QuickBooks file has been brought up-to-date:

- All deposits accurately recorded in your bank accounts

Entering Payroll Transactions

All payroll transactions must be entered before you begin using the QuickBooks Payroll feature.

If your start date is sometime after January 1 (and after the first day your company began doing business), you must enter year-to-date payroll amounts for all of your company's employees as of the start date. For example, if your company was in business all year and you choose April 1 as your start date, you have to enter January-to-March payroll amounts for all of the company's employees. In addition, you must enter every paycheck written after the start date, with full details of all tax and other withholdings.

If your start date is January 1 (or the first day your company began doing business), you will have no year-to-date amounts to enter, but you must enter every paycheck written since the start date.

Gather the details for every paycheck written since the start date as well as information relating to all payroll tax payments made since the start date.

To enter year-to-date payroll information for your employees, choose **Activities**, **Payroll**, **Set Up YTD Amounts**. The Set Up YTD Amounts window appears. See "Entering Starting Balances for Payroll" in Chapter 5, "Setting Up Accounts, Inventory, Fixed Assets, and Payroll" for the steps required for entering the year-to-date information.

Entering individual paychecks

1. Choose **Activities**, **Payroll**, **Pay Employees**. The Select Employees to Pay window appears.

2. Verify the dates for check and end of pay period. Also, verify that the correct bank account is chosen for this payment.

3. Click to the left of the employee you want to pay (see Figure 6.11). You can select more than one employee, but the payments you create for all selected employees will be recorded on the same date and for the same pay period.

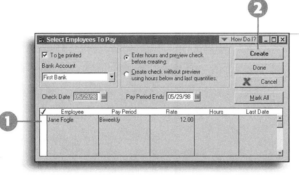

Set Up Payroll First

Payroll setup must be completed before you can begin entering historical payroll. This involves setting up individual payroll items such as types of withholding and benefits paid by the employer. The easiest way to set up payroll is by using the EasyStep Interview. If you need to set up payroll, choose **File**, **EasyStep Interview**, then click on the Payroll tab. See Chapter 5 for instructions for setting up payroll.

FIGURE 6.11

Choose which employees received checks during the stated pay period.

1. Click here to select the employees who received checks.

2. Click **Create** to proceed to the screen on which you will enter payroll detail.

4. Click the **Create** button. The Preview Paycheck window appears (see Figure 6.12).

5. Enter the appropriate information for this employee's paycheck. For a detailed example of paycheck creation, see Chapter 18, "Paying Employees and Contractors."

6. When you have completed this paycheck, click the **Create** button. If you selected more than one employee at step 3, the next employee screen appears; otherwise, you return to the Select Employees to Pay screen where you can change the dates and enter additional paychecks, or click **Done** if you are finished entering paychecks.

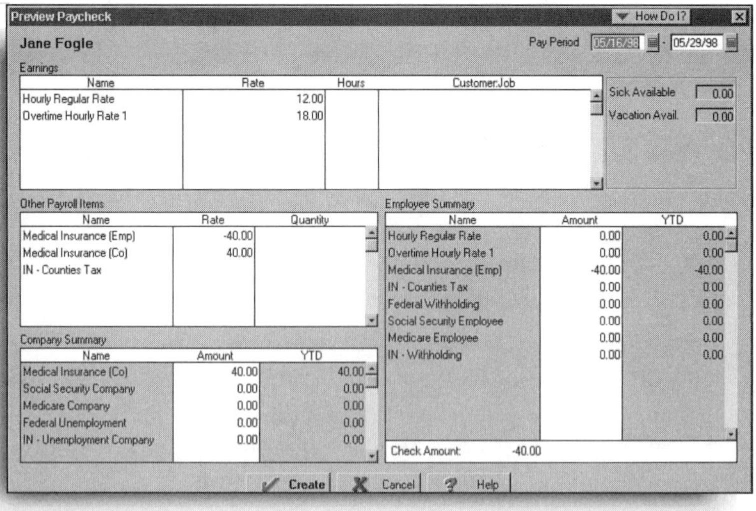

FIGURE 6.12

Enter all appropriate payroll information for this employee's paycheck.

When all paychecks and year-to-date payroll information have been entered into QuickBooks, the following areas of your QuickBooks file have been brought up-to-date:

- Year-to-date payroll records for each employee
- Complete payroll tax liabilities for the entire year

Entering All Other Payments Made

The final step in entering historical information involves entering any remaining payments that have been made since the start date. These payments might include rent, loan payments, loans to employees or owners, retirement contributions, and so on.

You need your check register or other record of checks written since the start date. You enter only the checks that have not been entered previously.

Entering checks not previously entered

1. Choose **Activities**, **Write Checks**. The Write Checks window appears. It looks just like a real check.

2. At the top of the screen, where it says **Bank Account**, select the bank account against which this check was written.

Deleting duplicate checks

It's possible that you might inadvertently enter a check that has been entered previously, in the form of a bill payment, for example. See Chapter 15, "Purchase Orders, Accounts Payable, and Paying Bills," for information on how to examine the checks that have been written and how to delete a duplicate check.

3. Verify that the correct date is displayed.

4. Enter the name of the payee at the top of the check.

5. Uncheck the **To Be Printed** box. This enables you to enter the correct check number for this check.

6. Enter the amount paid.

7. At the bottom of the window, enter a description of what you paid or purchased with this check, selecting the account to which the expense should be charged (see Figure 6.13). For more information about accounts, see Chapter 7, "Chart of Accounts."

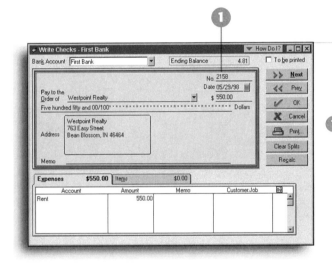

FIGURE 6.13

Enter all check information, just as it appeared on your original check.

1 Unchecking the **To Be Printed** box enables you to enter a check number here.

8. Click **Next** to enter another check, or **OK** if you are finished entering checks.

Repeat the preceding steps for all the checks you need to enter.

When all checks have been entered into QuickBooks, the following areas of your QuickBooks file have been brought up-to-date:

- Accurate ending balance in your bank accounts
- Company profit and loss statement for the year to date

Chart of Accounts

Basic accounting terms can be easy to understand when the concepts are useful to your business

QuickBooks provides you with a standard chart of accounts, which is a good springboard for customizing your own account list

Get rid of deadweight by removing accounts you no longer need

This is a chapter about scary accounting terms, such as *chart of accounts*, *assets*, *liabilities*, *equity*, *debits*, *credits*, and so on. As a former accounting instructor who taught introductory-level accounting courses to people who were new to these terms, I have a pretty good feel for just how obscure some of this stuff can seem to the uninitiated.

Before you skip ahead to future chapters, give me a few minutes to convince you that there are easy ways to look at these basic accounting concepts, and that your experiences using QuickBooks over the years will be better for having learned about them.

Understanding the Importance of Accounting

Accounting is the business of keeping track of all the financial activities of an entity. When you use accounting techniques, you provide an opportunity to obtain information about how your company is performing, and you can use that information to make intelligent decisions.

Without accounting, you would never know whether your business is profitable or losing money until you either find yourself with too many bills and not enough money to pay them, or find your cash register overflowing with no room to store all the cash. Chances are you will be met with the former scenario, if you have not kept track of your company's performance through basic accounting methods.

With an accounting system in place, such as QuickBooks, you can compare results from one year to the next, one month to the next, or even one day to the next. You can also do the following:

- Spot trends by comparing performance over time
- See areas of strength and weakness by identifying the costs of producing different types of income
- Budget your income and expenditures so that you will be sure to have enough money to meet your bills when they are due

- Plan for the future by forecasting anticipated revenue and expenses based on past performance
- Report on your performance to lenders and tax authorities

What Is an Account?

An account is a descriptive title for financial information. On a financial statement, which lists all the types of earnings and expenditures for a company, or a statement that lists the types of items a company owns and the amounts it owes to others, each individual category is known as an account.

Accounts simplify the way we organize financial information so that the information is easy to understand. For example, if you told your banker that your company earned $100,000 last year and spent $75,000, that probably wouldn't be enough to satisfy his curiosity regarding your ability to pay back a loan.

By separating your financial transactions into accounts, you can provide a more detailed picture of where the company got its money, how the money was spent, what possessions the company has (such as vehicles or office equipment), and what it owes lenders. Accounts provide the pieces that fit together to make a financial representation of the whole company.

Types of Accounts

There are five main types of accounts, and all your company's financial activity should fit into these five types. Within each type you can get creative, using descriptions that fit the kinds of financial transactions in which your company engages.

The five types of accounts are:

- *Assets*. Your company's possessions are assets. Quickbooks breaks this down into these categories: Bank (your company bank accounts), Accounts Receivable (amounts due from others), Other Current Assets (assets that will be replaced within one year), Fixed Assets (furniture, buildings, and other fixtures), and Other Assets (assets that don't fall into the preceding categories).

- *Liabilities.* Your company's debts are liabilities. QuickBooks breaks this down into these categories: Accounts Payable (amounts your company owes others), Credit Card (balance due on your company charge card), Other Current Liability (debts that will be liquidated within one year), and Long Term Liability (debts that will be around more than one year).

- *Equity.* The difference between your company's assets and liabilities equals your company's equity.

- *Income.* Your company's earnings are its income. QuickBooks breaks this down into the categories of Income and Other Income. Other Income is income that is not necessarily related to the main reason your business exists (such as interest income).

- *Expenses.* The costs involved in earning income are your company's expenditures. QuickBooks breaks this down into these categories: Cost of Goods Sold (costs of producing your company's inventory), Expense (all other business expenses), and Other Expense (expenses not necessarily related to the main reason your business exists).

Debits and Credits

The concept of debits and credits has confused many beginning accounting students, but it is simpler than you can imagine. Applying a strict accounting definition, debit means "left" and credit means "right."

Traditionally, accounts are viewed like the letter T, with the account name across the top of the T and changes to the account falling on the sides of the T—debits on the left and credits on the right. A dr (abbreviation for debit) and cr (credit) are placed at the top of the T.

Depending on the type of account it is, amounts on the left either increase or decrease the balance in the account, and amounts on the right do the opposite. For Asset and Expense accounts, an amount on the left side increases, an amount on the right side decreases. For Liability, Equity, and Income accounts, the opposite is true.

In Figure 7.1, the sales account has seen increases of $8,500 and a decrease of $600, for a credit balance of $7,900. Because credits increase an income account, income is increasing.

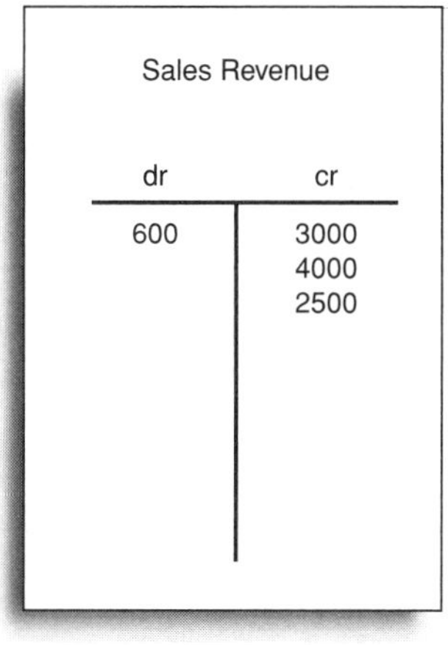

```
          Sales Revenue

       dr              cr
       600            3000
                      4000
                      2500
```

FIGURE 7.1

The way accountants see things: debits on the left, credits on the right. It's the same for every type of account.

Assets and Why We Care About Them

An *asset* is something that belongs to your company. It is part of what gives your company value. Following are examples of assets that your company might own:

- Cash in the bank, petty cash, cash in the cash register, cash in the safe
- Investments in stocks and bonds and mutual funds
- Inventory that is ready to sell, inventory that is in the process of being manufactured, pieces and parts that will eventually become inventory
- Accounts receivable—amounts owed to you by your customers
- Prepaid purchases or goods and services
- Amounts on deposit with suppliers

- Furniture, equipment, vehicles, building and building improvements, land and land improvements

- Loans that your company made to employees, shareholders, good friends…

Assets get used in the production of your company's income. Sometimes they are used and replenished quickly—for example, you use the cash that is in your bank to pay the expenses and payroll of your company, and you replenish the cash each time you sell a product or service. Your inventory (if your company has inventory) turns over quickly as well—you sell products and purchase or make new products to take their places.

Other assets are used up at a more leisurely pace—office furniture wears out over time, computer equipment becomes obsolete (all right, I admit that doesn't seem to happen at a very leisurely pace), and buildings get outgrown or need remodeling.

Your accounting records, over time, will show the pace at which assets turn over and need to be replaced, and from this information you can plan for future cash outlays. You can study the impact that time has on your assets and make decisions about how to slow down or speed up the pace at which you use assets.

SEE ALSO

➤ *For more information about using QuickBooks to forecast future performance of your company, see page 521*

Your Company's Liabilities

Liabilities are what you owe. When judging the viability of a company, one thing people look at is how great are the liabilities, and how well is the company able to meet those obligations. Following are examples of liabilities:

- Payables owing to your suppliers, vendors, utility companies, subcontractors

- Payroll owing to your employees

- Taxes owing to federal, state, and local government, including income taxes, payroll taxes, sales taxes

- Retirement contributions owing to your company retirement program

- Amounts your company has received as advance payments, retainers, and deposits from your customers and clients

- Loans owing to banks and other lenders

- Service and product warranties that you have issued to your customers

Just as with assets, some liabilities get turned over quickly—bills get paid and new bills take their places, paychecks get issued regularly, advances your company has received from customers turn into income as you fulfill your obligations.

Other liabilities stay around for a long time, such as mortgage loans on buildings and lifetime warranties.

By using QuickBooks to keep track of what your company owes and to whom, you can monitor how long it takes your company to meet its obligations and make decisions about what obligations you might be able to take on in the future.

Equity Is What Your Company Is Worth

When describing different types of accounts, the term *net worth* is often applied to the sum of a company's *equity* accounts. If you add up all the value of the company's assets (items that the company owns), subtract what the company owes (amounts due to others), what you are left with is the *book value* of the company, or equity.

Adding assets and subtracting liabilities is the back way into calculating equity. Equity itself is made up of the following types of amounts:

- Amounts contributed to the business by owners and shareholders, including the value of stock issued by the company

- Amounts earned by the company (the amount of income left over after the expenses are paid each year) and not distributed to owners

Adding up the preceding amounts gives you the same result as subtracting liabilities from assets.

Understanding Equity Accounts

There are some special account names given to equity accounts, including one account name that is unique to QuickBooks:

- *Capital Stock.* An account that appears only in corporations. It is the name given to the par value of shares issued by the company. Par value is the stated value of a share of stock, a value that is determined by the officers of a corporation and printed on the stock certificates. For example, if a company sells 1,000 shares of stock with a par value of $1 per share, the capital stock account shows a balance of $1,000. The amount in this account does not change with the market value of the stock.

- *Paid-in Capital.* An account that appears only in corporations. Paid-in capital describes additional amounts contributed to the company that exceed the cost of the stock. For example, the preceding stock, which has a par value of $1 per share, may actually have been sold at $10 per share. In this case, the paid-in capital account would reflect the difference between the amount paid for the stock ($10,000) and the par value of the stock ($1,000), or $9,000.

- *Retained Earnings.* Also a corporation account, retained earnings is the name given to the account that represents the net earnings of the company, or the total income minus the total expenses of the company. The amount in this account changes at the end of each year when a company determines its total income and expenses for the year. The difference between total income and total expenses for the year flows into this account and the income and expense accounts start over again with zero balances.

- *Partners' Capital Account.* Also referred to as a Capital Account or a similarly named account, it is the name given to the equity account in a business that is not a corporation.

- *Opening Balance Equity.* An account name that QuickBooks assigns to every type of business organization (see "Understanding the Type of Business" in this chapter). This is an account that is unique to QuickBooks and represents the value of opening balances that are given to accounts during the interview setup process. For example, if you indicate in your setup that your company has a starting balance of $3,500 cash in the bank, QuickBooks assigns an opening balance of $3,500 to your cash account. There must be an offset to this amount (refer to "Debits and Credits" in this chapter) and QuickBooks puts the offsetting $3,500 in this Opening Balance Equity account. After your entire setup is complete, a journal entry must be made to clear the opening balance equity account and transfer its balance to the retained earnings account.

Understanding the Type of Business

Your business falls into one of the following types:

- *Corporation.* A form of business entity that is separate and apart from its owners, the business has its own legal existence, files its own tax returns, and may acquire debt in its own name. Owners of a corporation are called shareholders.

- *Personal Service Corporation (PSC).* A special type of corporation that performs personal services in the areas of medicine, law, accounting, engineering, architecture, actuarial science, performing arts, or consulting. PSC's are subject to special tax rates and can use a cash method of accounting wherein they do not account for accounts receivable or accounts payable. They report their income only when it is received and their expenses when they are paid.

- *S Corporation.* Another special type of corporation that, for the most part, pays no income taxes. (However, state laws vary with regard to the tax treatment of S corporations.) Instead, an S corporation passes its earnings on to its owners who report the earnings of the corporation on their personal tax return. There are special limitations for S corporations; such as there can be no more than 75 shareholders.

- *Sole Proprietorship.* An unincorporated business in which there is only one owner (the "proprietor"). There are no legal forms required to establish a proprietorship—you simply begin doing business. Taxable income or loss of the business is reported on the owner's personal tax return, and the assets of the business are not protected should the owner default in some other, personal, area of his financial life.

- *Partnership.* A form of business in which a group of people (two or more) decide to form a business organization together. Partners (owners) of the business are personally responsible for the debts of the business (unless the partnership agreement that they all sign assigns a limited partnership role to certain owners, which protects them if the partnership defaults on its liabilities). The partnership files its own tax return, but pays no taxes—the income (or loss) of the business is passed through to the partners and is reported on their personal income tax returns.

- *Limited Liability Company.* A relatively new form of business entity in which all owners, called "members," are protected from creditors of the business. The business operates much like a partnership in that it pays no income taxes but passes income and losses on to its members, who report the activity of the business on their personal tax returns.

Income: Your Company's Bread and Butter

Have you ever filed an income tax return? I know you have—so this is a safe question. Think back to one of your tax returns. On the front page of the return you list different types of income, such as wages from your job, interest income, prize winnings, and so on.

If we were talking about accounts, each one of these types of income could be considered an *income account*—just a separate description for the different kinds of income you list on your tax return.

Rather that adding up all your income from all sources and placing one number on your tax return, you use separate lines and descriptions for different types of income, making it easy to see from where all your income is derived.

A business separates its income into accounts as well and uses those accounts as separate descriptions on the business financial statements, tax returns, and other reports that show the financial progress of the business.

The names given to business income accounts vary greatly, based on the type of business. A restaurant and catering business will have income accounts with names relating to catering services and food sales, whereas a manufacturing business will have income accounts with names relating to construction labor and materials.

Expenses Reduce Business Income

If you itemize your deductions on Schedule A, you have many types of expenses, such as real estate taxes, mortgage interest, or charitable contributions. Each of these can be considered an *expense account*, or a separate description for the different ways that you spend your money.

Businesses have expense accounts too. Expense accounts reflect the costs of generating income and therefore are shown on financial statements as reductions to income. On a business income tax form, for example, income appears first, reduced by business expenses, and the difference, called *net income*, is the amount on which you pay income tax.

Expense accounts, like income accounts, have names that vary depending on the type of business. A restaurant may have expense accounts for the cost of food, laundry (for its linens), printing (for menus), music and entertainment, whereas a construction company may have expense accounts for subcontractor fees, building permits, and tools.

QuickBooks Gives You a Standard List of Accounts

One of the biggest advantages to using the EasyStep Interview, rather that trying to set up your company from the ground up, is that QuickBooks assigns a standard list of accounts to your company, based on the company description that you provide.

This standard list of accounts includes accounts of all kinds previously mentioned (asset, liability, equity, income, and expense) geared to your type of company.

You have the option in the interview to not accept this list of accounts and create your own accounts instead, after the interview has finished. I recommend accepting the standard list and then deleting accounts you don't need and adding new accounts (the process for deleting and adding accounts is explained in the next section). You save a lot of time by using the standard list as a starting point.

Adding Accounts

Whether you choose the standard list of accounts for your company or decide to start from scratch, you no doubt have to add some accounts so that all your company's financial transactions can be properly classified.

Adding an account to your chart of accounts

1. Choose **Lists**, **Chart of Accounts**. The Chart of Accounts window appears, listing all account names currently available to your business.

2. Click the **Account** button at the bottom of the window, and a drop-down menu appears.

3. Choose **New**. The New Account window appears (see Figure 7.2).

4. In the Type field, select the type of account.

5. Enter the name you want to use for this account. This is the name that will appear on your company financial statements and other reports.

Add accounts now or add them later

You can add accounts all at once, or add them at a later date, as your business changes.

Keyboard shortcut

When viewing the Chart of Accounts List, press Ctrl+N to open the New Account window.

FIGURE 7.2

Enter all the information about your new account here.

① Click here if this is a subaccount.

② Choose a (optional) tax line by looking at a tax return for your type of company and determining on which line this account would appear.

6. If this account is to appear as a subaccount of another (for example, Room Additions might be a subaccount of New Construction)—the total of all subaccounts add up to the total of the main account—check the check box and fill in the account of which this is a subaccount.

7. Enter an optional description of the account in the designated field. You may also see a field for a note about the account, or a bank number. These fields may or may not appear depending on the type of account you select.

8. In the Tax Line field, choose the line of your tax return on which this account will be entered, if you plan to use QuickBooks to help you organize your tax information.

9. In the Opening Balance field, enter the balance (if any) in this account as of your start date. (The opening balance and start date fields only appear if the account is an asset, liability, or equity account.)

10. Verify that the start date is correct in the date field.

11. Click **Next** to add another account, or **OK** to close the New Account window.

Deleting Accounts

You may find that the standard list of accounts provided by QuickBooks includes some account names you don't want to use. If you have used an account (entered some transactions into the account), deleting the account is more difficult.

Keyboard shortcut

When viewing the Chart of Accounts List, click the name of the account you want to delete (or arrow down to it), and then press Ctrl+D to delete the account.

Deleting an account

1. Choose **Lists**, **Chart of Accounts**. The Chart of Accounts window appears.

2. Click once on the name of an account you are certain you no longer need.

3. Click the **Account** button at the bottom of the window. A drop-down list appears.

4. Choose **<u>D</u>elete**. A box appears asking if you are sure you want to delete this account (see Figure 7.3). Click **OK** and the account is removed from your Chart of Accounts.

FIGURE 7.3

Answering **OK** removes this account completely from your records.

Deactivating an Account That Has Seen Some Action

An account that has a balance in it (notice the balances across from the account names in Figure 7.4), cannot be deleted. You can't remove accounts that have balances associated with them—that would throw off the total company balances on your financial statements.

FIGURE 7.4

Accounts with balances cannot be deleted.

 Check this box to show inactive accounts. (This check box may be dim, if no inactive accounts are present.)

 This sign means an account is inactive.

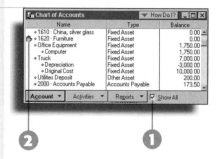

If the balance is zero, however, it seems like you ought to be able to remove the account from your records. Not so. As long as there has been activity in the account, QuickBooks insists that the account stay on your Chart of Accounts list, even if you don't expect to use it again.

For example, I charged my Rubbish Removal expense account with a $20 purchase of office supplies, then realized my mistake and reclassified the $20 to the correct account. My rubbish removal account now has a zero balance. I realize I'm not going to need that Rubbish Removal account after all because the property taxes my company pays cover the cost of rubbish removal. It seems I ought to be able to delete the Rubbish Removal account.

But when I try to delete the account, because there has been some activity in the account, I get the message you see in Figure 7.5.

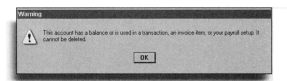

FIGURE 7.5

Warning from QuickBooks: You can't delete an account that has had transactions in it.

If I really want to get rid of that account, I have two choices. The first choice is to make the account inactive. Making the account inactive doesn't remove it from my Chart of Accounts list. Inactive status does, however, hide the account so that it appears that the account is no longer on my list.

Making an account inactive

1. With the Chart of Accounts window in view, click the **Account** button.

2. From the resulting drop-down list, choose **Make Inactive**. The account disappears from the Chart of Accounts list.

You can view inactive accounts on the Chart of Accounts list by checking the **Show All** box at the bottom of the Chart of Accounts window. Inactive accounts appear with a little gray hand to the left of the account name.

Inactive accounts can still be used

Inactive status applies only to the way accounts are listed in the Chart of Accounts window.

To make an inactive account active again, click the **A̲ccount** button in the Chart of Accounts window, and then choose **Make Ac̲tive**.

Deleting (Merging) an Account That Has Seen Some Action

Earlier in this chapter I indicated that QuickBooks doesn't want you to delete any accounts in which there has been activity, even if the balance in the account is zero. Although this is a true statement, there is a way around this dilemma, if you are bound and determined to delete an account.

The way to delete an account that has a zero balance, but in which there have been transactions in the past, is to *merge* the account into another account. By merging an account into another account, you transfer all the transactions from the original account into the new account, thus making it appear that there have never been transactions in the original account. During the merge process, QuickBooks automatically deletes the old account.

Before you begin merging an account, have in mind the names of the two accounts you use in this operation: the account you want to remove from the list and the account which will absorb the transactions in the deleted account.

Accounts that are being merged must be at the same level in the Chart of Accounts. If one account is a subaccount, the other account must be a subaccount too. The two accounts, however, do not need to be subaccounts of the same major account.

Merging an account into an existing account

1. From the Lists menu, choose **Chart of Accounts**. The Chart of Accounts list window appears.

2. Click the account you ultimately want to delete. This account must have a zero balance.

3. Click the **Account** button, and then choose **Edit Account**. The Edit Account window appears (see Figure 7.6).

Changing the hierarchical level of an account

You can easily move the level of an account from subaccount up to major account, from major account to subaccount, from subaccount to sub-subaccount, and so on. With the Chart of Accounts List window onscreen, drag the little diamond that appears to the left of the account name. If you drag to the right or left, the hierarchical level of the account changes accordingly. If you drag up or down, you can move the account to a new location (such as under a different major account) in the list.

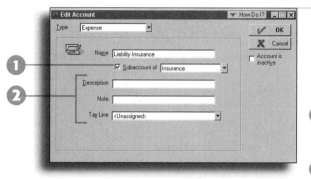

FIGURE 7.6

The name of the old account appears in the Na_me_ section. Replace this with the name of the account into which you want to merge.

1 Click here if this is a subaccount, and then enter the applicable major account.

2 These three areas may be left blank.

4. Change the name of the account you no longer want to the exact name of the account into which its transactions are to be merged. Make sure you spell the name of the new account correctly, and make sure you indicate the same subaccount level and position as that of the new account.

5. Click **OK**. You see a message that reads, "This name is already being used. Would you like to merge them?" Answer Yes.

All transactions of the original account are now a part of the account into which you merged. The original account has been deleted.

Numbering Your Chart of Accounts

QuickBooks doesn't assign numbers to your accounts when you set them up through the EasyStep Interview. You can assign numbers yourself in one of two ways:

- Let QuickBooks assign a numbering system for you.
- Choose your own numbering/lettering system.

Assigning Account Numbers with QuickBooks

The easiest way to assign numbers to your Chart of Accounts is to let QuickBooks do the work for you. QuickBooks assigns account numbers using the following numbering scheme, and you are welcome to accept these numbers. If you want to change the account numbers to your own numbering scheme, see the following section, "Assigning Account Numbers Yourself."

Assigning account numbers with QuickBooks

1. Create all the accounts you think you will want to use.

2. Choose **File**, **Preferences**.

3. Click the Accounting icon at the left side of the Preferences window.

4. Click the **Company Preferences** tab at the top of the window, and then click **Use account numbers**. QuickBooks assigns numbers to each existing account, based on a standard system of numbering as follows:

   1000s: Numbers in the 1000s are assets

   2000s: Liabilities

   3000s: Equity

   4000s: Income

   5000s: Cost of Sales

   6000s: All other expenses

Assigning Account Numbers Yourself

It's harder, but perhaps ultimately more useful to your business, to choose your own numbering/lettering system for account numbers, rather than letting QuickBooks choose account numbers for you. In both cases (easy way and hard way), you perform the preceding steps (go to the Preferences window and turn on account numbering). In addition to numbering all your existing accounts automatically, QuickBooks places a new field in your New Account window: the Account Number field.

Assigning account numbers yourself

1. For all new accounts, enter your own account number in this account number field when setting up the account.

2. For existing accounts, go to the Edit Account window and change the assigned account number to one you prefer.

When choosing account numbers, keep in mind the fact that any financial statements or reports you want organized by account name are going to now be organized by account number. This is because QuickBooks makes your account number part of the account name (almost like the first word in the name). If you like to have your accounts appear alphabetically on your financial statements, assign account numbers to the accounts in alphabetical order.

There is no provision for assigning account numbers during the EasyStep Interview. This is something you must do after the interview has been completed.

Printing a Chart of Accounts List

It is helpful to have a copy of your chart of accounts handy so that you can refer to the chart when assigning accounts to business transactions.

Printing a Chart of Accounts list

1. Open the Chart of Accounts List window, and then click **Reports**.

2. Choose **Account Listing** from the resulting drop-down menu. A report of your entire list of accounts appears onscreen.

3. Print the report by clicking the **Print** button that appears at the top-right side of the report.

Setting Up Services, Customers, and Suppliers

Understand how all transactions in QuickBooks are created as items and organized into lists

Learn different item types and how to create and save them conveniently

Apply items from the drop-down menus found in any of QuickBooks' forms

Create and apply subitems, and recognize the situations in which it's helpful to do so

Understand the activities associated with each list, and learn to locate them quickly

Identify reports associated with the various item lists, and select the most helpful report for any situation

Items are the backbone of QuickBooks, and all items in QuickBooks are organized in lists. If you've gone through the EasyStep Interview, having entered customers, employees, products, and vendors into their rosters, then you've already worked with lists. You'll be back from time to time when you hire a new employee, new vendors, and new customers, but unless situations in your company change drastically, you will not again have the chore of building up your lists from scratch.

Understanding Items

In QuickBooks, most everything is an item. Things you buy and sell are items. Discounts you apply and services you perform are also items, as are long-term loans and cash deposits you make to cover shortages. As such, you'll find them listed appropriately in the QuickBooks **List** menu.

Customers, vendors, invoices, purchase orders, and accounts are not items. Items are services or products that you sell or buy and the charges related to them.

Working with Items

A note to QuickBooks Standard Edition users

The examples used in this chapter are from the QuickBooks Pro sample company, "Rock Castle Construction." Your company data will appear differently.

Let's use preparing an invoice as an example of how to work with items. If you just finished a job with three components, perhaps Photography, Layout, and Publishing, you would have entered each of these tasks as items into QuickBooks (**Lists—Customers: Jobs**). These would be *service items*. These do not account for the equipment you purchase related to these jobs, but merely the time you spend on them, that is, a service.

In creating your invoice to charge for these services (**Activities—Create Invoices**), you'd click the invoice below and to the right of the word **Item** (see Figure 8.1), and then select **Photography** from the list. Because you've just entered Photography as an item, as previously noted, it is available to you here in the invoice you are creating.

Next, click the line right under Photography and a drop-down menu appears where you clicked. Choose **Layout**. To add the final task for this job, click the line below **Layout** and choose **Publishing**.

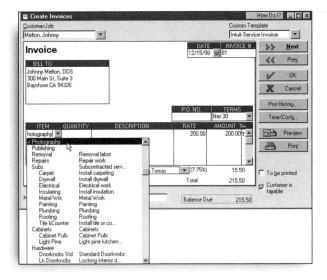

FIGURE 8.1
Charge for your services by adding an item to an invoice.

As soon as you create an item it becomes available for use in all the forms you have yet to create, such as sales receipts, checks, and invoices, as shown here. In this situation, we've created *service items* (Photography, Layout, and Publishing). A service item is a job you perform and charge a customer for. You would then associate these items with a charge (perhaps $30 per hour, or $500 per job) and any special purchases (paper stock, specialized film). Figure 8.2 shows a sales receipt generated from the same set of services previously discussed.

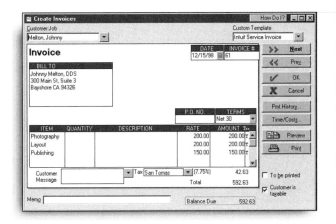

FIGURE 8.2
A sales receipt created for the same set of services previously outlined.

After you've created an item, you can conduct any business related to these tasks, or jobs, such as ordering supplies, billing clients, and paying back loans. You can also create accounts associated with these jobs, making sure that if you run to the store or make a special order on behalf of a customer, you can create a record and be reimbursed for all the "extras" you've spent on the project.

Getting back to our invoice, we'll see how other items can be applied to this job we've performed for a client, or customer. In these examples, terms of payment have been set up as an item, as well as sales tax.

QuickBooks lets you instantly choose from other items you've created and apply them to various customers and jobs as needed. Perhaps you've established terms of payment with a particular customer, offering them 60 days to pay you in full, with a 10 percent discount applied for early payment. In QuickBooks, you display this on an invoice, as an item, for example, and click the drop-down menu near the word **Terms**, as shown in Figure 8.3. That means QuickBooks updates the applicable accounts and customer lists, noting how much money is owed to you, by whom, and by what date.

Utilize standard terms

You may not have to make any changes to the **Terms** item QuickBooks provides. It's likely that the standard terms that come with QuickBooks will work just fine for you.

FIGURE 8.3

Displaying Terms that can be applied to an invoice.

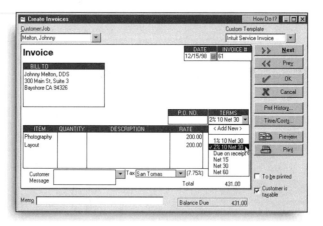

The **Tax** field at the bottom of the invoice also shows a drop-down arrow, in which you could have entered any applicable taxes to this customer's invoice. In creating a **Sales Tax** item, you type the percentages applicable to your city and state, and that tax item would be available to all your sales, calculating and applying the taxes you've set up in your tax item.

All the items we've discussed here—job components such as Photography and Layout, and special calculations such as Terms and Taxes—appear on **Lists**, and can be applied to any invoice, purchase order, credit slip, and so forth, as needed.

This same principle applies to checks, where payments (as **Items**) can be instantly credited and debited. Any inventory or noninventory part is ordered and recorded as an item. All the proper accounts are credited, and inventory lists are updated. The information you record for a particular item is available to all QuickBooks' accounts and record keeping.

Types of Items

There are 10 different types of QuickBooks Items:

- **Service**. Labor charges and professional fees.
- **Payment**. Payments are monies received that reduce the amount owed on an invoice.
- **Inventory Part**. Items you order in high quantity, track and resell, such as nuts and bolts, pencils, and paper clips.
- **Noninventory Part**. Products you do not sell regularly. For example, a mechanic who occasionally applies custom rims to a car upon request would consider the rims to be noninventory parts. Noninventory items include prepared food such as fresh-tossed salads (you can have the lettuce in inventory, but not the salad). Following are two examples of special noninventory parts:

  Livestock that you raise and ultimately sell. You didn't purchase the animals, so there was no inventory purchase cost, but the animals belong to you nonetheless and would be classified as noninventory parts.

An item you had a role in selling, but you were never the owner, for example, an expensive piece of medical equipment. As the Product Representative you brokered the deal, but never owned the machine.

- **Group**. A group of items can be saved all together as an item. This is helpful if you sell expensive china sets, for example. Most often, you sell the entire set of tableware, but occasionally, you do sell individual china pieces. So, your regular product set would be a group, and occasionally, you'd break down this group into individual pieces when needed. In QuickBooks, both the entire china set and the individual cups and bowls are called items.

- **Discount**. An amount of money subtracted from a total or subtotal cost of an item. Beyond the obvious 10 percent markdowns and such, discounts have multiple uses. Here are two examples:

    Tracking a Commission. If you are paid a commission for each sale of a product, create a discount item for the same percentage as your commission. QuickBooks tracks the discount for all your sales and keeps records of your total commission income.

    Forgiving a Charge. If you provide a service for a client and work 20 billable hours but decide as a courtesy to only charge for 15, you can create a discount item, deducting 5 hours from the final invoice. This way, you can keep track of both the hours you really did work, as well as the deduction.

- **Sales Tax**. When applicable, you can add a sales tax item to an invoice. Quickbooks automatically calculates the correct amount based on the percentage you set.

- **Sales Tax Group**. Often, the total sales tax we pay is actually a combination of state, county, and city tax. Customers are not accustomed to seeing three tax rates applied to their invoices (For example, 5 percent state tax, 1 percent county, and .6 percent city tax) Therefore, QuickBooks makes it easy to enter a sales tax group as an item.

- **Subtotal**. A subtotal item is important. If you apply shipping charges, discounts, credits, or tax, these items need to be applied after the goods or services themselves are totaled. The total charge before these "extras" are applied is called a subtotal.

- **Other Charges**. Freight, finance charges, late fees, special handling and rush charges can all be applied using an **Other Charge** item. **Other Charge** items can also be created to track unusual occurrences. Here are two examples:

> In the restaurant business, cash drawers often show overages or shortages at the end of the day. Use an **Other Charge** item to track these discrepancies. This enables you to create reports showing over/short trends in your business.

> If you are put on retainer, perhaps as a musician, prepaid to be available to record at a certain time of year, or as a scriptwriter, prepaid to turn in sitcom episodes before a particular date, the money you are paid is not really an asset. It's a liability, because you owe the service to the customer. You could create an **Other Charge** item to keep track of this special sort of income.

SEE ALSO

➤ *As an alternative to tracking different types of profits with items, consider dividing parts of your business into classes. See page 175 for a detailed discussion of this option.*

Creating Subitems

Subitems are created as easily as items themselves. Simply create an item, and then check the **Subitem of** check box, as shown in Figure 8.4. A drop-down menu appears, showing all QuickBooks items. Use it to select which item this subitem should appear under.

Creating items to track profits

To keep close track of where and how money is being made in your company, you may want to create several accounts that reflect income sources, and apply appropriate items to each account. For example, if you have one main office and smaller branches, you would expect supply usage and expenditures to be higher at the main office, but with good tracking, you can still know how profitable each office is without being confused by the differences in expenditures. You can guarantee this by creating unique inventory account items for both the home and satellite office. That way, each office can show its own scale of profitability.

FIGURE 8.4

Creating a subitem.

On your QuickBooks item lists, subitems appear neatly indented under the parent item.

Why would you create a hierarchy of items and subitems? Following are two examples:

- Most independent computer stores sell systems cobbled together from individual components, keeping an eye on the falling and rising prices of RAM, hard drives, monitors, and such. The profitability of the entire system sale is greatly dependent on the total cost of these components. To set a good price on a whole computer, you need accurate and up-to-date tracking of how you are being charged for each component. Use subitems to manage your inventory of parts and pieces, while the entire computer package can be presented as an item. Also, tracking RAM and hard drives as subitems enables you to sell these pieces individually and still keep an eye on how many entire computer systems (items) you can package and sell.

- As a service provider, subitems allow you to charge varying rates for different types of work you perform for a client. For example, a lawyer would charge one rate for her own time, and a lower rate for research conducted by a paralegal. Or, a medical office would charge one rate for a doctor visit, and another for a follow-up visit by a nurse practitioner. You could do this in two ways:

    The two rates could be a subitem of the entire charge, as shown in Figure 8.5. The secondary, lower rate could be a subitem of the primary, higher-paid professional.

FIGURE 8.5

An item called **_Legal_** shows two subitems beneath it. Each subitem can be charged at a different rate.

Locating Items with Lists

Items are organized into lists, and the three drop-down menus found on each list make it easy to edit items in all kinds of ways, even before you open an item for viewing. Items are found on the **Lists** menu, along with **Customer** lists, **Vendor** lists, and other important lists.

Figure 8.6 shows the menu options for the lists we'll be describing in some detail, although the contents of the **Other** submenu category might not be exactly as you see it here. Some lists may be missing, others added or in a different order.

Access lists

In QuickBooks, you may seldom have to access a list by clicking a menu at the top of the screen. Use the Navigator to conduct your day-to-day business with QuickBooks, and you'll be opening and editing lists of items on your actual forms.

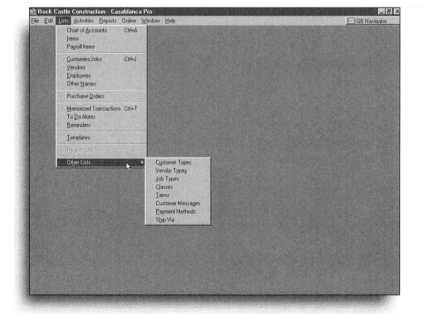

FIGURE 8.6

A look at QuickBooks' Lists.

To add, remove, or move lists as they appear in this **Other** sub-menu, select **File**, **Preferences**, **Menus**, and place a check by the items you'd like to have appear in the **Other** submenu, rather than in their own respective **Lists** or **Activities** menu (see Figure 8.7).

FIGURE 8.7

Use the **Preferences** menu option to change list items that appear in the **Other** submenu.

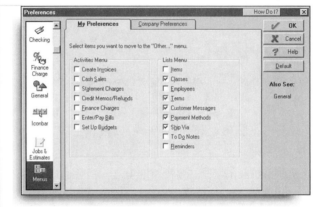

Before we look at specific features of lists, let's look at how to update lists as you work, merge lists, and view an entire list entry, rather than just a name.

Updating Lists

While working with any form, if you type a new entry in an appropriate field, QuickBooks checks to see if your entry is already part of a list. If not, you are prompted to add the entry using one of two methods (see Figure 8.8):

- **Quick Add**. This adds only that entry, exactly what you type, to the list. Later, you can add more supportive detail.

- **Set Up**. QuickBooks opens a window for recording an entire list entry with all pertinent information.

FIGURE 8.8

In any form, type an item that QuickBooks is not familiar with, and you see this prompt.

Merging Two List Items

Merging two list items can be helpful if you've been working a customer at two locations, and find she's consolidated her business into one. Or, if you've entered a client into your database twice, using slightly different spellings, merge the two entries into one, keeping pertinent information you might have recorded in both.

Merging list items

1. Locate the item whose name you *don't want to use*. Do this by selecting the **List** menu, then choosing the submenu containing that item.

2. Click once on the item in the list to select it.

3. Select the drop-down menu at the bottom left, and choose **Edit**.

4. Your goal is to change the name of this item to match the name of the item you *do want to use*. Select **Rename** from the **Edit** menu, and change the name to match the other item.

5. Click **OK**, and then click **Yes**, indicating that you do indeed want to merge the lists entries.

Viewing an Entire List Entry

If you are entering the name of a customer onto a form, for example, and you want to know whether they have any outstanding checks or back payments, click the field entry where you would type the customer's name. Press Ctrl + L, and the entire list appears in its own window. Locate the customer's name on the list. You see all available information about that customer, including a summary of any previous work you've done for them.

This technique works with any form (Estimates, Invoices, Cash Sales receipts, for example). Use this method to view whole lists in almost any field of the form, such as **Tax**, **Item**, **Customer Message**, and **Payment Method**, as well as **Customer**.

Working with Lists

Let's explore different types of items and lists, and focus on various ways you can put them to work for you. The QuickBooks manual does a wonderful job of touring each and every field and menu. We'll review some of the less obvious features, and emphasize those that bring you multilevel power for creating reports and getting information you want quickly. We'll see that you can tailor list items to very specific needs for your business.

Rather than start at the top of the **List** menu, we'll begin with lists that you are more likely to use regularly. First, we'll examine features common to all lists, taking the **Item** list as our example.

Features Common to All Lists

Like the others, the **Items** list (Select **List** from the menu and choose **Item**) shows a scrollable list of entries with three drop-down menus (**Items**, **Activities**, and **Reports**) at the bottom left (see Figure 8.9).

FIGURE 8.9

The Item list looks similar to other lists.

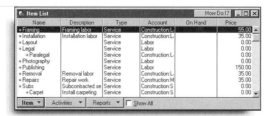

The items you see here are those you created when you walked through your EasyStep Interview when first installing QuickBooks, and any others you've added along the way. Or, if you are using the QuickBooks sample file (Rock Castle Construction, in QuickBooks Pro) to feel your way around the program, then you see the items created for that sample company.

Moving an Item in a List

You can move any list item by clicking and dragging with your mouse over the diamond that appears in front of each item name. When hovering over a diamond, your mouse turns into a four-way arrow (see Figure 8.10). Click and drag the item to a new location, up or down the list. If you click and drag an item with subitems, those will move as well. To return the list order to its original state, select **Resort** from the drop-down menu on the bottom left of any list.

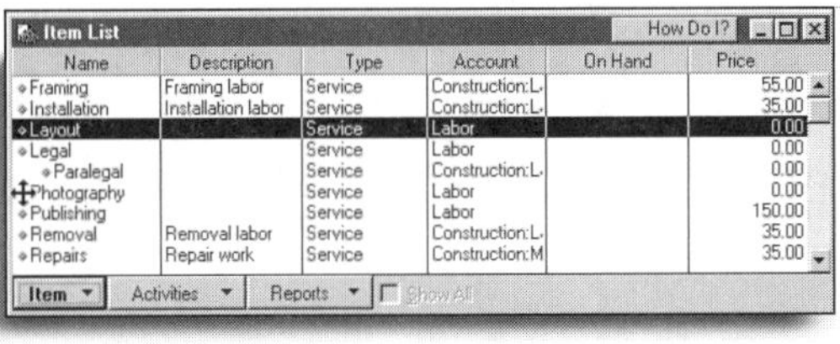

FIGURE 8.10

When hovering over an item in an item list, the mouse becomes a four-way arrow.

Listing Subitems

Subitems are indented, listed under their parent items. As you can tell from the example in Figure 8.11, "Wood Door" has two Subitems beneath it. Under "Wood Door," you can see the price and availability of two types of wood doors, Interior and Exterior. Look at the figure, and you can see that there are 6 Exterior and 14 Interior doors in inventory at the moment. To the right is the **Price** of each.

FIGURE 8.11

Subitems listed beneath parent items.

Finding a List Entry

QuickBooks' powerful **Find** feature (see Figure 8.12) enables you to choose **Filters** to locate just about anything—an individual check, bill, vendor, transaction, memo entry, or even a birthday or email address. **Find** is always available from the **Edit** menu, no matter what dialog box is open.

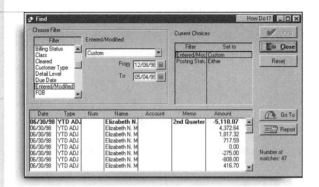

FIGURE 8.12

Set up **Filters** in the Find dialog box to locate transactions, vendors, bills, or just about any data you've ever entered.

Find works by selecting a filter from **Filter** list, and then typing text or using the drop-down menu to set criteria for that filter. You'll see your filter choice appear in a list at the upper right of the dialog box, under **Current Filter Choices**.

After a filter appears there, it is set, and you can use the **Filter** menu to choose an additional filter, providing another limit to your search. For example, your first filter could be a name of a customer, and the second filter could be a date range. Your search would bring up every document involving that customer that falls within that particular date range.

The filters provided by QuickBooks do a good job at predicting what a businessperson might need to know in a hurry. For example, **Aging** (for bills that are fast becoming due), **Cleared** (for checks that have cleared or not cleared), and **Detail Level**, which limits the number of duplicate entries you'd have to wade through.

After setting your filters, click **Find**, and entries that match appear in a list. You can generate a report on that list (click the **Report** button), or double-click any entry to view the document it refers to, such as a check or bill.

Quick Access to Editing

Double-click any item in the list to bring up the Edit Item dialog box. If you ever want to change the rate or price of an item, make it taxable, or to specify which account should receive monies when this item is sold, double-click its name in the item list.

Double-click **Exterior Door**, just as an example, and the Edit Item dialog box appears, with that item's data. You can see the cost of each door relative to its price (see Figure 8.13). The cost, as shown in the **Cost** data field of the Edit Item dialog box, is $105. And to the right you can see the **Sales Price** of $120.

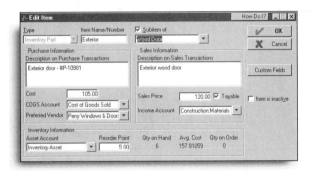

FIGURE **8.13**
Double-click any item in a list to view and edit its settings.

While we're here, notice that as soon as the inventory of these doors drops to five, a reminder is issued to reorder more (**Reorder Point**). You can also specify which vendor to regularly order doors from (**Preferred Vendor**), and which account to credit when a door is sold and installed (**Income Account**). If a drop-down menu appears next to a field, you can fill that field with a list item from the menu. Let's go on to explore how to create new items, and add them to your lists.

Creating a New Item

Creating a new item

1. Select the **Item** drop-down menu from the **Item** list, and choose **New**. The New Item dialog box appears (see Figure 8.14).

FIGURE 8.14

The New Item dialog box,
shown here with settings for
an Inventory Part item.

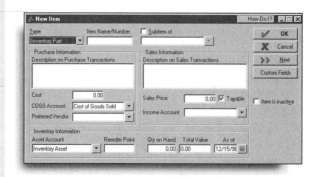

2. From this dialog box, you can specify item **Type**, using the drop-down menu, and provide a name and a description.

3. In the **Rate** field, type a rate (dollars per hour, for example) or price for this item, and click the **Account** arrow to pick which account to credit when the item is sold, or service performed.

4. If you click **Subitem of**, the drop-down menu below it becomes available. Use it to select a parent item from the list. Your new subitem appears indented, below the parent item.

5. Click the **Taxable** option if applicable.

Notice also the **Custom fields** button, for creating and applying custom fields to forms associated with this item. The custom fields do not appear in the Edit Item dialog box, but are available to forms involving this item.

Using the Item List

After creating the item, it appears with the others in the item list. By creating an item, you've not yet attached it to any form. It is now available, though, to any applicable form by using the drop-down menus.

Available fields will differ

The fields available in the New Item dialog box change depending on what type of item you are creating. Options available for **Inventory Parts**, for example, will differ from **Service Item** options.

Returning again to the **Item** list (select **List** from the menu, and choose **Item**), notice the **Item** drop-down menu at the bottom left. Use it to print a list, delete an entry and locate all the transactions in which a particular list entry is found (**Find in Transactions**). You'll find that every list has a menu offering similar functions, always found at the lower left.

Generating Sales, Invoices, and Price Changes

Creating a price change

1. Select any item entry, and click the drop-down **Activities** menu. Here you can quickly create an invoice for that item, receive items, enter bills, and change prices. Figure 8.15 shows the Change Prices dialog box.

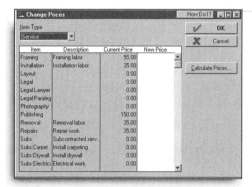

2. Select the **Item Type** to be affected by your price change. From the **Item Type** drop-down menu at the upper left of the screen, choose an **Inventory, Noninventory, Service Item** or **Other Charge**. You see a list of all the chargeable items pertaining to the item you clicked.

3. Select an item for a price change, and click across from it in the **New Price** column.

4. Change the price of an Exterior Wooden Door to $130 (see Figure 8.16).

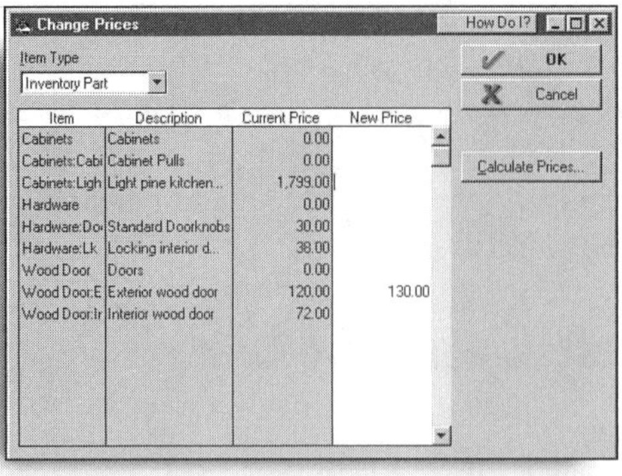

FIGURE 8.16
The changed price is displayed in the **New Price** column.

The Activities menu and other lists

All other lists, such as **Employees**, **Customers: Jobs**, and **Vendors**, have a drop-down **Activities** menu, similar to the **Items** list covered here. You'll find that in any list, chores related to paying or receiving money will always be found in the **Activities** menu. Here are some examples of what you'll find in a list's **Activities** menu:

Customers: Jobs list. Create Invoices, Receive Payments, Enter Cash Sales.

Vendors list. Write Checks, Enter Bills, Create Purchase Orders.

Employees list. Pay Employees, Pay Liabilities/Taxes, Process various tax forms.

Chart of Accounts. Write Checks, Make Deposits, Transfer Money.

Most often, businesses institute price changes on many items simultaneously. Customers seem less taken aback by one blanket price increase than many isolated ones. Also, an "across the board" change makes it easier for you to see its effect on your business. To calculate new prices on a range of items, see the following section.

SEE ALSO

➤ For more detailed information on using the invoicing feature in QuickBooks, see page 201

Calculating New Prices

Calculating new price markups or discounts

1. Click the **Calculate Prices** button. The Change Prices dialog box appears (see Figure 8.17). On the far left of the dialog box, check the items to receive the price change. (The accompanying Qcard and instructions seem to indicate that only price increases can be generated here, but that is not the case. You can lower prices as well.)

2. In the **Mark Up Sales of Checked Items by (amount or %)** field, type a dollar amount or a percentage. The item's price changes by that amount. (Type %10 in the $120 Exterior Door field, and the price rises to $132. Type -30, and the price falls to $90. Type -%15, and the door's price is reduced by $15.)

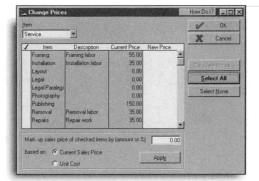

FIGURE 8.17

In the Change Prices dialog box, check the items set to receive price changes.

We've been discussing the Price Change window as if it applies only to prices you charge your customers for the item or service. However, at the bottom of the Change Prices dialog box shown previously in Figure 8.18, click **Unit Cost** to make your changes here apply to what you paid for each item, rather than the **Current Sales Price**, which is what your customers would pay.

When you click **OK**, you are not returned to the Change Prices dialog box. The program assumes you are done with editing, and you are returned to the **List** view.

Receiving Items, Bills, and Credit from a Vendor

In the **Activities** menu of the **Items** list, click **Receive Items & Enter Bill**. Here you can create receipts verifying that merchandise has been received, create a bill for it, and make a record of credit that a vendor has extended you.

The initial screen shows the Enter Bills dialog box (see Figure 8.18), enabling you to select the vendor who has billed you, the terms of the billing cycle, and the dates that the bill was received and due. You can also type the amount due, reference number, and memo message.

Quantity on hand

Notice the **Adjust Quantity/Value on Hand** menu item in the **Activities** menu. Here you can view the quantity On hand for each item. After scrolling down the list to see if there are any items you need to reorder soon, just create a **Purchase Order**, also found in this same **Activities** menu.

Enter bills

Why create a bill for an item in QuickBooks? After all, hasn't the vendor sent you his own bill? By entering a bill in QuickBooks, you can debit the appropriate accounts for the purchase, generate a check to pay the bill, examine and calculate the terms of payment, and receive a reminder telling you when the bill is due.

FIGURE 8.18

The Enter Bills dialog box lets you determine which of your accounts should shoulder this expense.

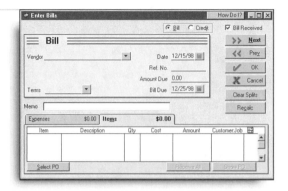

Memos appear in accounts payable register

The memo appears in the accounts payable register. This is a good way to write yourself an important note about the item.

Account crediting and customer information

If you filled out a purchase order for merchandise received, you might not have to enter detailed account crediting and customer information, because you probably already did so when you ordered the merchandise.

In the lower half of the Enter Bills dialog box (QuickBooks calls this the details area), you see two tabs: **Items** and **Expenses**. In the **Items** tab, use the drop-down menu under **Items** to specify the item you are being billed for. Quickbooks adjusts the **Quantity on Hand** to reflect that you've received this merchandise.

Here you can also include other information important for registering bills that have to be paid. Type the quantity of items you've received. The cost of each item appears in the **Cost** column, and QuickBooks calculates the total cost of the purchase in the adjacent **Amount** column. Select a customer to associate this purchase with, if applicable.

SEE ALSO

➤ For more detailed information on receiving, recording, and paying bills, see page 265 and page 268

Acknowledging Merchandise Received

If you received merchandise from a vendor and no bill, you still need to credit the appropriate accounts and inventory lists with the received merchandise.

Acknowledging received merchandise

1. From the **List** menu, chose **Vendors**. The **Vendors** list appears.

2. Select the **Activities** drop-down menu, then **Enter Bills**, which opens the dialog box shown in Figure 8.19.

3. Remove the check next to **Bill Received**, and this dialog box simply creates a receipt.

4. Just specify the vendor, and the items received, and if applicable, click the **PO** (Purchase Order, if available) button to view the purchase order that first generated this transaction.

5. Click **Next edit other Bills**, or **OK** to exit the dialog box.

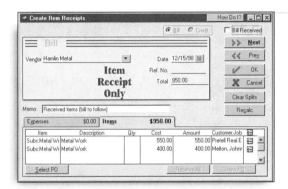

FIGURE 8.19

The **Select PO** button indicates that a purchase order is available for you to view.

Changing the Receipt into a Bill

Later, when the bill arrives, you can change the receipt into a bill.

Changing a receipt into a bill

1. Click the **Activities** menu here in the **Item** list, and choose **Enter Bill for Received Items**.

2. QuickBooks lists any receipts of unbilled, received merchandise. Click once, and the Enter Bills dialog box appears.

3. Click **Bill Received**, and the receipt turns into a bill. All the appropriate accounts reflect the fact that money is now due, and you are soon issued a reminder that the bill needs to be paid.

Entering Receipts and Credit from a Vendor

Up until now we've been discussing creating bills from vendors using the Enter Bills dialog box.

Viewing the associated purchase order

If a purchase order was created back when this item was ordered, the detail fields of this receipt will be automatically filled out from the details of the purchase order. That means you don't have to click the **Customer: Jobs** list and choose items and accounts manually.

Please note that clicking the **PO** button only applies the data from the appropriate purchase order to this receipt. It doesn't bring up the purchase order for you to view it. If you want to view the purchase order, click the **Select PO** button (refer to Figure 8.19). This button will not be available unless a purchase order was generated at the time of order.

Entering receipts and credits from a vendor

1. In the Enter Bills dialog box, check the **Credit** button, and the title of the form changes to **Credit**. A **Credit Amount** line appears.

2. Type the amount credited to your account by a vendor.

The Checking Credit in the Enter Bills dialog box is for recording amounts credited because you returned merchandise to a vendor. To set up a line of credit, open a line of credit account, specify a lender and a specific amount.

Adjusting Quantity/Value on Hand

To manually adjust the quantity or value of your inventory, select **Quantity/Value on Hand**, at the bottom of the **Activities** menu of the **Item** list. This enables you to update information in the Adjust Quantity/Value on Hand dialog box (see Figure 8.20). QuickBooks automatically adjusts your inventory whenever you make a sale or purchase new merchandise.

FIGURE 8.20

To manually adjust your inventory amounts, use the Adjust Quantity/Value on Hand dialog box.

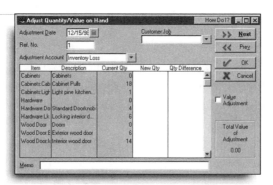

Following are three reasons you may need to adjust your inventory manually:

- *Theft*. To get an accurate recount of what was taken

- *Fire or Other Damage*. To accurately report inventory that is still available

- *Counting Discrepancies*. If you simply recounted and got a different total this time

Let's look at other features of the Adjusting Quantity/Value on Hand dialog box.

SEE ALSO

➤ *For more detailed information on counting and valuing your inventory, see page 237*

Adjusting New Quantity

To make an adjustment, locate the item whose numbers you want to change, and type a new quantity in the **New Qty** column. The **Qty Difference** column reflects your change. You may select as many items for adjustment as you like. You can also make an adjustment by typing a number in the **Qty Difference** column directly. QuickBooks calculates the correct quantity from that figure.

Adjusting Reference Number

In the Adjust Quantity/Value On Hand dialog box, QuickBooks creates a separate transaction record for each inventory adjustment. By noting the reference number, you can then access them later from this very same **Items** list, and create reports. Sequential reference numbers are generated automatically. If you'd like to type your own, you may do so.

Adjusting Other Important Fields

To associate this inventory adjustment with a particular customer's account, click the **Customer: Job** menu. To create a note regarding this adjustment that will appear in a report, explaining its circumstance and purpose, type text into the **Memo** field. Notice that a total value of adjustment panel appears in the lower right of the dialog box, providing a dollar amount based on your inventory changes. Please note that if none of your inventory items are associated with **Customer: Job** accounts, this option will not be available.

Adjusting Value Rather than Quantity

In the Adjust Quantity/Value on Hand dialog box, you may want to adjust the value of inventory, rather than the quantity on hand (refer to Figure 8.20). For example, if you sell computer parts,

Don't forget the Navigator

Because this chapter is discussing lists, it's easy to forget that many QuickBooks features are more easily accessed from the Navigator, including some discussed here. For example, to adjust quantity/value on hand, just click the Navigator's **Purchases and Vendors** Tab. Then click **Adjust Qty. on Hand**. You find that the Navigator often shortens menu option names, but the features accessed are the same.

Creating an inventory loss account

You may want to create a special account for recording inventory losses. Include this information in the **Adjustment Account** field. In the example shown in Figure 8.20, an account called "Inventory Loss" was created. Later, generate a report showing inventory losses separately, rather than burying them in some other account.

Warning: Before you adjust your inventory value

The IRS has specific rules about methods of valuing inventories, and changing the value of your inventory falls under these rules. See the section on "Adjusting Quantity and Value of Inventory Account" in Chapter 14 before you think about making adjustments to any of your inventory accounts.

prices of hard drives and RAM are apt to fluctuate wildly. You may want to periodically adjust the value of your stock on hand, according to the most current prices.

When you click the **Value Adjustment** check box (on the right side of the Adjust Quantity/Value on Hand dialog box), a **New Value** column is added. Here you may type in a new dollar value for an item's stock on hand. Please note that you are not changing the value of one item, but rather the entire inventory of that item. This procedure does not alter the number of items on hand, but rather the value of the items in dollars.

Making Reports Based on Items

The purpose of items in QuickBooks is not just to make forms more convenient, but to put more meaningful information at your fingertips. QuickBooks enables you to select particular items from lists and generate reports on all (or only) the data you want. Reports are the key and, as we shall see, are available from a drop-down menu on every list of items.

It's easy to create filters in reports, screening out information you don't need to see at the moment. After you've created a report, you can memorize it (retaining the format and scope of the report) even as the data changes over time. Also, you can graph your report. Viewing data pictorially can illumine seemingly insignificant differences in data.

Even something innocuous such as shipping charges can provide important data in a report. For example, you can learn what percentage of your customers requires out-of-state shipping, or, you can determine if you are getting the best deal from your shipping agency you are currently using.

SEE ALSO
➤ For more detailed information on creating and working with reports, see page 397

Creating Reports from the Item List

In this book, creating reports is thoroughly discussed as each topic arises. For now, we'll briefly touch on the reports that can be created from lists, and highlight some unique aspects of how each list can create unique reports helpful to your company. We will spend time on the **Item** list reports, using those to create a general picture of what you'll find in others.

Generating a QuickReport

Creating a QuickReport

1. Click once on any line in the **Item** list, and select the drop-down **Report** menu at the bottom (see Figure 8.21).

2. Click **QuickReport**. The name QuickReport appears with the name of the item you select, in this case, QuickReport: Drywall.

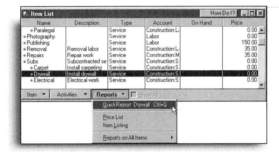

FIGURE 8.21

Generate a QuickReport on any item you click on from the **Item List Report** menu.

QuickBooks creates a report of every activity involving the item you've clicked. Here we see that customers requiring Drywall installation are included on the report (see Figure 8.22). Each line in the report represents a type of document that relates to the item, perhaps an invoice or bill.

Each line also shows a customer name, date of transaction, amount received, and quantity you billed for. A transaction number is also included. At the bottom of the report are totals and subtotals of each.

View any document up close

Double-click the magnifying glass on any line to see the document that the line refers to. Click a line that refers to an invoice, and the entire invoice appears. You can then edit the document as you like, although doing so affects other transactions as well. Edits you make are reflected on the report totals and subtotals, when applicable.

Type	Date	Num	Name	Memo	Qty	Amount
Service						
Framing						
Invoice	10/05/98	1	Abercrombie, Kris...	Framing labor	0	0.00
Invoice	10/15/98	4	Cook, Brian:Kitchen	Framing labor	-8	-440.00
Invoice	10/25/98	6	Abercrombie, Kris...	Framing labor	-16	-1,144.00
Invoice	10/26/98	7	Pretell Real Estate:...	Framing labor	-32	-1,760.00
Invoice	10/28/98	8	Ernesto Natiello:Kit...	Framing labor	0	0.00
Paycheck	10/29/98	170	Pretell Real Estate: ...		24	478.85
Paycheck	10/29/98	170	Cook, Brian:Kitchen		24	478.85
Paycheck	10/29/98	172	Abercrombie, Kristy		1.5	38.81
Paycheck	10/29/98	172	Abercrombie, Kris...		8	138.00
Paycheck	10/29/98	172	Pretell Real Estate:...		8	138.00
Invoice	10/30/98	10	Cook, Brian:Kitchen	Framing labor	-24	-1,320.00
Paycheck	11/12/98	173	Ernesto Natiello:Kit...		16	319.23
Paycheck	11/12/98	173	Melton, Johnny:De...		20.5	409.01
Paycheck	11/12/98	173	Pretell Real Estate:...		11.5	229.45
Invoice	11/15/98	12	Pretell Real Estate: ...	Framing labor	-19.5	-1,072.50
Invoice	11/16/98	14	Ernesto Natiello:Kit...	Framing labor	-32	-2,112.00
Invoice	11/23/98	17	Ernesto Natiello:Kit...	Framing labor	0	0.00

Rock Castle Construction
Item QuickReport
October 1 through December 15, 1998

Using Available Item List Reports

From the **Reports** drop-down menu of the **Item** list, a number of reports are available. Notice that quite a few reports branch out from the **Report on All Items** submenu, as shown in Figure 8.23.

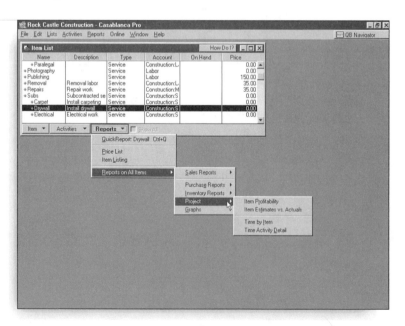

The following is a list of reports that are worth a special glance:

- **Viewing Your Inventory Prices**. To create a report that simply shows how much your inventory items cost (to you and your customers), click **Reports** on the **Item** list dialog box, and choose **Price List**.

- **Viewing Selected Item Details**. To create a report showing details you think are most helpful (use the **Customize** button to choose fields for viewing), click **Reports** on the **Item** list dialog box, and choose **Report on all Items**. You'll see several cascading submenus. Each submenu reveals a submenu for creating a detailed report, or a summarized report.

Item Sales Reports

From the **Item** list, **Reports** menu, there are two types of sales reports available. From the **Reports** drop-down menu, select **Report on All Items**, **Sales Reports**, and choose either **By Item Summary** or **By Item Detail**. Each is described as follows:

- **By Item Summary**. Includes Average Pricing, Gross Profit Margin and COGS information. Inventory items and complete products ready to be sold are summarized together (see Figure 8.24). Click the button at the top of the report to view even less detail about each product and its components.

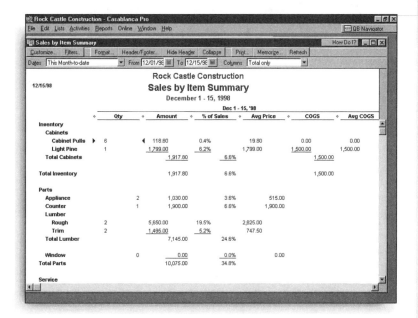

FIGURE 8.24

This sales report shows inventory information of all items to be sold.

- **By Item Detail**. Shows the date the item was acquired, memo if any, and also displays additional price and account balance information.

Item Purchase Reports

From the **Item** list, **Reports** menu, five types of **Purchase Reports** are available. Click **Report on All Items** from the **Reports** drop-down menu, and choose **Purchase Reports**. You'll see these five options:

- **By Item Summary**. You see a list of items and subitems, displayed with quantity and amount you paid for each item, summarized for quick viewing. Click the **Collapse** button at the top of the form to further abbreviate the information viewed.

- **By Item Detail**. You see each inventory item displayed with quantity information, source, purchase and sale price detail, and account balance totals.

- **By Vendor Summary**. Within the **Purchase Reports** menu, you can view how much you spent on vendors in any given accounting period using this report (see Figure 8.25).

FIGURE 8.25

The **By Vendor Summary** report summarizes how much you spent on vendors during a given time period.

- **By Vendor Detail**. Similar to the **By Vendor Summary**, but shows item name, purchase number and date, memo, and more detailed account information for each vendor.

- **Open Purchase Orders**. This report lists all orders for items that you have not yet received. It includes purchase order number and date you expected to receive the merchandise. Display a purchase order by clicking its name in this report.

Inventory Reports

Click **Reports** at the bottom of the **Items** list, and choose **Report on All Items**, **Inventory Reports**. You see several handy reports for showing which items are on back order, how many of each item you sold during a particular period, delivery schedules, and detailed asset value information. Reports dealing with inventory are covered in Chapter 14. Following are three of the most useful inventory reports:

- **Stock Status by Item**. Under the **Inventory Reports** submenu is the **Stock Status by Item** report, providing detailed quantity, reordering and item delivery information. Sales information for the week is also available.

- **Valuation Summary**. Generates a report for inventory asset value broken down into item types, percentage of total value, your own inventory costs, retail value, and average cost of each item.

- **Physical Inventory Worksheet**. This form contains a quick list of all your inventory items, featuring the reported inventory quantities. At the far right is a field for you to check off an actual physical count as you walk through the warehouse.

Project

Click **Reports** at the bottom of the **Items** list, and choose **Report on All Items**, **Project**. Here you can find out how profitable each item in your inventory is, estimated revenue versus actual revenue of inventory items, and how much time was spent on each job item. (This group of reports may not appear in QuickBooks Standard Edition.) Following are a few of the reports listed:

- **Item Profitability**. Under the **Project** submenu, click **Item Profitability** to see actual costs versus actual revenue, and a calculated dollar difference. Click the **Collapse** button to simplify the report for quicker data.

Zeroing in on data you want to see

Don't forget you can change the time scope of any report by using the drop-down **Date** menu, or typing new dates in the **From** and **To** fields at the top of the report. You can add filters to this vendor report by using the **Columns** drop-down menu, making this a very powerful reporting tool. For example, you can view money spent on your vendors according to **Terms** you pay them with, **Item Type**, **Shipping information**, and **Payment Method**.

Tracking down an order

If, while viewing a report, a specific purchase order jumps out at you, and you'd like to learn more about it, select **Reports** at the bottom of the Item List dialog box, choose **Report on All Items**, **Purchase Reports** and click **Open Purchase Orders**.

■ **Item Estimates vs. Actuals**. A more complete version of the previous report, featuring how much profit was estimated versus how much was actually realized on each set of transactions (see Figure 8.26).

FIGURE 8.26

Check profitability of your transactions using the **Item Estimates vs. Actuals** report.

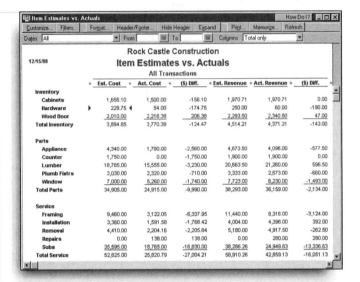

■ **Time by Item**. Click here to find out how much time was spent over a particular period on each type of job item.

Graphs

To see pie and bar graphs of your sales over a given period of time, click **Reports** at the bottom of the **Items** list, and choose **Report on All Items**, **Sales Graphs**. These graphs are a very powerful feature of QuickBooks, and the Sales Graph reviewed here is only one of many. QuickBooks graphs have amazing "drill down" capabilities, enabling you to click a pie chart for an entire year and continue clicking down for more detail until a specific invoice appears for a specific transaction. With a single mouse-click, you can print your graph as well.

Pictured in Figure 8.27 is a Sales Graph. When the graph first appears, you see a bar graph at the top showing **Sales by Month**. Each month's total is shown as a bar in thousands of dollars. You can change the date range by clicking the **Dates** button at the top of the graph, and choosing a new range. Type a custom range in the **From** and **To** fields if you like.

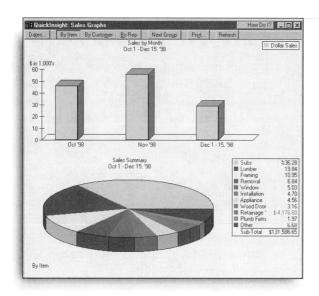

FIGURE 8.27

Graphs enable you to view data over time and by item simultaneously.

The lower half of the graph shows a pie chart breaking down all sales for a given period by item. Notice that you can change which data group is represented by clicking any of three buttons at the top of the screen: **By Item**, **By Customer**, or **By Rep**. Clicking these buttons only changes the data shown on the pie chart, not the bar graph, which measures time.

Going back and forth between these two graphs lets you narrow your view down to both a specific product or service—and a very specific time frame. Double-click any bar in the bar graph or "slice" of the pie to get a close-up view of that specific data group. For example, double-clicking the month of November will show a pie chart representing sales in that month only. Double-clicking the item "Framing" in the pie chart shows a new bar graph with the entire date range, but only data for sales of Framing services is shown.

If you've drilled down far enough (by double-clicking) to show a single month and data group, double-clicking again opens a list

A closer look at graphs

Although only a **Sales Graph** is available from the **Items** list, Quickbooks includes dozens of graphs. They are highly customizable. Graphs are covered in more detail in Chapter 21.

of invoices for that month. Double-click any invoice in the list to view it full screen. After it's open, you can edit it or simply view more details.

Customer, Vendor, and Employee Lists

Let's move on to look at other lists in the **Lists** menu, where you can quickly edit Customer, Vendor, and Employee information. Here, you can also see all your currently open Purchase Orders, Memorized Transactions, and Reminders.

Customer:Job List

The **Customer:Job** list (see Figure 8.28) is where you store information about a particular customer, such as name, address, credit limit, internal account info, for example. Information about jobs that you do for this customer is also stored here. This would include the type of job, its pending status, completion date estimate, and so forth.

FIGURE 8.28

The **Customers: Job** list. Leave yourself a note reminding you of important details regarding a particular customer or job.

After creating an entry in the **Customer:Job** list, you can access that entry from any form using the drop-down **Customer** menu. These include purchase orders, invoices, and cash sales forms. All the information you save with your **Customer:Job** list is available to these forms, as well as checks, bills, classes, and ledgers.

You probably made some entries into the **Customer:Job** list when you walked through your EasyStep Interview in setting up QuickBooks. It is those entries you see when you click **List**, **Customer: Job** list. However, one hopes you'll be adding new customers! To do so, from the **List** menu, click **Customer:Job**, and select **New** from the **Customer:Job** submenu. You see the three tabs of the New Customer dialog box (see Figure 8.29).

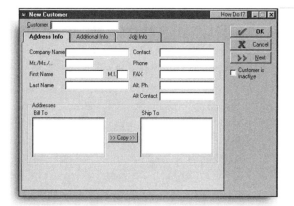

FIGURE 8.29

The New Customer dialog box contains three tabs for storing customer information.

Customer Field

Above the tabs is the **Customer** field. Type the customer's name. What you type here appears in the **Customer:Job** list, and is always the first field used any time you apply this entry to a form, check, or ledger.

Address Info

In the first tab, **Address Info**, you include company name, customer name and address, and contact information. If this customer's shipping address differs from his billing address, this tab is where you'd include both.

Additional Info

The second tab, **Additional Info**, is where you type a customer number (one you create your own internal reference), and choose Job Type, Terms and Sales Rep, if applicable. Custom fields that you design appear here by default for editing first.

Job Info

On the third tab, **Job Info**, type an estimated job completion date, start date, job status (awarded, pending, closed) and job description. This job description appears on many forms.

Associate all transactions with an account

Even your minor business transactions are on behalf of a particular customer or job. It must be to somebody's benefit that you are running to the hardware store for the third time today. In an effort to keep track of where your monies and energies are being spent, whenever possible, associate each task with a particular customer and job, even if that task or expense is not going to be billed to that customer.

Adding additional jobs

In the **Customer: Job** list, you can have more than one job associated with a customer. You have to fill out a new item for each job, though. In the **Customer: Job** list, each job appears indented below the customer associated with it.

Vendors and taxes

Dealing with vendors presents a special tax issue: the 1099 form. The IRS likes to make sure it gets its share of all transactions conducted by even the smallest, informal business relationships. Therefore, if you pay more than $600 per year to a unincorporated vendor, you are required to create a 1099 form for that vendor, reporting the income. QuickBooks keeps track of how much you've paid each vendor and helps modify 1099 forms as needed.

The $600 per year is subject to change. Needless to say, the 1099 forms issued by the IRS may not always reflect the new tax laws. To find out at which point you currently have to start reporting income to unincorporated vendors, call Intuit (800-771-7248), the IRS (800-Tax Form), or visit the IRS's Web site (www.irs.gov). If you think you will be using an unincorporated vendor frequently, click the **Vendor Eligible for 1099** check box on the **Additional Info** tab of the New Vendor dialog box.

Making a Note

In the Edit Jobs dialog box, at the far right is the **Notes** icon. Click it to type a note to yourself pertinent to this job. After you've done so, a small **Notes** icon appears next to that particular job in the **Customer:Job** list. Click the icon to view the note. This way, you can view the associated note without having to open the jobs entry itself because the note appears next to the description on the list of jobs and customers. Notes are helpful for reminding yourself of an agreed-upon time to make a delivery, call a business associate, or any small detail that defies categorization.

Notes and **To Do** lists are explored more thoroughly later in this chapter.

Vendor List

Besides creating new vendors and editing existing ones, the **Vendor** list is where you can print 1099, write checks, pay bills, enter credit card balances, print QuickReports on vendors, and create reports and graphs. These, as well as standard list activities such as making vendors inactive, deleting vendors, and finding specific vendors in any transaction.

When you set up QuickBooks, you entered vendors as part of the process. Vendors are businesses that regularly sell you goods. Most often with vendors, you've established a routine, a relationship of purchasing, billing, and paying. A vendor trusts you to pay within an agreed period of time. It's desirable to deal with vendors, rather than having to run to the store and pay cash for things.

Adding a New Vendor

To add a new vendor to the **Vendor** list, select **New** from the Vendor drop-down menu (see Figure 8.30), and type all pertinent contact information.

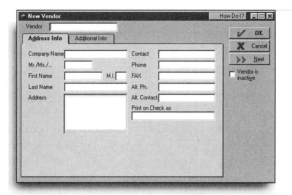

FIGURE 8.30
Create a new vendor, using the by-now-familiar tabs to include all necessary information.

The **Address Info** tab of the New Vendor dialog box prompts you for name, address, and phone information, as well as what you'd like printed on the checks you make out to the vendor. The **Additional Info** tab enables you to include an account number, email address, and lets you choose which Vendor type and credit terms to associate this vendor with. **Credit Limit** and **Tax ID** fields are also available. If your purchases begin to approach the figure you set in the **Credit Limit** field, QuickBooks issues a warning.

All the information you enter in these fields is used by QuickBooks in creating reports.

Editing A Vendor

To edit a vendor, select it from the list, and choose **Edit** from the **Vendor** drop-down menu. Make any changes you want in any of the fields. You can also add and customize fields using the **Define Fields** features on the **Additional Info** tab.

Employee List

When you first set up your QuickBooks company, you may have entered employees at that time. As your company grows, you'll perhaps hire more, and if you've never had an employee, the time may indeed come when you'll need to get some help. Let's look at how to add new employees to your company, and edit the information on those that you have. Setting up an employee can

Opening balance figures

Please note that you should only add an opening balance figure if you are just now beginning your QuickBooks company. Otherwise, leave this number zero and begin entering transactions, such as purchases and payments.

be a rather complex process because of the various agencies involved. State and federal withholding, health insurance, disability, and social security are some of the liabilities you are responsible for when you truly and officially "hire" someone.

When you add an employee to your company, choose **Employees** from the **List** menu, and click **New** from the drop-down **Employee** menu. The first two tabs, prompting you for name and address info, chargeable account number, and various fields such as **Date of Last Raise**, are filled out the same as any other new entry to a list. The third tab, **Payroll Info**, is where lots of unique information pertaining to employees must be spelled out. The complete job of setting up a new employee is explained in Chapter 17 of this book, but for now, we'll take a quick look at what's required.

In the **Earnings** field, use the drop-down menu to select a payroll item, such as **Salary**, **Sick Pay**, or **Vacation Pay**. This enables you to set one pay rate for each type of accrual. To the right, in the **Hour/Annual Rate** field, type the actual rate of each payroll item.

Use the drop-down menu to the right to specify pay period.

Use the bottom half of the **Payroll Info** tab to type additions and deductions just as they would appear on the employee's paycheck. These include health insurance deductions, bonuses, flexible spending account contributions, FSLA adjustments and such. You may type a percentage amount and a cap (limit) that a particular deduction or contribution should not exceed. To add a new type of deduction or contribution, click the drop-down menu arrow and choose **Add New**. The Add New Payroll Item Wizard appears. Here you can specify a **Type** and **Name** for your contribution or deduction, set a percentage or amount limit, and associate this payroll adjustment to a particular account.

Customer, Job, and Vendor Type Lists

In a submenu of the **Lists** menu, you find **Other Lists**. Of particular interest here are the **Type** lists. Types enable you to further break down your lists into subgroups that make sense for your business. Following are three examples:

- If you sell merchandise, you might have different terms for wholesale, commercial, and retail customers. QuickBooks could account for these as **Customer** types.

- As a wedding photographer, you might have a standard picture package you offer, and a deluxe package. Each service could be identified in QuickBooks as a **Job** type, under the main **Job Photography**.

- As a restaurateur, perhaps you purchase consultation and marketing services to come up with plans to bring in more customers. You would not group these transactions in the same expense category with ordering paper cups and food inventory. In this case, you'd set up two **Vendor** types.

As with other lists, click the drop-down menu at the bottom left to create new list entries, delete and deactivate old ones, as well as print the list contents. Use **Find in Transaction** to locate all active transactions using the item list you've specified.

When you create a new **Customer**, **Job** or **Vendor** type, it appears in the list, and is available to all relevant forms from the drop-down list. After it is created, you can associate charges with these new items, create estimates for such services, prepare invoices, receive payments, and otherwise include these new types in your daily business routines that you record in QuickBooks.

Next, let's briefly look at **Terms**, **Customer Messages**, and **Payment Method** lists. These are also found in the **Other Lists** submenu. We'll take a fast look at the **Ship Via** list as well.

Terms, Customer Messages, and Payment Method Lists

From the **Lists** menu click **Other Lists**, choose **Terms**, and you see the Terms List dialog box. You do not need to come here to apply terms to a transaction. To do that, simply open any form

(**Sales Receipt**, **Customer Payment**, or **Invoice**, for example) and click the **Terms** drop-down menu. However, to create a new set of terms, edit existing ones, or view a list of all transactions where certain terms have been applied, this list is where you'd come.

Editing and Creating Terms

Figure 8.31 shows the Terms dialog box. Double-click any existing term set to edit it. In this example the Term 2% Net 30 was double-clicked. Let's look at the dialog box to learn how to edit an existing term, as well as how to create new ones.

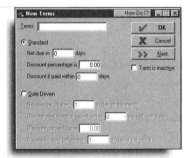

FIGURE 8.31

Create new terms to apply to customers from this dialog box.

Editing terms

1. In the **Terms** field, type what you'd like to call this term.

- This example, "2% 10 Net 30," means that if the customer pays the payment within 10 days, the total is discounted by 2 percent, and the total payment is due within 30 days.

- If the terms were "1% 10 Net 15," that would indicate that payment within 10 days brings a 1% discount, and that the entire payment is due within 15 days. What you type in the Term field, however, is simply a title. The term is set by filling out the fields that follow.

2. For creating standard terms, use the fields below the **Standard** radio button. In the **Net due in Days** field, type the number of days until the entire payment is due.

3. In the **Discount Percentage Is** field, type the percentage discount if payment comes early.

4. In the **Discount if Paid Within Days** field, type the number of days, starting today, that this discount is effective.

Click **Date Driven** if you want to set up your terms to apply to dates of the month, rather than days from the current date. Clicking **Date Driven** causes a new set of options to appear.

Creating a terms discount based on dates in the month

To create a terms discount based on dates in the month, complete the following steps:

1. First, type the day of the month that the entire payment is due.

2. Next, use the **Due Next Month if Issued within** field to create a condition enabling the customer to slide until next month. For example, let's say that you are accustomed to getting paid by all your customers on the 15th of the month, but this sale was made on the 14th. Rather than force this customer to pay by tomorrow, QuickBooks lets you specify that if a sale was made 10 or 15 days before the normal due date, you'll let it slide until the following month. This way you don't have to alter your payment routine just for one customer.

3. In the next field, type a discount percentage for early payment. Type zero if no discount is offered.

4. Below that field, type in on what day of the month this bill must be paid by to receive the discount.

You can create a new set of terms using this same dialog box. It would simply be accessed by choosing **New** from the **Terms** drop-down menu of the **Terms** list. After you've created new terms, they will be available on any applicable QuickBooks form, by clicking that form's drop-down **Terms** menu.

Printing, Deactivating, and Locating Terms in Use

Click the **Terms** drop-down menu from the **Terms** list, and options appear allowing you to print the terms currently in use on your QuickBooks forms. You can also make terms inactive

Creating term items specified by your vendors

We've emphasized creating terms in QuickBooks that you apply to your customers, relating to payments they make to you. You also need to make QuickBooks aware of terms that your vendors apply to you. To make your purchase orders and payments fully accurate, use the **Term** list to create a term item used by each of your vendors.

and use **Find in Transactions** to locate any current transaction that uses a set of terms you specify.

Viewing terms used by your customers and vendors

1. Click the **Term** item you want to run a report for, and choose **Quick Report** from the **Reports** drop-down menu. You see a list of all relevant bills, invoices, and payments.

2. From this report, double-click any document in the list.

3. The document opens, ready for you to edit. Make any changes you like, or just view the contents.

Customer Messages List

On most QuickBooks forms, you can type a message to your customers ("Thank you for your business," "Happy Holidays"), or use the provided drop-down menu to apply messages you've already created and saved. Customer messages can actually be created on-the-fly by clicking **Add New** from the **Customer Message** drop-down menu on any form, and typing a new message. Your message will be saved. To view and print all the customer messages you've created and saved, click **Other Lists** from the **List** menu, and choose **Customer Message**. From this list, you can also create new messages, delete old ones, make a message inactive, and print a list of all messages you use.

Payment Method List

This list lets you create new payment methods, delete and deactivate existing payment methods, and locate any transactions that use a payment method you specify. You can also view and print reports. To access the **Payment Method** list, click **Other Lists** from the **List** menu, and choose **Payment Method**. Typical payment methods are check, cash, and various types of credit cards. One of the principle conveniences of the **Payment Method** list is to create separate lists for each credit card you own, enabling you to keep track of what card got charged for which merchandise. However, when you are setting up a payment method, you are not creating an account, or terms for handling those methods. You are merely typing a name that appears in appropriate forms, and on reports.

To view all transactions conducted using a particular payment method, select from the list the **Payment Method** you want to track, and click the **Report** drop-down menu. Then choose **Quick Report**. To edit a payment method, double-click its name in the list.

When you create a **Payment Method** by clicking **New** from the **Payment Method** drop-down menu, you are simply providing a name. This name appears in the **Payment Method** drop-down menu found in many forms, such as Sales Receipts, Customer Payments, and Bills.

Separating Your Company into Logical Divisions

Use the QuickBooks Classes feature to keep track of income and expenses in different areas of your business

Set up classes all at once, or on-the-fly, as you enter transactions in QuickBooks

Prepare reports that emphasize the performance of your company's classes

Does your company have locations, divisions, departments, funds, or other areas that it needs to track separately? Perhaps you want to track income by the person who brings the income to your company (such as lawyers, accountants, sales people) for purposes of paying commissions and bonuses, or judging performance.

Or your company might engage in several types of business, such as a construction company that performs residential and commercial construction, and it would be beneficial to track the performance of each type of work.

If these or other scenarios apply to your company, you can use the QuickBooks class feature and report on each area of your business separately.

What's a Class?

A class is a label that you attach to your income, expense, and payroll transactions, to identify the transaction as belonging to a particular group. Only one class may be applied to a single transaction.

You have the option of setting up subclasses of classes, so as to further classify and separate income and expenses.

For example, a law firm that practices in the areas of criminal law, family law, and personal injury, may want to have a class for each of these types of law, and then a subclass for each attorney. That way the firm could create reports that show how the family law practice as a whole is doing, and then a report showing how each lawyer within the family law practice is doing.

Setting Up Classes

Before you can use classes, you must activate the QuickBooks preference for class tracking. During the EasyStep Interview, you were asked whether you wanted to use classes.

SEE ALSO

➤ *For information on setting up classes during the EasyStep Interview, see page 61*

If you answered the interview question about classes positively, the class preference has already been activated.

Manually activating the class preference

1. Choose **File**, **Preferences**. The Preferences window appears.

2. Click the **Accounting** icon at the left (you may need to scroll to find this icon). Make sure the **Company Preferences** tab is selected (see Figure 9.1).

3. Check the **Use class tracking** box to turn on the class tracking feature.

4. Click **OK** to close this window and save your settings.

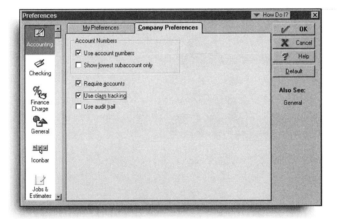

FIGURE 9.1
Turning on class tracking enables you to prepare reports showing how each class performs.

If class tracking is turned off, either inadvertently or intentionally, your class designations are still stored with your transactions, and you can still prepare reports based on class designations—you just can't assign future income and expense transactions to classes until you turn the feature on again.

Creating a List of Classes

When you are ready to set up your classes, you can open the Class List window and enter each class.

Setting up a list of classes

1. Choose **Lists**, **Other Lists**, **Classes**. The Class List window appears.

2. Click the **Class** button, and then choose **New** from the drop-down list (or press Ctrl+N). The New Class window appears.

3. Enter the name of the class you want to create in the Class Name field.

4. If this class is to be a Subclass of another class, check the check box and choose the name of the class from the drop-down list, or choose **<Add New>** to enter a new class name (see Figure 9.2).

5. To continue entering classes, click the **Next** button and another New Class window appears. If you are finished entering classes, click **OK** to close the window.

FIGURE 9.2

Create new classes in this window.

1 Click here to indicate that this new class is a subclass.

2 Click here to show a list of all existing classes, then click the class of which your new class will be a subclass.

3 Making this class inactive hides it on the list of classes.

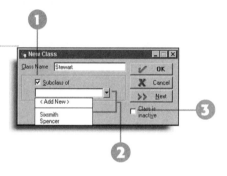

Other Features of the Class List Window

While in the Class List window, several other operations are available to you.

From the **Class** drop-down menu, you can perform these tasks:

- **Edit**. Click a class name on the list, and then choose **Edit** to change the spelling of a name.

- **Delete**. Click a class name that you no longer need, and then choose **Delete** to remove the name. You cannot delete a class name if transactions have occurred in that class.

- **Make Inactive**. Click a class name that you no longer want to see on the class list, and then choose **Make Inactive** to remove the name from the list. The name is still available for use on transactions, and still appears on reports.

- **Find in Transactions**. Click a class name, and then choose **Find in Transactions** to search for all transactions for this class.

- **Print List**. Print a complete list of all your classes.

From the Reports drop-down menu, you can prepare these reports:

- **Quick Report**. Click a class name, and then choose **Quick Report** to display a report of all transactions that refer to the selected class.

- **Profit and Loss by Class**. This is one of the most useful class reports you will find. Prepare the P&L by choosing **Reports**, **Reports on all Classes**. A side menu appears, from which you can choose **Profit and Loss by Class**. This report shows you all income and expenses for the year to date, with a separate column for each class. You can change the date at the top of the screen to select the time period that the report covers (see Figure 9.3).

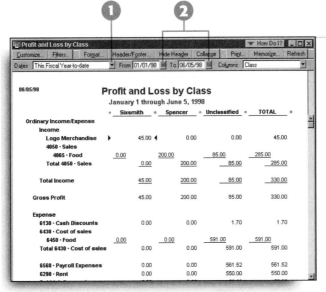

FIGURE 9.3

This useful report shows you all income and expense transactions, with a separate column for each class.

1 Click here to select a different time period for this report.

2 Click here to choose specific dates for this report.

- **Balance Sheet Itemized**. Choose **Reports, Reports on All Classes,** and then pick **Balance Sheet Itemized** to display a balance sheet with class listings. Most balance sheet accounts aren't affected by classes, but the detail of your accounts receivable and accounts payable includes class information, which may be useful to you.

- **Graphs**. Choose **Reports, Reports on All Classes, Graphs,** to select either graphs depicting **Income and Expense Items by Class**, or **Budget vs. Actual by Class**.

SEE ALSO

➤ For information on reports and graphs available in QuickBooks, see page 414

➤ For more information about performing various tasks within List windows, see page 133

Creating Classes On-the-Fly

If you want, you can just wait until you need a new class designation, and create it on-the-fly.

On an invoice, purchase order, bill, or any form on which you are entering a transaction that ultimately affects an income or expense account, a class field appears (see Figure 9.4).

FIGURE 9.4

Create a new class on-the-fly on any screen where you see a class field.

① Click here to view a list of existing classes.

② Choose **<Add New>** to create a new class on-the-fly.

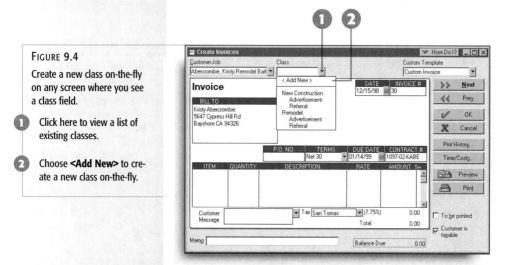

Click the drop-down arrow in the class field, choose **<Add New>**, and the New Class window appears. Enter the name and optional subclass information for the class you want to create, click **OK**, and presto! A new class is born!

Reporting on Classes

Many reports support reporting by classes, but here are some reports that might be especially useful to see with breakdowns by class:

- *Profit and loss statements.* From the **Reports** menu on your main QuickBooks screen (as opposed to the Reports button in your Class List window), choose **Profit and Loss**, and then choose from the reports listed. After it's onscreen, a report can be filtered to show only the results of a particular class or group of classes. QuickBooks has done part of this job for you already with one of its standard reports. If you choose **Reports**, **Profit and Loss**, **By Class**, your company profit and loss statement appears with a separate column for each class.

SEE ALSO

➤ *For guidance on filtering reports by classes, see page 409*

- *Sales reports.* From the **Reports** menu, choose **Sales Reports**, and then choose from the list that appears. You can request that any sales report be filtered by class, thus showing sales for only one or a selected group of classes.

- *Purchase reports.* From the **Reports** menu, choose **Purchase Reports**, and then choose from the list that appears. If you are interested in displaying purchase information by class, choose a purchase report and filter the report for a particular class or group of classes.

A much more detailed discussion of reports can be found in Chapter 21, "QuickBooks' Reports and Graphs."

You've done about everything you can do to get your company set up in QuickBooks. From here, it's time you got busy entering your day-to-day transactions.

PART

II

Taking Care of Business

Job-Cost Estimating and Tracking

Create a new job each time you offer an estimate

Use the QuickBooks Pro Estimates feature to create professional-looking estimates

Use an estimate as a starting point for preparing invoices

Revise estimates easily

Prepare reports to show your company's progress with ongoing jobs

Depending on the type of business yours is, you might find you have a need for keeping track of your costs on a per-job basis. Many businesses do this: construction companies, specialty manufacturing companies, architectural companies, caterers, law firms, accounting firms, and so on.

Any type of business that needs to keep track of separate jobs for the same customer can benefit from job-tracking. If you never do repeat business for a customer, you probably have no reason to track jobs. Or, if you want to reflect each job as if it were a separate customer, you can do that as well without the QuickBooks Pro job-costing feature.

With job-costing you can have the luxury of producing reports for a single customer, summarizing all the jobs performed for that customer, or you can produce reports for the individual jobs. Job-cost tracking gives you this choice.

Note that you must own QuickBooks Pro to do job-costing. The regular version of QuickBooks does not support this feature.

Setting Up Jobs

There is no limit to the number of jobs you can set up for a customer.

You learned how to set up your customer list in Chapter 8, "Setting Up Services, Customers, and Suppliers," and you might have taken the opportunity to set up some jobs during the EasyStep Interview (see "Entering Customers" in Chapter 5). This section presents the complete steps for setting up jobs.

You must have a customer already set up before you can set up a job for that customer. To review, you set up a new customer by opening the **Lists** menu and choosing **Customer:Job**. Then click the **Customer:Job** button in the window that appears, choose **New**, and enter the appropriate information for your new customer.

Setting up a job in QuickBooks Pro

1. Open the **Lists** menu and choose **Customer:Job**. The Customer:Job List window appears.

2. Click a customer for whom you want to create a new job (the customer must be on the list before you can add a job).

3. Click the **Customer:Job** button at the bottom of the window. A drop-down menu appears.

4. Choose **Add Job** from the menu. The New Job window appears (see Figure 10.1). The customer name appears in the **Customer** field of the **Address Info** tab. Verify that this is the correct customer.

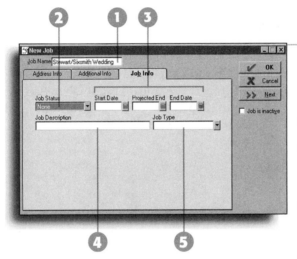

FIGURE 10.1

Set up a new job for an existing customer by choosing **Add Job** from the **Customer:Job** menu.

① Enter the new job name here.

② Choose a job status. You can update this field as the job progresses.

③ Enter dates relating to the start and completion of this job.

④ Enter an optional job description.

⑤ Select the type of job.

5. Enter a name for this job in the **Job Name** field at the top of the window. You are limited to 41 characters, including letters, numbers, and spaces. You may use a combination of upper and lowercase letters.

6. You can add optional job information (discussed in the next section) by moving to the **Job Info** tab. When you have finished entering information about this job, click **OK**. The job is added to the **Customer:Job** list, alphabetized, and indented under the name of the customer you have chosen.

Optional Job Information

You can add several pieces of information about a job when you are setting up the job. These include the job status, the dates of the job, a job description, and the job type.

Enter or update these options by clicking a job from the **Customer:Job** list, clicking the **C**ustomer:**J**ob button, and choosing **E**dit.

The following sections contain descriptions of the various descriptive job options.

Job Status

Job status is a distinction you can assign to a job to indicate where in the completion process this job falls. QuickBooks provides you with a standard list of job status options from which you can choose. You can also modify this list if your company uses different terms to identify job status.

The standard job status options offered by QuickBooks include

- *Pending.* Use this option to describe a job when you have provided an estimate but have not yet heard if your company has been awarded the contract.

- *Awarded.* Use this option to describe a job that has been awarded to your company but on which you have not yet begun working.

- *In Progress.* Use this option to describe a job on which you are currently working.

- *Closed.* Use this option to describe a completed job.

- *Not Awarded.* Use this option to describe a job on which you provided an estimate but for which you did not receive a contract.

- *None.* Leave None as the status if you do not use the job status option for your jobs.

Only five status options (plus **None**) are available for your use. If, however, the options you see are not appropriate for your business (perhaps your business is a law practice and you prefer to use terms such as Discovery, Pre-Trial, Trial, and Appeal to describe the status of a legal case), you can change any or all the five options to suit your business needs.

Changing a job status option

1. Open the **File** menu and choose **Preferences**. The Preferences window appears.

2. Click the **Jobs & Estimates** icon at the left of the window. You might have to scroll to find this icon.

3. Click the **Company Preferences** tab at the top of the screen to see the five job status options (see Figure 10.2).

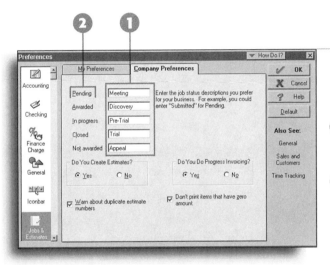

FIGURE 10.2

Enter your own job status descriptions in the Jobs & Estimates Preferences.

1. Create any status descriptions that will be useful to your business.

2. These standard descriptions for the fields don't appear anywhere in your lists and reports.

4. Change the name of any job status by deleting the name you see and entering your own choice for a job status. You are limited to 12 characters, including spaces. You may use upper and lowercase letters or numbers.

5. When you have entered all the job status options you plan to use, click the **OK** button to save your changes.

Any jobs for which you have already assigned a job status will be updated to reflect the changes you make to these options.

If you use the job status field to describe the progress of your jobs, you should remember to edit your jobs regularly, updating the status. Select a job in the **Customer:Job** list by clicking it, click the **Customer:Job** button, choose **Edit**, and update the status on the **Job Info** tab.

Whenever you display the **Customer:Job** list, you can quickly see the status of all jobs in the **Job Status** column.

Job Dates

If you want to use QuickBooks to help keep track of the dates on which you begin and end a job, you can enter information in the three date fields on the **Job Info** tab.

Enter a start date for the job. This is the date on which you actually begin or expect to begin working on the particular job.

Indicate an anticipated job completion date by entering a date in the **Projected End** field. This date is an estimate.

When the job is completed, enter the actual date by filling in the **End Date** field.

When you have entered dates in any or all these fields, you can produce reports based on these dates. See the "Reporting on Work in Progress" section later in this chapter for more information about different types of job-related reports you can create.

Job Description

You can enter an optional narrative description of the job. No standard entries are provided for this field, so you can be creative, or perhaps your company will want to set up some standard job descriptions of its own and make a printed list available to anyone entering job information in QuickBooks Pro (there is no provision for a drop-down list in this field).

For example, if you are a tax practitioner, some standard descriptions for the type of tax work you perform might include

- Quarterly Estimates
- Annual Tax Planning
- Individual Income Tax Returns
- Corporate Income Tax Returns
- Payroll Tax Forms

Job Type

The job type is another optional field you define. No standard entries are available in the **Job Type** field as they are in the **Job Status** field, so you can customize job types to go with your business. For example, a construction company's job types might include New Construction, Repairs, and Renovation. Job types can be subtypes of other job types; for example, the New Construction job type might include subtypes of Commercial and Residential.

You can create a job type on-the-fly by clicking the arrow in the **Job Type** field, clicking **<Add New>**, and entering a new job type in the window that appears.

An advantage to using job types is that QuickBooks considers job types to be an item. A drop-down list in the **Job Type** field provides an easy way to choose from existing job types. Also, if you open the **Lists** menu and choose **Other Lists**, and then choose **Job Type** from the submenu, you can create quick reports, easily edit job types, and search for job types in your transactions.

SEE ALSO

➤ *For more information about items, see page 134*

Creating an Estimate

When you use job-cost tracking, you have the option of preparing and working with estimates. An estimate is very similar in appearance to an invoice, but serves an entirely different purpose.

Just as an invoice is a final statement of work performed and materials purchased that are owed from the customer to your company, an *estimate* is a preliminary listing of the costs and time you anticipate will be associated with a particular job.

An estimate is prepared in advance of getting a job, as a summary of what the job is expected to cost. Typically, a businessperson or company presents a prospective customer with an estimate, hoping to get a job. The customer considers the estimate, often comparing it to estimates received from competitors, and decides whether to award the job.

A company might agree that the cost of the job will not exceed the amount on the estimate, or there might be agreement that the estimate can be exceeded with the customer's approval. Those terms should be decided before the job is accepted.

An advantage to creating an estimate in QuickBooks Pro, rather than just writing the estimate down on a piece of paper, is that you can create invoices right from the estimate. With the QuickBooks Pro Progress Billing feature, you can indicate which individual items on an estimate are to be invoiced, or you can request to invoice a percentage of an estimate (for example, if 40 percent of the job is completed, you could invoice 40 percent of the amount on the estimate).

Another advantage to using estimates in QuickBooks Pro is that you can create reports showing the amount of work in progress, based on the unbilled portions of your estimates.

QuickBooks Pro provides a way to revise an estimate at any time, if the job situation changes.

Creating an estimate

1. Open the **Activities** menu and choose **Create Estimates**. Or, from an open Customer:Job List window, right-click the customer job and choose **Create Estimates** from the pop-up menu. You can also click the ▦ **Estimate** button on the icon bar to open the Create Estimates window (see Figure 10.3).

2. Enter the job name in the **Customer Job** field at the top of the window (or verify the job name if one is already present).

3. If you use classes, choose a class in the **Class** field (or choose **<Add New>** to create a new class). If you want to activate the Classes feature, open the **File** menu and choose **Preferences**. Or you can click the Accounting icon and check the **Use class** tracking box.

4. In the **Template** field, choose the form of estimate you want to use. You'll find only one form to choose (**Custom Estimate**) unless you have created additional estimate forms yourself.

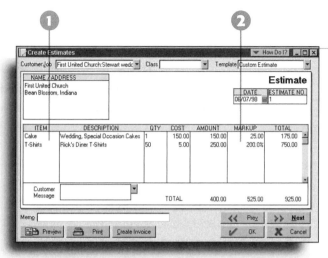

FIGURE 10.3

Enter all anticipated costs for this job in the Create Estimates window.

① Click in this column to display a drop-down list showing all your company's items.

② Enter a markup amount or percentage in this column. This figure won't print on the customer copy of the estimate.

5. Verify the date of the estimate.

6. Click in the **Item** field and choose from the drop-down list of available items (or create a **<New Item>**).

7. The **Description** field fills in automatically, as do the **Cost** and **Amount** fields if information for these fields is available. You can override any information in these fields by deleting the information that appears and entering what you want.

8. Enter an amount in the quantity field.

9. The Estimate form includes a **Markup** column. In this column you can enter either an amount or a percentage by which you want to increase the calculated cost of an item. The original cost and the markup amount do not appear on the printed estimate—this is for your information only. Only the amount in the **Total** column appears on the printed estimate.

10. If you like, enter an optional customer message that will print on the estimate. QuickBooks has chosen several friendly messages from which you can choose, or you can click **<Add New>** on the drop-down message list to create your own message.

11. You can also enter an optional **Memo** at the bottom of the Estimate form. This field is for your information only and will not print on the estimate.

Pressing Enter completes the form

If you press the **Enter** key while entering information on an Estimate form, QuickBooks thinks you have finished and takes you to the next form. If you press **Enter** inadvertently, click the **Prev** button to return to the form on which you are working.

12. Click the **Preview** button if you would like to see the estimate before printing it. Click the **Print** button to send the estimate to the printer. Click the **Create Invoice** button only if you are ready to invoice the customer for this estimate. Usually, you won't create an invoice until some portion of the job has been completed.

13. Click **Next** to proceed to the next Estimate form, or click **OK** to save this Estimate and close the window.

You can use the **Print** button on the Estimate form if you want to print the estimate right after you complete the form. Estimates don't queue for printing in QuickBooks the way other forms do (invoices, checks, and so on). If you want to print the estimate at a later time, first display the estimate onscreen by opening the **Customer:Job** List, clicking the job, opening the **Activities** menu, and choosing **View Estimate**. Then click the **Print** button.

SEE ALSO
➤ *To create your own forms, see page 374*

Invoicing Against an Estimate

If you have created an estimate for a customer, you don't have to start over when you are ready to send the customer an invoice. You can create an invoice right from the estimate—for the entire estimated amount, for a percentage of the amount, or for specific items on the estimate form.

If you plan to invoice the customer for the full value of the estimate, follow these steps:

Invoicing against an estimate

1. From the **Lists** menu, choose **Customer:Job**. The Customer:Job List window appears.

2. Click the job for which you want to prepare an invoice. Click the **Activities** button and choose **View Estimate**. The estimate you prepared appears in its Create Estimates window (as shown in Figure 10.3). If you need to make any changes to the estimate, you can do so at this time.

3. Click the **Create Invoice** button at the bottom of the Create Estimates window. (Note: If the Progress Billing window appears, you have turned on the Progress Billing feature in QuickBooks Pro. Choose **Create invoice for the entire estimate (100%)** and click **OK**.) If you make any changes in the estimate, you are asked to confirm that you want to record your changes. Click **Yes**. A notice now appears, indicating that the entire estimate has been copied to an invoice and reminding you that you can make changes in the invoice if necessary. Click **OK** when you see this notice (you don't have any other choice).

4. An invoice appears onscreen, listing all items from the estimate with prices that agree with the amounts in the Total column of the estimate. You can make changes if you need to; then click **OK**. The invoice is stored until you are ready to print it, or you can click the **Print** button and then click **OK** to print immediately.

At times you might want to create an invoice from an estimate before the job is completed. In situations like these, you will want to invoice only part of the estimate. You have two choices: You can either request an invoice for a percentage of the estimate (such as 40 percent or 75 percent) or you can request an invoice for particular items from the estimate (for example, the drywall and electrical work but not the flooring and ductwork).

Before QuickBooks creates an invoice for a portion of an estimate, you must turn on the Progress Billing feature. To turn on this feature, or to check to see if it has been turned on (you might have indicated that you plan to do progress billing when you answered the EasyStep Interview questions), follow these steps:

Turning on the Progress Billing feature

1. From the **File** menu, choose **Preferences**. The Preferences window appears.

2. Click the **Jobs & Estimates** icon on the left side of the window (you might need to scroll to find this icon).

3. Click the **Company Preferences** tab if it is not already selected.

4. Choose **Yes** in answer to the question, "Do You Do Progress Billing?"

5. Click **OK** to close this window and save your changes.

Now that you have turned on the Progress Billing feature, you can create an invoice from an estimate and use only part of the estimate.

To create an invoice for a portion of an estimate, follow these steps:

Creating an invoice for a portion of an estimate

1. Display the estimate from which you want to create an invoice (open the **Customer:Job** list, select a job, click the **Activities** button, and choose **View Estimate**).

2. Click the **Create Invoice** button at the bottom of the estimate form. The Create Progress Invoice Based On Estimate window appears.

3. Select from the following three choices:

- *Create invoice for the entire estimate (100%).* This option creates an invoice based on all the items on your estimate. This would be the Create an invoice for the remaining amounts of the estimate option, as in Figure 10.4, if you have already created a certain percentage.

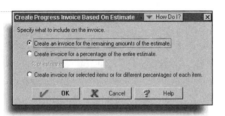

FIGURE 10.4

Indicate how much of this estimate you intend to invoice the customer for at this time.

- *Create invoice for a percentage of the entire estimate.* If you choose this option, you must enter a percentage (something less than 100%) in the **% of estimate** field.

- *Create invoice for selected items or for different percentages of each item.* Choose this option if you want to indicate which items on the estimate should be included in the invoice and at what percentage these items should be invoiced.

4. Click **OK** when you have made your choice. If you chose the third option, the Specify Invoice Amounts for Items on Estimate screen appears, listing each item on the estimate. Click the two check boxes on this screen so you can display a full view of the cost, quantity, and percentages for these items (see Figure 10.5). In the white columns (you can't make entries in the gray columns), enter the quantity or percentage of each item you want to invoice for at this time. Any amounts previously invoiced appear in the **Prior** columns in the center of the screen. Click **OK** when you have finished.

Which comes first, the invoice or the estimate?

If you start a new invoice (by either clicking the **Invoice** button on the iconbar or opening the **Activities** menu and choosing **Create Invoice**), you find that when you indicate a customer for whom an estimate is pending, QuickBooks Pro displays a message about that estimate and asks if you want to create the invoice from the estimate. If you answer positively, the estimate appears and you can follow the steps indicated in this section.

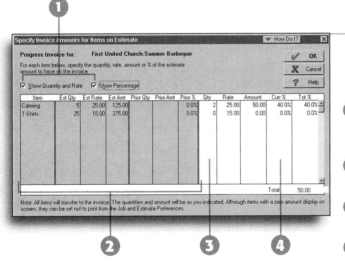

FIGURE 10.5

Indicate the quantity or percentage of each item you want to appear on the invoice.

1 Click these boxes to display all quantities and percentages for items on the estimate.

2 You can't change the amounts in the shaded area.

3 Enter the quantity you want to invoice in this column.

4 Enter the percentage of the item you want to invoice in this column.

5. The invoice appears, showing the items and amounts as you requested. Click **OK** to store this invoice for printing (or click **Print** and then **OK** to print the invoice immediately).

Changing your original estimate

You must be cautious about making decisions to change your estimate. Your company's reputation and future work for a customer might be affected by your decision to increase the cost of a job from your original estimate. If you think circumstances might warrant changing your estimate, put a disclaimer on the original estimate, noting that the prices are not guaranteed. You should also, of course, notify the customer of changes and receive approval before continuing the job.

Revising Estimates

In the normal course of business when you are working on a job, you might find you need to revise your original estimate. Perhaps the nature of the job has changed, the customer has asked you to perform more or less work, the price of parts you expected to purchase has increased, or you found the work is going to take longer (or not as long) as you originally anticipated.

Instead of waiting until you complete the job and prepare the final invoice, you can make adjustments to your estimate as you go along. This way, you can always bill from the estimate, eventually billing 100 percent of the job as estimated.

To change an existing estimate, view the estimate onscreen (open the **Customer:Job** list, select the job, click the **Activities** button, and choose **View Estimate**). Make any changes that are required, and click **OK** to save those changes.

Reporting on Work in Progress

One of the main reasons you will want to enter estimates into QuickBooks Pro instead of scribbling them on pieces of paper is so that you can view reports showing the status of your work as it is in the process of being performed.

Several interesting and useful reports are available to you when you use estimates:

- **QuickReports.** Display the Customer:Job list and click any job. Then click the **Reports** button and choose **QuickReport**, the first option on the list. A summary appears, showing all estimates and invoices issued on this job, as well as all payments received to date (see Figure 10.6).

- **Open Balance Report.** How much does this customer owe you? The Customer Open Balance report is the second report on the **Reports** drop-down menu in the **Customer:Job** list box. Choose this report to view exactly how much has been billed to this customer and how much is outstanding.

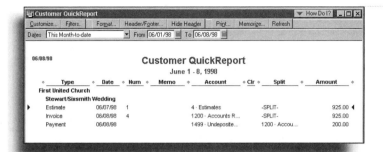

FIGURE 10.6
The Customer QuickReport gives you a detailed history of all estimates, invoices, and payments on the selected job.

- **Profit & Loss Statement by Job.** Take advantage of the fact that you have taken the time to set up separate jobs for each of your customers. The Profit & Loss Statement by Job gives you a complete breakdown of every job you have worked on in a designated time period, how much the job has cost you, and how much you have billed for the job. View this report from the Customer:Job window by clicking **Reports** (you don't need to select a job first) and then choosing **Reports on All Customer:Job**, **Profit & Loss**, **By Job**.

- **Job Profitability Summary.** Are you making any money on your jobs? The Job Profitability Summary provides a job-by-job report of how much you have earned on each job versus how much it cost you to get the job done. Prepare this report by opening the **Reports** menu, choosing **Project Reports**, and then choosing **Job Profitability Summary**.

- **Job Progress Invoices vs. Estimates.** Prepare a report showing all jobs in progress, their current status, the total of the estimate prepared for the job, the amount of the estimate that has been billed, and the percentage of the progress on the job (this calculation is based on the percentage of the amount of the estimate that has been billed). Open the **Reports** menu, choose **Project Reports**, and then choose **Job Progress Invoices vs. Estimates**.

- **Unbilled Costs by Job.** You might have assigned costs to a particular job (for example, you might have paid a subcontractor and indicated on the bill that the costs relate to a particular job), but perhaps those costs have not yet been billed. Your company is out the money and will eventually recoup it, but for now the costs are unbilled. To view a summary of all costs you have assigned to jobs but have not yet billed, open the **Reports** menu, choose **A/R Reports**, and then choose **Unbilled Costs by Job**. Each job is listed individually on the report, showing the source of the unbilled costs and the amount not yet billed to the job.

Invoicing, Monthly Statements, and Accounts Receivable

Use invoices to let your customers know how much they owe

Keep after customers with overdue balances by issuing monthly statements

Prepare accounts receivable reports to show how much is owed and how long overdue the payments are

Your company may be immensely successful at earning money, but that success will be diminished if you don't possess the tools for collecting the money in a timely fashion.

The process of collecting money includes preparing and sending invoices to your customers, following up on late payments with monthly statements, assessing finance charges to encourage timely payment of invoices, and learning to use an accounts receivable aging schedule to help you budget and plan for over-due payments.

Creating an Invoice

Unless your customers pay you in cash at the time of a sale or at the time you perform a service for them, you want to send invoices so that there is a paper record of the amount due.

The invoice provides your customer with a receipt for the purchase of merchandise or services and sets out exactly how much is owed.

When you create an invoice, your income account is increased by the amount of the invoice, and your accounts receivable account is increased as well.

Different form styles

Some of the fields that I refer to in the following steps may not appear on your invoice form. The style of form you choose controls which fields are present.

You may find it convenient to create an invoice every time you complete a sale or a project, or you may wait to create invoices on a schedule, such as one particular day a week. Whether you create one invoice at a time or prepare many invoices at once, the process is the same.

SEE ALSO

➤ *If you use the Estimating feature in QuickBooks Pro, and want to prepare invoices directly from your estimates, see page 194*

If you used the EasyStep Interview to set up your company, you were asked if you wanted to use one of four types of invoice forms: professional, service, product, or custom. Choosing an invoice style doesn't prevent you from using one of the other styles. The style you choose is the one that appears by default when you begin creating an invoice.

The following types of invoices are available in QuickBooks:

- **Professional invoice.** Includes the fields: Terms, Item, Description, Quantity, Rate, and Amount.

- **Service invoice.** Includes the fields: P.O. Number, Terms, Item, Quantity, Description, Rate, and Amount.

- **Product invoice.** Includes the fields: Ship To, P.O. Number, Terms, Rep, Ship, Via, FOB, Quantity, Item Code, Description, Price Each, and Amount.

- **Custom invoice.** Can be customized to include any of the fields from other invoice styles and any other fields that are useful to you.

SEE ALSO

➤ *For information about creating your own customized invoice form, see page 373*

Creating an invoice

1. Choose **Activities**, **Create Invoices**. The Create Invoices window appears (see Figure 11.1).

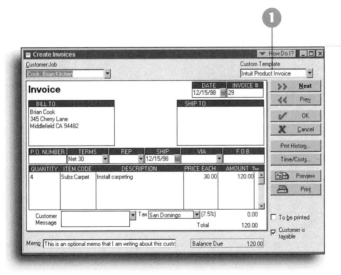

FIGURE 11.1

The fields you see on your invoice depend on the type of template you choose.

❶ Choose an invoice style by clicking here.

2. In the **Customer: Job** area of the invoice form, click the arrow to display a list of all customers (and jobs, if you use the job feature in QuickBooks). Choose a customer (and related job) from the list, or click **<Add New>** at the top of the list to set up a new customer name.

3. Verify that the correct template is in use by examining the list of available forms in the template area of the invoice form. To choose a different form, click the down arrow in the template area and choose from the drop-down list.

4. Verify that the date is the date you want to have appear on the invoice. Change to the correct date if necessary.

5. QuickBooks automatically assigns an invoice number and increments the numbers by one each time you create a new invoice. Verify that the number that appears is the correct number.

SEE ALSO

➤ *QuickBooks has a warning system to keep you from issuing duplicate invoice numbers. For information about this feature, see page 443*

6. The **Bill To** address appears automatically when you choose a customer for this invoice. Verify that the information is correct and make any necessary changes.

7. Depending on the type of invoice template you choose, there may be a **Ship To** address field (the product invoice form includes a **Ship To** address field, and your custom invoice form may include this area as well). If the **Ship To** address field appears, the address fills in automatically. Verify that the information is correct and make any necessary changes.

8. Enter a P.O. number, if applicable. This number appears on the purchase order issued by your customer.

9. In the **Terms** area of the invoice, click the down arrow to view a list of available payment terms, and then click the terms you want to use. This information may appear automatically, if you have already associated terms with this customer.

SEE ALSO

➤ *For more information about associating payment terms with a particular customer, see page 133*

What date should you use on your invoice?

Do you date your invoice as of the date you completed the job, as of the date on which you prepare the invoice, or as of the date on which you plan to put the invoice in the mail? The date you use on your invoice is especially significant if you assess finance charges for late invoices, and those finance charges are based on how many days past the invoice date a payment is received. Choose whether you want finance charges assessed based on the invoice date or the due date by setting a preference for one or the other. See "Sales & Customers Preferences" in Chapter 22 for more information.

10. In the **Rep** field, click the down arrow to see the initials of your sales representatives, and select the appropriate initials.

11. The **Ship** field should contain the date that the product shipped. Verify that this date is correct and change it if necessary.

12. Choose the appropriate shipment carrier by clicking the down arrow in the **Via** field. Enter the appropriate FOB status in the **FOB** field. You can instruct QuickBooks to fill in both the shipment carrier and the FOB status on your invoices by choosing **File**, **Preferences**, and clicking the Sales & Customers icon. Choose the **Company Preferences** tab and enter the standard shipment information that you want to appear automatically on your invoices.

13. Click in the **Item** column of the invoice and a down arrow appears. Click the arrow to display a list of all items your company sells. Click an item on the list to place the item on your invoice. Click **<Add New>** at the top of the list if the item you want is not on this list. The item name and description fills in automatically. The price may fill in as well. Verify that all information relating to the item is correct and make any necessary changes. Enter a quantity for this item, if the quantity field is available on this invoice form. QuickBooks calculates the amount due.

14. Click again in the **Item** column to add additional items to this invoice.

15. If you have charged time to this customer through the QuickBooks **Timer** feature, or through your payroll, or if you have charged expenses to this customer and are expecting reimbursement, you can automatically transfer these items to the invoice by clicking the **Time/Costs** button. Any amounts charged to this customer appear on a Choose Billable Time and Costs window where you can check off any items that you want to transfer to this invoice.

16. Click in the **Tax** column across from the item if you expect to collect sales tax on this item. A "T" appears in the field indicating the item is taxable. The "T" may appear automatically, depending on how the item was set up.

FOB

FOB is an abbreviation for the phrase, "Free on Board," and is a term used to describe when ownership of a product is transferred. Typically, if the FOB is your business location, the ownership transfers to the new owner as soon as the shipment leaves your location. If the FOB is the customer's location, the shipment is owned by you until it reaches the customer. The significance of FOB comes into play when determining who should pay the shipping costs for the item—typically the shipping costs are paid by the company that owns the product during transit. Additional concerns are liability and insurance. If the shipment is damaged, which company is responsible, and which company should insure the product during shipment? These are factors you should consider and discuss with your customers before a sale is consummated.

Deleting an item from an invoice

To delete an item from an invoices, click the line containing the item. Right-click to display a pop-up menu. Choose **Delete Line**. The item is removed from the invoice.

17. If you are charging sales tax, verify that the correct taxing authority has been selected in the **Tax** field under the item area of the invoice. To change the tax, click the down arrow in the **Tax** field and choose the correct taxing authority. Click **<Add New>** at the top of the drop-down list to add a new tax item.

18. Click the arrow in the **Customer Message** area to choose an optional customer message. Click **<Add New>** to add a new message.

19. The **Memo** area at the bottom of the invoice form is optional and you can enter any information you want in this area. The memo does not appear on the printed copy of the invoice. However, this information appears on statements issued to this customer (see "Creating a Monthly Statement" later in this chapter), and on reports that include this invoice. There is no limit to the number of characters you can enter in this field.

20. Click the **Preview** button to see what this invoice will look like before you print.

21. Click the **Print** button to print this invoice immediately. Alternatively, click the **To be printed** box, placing a check mark in this box, if you want to hold this invoice for future printing. The invoice is held by QuickBooks until you are ready to print invoices. To print all invoices, choose **File**, **Print Forms**, **Print Invoices**. The Select Invoices to Print window appears and you can check off all the invoices you want to print.

22. Click the **Next** button if you are finished entering information on this invoice and want to proceed to the next invoice. Click the **OK** button if you are finished entering all invoices and the invoice window closes. Clicking the **Cancel** button closes this invoice window without saving the invoice.

The invoice process may seem like a lot of steps, but as you use the form regularly, you find that the process becomes automatic to you.

Creating a Monthly Statement

Although it would be nice if everyone paid on time, chances are you will have customers who are slow with their payments. One way to remind customers that they have payments due is to send monthly statements.

You can create statements in QuickBooks that summarize all outstanding amounts for a customer. You can also instruct QuickBooks to assess finance charges to last invoices and list these charges on your statements.

Creating a monthly statement

1. Choose **Activities**, **Create Statements**. The Select Statements to Print window appears.

2. By default, QuickBooks uses a standard statement form (see Figure 11.2). If you have created a custom statement, or if you want to create a custom statement at this time, click the down arrow in the **Print format** field and choose the statement style you prefer.

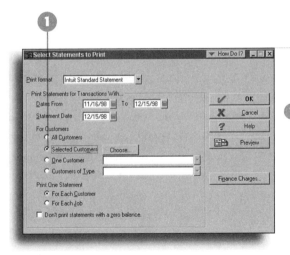

FIGURE 11.2

Choose which customers will receive statements.

① Click here to indicate which customers should not be assessed finance charges.

SEE ALSO

➤ *For more information about creating your own customized statement form, see page 373*

3. Click the **Finance Charges** button to pop up a window showing all customers with overdue balances (see Figure 11.3). Uncheck any customer who shouldn't be assessed a finance charge.

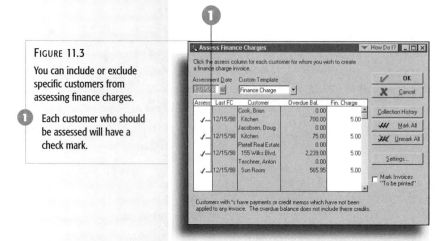

FIGURE 11.3

You can include or exclude specific customers from assessing finance charges.

1 Each customer who should be assessed will have a check mark.

4. Choose the range of dates for which you want to prepare statements. All customers for whom charges were assessed (finance charges or regular invoice charges) during the specified range are considered for statements.

5. Verify the date that should appear on the statements in the **Statement Date** field.

6. Select which type of customer for whom you want to prepare statements:

- **All Customers.** Statements are issued for all customers with outstanding invoices and finance charges issued during the period you indicated in step 3.

- **Selected Customers.** Click the **Choose** button (refer to Figure 11.2) to view a list of all customers. Click each customer or job for which you want to print a statement. This list is a little misleading because it lists all customers and jobs, even if there are no amounts due from the customers, and you can't see if any amounts are due or not. If you check a customer from whom no amount is due, a statement with a zero balance is prepared.

- **O̲ne Customer.** Choose this option if you want to prepare a statement for one particular customer, and then indicate the name of the customer or job for which you want to prepare the statement.

- **Customers of T̲ype.** If you designate types for your customers (this is a categorizing option available when you set up your customers), you can request that statements be prepared for customers of a particular type.

7. Indicate if you want to print statements for each customer, or separate statements for each job.

8. Check the box at the bottom of the window to prevent QuickBooks from printing statements with zero balances.

9. Click the **Preview** button to examine statements before printing.

10. Click the **OK** button when you have finished selecting statement options. The Print Statements window appears (see Figure 11.4). There is no option for saving statements to print at a later date—they must be printed at the time they are created.

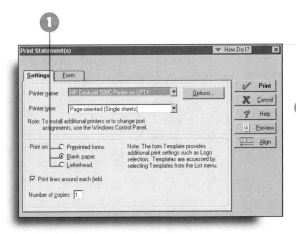

FIGURE 11.4

You must print statements at the time they are created.

1 Choose from one of these three paper types.

11. In the Print Statements window, indicate if the statements are to be printed on **Preprinted forms**, **Blank pages**, or **Letterhead**.

12. Click the **Print** button to print the statements.

Many companies find that if they follow a practice of sending monthly statements and assessing finance charges for late payments, their customers are more likely to pay on time.

Tracking Accounts Receivable

The balance in the accounts receivable account is the total of all amounts due to your company. Every time you record an invoice or a finance charge, this balance increases. Each time you record a payment against an invoice, the balance in accounts receivable is reduced.

SEE ALSO

➤ *For more information about recording payments, see page 216*

You can view all the transactions that have passed through your accounts receivable account by examining the accounts receivable register. In addition, there are several reports you can view or print that give you information about amounts currently due.

Viewing the Accounts Receivable Register

The accounts receivable register contains every transaction that has occurred in the accounts receivable account since you started recording information for your company. This means that the register information can go back several years.

You can easily obtain a customer's history from the accounts receivable register. You can also view and edit the form from which an accounts receivable transaction was created.

To open the accounts receivable register, choose **Lists**, **Chart of Accounts**. Click the **Accounts Receivable** account, and then click the **Activities** button in the Chart of Accounts window. Choose **Use Register** and the accounts receivable register appears onscreen (see Figure 11.5).

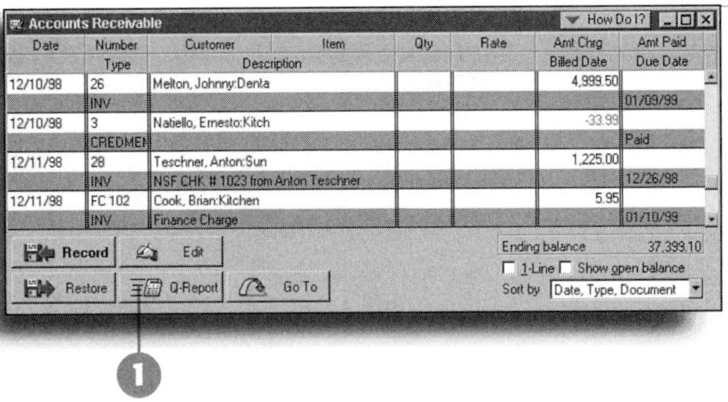

FIGURE 11.5

Use the accounts receivable register to view the details of every transaction that has passed through your accounts receivable account.

① Click a customer name, and then click here to produce a quick report showing all transactions for that customer.

Scroll through the register to view past transactions. Click a customer name, and then click the **Q-Report** button at the bottom of the register window to view a report showing all transactions for the customer.

To find a particular customer, click the **Go To** button. In the Go To window that appears, choose **Payee/Name** as the field to search, and then enter the customer name (and job name, if applicable) in the **Search for** field. Click the **Next** button to proceed through the register, stopping on each occurrence of that customer or job. Or, click the **Prev** button to progress backward through the register.

Double-click any entry in the accounts receivable register to view the form that created the entry. If there is an error on the form, you can edit the invoice, credit memo, or customer payment form and click **OK** in the form to save your changes.

Click the **x** in the upper-right corner of the accounts receivable window, or press the **Esc** key to close the window.

Accounts Receivable Reports

Several QuickBooks standard reports help you examine the contents of your accounts receivable register. Choose **Reports** from the overhead menu, and then **A/R Reports** to view accounts receivable reports. Depending on the information you want to find, choose from these reports:

- **Aging Summary.** The Accounts Receivable Aging Summary report shows the total amount due for each customer and job, with a breakdown of how much has been due for under 30 days, 31–60 days, 61–90 days, and more than 90 days. Use this report to determine which customers may be candidates for formal collection proceedings. Print this report monthly and examine the reports over a period of time to determine whether your collection processes are giving you the results you desire for your company. Determine when payments are normally received (more than 30 days but within 60 days, for example) to aid in budgeting and projecting cash flow.

- **Aging Detail.** The Accounts Receivable Aging Detail report gives you a breakdown of every amount due from every customer and job, with information on exactly how many days an amount is overdue. The report information is grouped by how many days the amounts are overdue (current receivables are listed first, then amounts up to 30 days overdue, and so on). Use this report in conjunction with the Aging Summary report to determine exactly which parts of a customer's billing are overdue and need collection attention. If a customer is late on paying for every bill, you may want to rethink the credit you extend to the customer. If the customer is late on only one bill, consider that the bill may have gotten misplaced.

- **Open Invoices.** Much like the Aging Detail report, the Open Invoices report shows the detail of all amounts due for each customer and job. The items on this report are grouped by customer and job whereas the items on the Aging Detail report are grouped by when the invoices are due.

- **Collections.** To be used when preparing to make contact with customers who have overdue balances, the Collections report includes the detail of all overdue amounts, grouped by customer and job, and includes the name and address and phone number of the customer.

- **Customer Balance Summary.** This report lists each customer with an accounts receivable balance and the total amount due.

- **Customer Balance Detail.** This report lists each customer and all the transactions that have occurred with each customer. View every invoice, credit memo, and payment made by each customer and a current balance due from each customer.

- **Unbilled Costs by Job.** View a detailed report of all amounts that have been incurred but not yet billed for your jobs. This would include time charged by employees and subcontractors that will be billed through to customers, and expenses that will be billed to customers.

You can view a graph of accounts receivable aging by choosing **R**eports, **G**raphs, Accounts **R**eceivable (see Figure 11.6). Right-click any bar or pie piece of the graph to see the dollar amount represented.

Double-click any bar on the main graph screen to see a pie graph of which customers make up the total. Double-click a resulting pie piece to see a detailed report of the transactions for that customer.

Double-click any piece of the pie on the main graph screen to see a bar graph depicting the aging for that particular customer. Double-click any bar of the resulting graph to see a detailed report of all transactions for that customer.

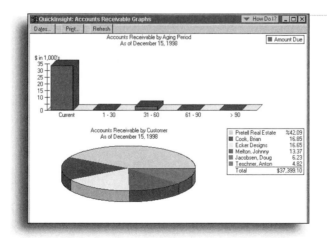

FIGURE 11.6

The bar graph shows how much of your receivables fall into each of the aging categories. The pie graph shows a section for each customer. Double-click the bars and pie pieces to get more detail.

Recording Income

Enter received payments

Enter cash sales

Deposit the cash and record the deposit in QuickBooks

Record a down payment for work you will perform in the future

Recording the fruits of your labors is one of the main reasons you invested in QuickBooks. In the last chapter you learned how to create invoices so you could let your customers know how much they owe you.

In this chapter you learn what to do when your company receives money. You learn how to record full and partial payments, down payments, and retainers. You read about making bank deposits and recording the receipt of cash that isn't associated with an invoice.

Receiving Payments for Your Invoices

When you record an invoice, an account receivable is formed, showing an amount owing from a customer. When you receive money from your customers and associate the receipt of that money with the appropriate invoice, the accounts receivable records are updated, with the amount you received no longer showing as being owed to you.

To record the payment of an invoice, follow these steps:

Recording invoice payments

1. Open the **Activities** menu and choose **Receive Payments**. The Receive Payments window appears (see Figure 12.1).

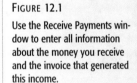

FIGURE 12.1

Use the Receive Payments window to enter all information about the money you receive and the invoice that generated this income.

2. Click the arrow in the **Customer: Job** area and choose the name of the customer from whom you received payment. Because you have previously entered an invoice for this customer, the customer name is on the list; you should not have to enter a new customer. Any outstanding invoices for this customer appear in the **Outstanding Invoices/Statement Charges** area of the screen.

3. In the **DATE** field, verify the date of this transaction and change the date if necessary.

4. Enter the amount received from this customer in the **Amount** field. The amount you enter should not exceed the amount shown in the **BALANCE** field at the top of the form. You may enter an amount that is less than the entire balance due.

5. In the **Pmt**. **Method** field, choose the method of payment (**Check**, **Cash**, or any of a variety of credit cards) or choose **<Add New>** to create a method of payment that is not on this list).

6. In the **Check No.** field, enter the number from the customer's check, if applicable.

7. If you like, type a memo in the optional **Memo** field.

8. If this payment is to be deposited in a group with other payments, choose the **Group with other undeposited funds** option. If you plan to deposit this payment immediately, click **Deposit to** and choose the name of the bank account to which it will be deposited.

9. If any credits have been issued to this customer, an amount appears in the **Existing Credits** area of the form. Check the **Apply existing credits?** box to apply credits to outstanding invoices at this time.

10. Click in the column to the left of any invoice(s) against which this payment should be applied.

11. Verify that the payment amount in the **Payment** column is correct and is applied to the correct invoice(s). Make any necessary changes, indicating the amount actually received for each invoice listed.

12. Click **Next** to save this receipt and proceed to the next one, or click **OK** to save the receipt and close the Receive Payments window.

Repeat these steps until all payments have been recorded.

Receiving Cash

Companies that do business in cash, such as retail stores and other types of companies that support walk-in business without prior invoicing, need to enter cash receipts so that income is properly recorded.

The example shown here assumes you are using the standard QuickBooks Cash Sales form. If you have customized the cash sales form to include fields that are different from the standard form, some of these instructions might not apply.

To enter cash received when there is no invoice relating to the cash, follow these steps:

Entering cash received

1. Open the **Activities** menu and choose **Enter Cash Sales**. The Enter Cash Sales form appears (see Figure 12.2).

FIGURE 12.2

Use the Enter Cash Sales form to enter information about money you receive when there was no previous invoice.

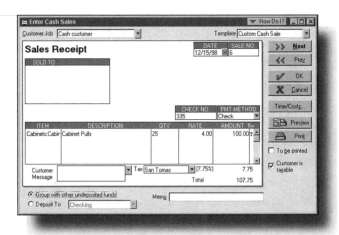

2. Click the arrow in the **Customer:Job** field and click a customer name (or, if applicable, a job name) from the resulting

drop-down list. If the customer name is not on the list, you can choose <**Add New**> to add a new customer to the list. If this is a cash sale for which you don't need a customer name, you can leave the customer field blank.

3. Verify that the date is correct. If necessary, change the date by clicking the little calendar icon to the right of the **DATE** field and then clicking the correct date.

4. The **SALE NO.** automatically increments each time you record a cash sale. You can override this number if you want to use a different number; however, if you override the automatic number with one of your own, QuickBooks ignores your number on the next cash sales form and continues incrementing from the number where QuickBooks left off. For example, if QuickBooks says this is cash sale number 12 and you change that number to 1012, the next cash sales form will display the number 13—not 1013.

5. In the **CHECK NO.** field, enter a check number that corresponds to the number on the check you receive from your customer. This field is optional.

6. Choose a method of payment (such as **Check**, **Cash**, or any of a variety of credit cards) in the **PMT METHOD** field if you choose to track the type of payment received.

7. Click in the **ITEM** column; an arrow appears. Click the arrow and choose an item from the drop-down list. If the item you sold or the service you provided does not appear on the list, click <**Add New**> at the top of the list and add the new item.

8. Verify that the description is correct, and make any changes that are necessary.

9. Enter a quantity of the item sold in the **QTY** column.

10. If the rate is not already filled in correctly, enter the correct amount in the **RATE** column. QuickBooks will calculate the amount based on the entries in the **QTY** and **RATE** columns.

11. If you like, enter an optional customer message. Some choices appear when you click the down arrow next to the

---

If you don't know the name of a customer

You might want to create a separate customer name for customers whose names you don't know. For example, if yours is a retail store where customers purchase items without disclosing their names, you might want to create a customer name such as "Cash Sale" or "In-store Purchase" to classify these customers. If all similar sales are grouped under one customer name, you will be able to produce reports by that customer name, showing how much you earned from cash sales.

Customer Message field—you can use one of these or add a new message to the list.

12. Check the box at the right of the form if this customer pays sales tax.

13. Choose the taxing authority if any items on this form are subject to sales tax. Verify the sales tax rate. QuickBooks will calculate the amount of sales tax.

14. If this payment is to be combined with other funds for deposit at a later time, click the **Group with other undeposited funds** button at the bottom of the form. Otherwise, click the **Deposit to** button and indicate the account to which this amount is to be deposited.

15. If you like, enter an optional memo at the bottom of the form. This Memo area is for your onscreen benefit only and will not print with the form.

16. Click the **Next** button to save this form and proceed to the next Enter Cash Sales form. Or, if you have finished entering cash sales, click the **OK** button to save and close this form.

Repeat the above steps until all cash sales have been recorded. In a retail setting, you might leave this form onscreen for the entire day while the store is open, recording all sales of the day.

Making Deposits

After you enter the payments you received (both payments against invoices and cash payments without invoices), you need to record a deposit to your bank account. Until you record the deposit in QuickBooks, the undeposited amount is listed on your balance sheet as an Other Current Asset called Undeposited Funds. Your cash balance is not affected by the deposit until the deposit is actually recorded.

When you are ready to make a deposit, follow these steps:

Making the actual deposit

1. Open the **Activities** menu and choose **Make Deposits**, and the Payments to Deposit window appears (see Figure 12.3). All undeposited funds are listed in this window.

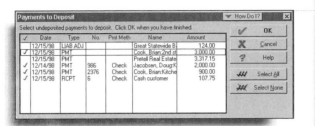

FIGURE 12.3
You can check any or all items on the Payments to Deposit screen to add them to your deposit.

2. Check to the left of all the items you want to deposit; then click **OK**. The Make Deposits window appears (see Figure 12.4).

FIGURE 12.4
The amounts listed in the Make Deposits window agree exactly with the amount you deposit in your bank account.

3. In the **Deposit To** field, select the account to which this deposit will be made. Deposits can only be made to one account at a time. If you plan to deposit to more than one account, you need to repeat these steps for the other account(s). For example, you might have received $5,000 from one customer and plan to deposit $3,000 to checking and $2,000 to savings. Make one deposit to your checking account, showing only $3,000 as the deposit (see step 5). Make a different deposit to your savings account, showing the remaining $2,000 as the deposit.

4. Verify that the date in the **Date** field matches the date of the actual deposit.

5. Verify that the amounts in the **Amount** column agree with the amounts you plan to deposit. If there is a discrepancy (as in step 3, for example), you can change the amounts in the amount column.

6. Did you forget to check something off on the Payments to Deposit window, or did you check something by mistake? Click the **Pmts** button in the Make Deposits window if you need to return to the Payments to Deposit window.

7. Click the **Print** button if you would like to print a deposit summary.

8. Click **Next** to record your deposit information and proceed to another Make Deposits window. Or click **OK** to record your deposit information and close the window.

I recommend printing deposit summaries (see step 7 in the previous exercise) and saving them in a notebook or file where they are easy to find. Deposit summaries provide useful information at the end of the month when you reconcile your bank account.

SEE ALSO

➤ *For more information on bank account reconciliation, see page* 277

Receiving Advances and Down Payments

Sometimes you might receive money in the form of an advance from a customer for whom you have agreed to perform some work, a retainer from a client who plans to use your services in the future, or a down payment on a future purchase.

If you created an invoice for a prepayment from a customer or client, treat the receipt of cash just as you treat any money received against an invoice (see the "Receiving Payments for Your Invoices" section).

If, however, the customer gives you a down payment and you have not created any paperwork for this amount, you can still deposit the money to your bank.

Depositing money received in advance

1. Open the **Activities** menu and choose **Make Deposits**. The Payments to Deposit window appears, with all undeposited funds listed. Because the advance payment is not related to an invoice, it is not listed with any other undeposited funds.

2. From the list of undeposited funds, you can check any items you want to deposit at this time. The list might be blank if all other money has been deposited. Click the **OK** button, and the Make Deposits window appears.

3. Choose the account in which you plan to deposit the money.

4. Verify that the **Date** field reflects the actual date of the deposit.

5. Click in the **Received From** column of the Make Deposits window. If items are already listed in this column, click in the white area beneath the list. An arrow appears.

6. Click the arrow in the **Received From** column and choose the name of the customer or client from whom you received this money. If the customer is not on the list, click **<Add New>** to add a new customer.

7. In the **Amount** column, enter the amount you plan to deposit.

8. Click in the **From Account** column, and an arrow appears. Click the arrow to see a drop-down list showing all of your accounts.

9. Click the account in which you want to record this advance payment. The account is probably a current liability account and might have a name such as Advances, Downpayments, Prepayments, or Retainers. If this is the first time you have entered a prepayment, you might need to click **<Add New>** to add the account to your account list.

10. In the appropriate columns, enter any optional memo, check number, and payment method information you want to record with this transaction.

11. Click **OK** when you finish entering information.

When you perform the work for which you received a prepayment, you will create an invoice for the work, just as you would under normal circumstances. The process of creating the invoice increases your income account by the amount of the job.

Creating an invoice also increases your accounts receivable account. Because you have already received the cash from your customer (so there is no accounts receivable), you need to create a general journal entry to remove the amount from your accounts receivable account (credit) and also to remove the amount from the down-payment liability account (debit).

SEE ALSO

➤ *To create general journal entries, see page 281*

Reporting Sales Tax

Collect state tax from customers and remit to the government

Set up your QuickBooks file in order to record sales tax

Charge sales tax to customers on invoices

Produce sales tax reports to help you determine how much tax you owe

Pay sales tax easily with the QuickBooks Pay Sales Tax feature

If you sell items at retail and the items you sell qualify for sales tax, you are expected to collect sales tax from your customers at the time of sale.

In QuickBooks, you can set up a sales tax item with a fixed percent so that QuickBooks can calculate the sales tax for you. You have the capability to set up more than one sales tax item, so if you sell in different localities, each with its own sales tax rate and taxing authority, QuickBooks will track the amount of sales tax you owe to each government.

Understanding How Sales Tax Works

When you issue an invoice or record a cash sale for a taxable item, QuickBooks adds the sales tax to the total sale and records an increase to your sales tax payable account.

At regular intervals, you will create sales tax reports and pay the amount due to each appropriate government agency. These payment intervals are determined by the government to which you pay the sales tax and are based on how much sales tax you charge over a certain period of time. Companies that don't have many taxable sales will not have to remit sales tax as frequently as companies that sell taxable items every day.

QuickBooks establishes a sales tax payable account when you set up your company. The government to which you pay the sales tax is set up as a sales tax item. Sales tax reports are created based on each government agency or each sales tax item.

Getting Ready to Collect Sales Tax

In the EasyStep Interview, if you indicated that you plan to collect sales tax, QuickBooks set up a sales tax payable account for you. This liability account tracks the sales tax you bill to your customers and is relieved each time you make a remittance of sales tax to the taxing authority. If you already have a sales tax liability account, you can skip this section.

If you didn't set up sales tax initially but want to set it up now, follow these steps to create your sales tax payable account.

Creating your sales tax payable account

1. Choose **Lists**, **Chart of Accounts**. The Chart of Accounts window will appear.

2. Click the **Account** button at the bottom of the window and choose **New**. The New Account window will appear (see Figure 13.1).

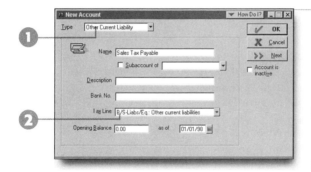

FIGURE 13.1

Set up your Sales Tax Payable liability account so that QuickBooks can track how much sales tax you owe to the government.

1 Sales Tax Payable should be classified as an Other Current Liability.

2 Fill in the tax line information if you plan to use QuickBooks to help prepare your income tax return.

3. Click the down arrow in the **Type** field and choose **Other Current Liability**.

4. In the **Name** field, enter "Sales Tax Payable" as the name of the new account.

5. If you use tax lines and your business entity type is something other than a sole proprietorship (such as a corporation or a partnership), choose **B/S-Liabs/Eq.: Other current liabilities** for your **Tax Line**.

6. If you have already been collecting sales tax and a balance exists in your liability account, enter that amount as the **Opening Balance**. Choose the date that you want to use to start tracking sales tax liability.

7. Click **OK** to close this window and save your entries.

The next step is to set up your sales tax items. The items are the actual rates you will charge your customers.

Paying sales tax at different rates

Some companies have to charge different rates of sales tax for the various types of items they sell. Food sold in a food store may be taxed at one rate, for example, but food prepared and sold for consumption in a restaurant may be taxed at a different rate. If you own a restaurant that is combined with a specialty food store, you may be required to charge sales tax at two different rates. Each rate is set up as a separate item in QuickBooks.

Creating a Sales Tax Item

A sales tax item is created for each type of sales tax you pay. Depending on where you do business, you may pay sales tax to many different states—or one state may require different sales tax rates for different types of taxable items. Each rate and each government require a separate sales tax item.

By creating separate sales tax items for each rate and government you pay, charging sales tax to your customers is a simple matter of selecting the appropriate sales tax item from a drop-down list on the invoice or cash sale form. QuickBooks takes it from there, calculating the sales tax due and adding it to the balance due from the customer. At the same time, your sales tax payable account is increased, indicating the amount you owe to the government for tax on items sold.

Setting Up a Sales Tax Item

The EasyStep Interview doesn't help you create sales tax items, so this is a procedure you must perform after the interview to set up your sales tax.

Setting up a sales tax item

1. Choose **Lists**, **Items**. The Item List window will appear.

2. Click the **Item** button and choose **New**. The New Item window will appear.

3. From the **Type** list, choose **Sales Tax Item** (see Figure 13.2).

FIGURE 13.2

Sales Tax items appear on your customer invoices.

4. Enter a name for the type of tax. You are limited to 13 characters, including spaces. This is the name you will refer to

when choosing which tax to apply. If I am charging Indiana Sales tax of 5%, for example, my name might be "Ind Tax 5%."

5. Enter a description for the tax. The description will appear on your customer invoices.

6. Enter the rate at which this tax is to be calculated. Five percent would be entered as **5**, five and one-half percent would be entered as **5.5**, and so on.

7. Enter the name of the tax agency to which you will make payments of this tax. This tax agency will be set up as one of your vendors.

8. Click **OK**. If the tax agency has not yet been set up as a vendor, you will be asked to set it up at this time (see Figure 13.3). Choosing **Quick Add** will enable you to set up only the name of the vendor, but no additional information (such as the agency address). Choosing **Set up** will provide you with a setup screen for entering all pertinent information about the tax agency.

SEE ALSO

➤ *For more information about setting up vendors, including sales tax agencies, see page 166*

FIGURE 13.3

Choose **Quick Add** to add only the name of the taxing agency to your vendor list; choose **Set Up** to enter detailed information such as the address and telephone number of the agency.

Telling QuickBooks to Charge Sales Tax

Before you can begin using the sales tax feature in QuickBooks, you must indicate to QuickBooks that you plan to charge sales tax. Otherwise, no option will be available for charging tax on your invoice forms.

Note that you must set up your sales tax items before completing these steps.

Using a sales tax group

If you need to charge your customers more than one type of sales tax, you might want to consider setting up a sales tax group. With a group, you include multiple tax assessments under one title. If you need to collect both county and state sales tax, for example, your group might be called simply "Sales Tax," and that is the name that would appear on invoices. The assessment, however, would combine rates from both taxing authorities. To create a sales tax group, set up a new item by choosing **Sales Tax Group** as the item type. A checklist will appear in which you check off each of the sales tax items you want to include in the group. All your sales tax items must be set up before you can create a group.

Advising QuickBooks that you plan to charge sales tax

1. Choose **File**, **Preferences**. The Preferences window will appear.

2. Click the **Sales Tax** icon on the left. You may need to scroll through the list to find this icon. Choose the **Company Preferences** tab.

3. Choose **Yes** in answer to the question, "Do You Charge Sales Tax?"

4. Indicate whether you expect to pay sales tax **monthly**, **quarterly**, or **annually**. If you are new to collecting and paying sales tax, your state government will provide you with this information.

5. Indicate that your company is a cash basis or accrual basis company by choosing whether you owe sales tax **As of invoice date** (accrual basis) or **Upon receipt of payment** (cash basis).

6. Choose the sales tax item you charge most frequently as the **Most common sales tax**. If you don't charge one type of sales tax any more frequently than any other type, you must still select one sales tax item here. This item will appear automatically on your invoice forms, but you can choose a different tax item if necessary.

7. If you want QuickBooks to print a "T" on customer invoices next to taxable items, check the box at the bottom of the window.

8. Click **OK** to save your changes. The Updating Sales Tax window may appear (see Figure 13.4).

FIGURE 13.4

Check these boxes to update your customer and item list for sales taxes.

9. In the Updating Sales Tax window, indicate whether all current customers should be designated as subject to sales tax,

and whether all existing inventory and non-inventory part items that you sell should be designated as taxable. Click **OK** to close this window.

In the future, when you set up new customers, you will notice an option in the customer setup screen for designating the customer as subject to sales tax (see Figure 13.5). Check the box to enable QuickBooks to charge sales tax to this customer.

FIGURE 13.5

The customer setup screen includes an option to designate whether a customer is subject to sales tax.

① Click here to turn on sales tax for this customer.

When you set up new inventory or non-inventory part items, you will have an opportunity to indicate whether the item is subject to sales tax (see Figure 13.6).

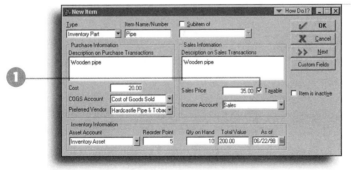

FIGURE 13.6

This item setup screen includes an option to designate whether an inventory item is taxable.

① Click here so that Quick-Books will charge tax when you sell this item.

Using more than one sales tax rate per invoice

If you have customers who purchase various items that are subject to different sales tax rates, you can't use the sales tax rate at the bottom of the invoice. This rate applies to the entire invoice. To apply separate rates to different items on the invoice, create a sales tax rate of 0% to use as your tax rate at the bottom of the invoice, then enter tax items as needed in the item list of the invoice (see Figure 13.8). You may need to subtotal items subject to tax, then apply the tax rate to the subtotal.

Charging Sales Tax to Customers

When a customer purchases a taxable item from you, indicate the correct tax amount on the invoice or cash sale form.

Applying sales tax to a purchase

1. Prepare the invoice as you normally would, including the customer name, job name (if applicable), terms, and items sold.

2. In the Tax area at the bottom of the invoice form (see Figure 13.7), the tax you set up as the common sales tax will already be chosen. To accept this tax, do nothing. To switch to a different sales tax, click the drop-down arrow and choose from existing tax items, or click **<Add New>** to add a new sales tax item.

FIGURE 13.7

QuickBooks calculates sales tax based on the rate selected in the tax area.

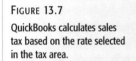   Click here to choose a different tax rate.

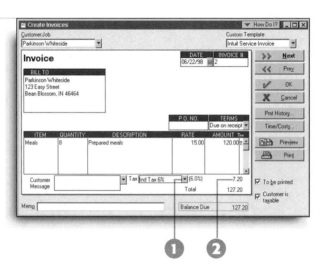   Tax as calculated by QuickBooks.

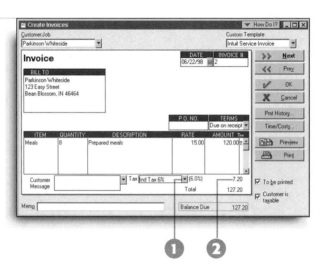

3. All items subject to sales tax are marked with a "T" in the item area of the invoice. If some items should be excluded from tax, click the "T" to remove it. If some items should be taxed but are not marked, click in the Tax column to place a "T" next to the item.

SEE ALSO

> *For more information about creating subtotals to use as items on a form, see Chapter 8, "Setting Up Services, Customers, and Suppliers."*

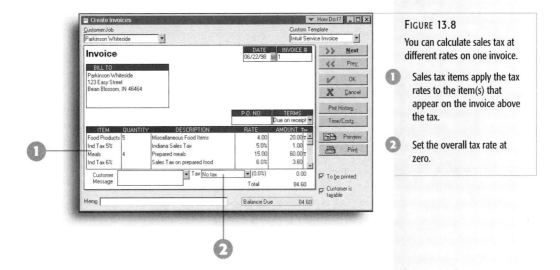

FIGURE 13.8

You can calculate sales tax at different rates on one invoice.

① Sales tax items apply the tax rates to the item(s) that appear on the invoice above the tax.

② Set the overall tax rate at zero.

Taxable Versus Non-Taxable Sales

If an item you are selling is not subject to sales tax (services such as consulting, legal, or accounting services often are not subject to sales tax), you should set up this item as non-taxable when it is created (refer to Figure 13.6). In addition, you can double-check your customer invoice to make sure no "T" is next to the item, which would generate a sales tax charge.

To determine which items are subject to sales tax, contact your taxing authority. Usually this is the department of revenue for the state in which you live. Each state has different rules regarding which items are subject to sales tax, and sometimes different rates apply to different types of items.

Tax-Exempt Sales

Sometimes you will sell items that are subject to tax, but you will sell them to customers who are exempt from paying sales tax. It is important that you check with your state taxing authority regarding the rules for dealing with tax-exempt customers.

In general, before you can permit a tax-exempt sale, you must request a tax resale number from the customer and keep that number on file. The customer should be happy to supply you with this number.

Entering the customer's tax-exempt number

1. Choose **Lists**, **Customers:Jobs**. The Customer:Job list window will appear.

2. Click the customer name, then click the **Customer:Job** button and choose **Edit**. The Edit Customer window will appear.

3. Click the **Additional Info** tab. At the bottom of the window (as shown in Figure 13.5), uncheck the box indicating that the **Customer is taxable** and enter the customer's resale number in the space provided.

4. Click **OK** to save your changes.

The next time you issue an invoice to this customer, no sales tax will be calculated.

Monthly Sales Tax Reports

You will need to prepare sales tax reports and submit them to your taxing government agency. Generally, these reports are prepared monthly; however, you may report sales tax less frequently depending on the rules of your state.

SEE ALSO

➤ *For a complete listing of taxing agencies for all states, see Appendix D, "State Revenue Agencies," page 569*

Although QuickBooks will prepare your sales tax payment for you (see "Paying Sales Tax" later in this chapter), it is up to you to prepare the tax form required by your government.

Because each state requires a different tax form, QuickBooks is not equipped to produce the actual forms for you. However, you can produce reports in QuickBooks that will provide you with all the information you need to prepare your monthly sales tax reports.

Producing the Sales Tax Liability report

1. Choose **Reports**, **A/P Reports**. A side menu appears.

2. Choose **Sales Tax Liability Report**. The report that appears includes total sales, non-taxable sales, taxable sales, tax rate, the total tax due for the current period, and the total tax due for all your taxing jurisdictions (see Figure 13.9).

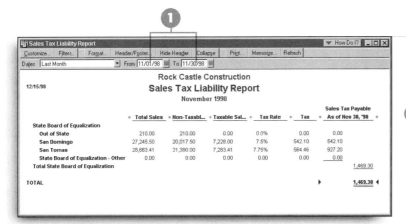

FIGURE 13.9

Prepare this report so that you can see exactly how much sales tax you owe.

① Set the dates that agree with the period for which you are paying tax.

3. At the top of the report window, you should verify that the dates agree with the period for which you are paying tax. If you pay monthly, you will want to produce a report for the prior month. However, if you want to view the amount of tax you owe so far for the current month, you should change the dates to reflect the current date.

4. Print a copy of the report by clicking the **Print** button at the top of the report.

In addition to the Monthly Sales Tax Report, you can produce a quick report showing the detailed transactions that make up your tax liability. Choose **Lists**, **Items**, click the name of the taxing authority, click the **Reports** button, and choose **QuickReport**. Adjust the dates on the report so that the detail you view is for the correct time period. Double-click any item on this report to see the invoice or cash sale form that generated the tax.

Paying Sales Tax

QuickBooks is ready to help you make your sales tax payments. Choose **Activities**, **Pay Sales Tax,** and the Pay Sales Tax window will appear (see Figure 13.10). Verify that the date shown in the **Show sales tax due through** area coincides with the end of the period for which you are paying sales tax (usually, this will be the last day of the prior month).

FIGURE 13.10

Check off the sales tax amounts you wish to pay at this time.

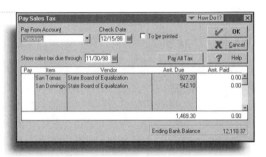

Sales tax liability

The frequency with which you must make sales tax payments is determined by the laws of the taxing agency. Many state and local taxing agencies require monthly payments of sales tax, but you should check with your government tax agency to be sure. Late sales tax payments are subject to costly fines, so it is imperative that you learn the laws governing your situation.

Penalties for not paying sales tax on time

Taxing agencies take a pretty hard line when it comes to collecting tax on time. Particularly with sales tax, because you have already collected the tax from your customers, the government accepts few excuses for late payments. Penalties are harsh, and the government has the right to seize your company's assets when taxes are not paid. If your company is having cash flow problems, look for other ways to make ends meet rather than holding back taxes owed to the government. And while you're at it, take a look at Chapter 26, "Budgeting," where you can find some advice for getting a handle on your finances.

If you pay tax to more than one agency, each agency will be listed. Check off all items you intend to pay at this time. Adjust the amount if you do not intend to pay the full amount due.

Verify that the account shown at the top of the window is the account from which you want the payment to be drawn. Check the To be printed box if you want QuickBooks to print this check. Leave the box blank if you plan to prepare the check by hand. Click **OK** and QuickBooks issues the payment for your sales tax.

SEE ALSO

➤ *For more information about writing checks in QuickBooks, see Chapter 15, "Purchase Orders, Accounts Payable, and Paying Bills," page 257*

Keeping Track of
Your Inventory

Inventory items are the things you sell, whether
you produce them or purchase and resell them

Value your inventory by calculating the average cost of all
items on hand

Set up as many inventory items as your company needs

Take a physical inventory count at least once a year

Consider alternatives such as spreadsheets, databases,
and inventory programs to help value your inventory

QuickBooks provides a full, interactive inventory feature that constantly tracks and updates your company's inventory totals. Each time you receive new items in stock, your inventory quantity increases; each time you sell an item, your inventory quantity decreases. A reorder feature reminds you when supplies are getting low and you need to order more.

QuickBooks also comes with a serious shortfall in the area of valuing inventory: The only way QuickBooks provides to value inventory is the *weighted average* method. This method of valuation is described in this chapter, along with other common methods. The chapter also discusses alternatives to using QuickBooks to account for the value of your inventory.

What Is Inventory?

Merchandise you own and expect to sell to others is *inventory*. Inventory includes finished goods or partly finished goods you produced. Raw materials and supplies that will eventually become part of goods available for sale are also considered to be inventory.

Items you own but have placed on consignment with someone else or on display in a showroom or booth away from your place of business are part of your inventory.

Inventory includes items you have contracted to sell but to which you have not yet relinquished ownership.

If a container is sold as part of the inventory item, the container itself is also considered inventory. A container on which a deposit has been received from the customer to guarantee the return of the container is not considered part of inventory.

Inventory is considered a current asset; its value is presented on your balance sheet. The value of your inventory increases the value of your business.

Raw Materials, Work in Progress, and Finished Goods

If your company is a manufacturing company producing products from raw materials or parts and supplies, you will find that QuickBooks falls short of being able to provide you with the inventory accounting you need. You can keep track of individual raw material items with the QuickBooks inventory feature, but no provision is made for transferring these items to a Work in Progress or Finished Goods status.

The only way to properly account for manufactured goods in QuickBooks is to record raw materials or parts as inventory items at acquisition. Then when the end product has been manufactured, create a sale to yourself of all the individual parts and create a purchase of the finished product item into a new inventory account.

This process of selling yourself parts and purchasing a finished product as a way to record items in inventory is cumbersome, subject to error, and not the way we envision a manufacturing process to work. No sale actually occurs—just a change in the status of the inventory items.

QuickBooks doesn't pretend to offer this scenario as a solution to accounting for manufactured inventory. Instead, the makers of the program (in their printed material) recommend against using QuickBooks for tracking manufactured inventory: "If you do manufacturing, you should not use the QuickBooks inventory feature."

Determining the Average Cost of Inventory Items

The cost of your inventory is determined by the cost of the merchandise you purchase for resale. If you are a manufacturer, the cost of your inventory is represented by the cost of materials and supplies that will ultimately become part of your finished goods.

FIFO, LIFO, and Specific Identification

The three most popular methods of inventory valuation are not supported by QuickBooks:

- *FIFO (First In, First Out)*. The first items you purchase are the first items you sell. A grocery store prefers to sell items on this basis, always moving the items with the earliest date to the front of the shelf so there is never any old stock on hand. The value of inventory at the end of the year (or reporting period) is determined by taking a physical inventory count and then matching the costs of items most recently purchased to the quantity of items on hand. The cost of the earliest items purchased is then added to the cost of sales. By using this method, your inventory is always valued at its most current cost.

- *LIFO (Last In, First Out)*. The last items (the most recent items) you purchase are the first items you sell. Imagine a clothing store, where the latest fashions are the ones that sell, whereas the older articles of clothing stay on the racks. Items remaining in your inventory are assumed to be the oldest items and are valued at the cost of the oldest items purchased.

- *Specific Identification Method*. The inventory that lends itself to tracking of individual items. As each item is sold, the value of inventory on hand is reduced by the actual cost of the specific item. For example, all automobiles have a VIN (Vehicle Identification Number) so it is easy to track automobiles that go in and out of inventory.

As business unfolds on a day-to-day basis, QuickBooks constantly updates the value of your inventory asset account by using a *weighted average* method of valuing your inventory on hand.

As each item is added to the total inventory, the cost of the new item is added to the cost of all pieces of the same item on hand to provide a total. When an item is sold, the total cost of all inventory items is divided by the number of pieces on hand to determine an average cost. This cost is reflected at the time of sale as the cost of sales for the item sold.

This method is contrary to more traditional methods of inventory costing on two levels:

- Although the averaging method of determining the cost of items sold is not uncommon in very small businesses or in businesses where sales of inventory are not a major part of the operation, many companies prefer to use methods of inventory costing that perhaps more accurately reflect the way the company or the industry performs, such as FIFO, LIFO, and Specific Identification.

- The more traditional method of accounting is to charge all purchases of inventory items during the year to a purchases expense account. Then determine the value of your inventory at the end of the year by taking a physical inventory count and using one of the valuation methods to calculate the value of the inventory on hand. The difference between the value of the inventory on hand and the value of the inventory the last time you counted gets added to—or deducted from, if the value of inventory has decreased—the purchases expense to determine the cost of sales for the year.

Because QuickBooks does not address these issues of alternative costing and year-end adjustments, you might find the accounting method used for inventory in QuickBooks unacceptable. If that is the case, see the "Alternatives to the QuickBooks Inventory Feature" section later in this chapter.

If the average-costing method of valuing inventory is acceptable to you and you appreciate the opportunity to have your inventory updated instantly each time a sale is made, continue with this chapter for more detailed information about how this inventory feature works.

Using the QuickBooks Inventory Features

If you choose to use QuickBooks to keep track of your inventory, you will find it is a luxury to know that every single item of your inventory is accounted for on an individual basis. At any time, you can request a report of all inventory items in stock or a complete listing of all items on order.

With the QuickBooks reorder feature, you can indicate a point at which new stock should be ordered for each inventory item. Then, when sales of your inventory indicate quantities are running low, you will receive a reminder from the program that it is time to reorder.

Although you can create invoices in QuickBooks for inventory you do not have in stock, the program gives you a message indicating present quantities are too low to fill the order for which you are invoicing.

SEE ALSO

➤ *To set up inventory and reorder points, see page 76*

Setting Up Inventory Items On-the-Fly

When you set up your company with the EasyStep Interview, you may have set up several inventory items. As your business grows, you will probably need to set up additional inventory items. You can do this on-the-fly by waiting until you are ready to use the item on a form (such as a purchase order or invoice) and then entering the name of the new item in the **Items** area of the form. You'll see an Item Not Found window onscreen (see Figure 14.1). To add the item to your inventory list, click the **Set Up** button. (Items must be set up before you can use them; if you click the **Cancel** button, QuickBooks does not allow you to use the item on your form.)

FIGURE 14.1

Click **Set Up** if you want QuickBooks to let you use your new item.

When you click the **Set Up** button in the Item Not Found box, the New Item window appears. In this window you will set up all the information you have about this new inventory item.

To move from one field to the next in the New Item window, press the **Tab** key (or press Shift+Tab to move backward through the fields). You can also click in each field. Do not press the **Enter** key until you are finished entering all information about this item.

Setting up your new inventory item

1. Verify the description "Inventory Part" that appears in the **Type** area of the New Item window. If something else appears here, click the drop-down arrow and choose **Inventory Part** (see Figure 14.2).

FIGURE 14.2

Enter all the information about your inventory item in the New Item window.

1. Choose **Inventory Part** to set up a new inventory item.

2. When do you want to be notified to order more of this item?

3. How many of this item are on hand as of this date?

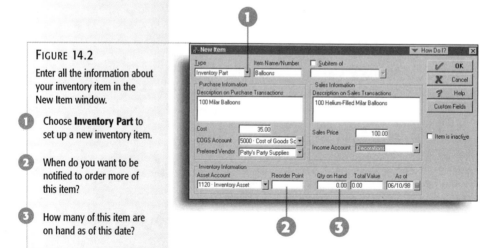

2. The item name you entered on your transaction form appears in the **Item Name/Number** area. You can revise this if necessary. If this item is to be a subitem of another

item, check the **Subitem of** box and choose the item that is the parent of this item.

3. Enter a **Description for Purchase Transactions**. This description appears on your purchase orders when you order the item and on your bills when you enter bills you receive for the item. This description also appears on inventory and purchase reports.

4. Enter the cost you typically pay for this item. You can override this amount when it appears on a purchase form, and you can also change the amount by editing the item in your **Items** list (explained later in this chapter). If cost of the item changes frequently, you might want to leave this area blank; however, QuickBooks uses this amount to estimate the value of any of these items you currently have on hand (see step 12).

5. Verify that the Cost of Goods Sold (COGS) account shown is the account in which you want to record the cost of purchases of this item. You might have designated subaccounts to identify cost of specific items sold, or perhaps you set up an account called Purchases instead of Cost of Goods Sold. If the account needs to be changed, click the arrow at the end of the **COGS Account** field and choose the appropriate account.

6. From the drop-down list in the **Preferred Vendor** field, choose the name of the vendor you use most frequently for purchases of this item. If you use this optional field, QuickBooks displays the name of the vendor on your stock status report and your physical inventory worksheet (these reports are discussed later in this chapter).

7. Enter a description you want to see on sales transaction forms. This description also appears on the invoices you present to your customers. You can use the same description as on your purchase transaction forms.

8. Enter the **Sales Price** you generally charge for this item. The amount you enter appears automatically on invoices for this item. If necessary, you can override this amount on the invoice form. If the sales price changes frequently, you can leave this area blank and fill in the sales price each time you invoice for the item.

9. Choose an **Income Account** for this item. This is the account where income from sales of this item will be reported.

10. Indicate the **Asset Account** in which to record the value of this asset. QuickBooks has already chosen an inventory asset account for you, but you might have a specific subaccount where you want to track information about this particular inventory item.

11. Enter a **Reorder Point**. If the number of pieces of this item drops below this reorder point, you will receive a reminder that it is time to reorder.

12. In the **Qty on Hand** area, enter the number of pieces of this item you currently own, if any. QuickBooks uses the cost you entered earlier when calculating the total value of the items you have on hand.

13. QuickBooks assumes the information you are entering is current as of today's date. If another date is more appropriate, change the date in the **As of** field at the bottom of the New Item window.

14. If you want to enter more information about this item but no field is available, you can click the **Custom Fields** button and then the **Define Fields** button to designate up to five custom fields. Enter a description for the field you want to create (see Figure 14.3), check the **Use** box to indicate you want to use this custom field, and then click **OK**. The custom field(s) you define won't appear on the New Item screen but will now be available if you click the **Custom Fields** button. Any custom fields you create will also appear as a choice if you customize a form such as an invoice so you can choose to have the custom field actually appear on the form.

15. When you finish entering all information for this new item, click the **OK** button. The information is saved, the inventory item is added to your **Items** list, and you are returned to complete the form on which you were working.

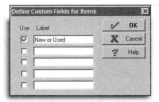

FIGURE 14.3
Create up to five fields that request any information you need.

SEE ALSO

➤ *To add customized fields to forms, see page 373*

Setting Up Inventory Items in General

If you prefer to set up your inventory items all at once rather than on-the-fly, you can open the **Items** list (from the **Lists** menu, choose **Items**, or click the **Item** button). Click the **Item** button and choose **New** (or press Ctrl+N). The New Item window appears.

Select **Inventory Part** from the **Type** drop-down list. Enter all the information for a new item. The fields will differ on this screen, depending on the type of item you choose. Click **Next** when you're ready to proceed to the next new item. When you have finished entering all items, click **OK** to close the New Item window.

Editing Items

You can change the specifications of any of your inventory items by displaying the Items List window, clicking the item you want to change, opening the **Item** menu, and choosing **Edit** to open the Edit Item window. Make your changes to any of the fields in this window and then click **OK** to save your changes.

Adding to Your Inventory

Whether you receive a bill when you receive items of inventory determines how the receipt of inventory is recorded.

Receiving Items Without a Bill

If you receive the items without an accompanying bill from your supplier, follow these steps to record the receipt of items:

1. Open the **Activities** menu and choose **Inventory**; then choose **Receive Items** from the submenu. (Or with the Items List open, click the **Activities** button and choose **Receive Items**). The Create Item Receipts window appears.

2. Select from the **Vendor** drop-down list (see Figure 14.4). If a purchase order has been issued for this vendor and items ordered on the purchase order have not yet been received, you see a message onscreen asking if you would like to receive against the outstanding order(s) (see Figure 14.5). Click **Yes** to verify the purchase order(s) to which the received items relate. If no outstanding purchase orders exist for this vendor, skip to step 5.

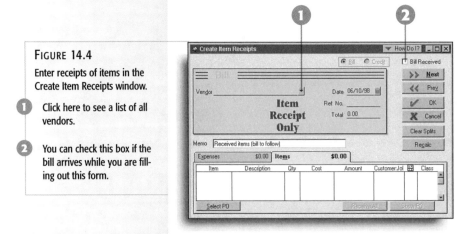

FIGURE 14.4

Enter receipts of items in the Create Item Receipts window.

1 Click here to see a list of all vendors.

2 You can check this box if the bill arrives while you are filling out this form.

3. If you have open purchase orders against which you are receiving items, the Open Purchase Orders screen appears, listing the date and purchase order number of each outstanding purchase order for this vendor. Click in the check mark column next to the purchase order you want to associate with this order (see Figure 14.6). Click **OK** to return to the Create Item Receipts screen.

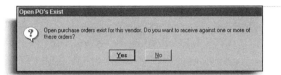

FIGURE 14.5

The Open POs Exist message appears if a purchase order exists for items that have not yet been received.

FIGURE 14.6

Click in the check mark column to associate a purchase order with the receipt of the item(s).

4. If you indicated a purchase order in step 3, the items listed on that purchase order appear in the **Items** area at the bottom of your Create Item Receipts screen. You can change any information in this area so the items noted on this form correspond to the items actually received. If you would like to view the purchase order from which these items were generated, click the **Show PO** button to display the original purchase order form. Click **OK** to close the purchase order form.

5. If you did not indicate a purchase order in step 3, click the **Items** tab in the center of the Create Item Receipts screen. Click in the **Item** column and then click the arrow to open a list of all items. Choose an item by clicking it, or set up a new item by clicking **<New Item>**. Enter the quantity and, if necessary, the cost of the item in the appropriate columns. Repeat this step for as many different items as were received in this shipment.

6. When all items have been entered, click **Next** to proceed to the next Create Item Receipts screen, or click **OK** if you have finished entering receipts.

After you have completed all the preceding steps, your inventory records are increased by the quantity of items you indicated your company received.

Receiving Items with a Bill

If you receive a bill at the same time you receive your inventory items, you want to enter both the items and the bill in the system. Open the **Activities** menu and choose **Inventory**. Then choose **Receive Items and Enter Bill**. The Enter Bills window appears.

Follow steps 2–6 in the preceding section to enter all information from the bill and to record the receipt of inventory items, but use the Enter Bills window rather than the Create Item Receipts window.

Reports About Inventory

Activating Inventory feature

The inventory reports are not visible on your **Reports** menu if you have not activated the Inventory feature for your company. To activate Inventory, open the **File** menu and choose **Preferences**. Click the **Purchases & Vendors** icon at the left of the window. On the **Company Preferences** tab, click the **Inventory and purchase orders are active** box.

QuickBooks provides several standard inventory reports with which you can obtain information about your inventory. Find out how many items you have on hand and what your inventory is worth by choosing from these inventory reports:

- **Inventory Stock Status by Item.** This report lists each item in your inventory and lets you know how many are currently in stock, how many are on order, and when you can expect to receive the orders. The report also calculates the average sales of each item on a per-week basis. Open the **Reports** menu, choose **Inventory**, and then choose **Stock Status by Item** to display this report.

- **Inventory Stock Status by Vendor.** This report displays the same information as the Stock Status by Item report, but the items are grouped by vendor so you can quickly find out how many items are on order from a particular vendor and which inventory items get ordered from each vendor. Open the **Reports** menu, choose **Inventory**, and then choose **Stock Status by Vendor** to display this report.

- **Inventory Valuation Summary.** This report shows the worth of each item in your inventory, based on the average cost method. The report also shows what percentage of the total inventory each item accounts for, what the items retail for, and what percentage of the total retail value each item accounts for. Open the **Reports** menu, choose **Inventory**, and then choose **Valuation Summary** to display this report.

- **Inventory Valuation Detail.** This report takes the Inventory Valuation Summary one step further and shows you the complete details of every inventory transaction (each purchase and each sale) for the requested period of time. Open the **Reports** menu, choose **Inventory**, and then choose **Valuation Detail** to display this report.

- **Item Price List.** Prepare a report that shows the price of each item in your inventory as well as all your company's other items. Open the **Reports** menu and choose **List Reports**, **Item**, **Price List** to display the report. To display a price list of only inventory items, click the **Filters** button, choose **Item** in the Filter box at the left, then select **All Inventory Items** as the Item filter.

Taking a Physical Inventory Count

Typically, the value of the inventory is determined by taking a count of physical inventory items on hand at a specific time (year-end is most common). Quantities of inventory items are confirmed, and cost is determined by using one of several costing methods described earlier in this chapter.

The more frequently you count inventory, the more likely you will be aware of any loss or damage to your inventory. Most companies count inventory once a year, at the end of the year when they are preparing their year-end financial statements.

QuickBooks makes taking a physical inventory easy by providing you with a physical inventory worksheet as one of its standard reports. The worksheet, shown in Figure 14.7, lists all inventory items you have set up for your company. From the **Reports** menu, choose **Inventory Reports**, and then choose **Physical Inventory Worksheet** to produce this report; then print a copy so that you can use it while you count your inventory.

FIGURE 14.7

A sample worksheet for use in counting inventory on hand.

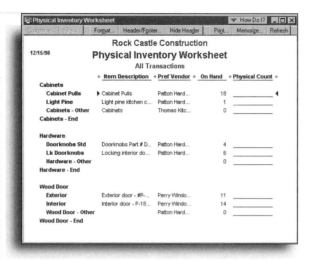

The Physical Inventory Worksheet includes any descriptive information that has been set up for these items, the preferred supplier of each item, and the quantity QuickBooks thinks is on hand as of the date you request the report.

In the far right column, next to the amounts expected to be on hand, is a series of blank lines where you can fill in the actual amounts on hand as you make your count.

As you make your physical inventory count, you might find a disagreement between the inventory in QuickBooks and the inventory you actually have in your warehouse or other business premises.

Large discrepancies must be explained, and it is up to you and the other members of your company to determine what constitutes a large discrepancy to your business. If your inventory is made up of many small parts, such as nuts and bolts and screws, you might not feel a discrepancy of 20 bolts is worth investigating. If your inventory is made up of computers and printers and other high-tech equipment, you'll probably consider 20 missing computers an unacceptable loss.

Adjusting Quantity and Value of Inventory Account

When you take your physical inventory count, you might find that your actual inventory totals don't agree with the quantity of items QuickBooks thinks you have. Perhaps some items were damaged or lost, perhaps there was a theft, or there might be other reasons—which you will want to determine—for the discrepancies in your inventory totals.

QuickBooks adjusts your inventory quantities whenever a sale takes place. When changes in quantity occur that aren't attributable to a sale, you have to adjust your QuickBooks records yourself so they show the exact quantity on hand.

To make an adjustment in the quantity of inventory items on hand, follow these steps:

Making quantity adjustments

1. Open the **Activities** menu and choose **Inventory**; then choose **Adjust Qty/Value on Hand** (the Inventory feature must be activated for this menu option to be available). The Adjust Quantity/Value on Hand window appears (see Figure 14.8). All inventory items owned by your company are listed in the **Item** column at the left. The quantity on hand, according to QuickBooks, is shown in the **Current Qty** column.

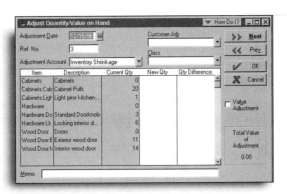

FIGURE 14.8

Adjust your inventory quantities based on the difference between your physical count and the amounts QuickBooks shows in the Adjust Quantity/Value on Hand window.

2. If your physical count shows the quantity on hand to be different from the quantity on hand according to QuickBooks, enter the correct quantity in the **New Qty** column. QuickBooks makes the necessary changes to your records to reflect this change.

3. In the **Adjustment Account** field, enter the name of the account you want QuickBooks to use when making an adjustment in the value of your inventory. QuickBooks adjusts your inventory by the average cost of the items you enter. You might want to set up a new account called Inventory Shrinkage or something similar so you can easily spot the changes in inventory. The account you create to track inventory shrinkage will typically be an expense account.

4. Click **OK**.

Note that there is also a **Value Adjustment** check box on this screen. If you check this box, two more columns appear: **Current Value** and **New Value**. The **Current Value** column shows the total cost of all inventory items. You can use this column to adjust the value of your inventory.

If you use an outside program to value your inventory, as discussed in the "Alternatives to the QuickBooks Inventory Feature" section, you might find you can make your year-end adjustments right on the Adjust Quantity/Value on Hand screen, rather than making an adjustment in the general journal (also discussed in the next section).

SEE ALSO

➤ *For more information on passwords and limiting access to the file, see page 535*

Alternatives to the QuickBooks Inventory Feature

As mentioned earlier in this chapter, some inventory matters can't be accomplished with QuickBooks. Manufacturers are encouraged to seek other methods of accounting for inventory.

And it is very difficult to account for inventory if you use a valuation such as LIFO, FIFO, and Specific Identification with QuickBooks.

So how should your company proceed if you want to use QuickBooks for other accounting but find the inventory feature unacceptable?

Several alternatives to QuickBooks are available, all of which require you to account for inventory outside of QuickBooks and then make a year-end general journal entry to adjust inventory and cost of sales amounts.

For example, if the value of inventory at the end of the year is $5,000 more than the value of inventory at the beginning of the year, you need to make a general journal entry to adjust the amount in your inventory account on your balance sheet. The journal entry debits inventory by $5,000 (increasing the account, because debits increase assets) and credits cost of sales (decreasing the account, because all purchases were charged, or debited, to the cost of sales account during the year, but $5,000 of these purchases presumably are still in inventory and should be reclassified to the inventory asset account).

SEE ALSO

> *For more information about making general journal entries, see page 293*

> *For more information about debits and credits, see page 116*

The Spreadsheet Alternative

You can use a spreadsheet program, such as Microsoft Excel, Lotus 1-2-3, or Corel's Quattro Pro, to track your inventory. If you use a spreadsheet program, you might want to set up a separate sheet for each inventory item or a separate column on one large sheet for each item.

All purchases of inventory items are recorded on these spreadsheets, which carry over from year to year as long as the inventory items are carried in your stock.

If you change your inventory items frequently, selling out of older items and not replacing them but acquiring newer models

---

Tracking inventory tiers

Although it is difficult, it is not impossible to track inventory in QuickBooks using a LIFO or FIFO method. You can choose to set up each differently-priced set of inventory items as separate items, thus establishing what is known as tiers of inventory. For example, suppose you are in the business of silk-screening T-Shirts and you purchase solid-colored T-Shirts from a supplier. Your purchases include 1,000 T-Shirts acquired at $3.29, 1,000 T-Shirts at $3.33, and 1,000 T-Shirts at $3.37. QuickBooks would indicate that you own 3,000 T-Shirts valued at $3.33 (the average cost). If you set up each block of T-Shirts as a separate item with its own price, you can track each group of shirts individually and the cost will not be averaged. There will be a lot more work on your part, having to identify from which lot a shirt is chosen, but at least the accounting will be accurate.

instead, it makes sense to use a separate spreadsheet for each item rather than one sheet with a column for each item. By using separate sheets, you can stop using a particular sheet altogether when an item is retired.

In a FIFO environment, the oldest items on the spreadsheet are retired after the physical inventory count at the end of the year. Some notation shows these are the items that were sold during the year. The rest of the inventory carries forward to make up the beginning inventory for the next year.

Companies using LIFO calculations show a retirement on their spreadsheets of recent acquisitions, while maintaining a value for their year-end inventory made up of the cost of the earliest purchases.

Companies that use the Specific Identification method of costing inventory note on their spreadsheet each individual item sold, adding up the cost of each remaining item to arrive at a total for valuing their inventory at year-end.

Creating a spreadsheet system for tracking and costing your inventory might require the time and expense of an outside programmer.

If you have a large inventory with thousands of different pieces, large quantities of each piece, and frequent turnover of the pieces, you will find a spreadsheet a time-consuming method of evaluating inventory costs. Also, spreadsheets have size limitations: a maximum of 16,384 rows (some have only 8,192 rows) and 256 columns. When you consider that you intend to track your company's inventory for many years, you might find these limitations to be a problem.

The Database Alternative

Database programs, such as Microsoft Access, Corel's Paradox, Oracle, and others, can accommodate millions (and even billions) of records, thus lending themselves much more easily to tracking large inventories.

A database can be created that retires inventory items as they are sold. Ending inventory quantities can be compared to the quantities determined in the physical inventory count, adjusted as necessary, and the value calculated instantaneously, based on the valuation method your company uses.

Many retail stores use point-of-sale database programs that keep track of each item of inventory, providing cost and availability information right at the cash register. Although QuickBooks can provide this point-of-sale information, a sophisticated database program can go farther by tracking raw materials and transferring the materials into finished goods as inventory is produced.

Creating a database program for tracking and costing your inventory might require the time and expense of an outside programmer.

Other Software Alternatives

Several programs on the market are designed specifically to track inventory. A little time searching through software stores or poring over computer catalogs might result in a program that fits the needs of your company.

I have found, through searching the Internet, several inventory programs, including some specifically designed for users of QuickBooks. An easy search for "Inventory AND Software" yielded a dozen or so links to companies providing software programs designed to combat the shortcomings of accounting programs such as QuickBooks.

Some programs are specifically designed to track manufacturing inventories, with easy transitions for raw materials becoming finished goods.

Many of the programs I found on the Internet offer demos and limited-time samples of the programs so that you can try out the programs and see if they will do the job you need.

Purchase Orders, Accounts Payable, and Paying Bills

Use purchase orders to keep track of items on order

Enter all received goods in QuickBooks so that your inventory records will always be up-to-date

Record bill payments in QuickBooks

Use QuickBooks to write checks and print them as well

Find specific transactions in the check register

Void checks, if necessary

Reconcile your bank account the easy way with QuickBooks

There's an old saying that goes, "It takes money to make money." It costs money to develop, build, or purchase the things you sell. In addition, the overhead cost of operating a business includes rent, utilities, office salaries, equipment, supplies, repairs, cleaning—and so on.

When you record your company's income, you know how much money is coming into the business. But you can't get a sense of how much money the business is actually making without recording the expenses as well. All the costs of operating a business must become a part of your QuickBooks record-keeping.

Using Purchase Orders

Purchase orders are an optional part of QuickBooks. The idea behind a purchase order is that you issue a document that lists the items you are ordering and send that document to your supplier. The purchase order acts as a written record of your order, providing more accuracy than a verbal order might offer.

If you have not yet advised QuickBooks that you plan to use the Purchase Orders feature, you should do so now.

To turn on the preference for purchase orders or to check to see whether this feature has been activated, follow these steps:

1. Choose **File**, **Preferences**. The Preferences window will appear.
2. Click the **Purchases & Vendors** button at the left side of the window. You may need to scroll to locate this button.
3. Click the **Company Preferences** tab at the top of the window.
4. Check the first box, **Inventory and purchase orders are active**.
5. Click **OK** to save your changes and close the window.

After the Purchase Order feature has been activated, you can create purchase orders in QuickBooks.

Creating a purchase order

1. Choose <u>A</u>ctivities, **Create P<u>u</u>rchase Orders**. The Create Purchase Orders window will appear (see Figure 15.1).

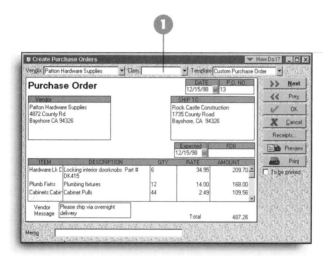

FIGURE **15.1**

Create a purchase order with this form.

This **Class** field only appears if class tracking has been turned on.

2. Select the vendor by clicking the arrow at the right of the **Ven<u>d</u>or** field. If the vendor from whom you are purchasing is not on the list, click the **<Add New>** button and enter information for a new vendor.

3. Choose a class if you use the QuickBooks class-tracking feature (described in Chapter 9, "Separating Your Company into Logical Divisions"). The class field will not be visible if this feature has not been activated.

4. If you plan to use something other than the standard purchase order template, click the arrow in the **Template** field to choose another template.

SEE ALSO

➤ *For more information about creating custom templates, see Chapter 20, "Customizing QuickBook Forms," page 373*

5. Verify the address information in the **Vendor Address** area. This information will fill in automatically when you select a vendor and is based on the information you entered when you set up this vendor. If you change the information in this

Using QuickFill

As you're entering information in QuickBooks, you may notice occasions when QuickBooks seems to know just what you're thinking because it fills in the rest of the name or item. This feature is known as QuickFill. If you type a **P** in the **Ven<u>d</u>or** area, for example, QuickBooks will search the vendor list for the first name beginning with a "P" and fill in the rest of the name, which may be "Partington Supply." If the vendor you are really trying to type is "Pranitis Heating and Cooling," continue typing. By the time you have typed **Pr**, QuickBooks will have filled in the rest of the name; you don't have to type anything more. Just click the next field or press Tab to proceed.

field, a message will appear onscreen when you attempt to save this purchase order, asking if you want to see the changed information next time (see Figure 15.2). If you answer **Yes**, the permanent address information for this vendor will be updated to reflect your changes.

6. The **Date** field contains today's date, which QuickBooks fills in automatically. Change the date of the purchase order, if necessary.

FIGURE 15.2

Click **Yes** to update the permanent information for this vendor. Click **No** to leave the vendor file intact. Click **Cancel** to return to the purchase order form.

7. If a **Ship To** field appears on your purchase order, verify that the information in this area is correct. This is the address to which you want the ordered items shipped. QuickBooks automatically fills in your company name and address, but your company may have additional locations, or you may want the items shipped directly to a customer. You can change any information in this area. (Note: Remember that you can add fields, such as the Ship To field, to your purchase order. Chapter 20 discusses this process.)

8. If the **Expected** area appears on your purchase order, enter the date you expect the order to arrive. QuickBooks automatically fills in today's date, but you can change this information. If you expect the ordered items to arrive on different dates, decide whether you want to enter the first date of arrival or the last date of arrival. QuickBooks uses this date on inventory stock status reports to show the date on which ordered items are expected to arrive.

9. If an **FOB** field appears in your purchase order, enter the FOB status for this order, if you know it. Sometimes the vendor determines this status, so you may not have this information when you place the order.

SEE ALSO

➤ *For more information on FOB status, see the sidebar, "FOB," on page 205, in Chapter 11, "Invoicing, Monthly Statements, and Accounts Receivable"*

10. Click in the **Item** area. An arrow will appear. Click the arrow to display a drop-down list of all items you have entered in your QuickBooks file. Choose an item from this list by clicking it. If the item you wish to order is not on this list, click **<Add New>** at the top of the list and enter information for a new item.

SEE ALSO

➤ *For more information about setting up new items, see page 147*

11. The item description should fill in automatically. You can alter this description, if necessary.

12. In the **Quantity** area, enter the number of pieces of this item you wish to order.

13. Verify that the rate is correct. QuickBooks will fill in the rate automatically if this information was entered when you set up the item. If no amount appears in the **Rate** column, enter the appropriate amount at this time. If you do not know the cost of the item(s) you are ordering, you can leave this column blank.

14. The amount will calculate automatically based on the rate you fill in. You can override the amount, if necessary.

15. Repeat steps 10–14 until all the items you wish to order from this vendor are listed.

16. Enter an optional message in the **Vendor Message** area. You may want to provide special shipping instructions, (for example, "Our warehouse will be closed the week of July 17. No deliveries will be accepted that week." or "Please ship via overnight delivery."), or you may want to enter other information here. Your message will appear at the bottom of the printed purchase order.

17. Enter an optional memo in the **Memo** area at the bottom of the purchase order form. This memo is for internal use only and will not print on the purchase order form.

18. Check the **To be printed** box (see Figure 15.3) unless you plan to print this purchase order immediately. Checking this box places the purchase order in a holding area, and QuickBooks will remind you that the form is waiting to be printed. To print a purchase order after you have closed the Create Purchase Order form, choose **File**, **Print Forms**, **Print Purchase Orders**. Click each purchase order on the list to select that document for printing. Then click the **Print** button to print the selected forms.

FIGURE 15.3

Enter all information about the item(s) you wish to purchase on this form.

① Click here to request that the form be printed later.

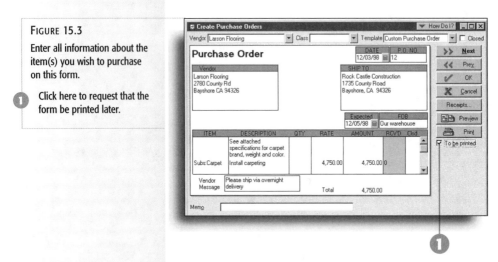

19. After you have entered all pertinent information on this purchase order, choose from the buttons at the side of the purchase order form:

- **Next.** Click **Next** to save your changes on this purchase order and display the next available purchase order form.

- **Prev.** Click **Prev** to save your changes on this purchase order and display the order that was created just before this one.

- **OK.** Click **OK** to save your changes on this purchase order and close the Create Purchase Order window.

- **Cancel.** Click **Cancel** to close the Create Purchase Order window without saving this purchase order.

- **Receipts.** After you have received items from this purchase order and have noted those receipts in QuickBooks (discussed later in this chapter), you can check to see which items have been received by viewing this purchase order and clicking the **Receipts** button.

- **Preview.** Click **Preview** to see what the purchase order will look like before you print it.

- **Print.** Click **Print** to print the purchase order immediately. If you do not plan to print the purchase order at this time, be sure to check the **To be printed** box.

After you have created purchase orders in QuickBooks, you can take advantage of their existence and quickly see what items have been ordered.

What's On Order?

When you issue a purchase order for inventory items, QuickBooks keeps track of the quantity of items on order. At any time, you can get an update of the number of items in stock and the number on order by following these three steps:

1. Choose **Lists**, **Items**. The Items list window will appear.

2. Click an item for which you want to check the quantities on hand and on order.

3. Click the **Reports** button at the bottom of the window and choose **QuickReport** at the top of the drop-down menu. A quick report for the particular item will appear (see Figure 15.4), listing all activity relating to the in-stock quantities and outstanding orders for the item.

FIGURE 15.4

QuickReports for inventory items show how many items are in stock and how many are on order.

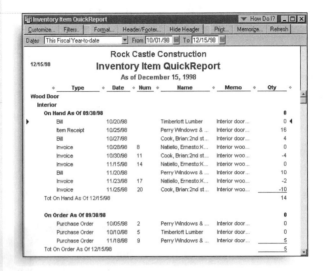

State resale numbers

The state in which your company does business will provide you with a resale number when you register to collect sales tax from your customers. See Appendix D, "State Revenue Agencies," for a complete list of state revenue agencies that can provide you with more information about registering to do business in a state.

Tax-Exempt Purchases

Some organizations are entitled to make purchases that are exempt from sales tax. If your company purchases items that will ultimately be sold to your customers, for example, you are considered a reseller, and your purchases are not subject to sales tax. The reason is that you presumably collect sales tax from your customers when you sell the items, and sales tax needs to be collected only once on the sale of an item.

Your organization may be tax exempt under IRS rules that protect schools, churches, and other charitable organizations from paying tax.

If you are exempt from sales tax, you will need a tax-exempt number from your state revenue department. This number should be provided to each of your vendors whenever you make a purchase.

The **Vendor Message** area near the bottom of the purchase order form is an excellent place to display your tax-exempt number.

Receiving Goods

When you receive inventory items, your QuickBooks records
need to be updated so that your listings of available inventory
items will be up-to-date. When you make a sale, QuickBooks
checks against the quantity of items you have in stock and determines if you have enough items to sell.

You can record the receipt of goods in two ways: goods received
before you are billed, and goods received with a bill. The
processes for entering both types of goods are almost identical.

When you enter goods before receiving a bill, QuickBooks
increases the value in your inventory account and increases your
accounts payable account. The quantity of items on hand in your
inventory records is increased so that your inventory records will
be accurate.

Entering goods received without an accompanying bill

1. Choose **Activities**, **Inventory**, **Receive Items**. The Create
   Item Receipts window will appear (see Figure 15.5).

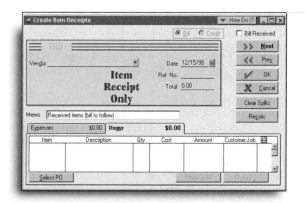

FIGURE 15.5
Enter items received in this
window so QuickBooks can
update your inventory records.

2. In the **Vendor** area, enter the name of the vendor from
   whom the items were received. If you have entered purchase
   orders for this vendor, a message such as the one displayed
   in Figure 15.6 will appear.

FIGURE 15.6

Click **Yes** when this message appears to display a list of open purchase orders. Click **No** if you are receiving items for which a purchase order was not prepared.

3. If you received the message described in step 2 and chose **Yes**, the Open Purchase Orders window will appear (see Figure 15.7). In the Open Purchase Orders window, check off each purchase order against which you are receiving items. Then click **OK**. These items will appear on the Item Receipt form where you can adjust the quantity to reflect the amount actually received.

FIGURE 15.7

Click to the left of any purchase order against which you received items. The items from this purchase order will appear on your Item Receipt form.

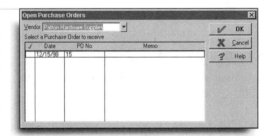

4. If you chose not to record items received against a purchase order and clicked **No** in step 3, but later realize you are receiving against a purchase order—or if you just want to view a list of all outstanding purchase orders for this vendor—click the **Select PO** button at the bottom of the Create Items Receipts screen. The Open Purchase Orders window will appear.

5. To add items to your Item Receipt form, click in the **Item** area. An arrow will appear. Click the arrow to display a drop-down list of all items you have entered in your QuickBooks file. Choose an item from this list by clicking it. If the item you have received is not on this list, click **<Add New>** at the top of the list and enter information for a new item.

6. Enter the quantity of any items received in the **Qty** column. Adjust the cost to reflect the cost per item. QuickBooks will automatically calculate the total amount.

7. If, as you're entering information on this form, you realize you have received a bill for this shipment, check the **Bill Received** box at the top of the form. Two extra fields will appear on the form if you check this box—the date on which the bill is due and the terms of payment.

8. Click **Next** to save this receipt form and advance to the next form; click **Prev** to save this receipt form and view a prior form; or click **OK** to save and close this window.

Entering goods received at the same time as the bill is received

1. Choose **Activities**, **Inventory**, **Receive Items** and **Enter Bill**. The Enter Bills window will appear.

2. Enter the vendor in the **Vendor** field. If an open purchase order exists for this vendor, the message shown in Figure 15.6 will appear. Check **Yes** or **No** to indicate whether you want to receive items against the open purchase order(s).

3. Verify and change, if necessary, the Amount Due, the date on which the bill is due, and the Terms of payment. If any items appear on the **Items** tab in the lower portion of the screen, verify the description, quantity, and cost of all items received in this shipment. To remove an item from the bill, click the item to be removed, and choose **Edit**, **Delete Line**. Alternatively, you may want to leave an unreceived item on the bill but change the quantity to zero.

4. To charge this amount to a **Customer:Job**, click in the **Customer:Job** column and choose a job from the drop-down list. When you charge items to a job, a little invoice icon appears in the column to the right of the job name. This icon indicates that the amount will be automatically billed to the customer. To override that decision and tell QuickBooks not to automatically invoice the customer, click the invoice icon and an "x" will appear over the icon.

5. Click **Next** to save this bill and advance to the next bill; click **Prev** to save this bill and view a prior bill; or click **OK** to save and close this bill window.

Paying Bills

Receiving merchandise and bills is only half the fun! Now that you have a pile of bills, you need to figure out how to pay for all this fun.

Paying bills is more than simply writing checks when the mood strikes. Well-run businesses plan for their expenses by budgeting and predicting cash flow.

Many businesses pay bills on certain days of the month, such as the 15th and the last day of the month. Paying bills on a regular, predictable timetable can help you plan for times you need to have cash on hand and can allow your vendors to depend on the knowledge that their bills will be paid on a particular day.

When you pay a bill in QuickBooks, your cash account is reduced by the amount of the payment, and your accounts payable account is reduced to reflect the bill that is no longer due.

Paying bills in QuickBooks

1. Choose **Activities**, **Pay Bills**. The Pay Bills window will appear (see Figure 15.8), listing all bills currently due. This list is not comprehensive because bills that have been received but have not reached their due date are not included in the list.

2. In the **Pay By** area, indicate your preferred method of payment: **Online**, **Check**, or **Credit card**. Also indicate which bank account you plan to draw from, or which credit card you plan to use. If you plan to print this check in QuickBooks, check the **To be printed** box.

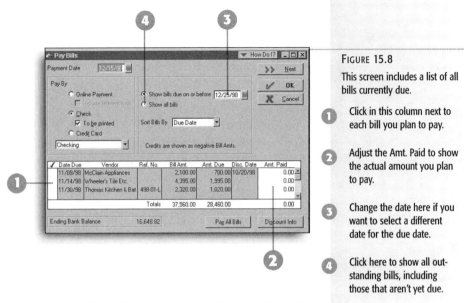

FIGURE 15.8

This screen includes a list of all
bills currently due.

1 Click in this column next to
each bill you plan to pay.

2 Adjust the Amt. Paid to show
the actual amount you plan
to pay.

3 Change the date here if you
want to select a different
date for the due date.

4 Click here to show all outstanding bills, including
those that aren't yet due.

3. Select the due date for which you want to display bills. All
bills due up to the selected date will appear in the bills list at
the bottom of the screen. Alternatively, you can choose to
display all bills (Show all bills), whether or not they are currently due. Note: If you choose a due date other than the
one QuickBooks has chosen for you, the screen does not
automatically refresh to show the bills that fit the new date
you have chosen. To be sure you see all the correct bills,
change the due date, choose **Show all bills**, then click the
top option to show bills on or before the selected date.

4. Check off each bill you intend to pay, and change the
amount in the **Amt. Paid** column if you don't intend to pay
the full amount. If you choose to pay less than the full
amount, the bill will remain in this list. If an error exists in
the amount shown as due for this bill, you should reopen the
bill and correct the amount.

5. If you plan to take a discount on a bill, click the bill, then click the **Discount Info** button at the bottom of the window. The Discount Information window will appear (see Figure 15.9), displaying the available discount for this bill. In this window you can choose to accept or override the calculated discount amount. Choose a discount account for recording the discount. You may have to set up an account if this is the first time you are recording a discount. Click **OK** to save the information in this window.

FIGURE 15.9

The discount terms that appear here were derived from the bill.

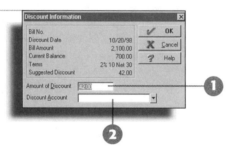

 QuickBooks has calculated the discount amount. You can revise this amount, if necessary.

 Enter the name of account where the discount should be recorded.

6. Click **Next** to save your payment choices and refresh the Pay Bills window, removing all bills you have indicated you want to pay in full. Or click **OK** to save your payment choices and close the window. **Cancel** closes the window without recording any of your payments.

Writing Checks in QuickBooks

All your company checks won't be written in response to bills. Some checks you write regularly without ever receiving a bill—rent, for example. Or perhaps you have to run out to make a quick purchase and you don't plan to bother with a purchase order or entering a bill—you just want to write the check for the purchase and be done with it.

Entering checks in QuickBooks without the formality of entering a bill

1. Choose **Activities**, **Write Checks**. The Write Checks window will appear (see Figure 15.10).

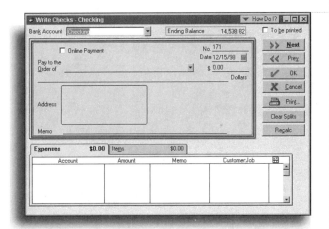

FIGURE 15.10

Write checks on this form, which looks the same as a real check.

2. In the **Bank Account** field, choose the account from which the money for this check will be drawn.

3. Verify the check number and the date of the check. Change this information, if necessary.

4. Enter the name of the payee in the **Pay to the Order of** field. A drop-down list of all your vendors is available in this field, or you can choose to enter a name not on the vendor list. If you enter a new name, QuickBooks will display the message shown in Figure 15.11. The Select Name Type window will then appear (see Figure 15.12), asking you to indicate if this is a vendor, a customer, an employee, or something else.

Quick Add versus Set Up

When entering a new payee, you are prompted to either **Quick Add** or **Set Up** this payee in the QuickBooks file. You must choose, or QuickBooks won't let you use this payee name. Choose **Quick Add** if this payee is someone to whom you will not write additional checks, or if this is someone for whom you don't need to save any additional information. Choose **Set Up** if additional information about this payee, such as address, phone number, personal contact, and so on, would be useful to you.

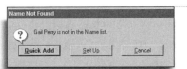

FIGURE 15.11

Click **Quick Add** to add this name to your vendor list; click **Set up** to enter additional information about this vendor, such as address and phone number.

FIGURE 15.12

Choose the type that applies to this payee.

5. Enter an amount for this check.

6. Verify that information in the **Address** area is correct and that you want this information to print on the check. You have the option of deleting information in the **Address** area and leaving this area blank. If you plan to use the QuickBooks online payment feature, the payee's name and address must be filled in.

SEE ALSO

➤ *For more information about online bill paying, see page 451, Chapter 23 "Going Online with QuickBooks."*

7. In the lower part of the Write Checks dialog box, choose whether you are paying for **Expenses** (such as rent and repairs) or **Items** (such as inventory, shipping, or subcontract work) by clicking the appropriate tab.

8. Enter the items or expenses for which you are paying with this check by filling in the appropriate information at the bottom of the check form.

9. Click the **Print** button if you plan to print this check immediately. If you want to print this check later, check the **To be printed** box at the top of the form. If you will write this check by hand, don't click either print option.

10. Click **Next** to save your information and proceed to the next check; click **Prev** to save your information and view the prior check; click **OK** to save your information and close this window; click **Cancel** to close the window without saving your check.

Printing Checks

When you write checks in QuickBooks, you indicate whether you want to print the check immediately (by clicking the **Print** button), print it at some future date (by checking the **To be printed** box), or not print at all (by not choosing either print option).

If you have indicated that you want checks to be printed, QuickBooks will provide you with a list in your Reminder window of the outstanding checks that are waiting to be printed. Don't overlook this task!

Creditors won't look too favorably on someone who says he entered the information for the check in QuickBooks weeks ago but forgot to print the check.

Printing checks that have already been entered in QuickBooks

1. Choose **File**, **Print Forms**, **Print Checks**. The Select Checks to Print window will appear (see Figure 15.13).

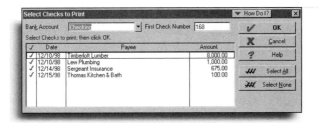

FIGURE 15.13
Click **OK** to print the selected checks.

2. Verify that the account listed in the **Bank Account** area is the one from which you want to print checks.

3. If you use preprinted check forms that are already numbered, verify that the first check number shown in this window corresponds with the check number on the first available preprinted check form.

4. All checks that are awaiting printing have been check marked. If you don't want to print some checks at this time, click the checks and the check mark will disappear. Only check-marked checks will be printed.

5. Click **OK** when you are ready to print the checks. The Print Checks window will appear. (Alternatively, click **Cancel** if you've changed your mind and don't want to print checks at this time).

6. On the **Settings** tab (see Figure 15.14), choose the printer, the type of sheets you use, and the style of checks you use. Indicate how many checks are on the first page of checks. Also indicate whether you want QuickBooks to print your company name or a logo on your checks. If you choose to print a logo on your checks, you will be asked to direct QuickBooks to a bitmap (.BMP) file that contains the logo.

FIGURE 15.14

Use this window to let QuickBooks know what kind of checks you use and where to print them.

1 Notice that QuickBooks tells you how many checks will print and the sum of those checks.

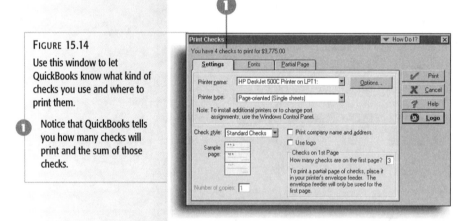

7. If you want to choose the typeface that will print on the checks, click the **Fonts** tab, then click the **Font** and **Address** font buttons to change the fonts on the main part of the check and the company name and address section, respectively.

8. You can print less than a full page of checks without confusing QuickBooks by clicking on the **Partial Page** tab and choosing the type of check form you plan to use.

9. Click **Print** when you are ready to print your checks. Or, click **Cancel** to close the window without printing.

The QuickBooks Check Register

In the good old days of writing checks by hand, we always kept a check register where we recorded each check, the number, the date, the payee, the amount, and maybe a little memo about what the check was for. We also recorded every deposit we made, the date, the amount, and the source of the deposit.

QuickBooks still keeps that check register for you, and you can view it at any time.

Opening the QuickBooks register for your checking account (or any bank account)

1. Choose **Lists**, **Chart of Accounts**. The Chart of Accounts list window will appear.

2. Click the name of the account for which you want to view the register.

3. Click the **Activities** button at the bottom of this window, and choose **Use Register** from the drop-down menu. The QuickBooks register for the chosen account will appear (see Figure 15.15).

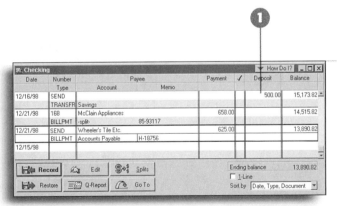

FIGURE 15.15

Just like a hand-written check register, the QuickBooks register records all transactions in and out of the account.

1 Deposits to the account appear in this column.

4. After you have finished examining transactions, click the **x** button in the upper-right corner of the window to close it.

If you are looking for a particular transaction, you can search for items in your check register. Click the **Go To** button at the bottom of the screen. The Go To window will appear (see Figure 15.16).

FIGURE 15.16

Enter the search criteria for finding an elusive transaction in your register, then click **Prev** to search the register backward, or **Next** to search forward.

Choose a field in which to search. You may want to search for transactions of a particular amount, in which case you would choose the **Amount** field. To search for checks payable to a particular party, search the **Payee/Name** field. In the **Search For** area, enter the amount or name for which you are searching. Then click **Prev** to search backward or **Next** to search forward for your missing transaction.

Although you can make entries directly in the register, such as recording checks you wrote by hand or deposits you made to your account, you will ensure a more complete accounting of transactions if you use the standard QuickBooks forms, such as the bill paying form, the invoice form, the cash receipt form, and so on.

Voiding Checks

At times, you may write a check and discover later that you must void the check. Perhaps you paid for an order, only to find the order was defective and the supplier told you he would tear up your check.

The process for voiding a check involves finding the check in QuickBooks, then requesting that QuickBooks void the check. It is possible to delete a check in QuickBooks, but deleting is irreversible and leaves a more difficult trail to follow. Because voiding a check leaves a record of the existence of the check, it is the preferable method.

Voiding a check in QuickBooks

1. Find the check that you want to void. Probably the easiest way to do this is to open the register (see "The QuickBooks Check Register," above), scroll through or search the transactions until you find the check you wish to void, and double-click the check. The check will appear onscreen.

2. Choose **Edit**, **Void Bill Pmt-Check**. The amount of the check will change to zero, and the **Amt. Paid** area at the bottom of the check will also change to zero. All other information on the check will remain intact.

3. Click **OK** to save your changes and close the check window. A message will appear asking you to confirm your actions. Click **Yes**. You will be returned to the register where you will see that this check appears with a zero amount.

4. Click the **x** at the top of the register window to close the register.

The Monthly Ritual of Bank Account Reconciliation

Reconciling your bank account has never been so much fun. Fun? QuickBooks makes it seem like fun because it is quick and easy. After you get your bank statement and are ready to begin the reconciliation process, follow these steps:

1. Choose **Activities**, **Reconcile**. The Reconcile window will appear (see Figure 15.17).

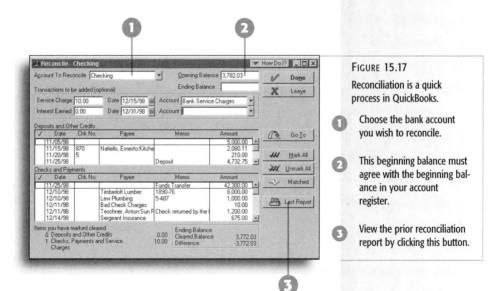

FIGURE 15.17

Reconciliation is a quick process in QuickBooks.

1. Choose the bank account you wish to reconcile.

2. This beginning balance must agree with the beginning balance in your account register.

3. View the prior reconciliation report by clicking this button.

2. In the **Account to Reconcile** area, choose the account for which you received a bank statement.

3. Verify that the opening balance agrees with your bank statement. If you find a discrepancy, you must make a change in your register so that the amounts agree. The only time you should see a discrepancy is the first time you reconcile this account. Transactions that were outstanding with the bank may not have been entered in your register. Make sure all transactions have been entered and the opening balances agree.

4. Enter the **Ending Balance** from your bank statement.

5. In the **Service Charge** area, enter any service charge applied by the bank and the date it was applied. This information will appear on your bank statement.

6. In the **Interest** area, enter any interest income that your bank account earned and the date it was received. This information will appear on your bank statement.

7. The amounts you see in the **Deposits and Other Credits** area represent the amounts from your register. Check off all items that appear on your bank statement. Click an item to check it off.

8. The amounts you see in the **Checks and Payments** area represent the amounts from your register. Check off all items that appear on your bank statement. Click an item to check it off.

9. At the bottom of the screen you will see a running balance of all deposits and checks you have checked off. You will also see an Ending Balance (the amount from the bank statement), a Cleared Balance (the amount of items you checked off) and a Difference amount. When all items from the bank statement have been checked off, the Difference amount should be zero. If it is not zero, you should go back through every transaction on the bank statement, comparing it carefully to the items you checked off. Correct any discrepancies.

Bank and register don't agree

When reconciling, you may find discrepancies between your bank statement and the amounts you recorded in QuickBooks. When this happens, first verify who is right. Banks can make mistakes, and you shouldn't take their word for it that they are correct. However, if you find that the bank is right and your transaction was entered incorrectly, open the register (leave the reconciliation window open as well), find the transaction in question, double-click it to get to the original entry form, and make a correction. The correction will flow through to your register and, ultimately, to your reconciliation. If you find you are missing an entry, open the appropriate window and enter the transaction in QuickBooks, making sure the transaction is dated properly. The transaction should then appear in your reconciliation when you return to it.

10. After the reconciliation is finished (and the Difference amount at the bottom of the window is zero), click the **Do<u>n</u>e** button to save your work and close the reconciliation window. If you need to close the reconciliation window before you have finished, click the **Lea<u>v</u>e** button. Your work will be saved, and when you return you can start right where you left off.

11. When you have finished, you will be given an option to print a reconciliation report (see Figure 15.18). The Full reconciliation report gives you a detailed list of all transactions that cleared your account during this time period as well as all outstanding transactions (amounts that have not yet cleared the bank). The Summary reconciliation report gives you the totals of all amounts deposited to and deducted from your account during the time period. Printing either report is optional.

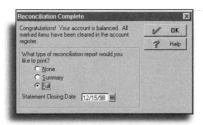

FIGURE 15.18

Choose from a **Full** report which shows all transactions, a **Summary** report which gives only totals, or no report at all.

You will find that when you get in the habit of reconciling your bank account with the QuickBooks reconciliation feature, you actually look forward to this process because it is such an easy task.

Managing Fixed Assets

Fixed assets are assets of a durable nature acquired for use in the business rather than for resale and expected to last for a number of years. Rather than taking a deduction for the cost of a fixed asset in the year it is acquired, as you might for the cost of office supplies or small tools, the investment for these assets is assigned to future periods and deducted through periodic charges to a depreciation expense account.

Examples of fixed assets include furniture, equipment, buildings, large tools, vehicles, computers, machinery, and animals.

A company's balance sheet lists the cost of the asset in total, with the accumulation of depreciation charges summarized beneath the cost. A net asset value, commonly referred to as *book value*, is shown as the difference between the original cost and the depreciation charges to date. Even after a fixed asset has been fully depreciated, the asset and its accumulated depreciation remain on the company balance sheet as long as the asset is still in use, with a net value of zero.

Why Do We Have to Use Depreciation?

The purpose of using depreciation accounts to report the expense of the cost of assets is to match the cost of the asset with the income it produces.

If an asset is expected to function and produce income for several years before it becomes outdated or no longer works properly, spreading the cost of the asset over a similar period of time seems reasonable. Deducting the cost of the asset all in one year would distort the process of matching income with expenses.

Accounting for Fixed Assets

When you use QuickBooks to account for fixed assets, you group similar assets in a single account. For example, you might have one account for office furniture, another for computer equipment, and so on. As you purchase new assets, the cost of each new asset gets added to the appropriate account. If you purchase five office desks, each costing $400, your office furniture account increases in value by $2,000 (5 times $400).

Depreciation expense for all assets is added to a single depreciation expense account. At the time the depreciation expense account is increased, an *accumulated depreciation* account is increased by the same amount. The accumulated depreciation account is a type of asset account, but because its purpose is to offset the value of the assets by the amount of the accumulating depreciation, it is referred to as a *contra asset* account.

On the balance sheet, the accumulated depreciation account is listed with the assets, reducing the value of the related fixed asset account. The following is an example of how fixed assets might appear on your balance sheet:

Fixed assets

Office furniture	$ 4,000
Accumulated depreciation	3,000
Total office furniture	1,000
Computer equipment	12,000
Accumulated depreciation	12,000
Total computer equipment	0
Total fixed assets	1,000

Calculating Depreciation

The accounting profession, in conjunction with the IRS, has established many complicated rules for calculating depreciation expense—rules certain to confuse even the most savvy businessperson. Following are some of the basics.

Even though the process of calculating depreciation is designed to spread the cost of a fixed asset over the useful life of the asset, you don't need to guess about the useful life of your assets. The IRS has already decided what the useful life is for most assets, and you are expected to use these standard lives when determining your depreciation expense. The following is a list of several common asset types and the standard lives assigned to those types, courtesy of the IRS:

Depreciable asset	Depreciable life
Automobiles	5 years
General-purpose trucks	5 years
Computer equipment	5 years
Office equipment	5 years
Office furniture	7 years
Residential rental property	27.5 years
Office buildings/factories	39 years

Depreciation rules can change

The standard lives are the lives currently recognized by the IRS. The rules for determining standard lives and calculating depreciation are always subject to change, and you should consult with an accountant to determine the rules in place when you purchase assets.

Depreciation was originally established as a means of spreading the cost of an asset evenly over the expected useful life of the asset. Over the years, Congress has enacted laws that enable you to accelerate the rate at which assets are depreciated—taking larger deductions in the earlier years of asset ownership.

Businesses often use accelerated methods of depreciation for calculating the depreciation expense they will take on their business income tax returns, while using a more even, conservative depreciation expense for the amount they show on the company's financial statements. Deciding which method of depreciation to use and when to use it is a decision you should make with the help of an accountant.

Because of the complications in this area of accounting and tax law, I've limited the discussion in this chapter to the two most common methods of calculating depreciation: straight-line and Modified Accelerated Cost Recovery System (MACRS).

Straight-Line Depreciation

A straight-line method of calculating depreciation expense results in spreading the cost of an asset evenly over the anticipated useful life of the asset.

The cost of the asset is divided by the number of years of estimated useful life (following the IRS guidelines). For the first and last year of depreciation expense, only half a year of expense is taken. For an asset that cost $5,000 with a useful life of five years, the depreciation expense calculation using the straight-line method actually results in six years of depreciation deductions, calculated as follows:

Year 1	$500
Year 2	$1,000
Year 3	$1,000
Year 4	$1,000
Year 5	$1,000
Year 6	$500

MACRS Depreciation

Depreciation expense calculated by using the MACRS method of accelerated depreciation results in greater deductions in the earlier years of asset use. Some negative side effects of using MACRS include a greater taxable gain if the asset is sold before its useful life is over and some potential additional adjustments for tax purposes.

The company choosing to use MACRS depreciation calculations is well advised to obtain a copy of IRS Publication 946, "How to Depreciate Property." This publication can be obtained by calling the IRS at 1-800-TAX-FORM, or it can be downloaded from the IRS Web site on the Internet at www.irs.ustreas.gov. You might also find it useful to seek advice about depreciation from an accountant.

If you choose to use the MACRS method for calculating depreciation, you can use tables published by the IRS to perform the calculations. Some of these tables are reproduced here; others are available in the IRS publication mentioned earlier.

MACRS Depreciation Tables

The MACRS depreciation tables reproduced in this book are the tables most commonly used for 3-, 5-, and 7-year assets (see Tables 16.1, 16.2, and 16.3, respectively). However, additional tables are available for use in situations in which the majority of assets are purchased in a particular quarter of the year. The best approach is to consult an accountant when determining which method of depreciation fits your situation.

TABLE 16.1   MACRS depreciation deduction for 3-year property

Year	Percentage (this percentage multiplied times the cost of the property provides the depreciation deduction for the year)
1	33.33%
2	44.45%
3	14.81%
4	7.41%

TABLE 16.2   MACRS depreciation deduction for 5-year property

Year	Percentage (this percentage multiplied times the cost of the property provides the depreciation deduction for the year)
1	20.00%
2	32.00%
3	19.20%
4	11.52%
5	11.52%
6	5.76%

TABLE 16.3   MACRS depreciation deduction for 7-year property

Year	Percentage (this percentage multiplied times the cost of the property provides the depreciation deduction for the year)
1	14.29%
2	24.49%
3	17.49%
4	12.49%
5	8.93%
6	8.92%

Year	Percentage (this percentage multiplied times the cost of the property provides the depreciation deduction for the year)
7	8.93%
8	4.46%

Recording Depreciation

After you figure out how much depreciation expense you will deduct for each of your assets, you must record this depreciation.

You may choose to record an entire year's worth of depreciation at the end of the year, or you may make monthly or quarterly adjustments for depreciation so the financial statements you produce during the year reflects an accurate amount for depreciation.

In QuickBooks, you make a *general journal entry* to reflect the depreciation expense and the adjustment to your accumulated depreciation account. General journal entries are adjustments made to the balances in your accounts without the use of forms such as invoices, bills, and checks. A general journal entry must always have two sides—a debit and a credit.

SEE ALSO

➤ *For more information on debits and credits, see page 116*

If an amount was misclassified, for example, a general journal entry can be made to correct the classification of the amount. If $100 was recorded as a repair expense when it should have been an expense for office supplies, a general journal entry can be made to reduce the repairs expense account by $100 and increase the office supplies account for $100 without your having to open any forms.

A general journal entry is necessary to record depreciation, because depreciation isn't generated by any of the traditional forms. When you record depreciation expense, an offsetting amount is recorded as accumulated depreciation.

For example, if your depreciation expense for the period is $500, of which $300 is for computer equipment and $200 is for office furniture, a general journal entry would look like the one in Figure 16.1.

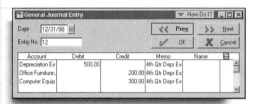

Creating a general journal entry

1. From the **Activities** menu, choose **Make Journal Entry**. The General Journal Entry window appears.

2. Verify that the date of the entry is correct. The entry date doesn't always coincide with today's date. For example, you might have some end-of-the-year journal entries to make, which should be dated 12/31, but not actually have the information to make these entries until sometime in January (see the following section, "Following the Audit Trail").

3. Enter a number for this journal entry in the **Entry No.** area. Typically, general journal entries are numbered consecutively.

4. Click in the **Account** column; an arrow appears. Click this arrow to display the drop-down list and click the name of the account to be debited (**Depreciation Expense** is being debited in Figure 16.1).

5. Click in the **Debit** column and enter the amount of the debit.

6. If you like, enter a memo in the optional **Memo** column across from the debit amount. In the example shown in Figure 16.1, the memo description is **1998 4ᵗʰ Qtr Depr**.

7. Use the **Name** column if this journal entry is to be charged to a specific customer or job. Depreciation expense would probably not be charged to a job unless a piece of equipment

was purchased for a specific job and will only be used for that job.

8. Repeat steps 4–7 if more than one account is to be debited.

9. Click in the **Account** column again and choose the name of the account to be credited.

10. Click in the **Credit** column and enter the amount of the credit.

11. If you like, enter a memo in the optional **Memo** column across from the credit amount.

12. Use the **Name** column to choose a customer or job if this amount is to be reflected on the records for a specific customer.

13. Repeat steps 9–12 if more than one account is to be credited. In the example shown in Figure 16.1, two different accumulated depreciation accounts are being credited.

Following the Audit Trail

QuickBooks comes with a feature called the Audit Trail, which is a summary of all the transactions and changes to transactions made in your QuickBooks file. If you have a tendency to change transactions (go back to previous forms and make changes), you might find the Audit Trail useful in identifying when these changes occurred. If more than one person has access to your company's QuickBooks file, the Audit Trail provides a certain amount of security in that no changes can be made to any forms or amounts in your file without a record of the changes appearing in the Audit Trail.

If you use an outside accountant to examine your records and help with year-end adjustments, your accountant will probably request that you use the Audit Trail.

To turn on the Audit Trail, open the **File** menu and choose **Preferences**. When the Preferences window appears, click the **Accounting** icon at the left side of the window. On the **Company Preferences** tab, check the box next to **Use audit trail**.

Only transactions that occur while the audit trail is turned on are stored in this list. To view the listed transactions, open the **Reports** menu and choose **Other Reports**. Then select **Audit Trail** from the submenu.

Selling Depreciable Assets

When you sell an asset you have been depreciating, the sale of the asset must be recorded in such a way as to relieve both the asset account and the accumulated depreciation account of the value of the sold item.

Consider this example. You purchased a piece of equipment for $3,500, and over the years you took deductions for $1,250 in depreciation expense relating to this piece of equipment. The book value of the asset is therefore $2,250 ($3,500–$1,250), and you sell the asset for $1,700. The following accounts would be affected by the sale:

Cash	$1,700 (debit)
Fixed asset: Equipment	$3,500 (credit)
Acc. depreciation: Equipment	$1,250 (debit)
Sale of assets	$550 (debit)

The cash account is increased (debited) as cash is received in the company. The fixed asset account is decreased (credited) to remove the asset from the company balance sheet. The accumulated depreciation account is decreased (debited) to remove accumulated depreciation relating to this asset from the company balance sheet. The sale of assets account is decreased (debited) to reflect a loss (amount by which the book value exceeds the sale price) on the sale of the asset.

If the previous asset had been sold for $3,000 instead of $1,700, the cash account would show an increase of $3,000 instead of $1,700, and the sale of assets account would show a increase (credit) of $750 to reflect the gain (amount by which the sales price exceeds book value) on the sale.

Alternatives to QuickBooks for Fixed Asset Tracking

You will notice that there is no provision within QuickBooks for calculating depreciation on assets. The information provided in this chapter relating to calculating depreciation might be enough to get you started, or you might feel the need to consult with an accountant who can advise you in this area.

If you know the calculations you need to make, you can use a spreadsheet program to create a spreadsheet that calculates and keeps track of depreciation for you. An accountant or a computer professional can help you set this up.

An alternative to using outside resources to help you with your depreciation calculations—especially if you have many assets for which you need some method for tracking depreciation—is to seek out another software program to help with depreciation.

An Internet search for depreciation yields several programs designed to perform depreciation calculations. Many of these programs offer demonstration disks or trial periods so you can test the software and see if it will be helpful to you. Intuit's TurboTax program also provides depreciation calculations.

Uncle Sam is watching

In the previous example, an asset and its related accumulated depreciation are both reduced to zero to remove them from the company's balance sheet, cash is increased to reflect the cash received, and a gain or loss is recorded for the difference.

You should be aware that sales of assets are often recorded differently on a company's tax return than they are on a company's balance sheet. This is especially common when a company uses an accelerated method of depreciation. When selling assets, you should consult a tax professional to determine the proper treatment of the sale for tax purposes.

Entering Cash Transactions

Record cash sales in QuickBooks

Create a daily cash summary to record many sales at once

Set up an account to record cash overages and shortages

Record credit card payments just as you would any cash payment

Many businesses deal in cash—retail stores, filling stations, lawn care services, and more. When these businesses receive cash, they must have a method of recording the cash and reporting the amount received.

Forms of Cash

Cash is more than just a handful of bills and coins. You can receive cash in any of several guises:

- Currency, including bills and coins
- Checks
- Traveler's checks
- Credit card transactions

When you receive cash, your immediate reaction may be to run to the bank to make a deposit. Before you make that trip, however, you should perform some QuickBooks tasks that will help you keep track of all this cash, where it came from, what it was from, and what you plan to do with it.

Quick Cash Entry

One way to enter cash in your QuickBooks company file is to use the Cash Sales form. This form is similar in appearance to the invoice form, but some major differences exist between an invoiced sale and a cash sale:

- When you enter a sale on an invoice, it is for the purpose of billing the customer, so it is important that you know the name and other pertinent information about the customer. In fact, QuickBooks will not accept an invoice that does not have a customer name filled in. In the case of a cash sale, you may record the sale without filling in the customer area of the form. Cash sales often occur without the vendor (you) knowing who the customer is. The Enter Cash Sales form has a field for Customer:Job entry, but the form can be prepared with this field left blank.

- The accounting for cash sales is different from the accounting for invoices. When you record an invoice, QuickBooks increases an income account by the amount of the sale and increases accounts receivable for the same amount. With a cash sale, income is increased, but accounts receivable is not affected. Instead, cash received but not yet deposited goes into an asset account called Undeposited Funds (or you may have set up a cash-holding account with a different name).

For a comprehensive example of entering a cash sale in QuickBooks using the Enter Cash Sales form, see "Receiving Cash" in Chapter 12, "Recording Income."

Daily Cash Summaries

During the day, you may collect money in your business establishment by placing cash in a cash register (or your pocket!). At the end of the day, you need to get all that cash information into QuickBooks.

One way to enter your day's cash activities into QuickBooks is to prepare a daily cash summary. The summary is like creating one giant sales form that adds up all the sales for the day. This may be sufficient in terms of tracking sales, unless you need to track each individual sale.

Creating a summary of daily cash sales

1. Choose **Activities**, **Enter Cash Sales**. The Enter Cash Sales window will appear, the same as it does when you plan to enter only one sale at a time.

2. In the area labeled **Customer:Job**, enter a name that describes this cash sale summary (see Figure 17.1); for example, you may want to enter "Daily Sales Summary" or "Summary of Cash Sales." If this is the first time you have used this description, you will be notified that no customer with that name exists. Choose **Quick Add** to add the name to your customer list so that it will be accessible to you in the future.

Should you use a daily summary?

Some companies don't need a specific record of each sale; they find that a daily summary gives them all the information they need. Others find the information about individual sales necessary and useful. If the time that each sale occurs is important to you–so that you can see which times of the day your store is busy, for example–then you will want an individual record of each sale. Alternatively, if your business flows evenly throughout the day, or if you already know your peak periods, you may not need to know at what time sales occurred. If you have employees who are paid on a commission, tracking individual sales will be important to that calculation. But if your employees are all paid at the same rate and are all considered to be adding to the value of the sale, then the individual sales by employee will not be useful to you.

FIGURE 17.1

Use a cash sales form to
create a daily cash summary.

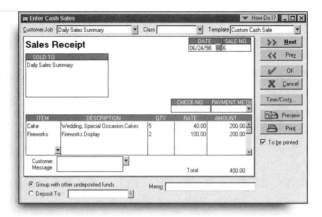

3. If you use classes, enter the correct class in the space provided. You may be entering the daily cash sales from your downtown division, for example, which falls into a class you have named "Downtown."

4. Verify that the date is correct. The date that appears on this form should be the date on which the sales were made, which is not necessarily today's date.

5. If you use a cash sales template that you have designed especially for recording the cash sales summary, choose the template you want by clicking on the arrow in the template area. If you choose a template that you have customized, the steps that follow may differ, depending on which fields appear on your customized cash sales form.

SEE ALSO

➤ *For more information on customizing forms such as cash sales entry forms, see Chapter 20, "Customizing QuickBook Forms", page 373*

6. You can leave the **Check No.** and the **Payment Meth** areas blank.

7. In the **Item** area at the bottom of the form, list each item that was sold during the day and the quantity. In this way, QuickBooks can update your inventory records to reflect items sold and no longer in stock. If you don't use

QuickBooks' inventory-tracking feature, the information in this **Item** area can still be useful by telling you which services or non-inventory items you sold during the day.

8. If the amount you received is to be deposited immediately to your bank account, you can choose the name of the account at the bottom of the window in the **Deposit To** area. If you plan to hold the deposit so it can be combined with other deposits, click the **Group with other undeposited funds** button.

9. To enter another daily summary (from a store at a different location, for example), click the **Next** button. Otherwise, click **OK**. Your entries have been saved, and you're ready to read the next section, "Depositing Cash."

When you create the daily cash summary, QuickBooks enters the total amount as income and offsets that amount with an entry to your Undeposited Funds account.

Cash Over or Short

What happens if the actual cash you count up doesn't agree with the amount reported on your cash sales forms for the day or your daily cash summary form? This is a frequent occurrence, especially in retail stores where a large quantity of cash is handled each day.

You need to create an account that will give you a place to report these overages and shortages. You can then note a discrepancy in cash when you fill out your daily cash summary form.

Creating a new account to track cash overages and shortages

1. Choose **Lists**, **Chart of Accounts**. The Chart of Accounts list window will appear.

2. Click the **Accounts** button at the bottom of the window and choose **New**. The New Account window will appear (see Figure 17.2).

FIGURE 17.2

Create a new account for
recording cash discrepancies.

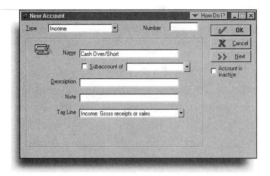

3. Decide whether you want this account to reside with your income accounts or your expense accounts. Consider past performance, and if your company seems to experience more cash overages than cash shortages, choose **Income** for the type of account. If the opposite is true, choose **Expense** for the type of account.

4. Enter a name for this account—such as "Cash Over/Short"—so that its purpose will be easy to understand.

5. Enter a tax line if you plan to use QuickBooks to help with your income tax return.

6. Click **OK** to save your new account information and close the window.

Before you can use your new cash over/short account, you should create an item so that you can apply the cash overage or shortage right on a cash sale or daily cash summary form.

Creating a new item for cash overages and shortages

1. Choose **Lists**, **Items**. The Item list window will appear.

2. Click the **Item** button at the bottom of the window and choose **New**. The New Item window will appear (see Figure 17.3).

FIGURE 17.3

Creating an item for cash discrepancies enables you to enter the item on a cash sales form.

3. Choose **Other Charge** for the type of item.

4. In the **Item Name/Number** area, enter a name for this item. Cash Over/Short won't fit because the item name can have a maximum of 13 characters, including spaces. Instead, think of some other appropriate name, such as "Over/Short," "Adjustment," or "Reconcile."

5. In the **Account** area, choose the **Cash Over/Short** account you just created.

6. Click **OK** to save your new item and close the window.

Now that you've created both a new account for recording your cash overage and shortage amounts and a new item so that you can enter these amounts right on your cash sales form, you're ready to record a cash discrepancy.

Imagine it's the end of the day and you have created a daily cash summary report, such as the one described in the last section. You arrive at a total for the cash you expect to deposit for the day. But when you count your cash, you find you are $2.00 short of the expected total.

You open your Enter Cash Sales window and choose your daily cash summary as the Customer:Job. After you enter all the items you sold today, click again in the item area of your cash sales form, and choose your new **Over/Short** item. In the **Amount** column, enter the amount of an overage as a positive number. Enter a shortage as a negative number by entering a minus sign before you enter the number.

Shortage too large

You cannot create a cash sales form with a net balance that is a negative number. Therefore, a cash shortage must be reported on a cash sales form that has sales numbers at least equal to or in excess of the shortage. You could enter a cash shortage on a credit memo/refund form, but if you choose to use a cash sales form, you must offset the shortage with sales.

Depositing Cash

After you've entered your individual cash sales or your daily cash summary in QuickBooks, you need to deposit the money you received.

For detailed steps in making and recording a deposit in QuickBooks, see "Making Deposits" in Chapter 12.

Credit Card Payments from Customers

When a customer uses a credit card such as MasterCard or Visa to pay you, the credit card receipt gets deposited the same as cash.

Later—usually monthly—you will receive a statement from the institution where your credit card payments are deposited. The statement will include a fee. If you pay this fee by writing a check, you will follow the procedure for paying bills, which is described in Chapter 15, "Purchase Orders, Accounts Payable, and Paying Bills."

On the other hand, if the bank withdraws the fee from your deposited money, you must make a general journal entry to record the increase in your expense account for the bank fee (a debit) and the reduction in your cash account (a credit).

Examples of general journal entries and a discussion of this type of accounting procedure appear in Chapter 16, "Managing Fixed Assets."

III

Paying Employees and Contractors

Paying Employees and Contractors

Understand how QuickBooks handles payroll, tracks various payroll expenses, and creates payroll items

Enter year-to-date payroll expenses into QuickBooks and other steps before writing paychecks

Understand the accounts QuickBooks creates for accurate Payroll

Set up employees, specify their deductions, and write paychecks

Gather information necessary for W-2s and print them

Set up independent contractors to be paid correctly, prepare and print 1099 forms

When you first set up your QuickBooks company with the EasyStep Interview, part of that process is choosing how to pay the people who work for you. Not everyone that works for you is an employee. QuickBooks defines employees as people you pay for services and deduct taxes from, sending that money in his or her name to state and federal tax agencies. Therefore, independent contractors (people you hire to do a particular job and send them on their way) are not your employees because you don't withhold taxes from their paychecks. Additionally, you should not consider yourself an employee of your own company unless you pay yourself via payroll accounts as you would all your other employees. Nor is a business partner an employee, unless she or he is actually on the payroll.

Determining Employees and Independent Contractors

Sometimes it's difficult to determine whether someone who works for you is an employee or an independent contractor. The IRS has published a list of 20 questions to help answer this question. The more positive answers you get to these questions, the more likely the person is an employee rather than an independent contractor. The following are some questions you can ask:

1. Do you (as the person paying the worker) give the worker instructions that he is expected to obey?
2. Does your company provide the worker with training?
3. Are the worker's services integrated into the regular business operation of your company?
4. Is it a requirement that the worker, personally, provide the services?
5. Is the worker prohibited from subcontracting the work?
6. Is the business relationship between your company and the worker an ongoing one?
7. Do you set the hours for the worker?
8. Is the worker expected to work full-time for your organization?

9. Is the work performed on your company's premises?

10. Do you instruct the worker regarding the order in which to perform his tasks?

11. Is the worker expected to submit reports (oral or written) summarizing his work progress?

12. Does the worker receive payments at regular intervals, such as weekly or monthly?

13. Does the worker get reimbursed for business and travel expenses?

14. Does your company supply the tools and supplies for this worker?

15. Does the worker have little or no significant investment in the tools used to perform the job?

16. Is the company responsible for absorbing any loss resulting from the work performed?

17. Is the worker prohibited from working for more than one company or person at a time?

18. Is the worker prohibited from making his services available to the general public?

19. Is it the company's responsibility if the worker does not perform to the specifications of the project?

20. Is the company responsible if the worker causes any damage?

Gathering Payroll Information

When you first began setting up your QuickBooks company, you began reading about payroll, tax, and insurance withholding, and perhaps you didn't have all the information handy for setting up your payroll. It might appear that if you answered QuickBooks' questions the wrong way, undoing what you've done would be a major chore. Not so!

If you chose to learn more about payroll, or take the time to gather more information, before responding to some of the payroll questions, rest assured that your EasyStep Interview remembered everything you answered, and all the information you provided will still be there when you come back. Pressing the **Leave** button in the EasyStep Interview does not mean you have to start from scratch. When you return to the interview (by choosing **File**, **EasyStep Interview**), you can continue entering payroll information where you left off.

Your Personal Experience with Payroll

Skipped the interview?

If you did not do an EasyStep Interview for your company and are entering company information as you go, we'll address special tasks throughout this chapter that you need to go back and do.

If you've never set up a payroll before, you'll read through this chapter and realize that the onerous task of deducting money from people's paychecks and making sure it gets sent to the right agencies is now part of your job. Payroll is serious business; it's dealing with other people's money. You might never appreciate having QuickBooks so much as when an employee comes to you about discrepancies in her paycheck. QuickBooks makes record keeping of that sort virtually painless. It is easy to draw up reports and show exactly how much sick time an employee has coming, how much overtime was worked, and exactly when it is time to send the government its quarterly tax payment for each employee.

If you have worked with payroll before, perhaps using another program, or with a couple of bank accounts and a calculator, you've already had a taste of having to keep track of health insurance premiums, state disability payments, worker's compensation, accrued vacation time, and the like. You'll enjoy how easy QuickBooks makes it to create separate payroll items for all those deductions, printing out paychecks that accurately break down what each person is really owed month after month. QuickBooks makes it easy to provide mileage reimbursements, set up voluntary contribution accounts that are specific for each employee, such as Flexible Spending accounts, and determine AEIC eligibility. You can even automate bonuses and create different commission rates for each employee. You'll be happy to learn that QuickBooks generally knows which payroll adjustments are computed on gross pay and which are computed on net. After you do the initial fingerwork of setting up employees and their payroll deductions and contributions, you'll find that regular payroll tasks can become fairly automated.

Planning Payroll

Whether you use the EasyStep Interview or not, there are several steps for setting up and paying employees. The following are tasks you must accomplish before using QuickBooks payroll. These are necessary to keep accurate records of how much you've paid each employee and accurate totals for taxes, contributions, and accrual of benefits such as sick time and vacation. After listing these tasks, we'll explore them step-by-step in the following sections:

- Determine who is an employee and who isn't. Understand the distinction between paying an employee and a contractor (see previous sidenote).

- Make sure **Payroll** is turned on in the **Preferences** menu.

- Make final decisions about how often you'll pay your employees, and think about which employees are salaried and which are paid by the hour.

- Determine if you want to have special types of payroll accounts (one for supervisors, another for labor, for example), rather than the standard payroll-related accounts QuickBooks automatically creates.

- Review the payroll items that QuickBooks sets up. These are the items QuickBooks uses to make deductions from employee paychecks, generate reports, and make payments to tax agencies, insurance firms, and so on.

- Determine if you think you need to create other payroll items. When QuickBooks sets up payroll, it includes familiar payroll items such as Federal Income Tax and Medicare contributions, state tax deductions, and so on. However, QuickBooks needs to know about all deductions and contributions, such as 401Ks, mileage reimbursement, and anything that has a positive or negative effect on your payroll and liability accounts.

- Create new items if needed. Examples of these might include company-paid insurance or union dues.

- You can then enter data for all your employees and make individual changes in their deductions and contributions, as you deem necessary. Use the Employees List to add new employees or edit existing ones.

Create new payroll items

If you pay your employees variable commissions or bonuses, or reimburse mileage at different rates for each employee, you don't need to create new payroll items to account for each variable. You can set a distinct rate for each employee in the employee information section, using the same payroll item.

- Decide on a company "start date," if you haven't already. That's the date that QuickBooks should have begun "knowing" about your company, calculating data, and generating reports.

- In the Set Up YTD Amounts dialog box, determine which adjustment period is best for your company (we'll go over this step-by-step).

- Enter all payroll history from the beginning of the year, up to the start date of your QuickBooks company. This includes all wages paid to employees, taxes, deductions, and contributions. This needs to be done before you use QuickBooks payroll, so QuickBooks knows when to stop deducting certain taxes and withholdings for that year. This payroll history includes money paid to any employees who have worked for you during the current year, even if you no longer employ them. You need not create adjustments for new employees whom you have not paid yet.

- Determine how you want to use timesheets. Do you want to print them for each employee? Do you want to use the QuickBooks Timer to have employees enter their hours from the Timer? Do you want employees to enter their own hours into QuickBooks, or should you be the one doing it?

- Finally, QuickBooks generates regular paychecks using either the Timer, hours you manually enter, or by salary or project. All you need to do is select **Pay Employees** from the Employees Items list. All accounts are appropriately debited and credited, and checks are printed.

- QuickBooks also generates checks to tax agencies and other payroll liabilities such as insurance and retirement plans. This occurs at intervals that you set, or when you click **Pay Liabilities/Taxes** from the Employee Item List.

Let's look closely at these steps in the following sections.

SEE ALSO

➤ *If you haven't done so already, this is a good time to think about keeping your payroll information secure. See Chapter 28, "Security," for tips on setting up passwords and limiting access to parts of your QuickBooks company file.*

Paying Employees Versus Paying Independent Contractors

If someone is an employee of yours, you pay his taxes as well as his wages. The complexity of setting up payroll encourages lots of businesses to work with independent contractors whenever possible. However, there are some tax issues at stake when you employ a contractor. If you pay an independent contractor more than a certain threshold amount (currently $600 in one year), what you pay him must be reported to the IRS by the contractor as income. Tax rules regarding this "threshold amount" may change. To find out the current threshold amount, call Intuit at 1-800-771-7248, or the IRS at 1-800-TAX-FORM.

QuickBooks enables you to track all payments that affect this IRS threshold amount. Your independent contractors expect to receive 1099 forms from you at the end of the year, indicating how much you've paid them. You can easily set up QuickBooks to print out these 1099 forms, with the appropriate totals, ready for you to send. We'll explore this in detail at the end of this chapter.

QuickBooks Payroll and Employee Setup

Before we get into the nuts and bolts of actually setting up employees, we're going to take a minute to explore the two accounts QuickBooks sets up when you turn on payroll. You'll see that QuickBooks can do so much more than simply set up a roster of people who work for you. QuickBooks creates vitally important accounts that help you keep track of all employee deductions, and makes it easy for you to make sure that all money gets sent to the right agency. If this is not of interest to you at the moment, you can skip the following section, "Payroll Expense and Liability Accounts," and move right to the "Setting Up Employees" segment.

Payroll Expense and Liability Accounts

When you first turn on QuickBooks' payroll feature, QuickBooks creates two new accounts: Payroll Expense and Payroll Liability accounts. (Figure 18.1 shows the Payroll Liability account in the

Set up independent contractors as vendors

The best way to work with independent contractors in QuickBooks is to set them up as vendors. You can pay your contractors just as if you were paying a bill to a vendor. This enables you to keep track of the yearly totals, seeing separately how much money you pay out to contractors and how much is paid as wages and salary to employees. We'll explore how to pay independent contractors later in this chapter.

Chart of Accounts. The Payroll Expense account is much farther down the list, appearing with other expense accounts.) Also, upon turning on Payroll, QuickBooks automatically assigns the most obvious payroll expenses (wages, company-paid payroll taxes, employee deductions) to one of these two accounts.

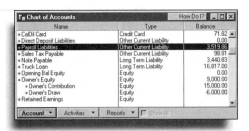

Understanding Payroll Expenses and Payroll Liabilities

When you issue paychecks, each of these accounts has its balance decreased or increased appropriately. If you create additional payroll items (perhaps union dues, voluntary employee deductions such as United Way, or 401K plans), QuickBooks assists you in choosing the right account. Here's why, and here's what's at stake:

QuickBooks sets up the Payroll Expense account to handle pure company expenses. These would be wages you owe to employees, company bonuses, and so on. In QuickBooks, an expense is an amount you record and pay as it occurs. For example, when it's payday, you pay your employees. The company-paid portions of taxes, such as social security and Medicare, are also expenses that are paid when they are due (usually quarterly).

QuickBooks sets up a Payroll Liability account to handle amounts you owe, but have not yet paid. These include each employee's share of state and federal taxes. The Payroll Liability account helps you keep track of money that is not your own and is just waiting to be sent to the appropriate tax agencies in due course. QuickBooks calculates and deducts the correct amount for taxes from each employee, based on your choices in Employee Setup, which we are exploring shortly, and records the totals in your Payroll Liability account. When you issue paychecks, you see your Payroll Liability account increase, because you are now holding onto even more of your employee's money than you were before, so it's considered an increased liability.

Setting Up Employees

Setting up employees first involves making QuickBooks aware of all paychecks you've written since the beginning of the year, until the date you designate as your QuickBooks *start date*. You can't record paychecks written to employees unless QuickBooks knows the history of the employees first, so we'll learn how to set up employees and enter all payment data since the beginning of the year. The purpose of this long way around is to ensure that at the end of this process, you'll be able to issue paychecks to your company's employees, with all deductions accurately accounted for and credited.

For the purposes of bringing QuickBooks up to speed with where your business is in the real world, this employee list would have to include all employees that have worked for you during the current year, including those who no longer do.

From the QuickBooks Navigator, select the **Payroll and Employees** tab, and click the **Employees** Icon. The Employee List appears (see Figure 18.2).

Tracking deductions using the Payroll Liability account

Sometimes an employee may come to you questioning a specific deduction. To track a particular deduction using the Payroll Liability account, view a check before sending it to an employee. (Select **Pay Employees** from the **Activities** menu of the Employees List. Place a check by an employee whose deduction you want to track, and click **Create**.) In the Other Payroll Items panel, you see the deductions for that paycheck. Make a note of a particular deduction amount and its date. Close that dialog box, select **Chart of Accounts** from the **List** menu, and click the **Payroll Liabilities** account to open it. Click the **Q-Report** button and you see a list of all Payroll Liability deductions for that employee. Using the date as your guide, find that same deduction amount in that list. In the **Type** field, look specifically for "Paycheck." Click it, and the paycheck in question appears on the screen. Use this same Quick Report to open other paychecks that deducted similar amounts. This is how you can locate any deduction and quickly track the paycheck affected by it.

FIGURE 18.2

Set up employee data from the Employee List.

From the Employees drop-down menu at the lower left, select **New**, and you see the New Employee dialog box. It has three tabs:

- **Address Info**. Fill in basic statistics such as Name, Address, Initials, and Phone Number. Also include Social Security Number and Hire date. If the employee ever leaves, you'll record that information here as well.

- **Additional Info**. This tab has "extras" such as Birthday, Date of Last Raise, and Spouse's Name. If there is other incidental information you'd like to keep track of for each employee, perhaps department, team, or travel preferences, here's where you create it. The **Define Fields** button enables you to create new fields that appear on the **Additional Info** tab of each employee. Note that you can create fields for Customer and Vendor forms from this same dialog box. Employee Account Numbers can be recorded here, if your company uses them.

- **Payroll Info.** The **Payroll Info** tab is where you record how much you pay this employee, how often, and what deductions you remove from his regular paychecks. You also manage employee sick time and vacation time pay rates from this tab, specifying at what rate these items should accrue for this employee and whether you want unused sick time and vacation to "zero out" at the year's end. Tax withholdings and preferences are also managed from the **Payroll Info** tab. Specify how often this employee is to be paid by choosing a Pay Period from the drop-down menu.

SEE ALSO

➤ *For more information on creating custom reports, see page 406*

Specifying Earnings

To specify how much you are going to pay this employee, click the top line in the **Name** field of the Earnings panel. A drop-down menu appears.

- To pay this employee a particular hourly wage, select **Regular Pay** from the drop-down menu. Specify an hourly

---

Additional Info tab

If you create a new field for one employee, it is available for you to use with every employee. When filling in data for the **Additional Info** tab, consider if there is any sort of useful information you might want to track. For example, if your company has to relocate, you may want to speak with each employee about the chances of them relocating with you. Create a field here to keep track of the results of those conversations.

Use the Define Fields

After you create a new field with **Define Fields**, how will it be used? What employee form will your new field appear on? You can place the data in each employee item, of the type we are building here, and view your new field one by one, but what if you wanted to view a report that included data from the new field you just created? For example, if you needed to fly your staff somewhere and you wanted to know the travel preferences of each employee, how could you see them all at once? You'd have to create a custom report that includes that field.

rate by typing a number into the **Hour/Annual Rate** field. The number you type there will be how much this employee makes per hour.

- To pay this employee a yearly salary, select **Salary** from the drop-down menu. After determining how much per year you want to pay, type that number into the **Hour/Annual Rate** field.

Use this same Earnings panel to specify an overtime, a sick time, and a vacation time pay rate for this employee (see Figure 18.3). You should type an hourly rate even if the pay rate for sick and vacation time is the same as the regular hourly rate.

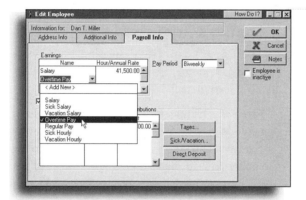

FIGURE 18.3

Creating a new overtime item for an employee.

Remember that in the **Earnings** field, the title **Name** does not refer to the name of the employee, but to the name of the payroll item you are applying to this employee.

If you are using QuickBooks Pro, you'll see a check box "Use Time Data to Create Paychecks." Click this if you want to calculate paychecks from QuickBooks time tracking.

SEE ALSO

➤ *For more information on using QuickBooks to track time, see page 489*

Applying New Payroll Items

If you've created other payroll items that apply to earnings, such as a special rate for working weekends, holidays and night shift, use the drop-down menu to include those rates as well. To include more than one type of payroll item in the **Earnings** field, just click the line below the item you just added, and you see a new drop-down menu as shown in the preceding figure. The same choices are available from this menu, but will apply to this new line. Don't forget to type an hourly rate for each new item you add. If the number of items you use exceeds the number of visible lines, just use the scrolling button to see the lower ones.

Each payroll item and rate that you add to this employee's record will be available for you to apply to his paycheck.

To learn how to create a new Payroll Item of this sort, see the following section.

Creating a New Payroll Item

The **Payroll Info** tab of the New Employee dialog box enables you to create new Payroll Items on-the-fly by clicking **Add New** at the top of each drop-down menu.

From the **Names** field of the Earnings panel, you can create a new **Hourly** or **Yearly Salary Payroll Item**. This adds a new category of payment that you can apply to any employee's paycheck. You can make a new salary or hourly wage item if you are creating a new job and job description in your company, one that would be easier to manage if you could track it separately from other employees. When you create the new item, you are asked to specify either hourly wage or salary and choose which account this new payroll item will be paid from. As you choose an account type, explanations as to the purpose of each account appear beneath your choice.

If you want to create a new **Additions, Deductions, and Company Contributions** item, click in an empty line below the Earnings panel, and choose **Add New**. A dialog box appears. Each of these items has features that should be pointed out:

- **Commission.** When creating a new commission item, the rate you enter here can be overridden on a paycheck-to-paycheck basis. You can create a new commission rate on-the-fly for each employee, if you like. The rate you type here only applies if no other rate is chosen on the paycheck itself. Again, click **Track Expense by Job** if you want more powerful reports that associate this payroll expense with an employee's job.

- **Addition.** Fill in similar fields as you would for a deduction, but in this case, the Calculation Type feature becomes more important. For example, if you are creating a new mileage reimbursement item, click **As a Dollar Rate Times a Quantity**, you are prompted to enter the number of miles this employee drove, and thus, pay her for every mile she drove, rather than just one. Also, if you are planning to pay an employee for piecework, for example, $5 for each blouse sewn, click **Based on Quantity**, so you can specify in each paycheck the number of blouses sewn. Click **Track Expense by Job** if you want to create reports that link this addition to the job accounts that this employee has been working on.

- **Deduction.** When you create a new deduction, specify its name, who the deduction should be paid to, and whether the deduction should be applied to Net or Gross pay. Also include an amount or percentage for this deduction and an annual limit dollar amount, if it's the same for each employee.

- **Company Contribution.** The Company Contribution dialog box requires the same type of input as the preceding payroll items. Create a new company contribution item if your company is contributing to a particular fund or company on behalf of its employees.

Creating Items for Weekend Pay and Shift Differentials

Many employers pay more per hour for working weekends and night shifts, and sometimes, employees who work holidays get extra compensation too. Often, these amounts are calculated as an additional amount per hour. For example, an employee whose *base pay rate* is $16 per hour might make an additional $8 per hour for working overtime. With QuickBooks, it's best to create an item called overtime that pays out at the full $24 an hour rate, rather than creating an item for $8 an hour that you can tack on as extra when applicable.

Additions, Deductions, and Company Contributions

Use the **Additions, Deductions, and Company Contributions** portion of the **Payroll Info** tab of the New Employee dialog box to specify all types of regular adjustments to an employee's paycheck, except for taxes. Apply payroll items such as union dues, 401K deductions, health insurance, mileage reimbursement, and employee bonuses.

To apply an addition, deduction, or company contribution to an employee, click the first available blank line in the **Names** field, as shown in Figure 18.4. A drop-down menu appears. From this list, select any item to make it appear on that line. In the fields to the right of the Name field, type an amount and yearly limit for this item. When you type an amount for a deduction, the number automatically turns to negative. Rather than a simple dollar amount, you can also specify a percentage.

FIGURE 18.4

Adding a deduction or addition item to the employee's paycheck.

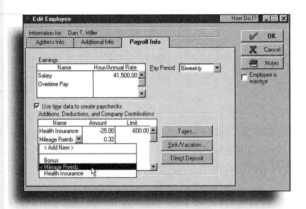

To learn how to create a new payroll item of this sort, see the preceding section, "Creating a New Payroll Item."

Setting Up Payroll Taxes

Chapter 19, "QuickBooks and Taxes," is dedicated entirely to payroll taxes. For now, we'll point out that to set withholdings, allowances and filing status, click the **Taxes** button, found on the **Payroll Info** tab. You see three separate tabs for setting up taxes: **Federal**, **State**, and **Local**.

Establishing Sick and Vacation Time

Click the **Sick/Vacation** button to open the dialog box shown in Figure 18.5.

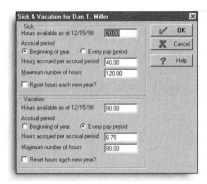

FIGURE **18.5**

Setting up sick and vacation time for an employee.

Here is where you determine the accrual rate for sick and vacation time and type the number of hours available as of the current date. Click the **Every Pay Period** button to allow the employee to accrue a certain amount of hours per pay period toward this benefit, or click **Beginning of Year** to front load the employee with a certain number of hours for the entire year. You can also specify if sick and vacation time should *zero out* (start over) at the beginning of the year.

Updating Year-to-Date Amounts

After completing the previous sections, an employee is set up for regular payroll activity. (You might want to review Chapter 19 on payroll taxes before actually printing out checks.)

Because we are moving through the process of initially setting up payroll, we'll explore how to enter information about all employees so that your withholding, contribution, and deduction totals are all up-to-date.

Entering Year-to-Date Paycheck Amounts

At this time, go through your file cabinet or shoe box and locate records for any paychecks you've written to any employee from

Company sick time contribution

Some companies institute a *sick bonus* for those employees who seldom call in sick. After resetting sick hours at the beginning of the year, a bonus is awarded to the employee. This bonus can be set up as a payroll item, or simply applied spontaneously to the final paycheck of the year, for example. If you were to set up such an item as a company contribution, a certain dollar amount per hour, for example, make sure you've clicked the **Based on Quantity** button, which would apply this set dollar amount to every hour of remaining sick time.

January of the current year, to your QuickBooks start date. You need total amounts you paid to each employee, as well as all deductions and contributions during that period.

Updating year-to-date paycheck amounts

1. Click the **Payroll and Employees** tab of the QuickBooks Navigator and choose the **YTD amounts** icon. You see the dialog box shown in Figure 18.6.

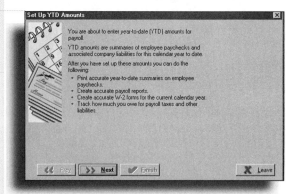

2. Read the instructions and click **Next**. The next two dialog boxes prompt you for three dates:

- Your QuickBooks start date
- The date you'd like to show that QuickBooks Year-to-Date summaries as truly affecting your bank accounts
- The day you'll start paying employees with QuickBooks paychecks

After answering questions about these dates, you see a dialog box for entering data about each employee (see Figure 18.7).

3. Double-click an employee's name to enter new data. Just like the **Payroll Info** tab of the New Employees dialog box, use the drop-down menus that appear to enter wage data in the upper fields, and use the lower fields to enter deductions and contributions (see Figure 18.8).

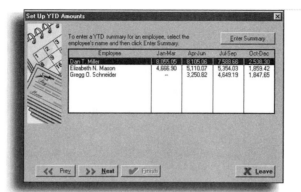

FIGURE 18.7

Getting ready to choose which employee to update data for. Click **Enter Summary** when an employee is selected.

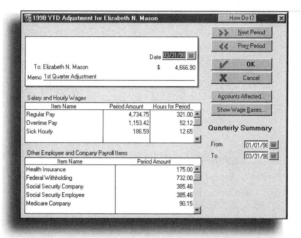

FIGURE 18.8

Adding employee payment data from the beginning of the year, up to the QuickBooks start date.

4. Use the Pay Period Summary panel at the lower right to specify how large a time frame should be covered by each adjustment. This is your adjustment period. In the following sidenote, learn the pluses and minuses of choosing monthly, quarterly, or a single adjustment period starting at the beginning of the year.

5. After you choose that adjustment period, use the **Next Period** button to move from one time period to the next. For example, if you've used the pay period summary dates to indicate that you want to enter data for the entire year up to now in one summary, you won't need to use the **Next** button because you've chosen to type all yearly figures in one summary. However, if you've chosen a monthly or quarterly

Choosing an adjustment period

Before you begin entering YTD amount data, you have to choose an adjustment period. You can enter a sweeping sum for each employee from the beginning of the current year until now, or you can break down the data into quarterly (or even monthly) chunks and enter it that way. The amount of detail available for QuickBooks reports depends on this choice. The smaller your adjustment period is, the more accurate QuickBooks can be with its projections and period summaries. Breaking down your adjustment period into shorter periods is more work, and you may not have detailed enough paper documents to warrant it, but if you do, your QuickBooks reports will be of more help to you.

Keep in mind that this is a different question from choosing a QuickBooks *start date*. You can choose to start your QuickBooks company mid-year, or at the previous quarter, if you choose, but in this Year-to-Date Amount dialog box, employee data should be entered for the entire year up to the QuickBooks start date.

Keep in mind that after you choose an adjustment period and have entered employee data, you cannot change it unless you delete all YTD adjustments for every employee.

adjustment period, then make sure you have your figures from your older documents divided into these periods, and enter data for only that one period. Then, use the **Next Period** button to move forward to the next quarter, month, or pay period.

6. Add all relevant data for an employee. Then click **OK**, and move on to another employee.

When you've updated payroll for your entire work force, you'll be back at the Set Up YTD Amounts dialog box pictured preceding Figure 18.8.

Entering Prior Payments of Taxes and Liabilities

Entering prior payments of taxes and liabilities

1. Click the **Next** button in the Set Up YTD Amounts dialog box. You see a dialog box prompting you to enter data for all special payments you've made toward health insurance for your employees, pensions, or any company contributions for which you want it understood that you've already made payments toward.

2. Click the **Create** button and you see the Prior Payments of Taxes and Liabilities dialog box (see Figure 18.9).

3. Select any blank line to choose a contribution type from the drop-down menu. Again, use the date boxes to choose an adjustment period. Here you should enter any checks you've mailed this year to tax agencies, insurance groups, or any payment that would help QuickBooks create a correct up-to-date picture of where your payroll accounts stand as of the start date. Write a memo to yourself regarding this

FIGURE 18.9

Use this dialog box to enter all company contributions you've made since the beginning of the year.

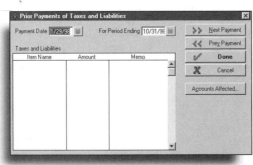

adjustment if you'd like. To add more adjustments, click the line under the adjustment you just created, and a new drop-down menu appears.

4. If applicable, you may see a dialog box prompting you to enter any unpaid carryover liabilities from the previous year. You need to enter this as well to make QuickBooks aware of any payments from last year's payroll liabilities that you have yet to make. Again, choose an item to add and adjust by clicking the top line in the **Item Name** field. A drop-down menu appears, as usual.

Updating Payroll Tax Tables

When you use the **Employee List** to add a new employee or edit an existing one, click the **Taxes** button on the **Payroll Info** tab to specify withholding and deduction information for each employee (see Figure 18.10). Based on your choices, QuickBooks accurately calculates the amount of taxes owed, deducting the correct amount from each check, and places the sums in the correct accounts. It does this for state taxes, as well as federal, simply by selecting a state from a drop-down menu. You might be wondering how QuickBooks does this. After all, aren't tax withholding calculations time-sensitive, subject to new congressional laws and changes in the tax code?

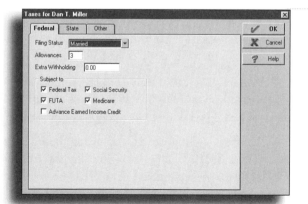

Quarterly adjustment period

Before going too easy on yourself and choosing **Year To Date** as an adjustment period, remember that tax agencies such as the IRS often expect you to pay employee taxes *quarterly*, so you might as well set up QuickBooks employee records to create quarterly reports for tax deductions. And when those taxes are due, this makes it easy for QuickBooks to calculate how much to pay.

Accounts Affected button

Some of these dialog boxes have an **Accounts Affected** button. Click it if you want these payments you've made to affect an account *other than* the Payroll Expense and Payroll Liabilities accounts. If you do not want the adjustments you are making here to affect the Payroll Expense and Payroll Liabilities accounts, click this button and choose another account from the list. The adjustments you make here still affect the amounts on your Year–to-Date Payroll Reports.

FIGURE 18.10

Enter Employee Tax Deductions with the Taxes dialog box.

Payroll tax table updates

You can verify if the tax tables you are using are up-to-date by calling Intuit at 800-771-7748. To subscribe to the update service, if you don't have Internet access, call 800-644-8371.

It is true that tax withholding calculations are time-sensitive. QuickBooks maintains a Tax Table (select **Payroll and Employees** from the Navigator, and click the **Tax Table** Icon, see Figure 18.11), and uses it to calculate all federal and state taxes. When you first purchase QuickBooks, you need to make sure your version comes with the latest tax table. Just because you are using QuickBooks 6 does not mean you have the latest version of the table. Intuit updates QuickBooks from time to time by issuing *maintenance releases* that you can download from their Web site (www.intuit.com). In between full new versions of its products, Intuit can offer several maintenance releases to fix small problems and offer the latest information to its customers.

FIGURE 18.11

The QuickBooks Tax Table, which is used to keep your tax deduction rates up-to-date.

As a QuickBooks owner, you can download one Tax Table update from its Web site for free. You must do this within 60 days of your purchase. After downloading one new Tax Table, you must subscribe to Intuit's Update Service to obtain later versions, which currently costs $59.95 for 12 months.

You might want to wait until that 60 day period has nearly arrived, so you'll stand the greatest chance of obtaining the newest Tax Table before the offer expires.

How do you know if you are using the most recent Tax Table? Click the **Tax Table** Icon from the **Payroll and Employees** tab, and you see a panel indicating which version you are using. Then, log on to Intuit's Web page. You are prompted to search for a product or a service. Click **Tax Table Service**, and locate the page where you are prompted to type your current Tax

Table number (see Figure 18.12). If your number matches its most recent release, you need not download the new one. If you do need to replace your Tax Table, download the newest one, and follow the directions for installation.

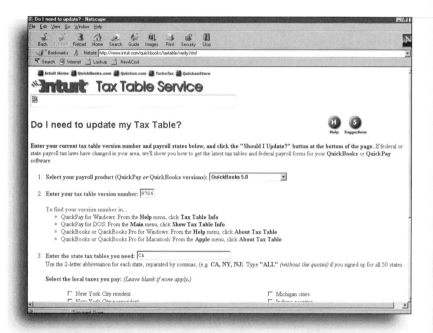

FIGURE 18.12
Intuit's Tax Table Service Web page, where you can make sure your QuickBooks Tax Table is up-to-date.

Payday

If you fully set up Payroll, entering each employee's past and current data, creating any additional payroll items you need in addition to the ones generated by QuickBooks, you are pretty much ready to print checks and pay your employees.

Preparing Paychecks

QuickBooks knows your employees are due paychecks when hours have been entered into weekly timesheets, or when they've performed billable activities (this topic is also covered in Chapter 25). So after having set pay rates and salaries for each employee, as well as setting up vacation and sick time accrual rates, payday is simply a matter of preparing the paychecks and printing them.

Maintenance release version

Although you are using QuickBooks 6, it's helpful to know which maintenance release you are using also. Before downloading a new version from Intuit, find out which version you have running. To do this with QuickBooks running, press Ctrl + 1. The information you want appears at the top of the panel. Then log on to Intuit's Web site, locate their Service and Update page (currently, the URL is `http://www.intuit.com/support/updates`), and see which version Intuit is offering as the latest.

Paying your employees

1. Click the **Payroll and Employees** tab on the QuickBooks Navigator and select the **Create Paychecks** Icon. You see the Select Employees to Pay dialog box (shown in Figure 18.13).

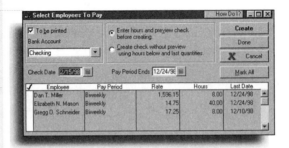

FIGURE 18.13

Review a list of all employees who are due paychecks, and the amounts.

Automate payroll hours

Please take a look at Chapter 25, "QuickBooks and Time Tracking," to learn how to set up timesheets, use the QuickBooks Pro Timer, and associate payroll time with a single job and customer. After reviewing that chapter, you'll know how to automate payroll hours.

---

2. Select which **Bank Account** these checks will be paid from. In the example shown here, **Checking** is selected. Of course, you need to make sure you've got the money in this account to cover the checks.

3. Verify the **Check Date**, as well as the pay period dates covered by this paycheck. QuickBooks tracks pay periods by indicating the final day of that pay period (**Pay Period End**). You'll be drawing up checks for that pay period shown.

4. Specify if you want to preview the paychecks before they fly out to your printer, or just view the information here in this dialog box and be done with it.

5. Place a check to the far left of each employee who is due a paycheck. If every employee visible in this dialog box is going to be getting a check today, then click the **Mark All** button.

6. View and verify the employee information available here: name, pay rate, pay period covered by this paycheck, and pay period type, in this case it is biweekly. If you see something amiss, you can fix it later in this process.

7. Click **Create**, and you see the Preview Paycheck dialog box.

Previewing Your Checks

In the Preview Paycheck dialog box (see Figure 18.14), each check is presented in sequence, with the employee's name at the top. When you are done previewing and adjusting, click **Create** (at the bottom of the dialog box) to go to the next employee.

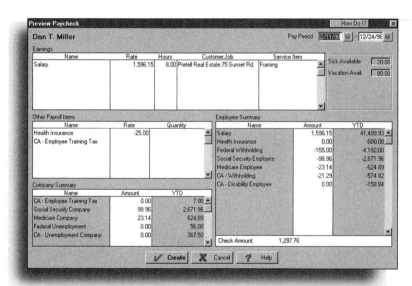

FIGURE 18.14

Review all employee deductions and totals before printing the check.

This is pretty much your last chance to gracefully edit paycheck components and totals. Here you can change hours, regular deductions, and add new payroll items. Payroll items such as health insurance, mileage reimbursement, and even sums you'd think of as being written in stone—such as Social Security and Medicare deductions—all can be edited here.

Reviewing and editing paycheck amounts

1. Review the amounts in the Earnings panel of the Review Paycheck dialog box. Type a new amount if you like. Also, use the Customer: Jobs area and Service Item to assign this paycheck to a particular job account. Use the drop-down menu to select a customer account and item, if needed.

2. Review the Other Payroll Items and Company Summary panels, and use the drop-down menus to make changes. (Menus appear when you click a line.) Manual adjustments can be helpful if you realize it's someone's bonus day, and you just want to tack it on quickly, or if someone came in on a weekend and forgot to let you know about it formally, but you still want to pay them.

3. Quickly compare the Company Summary, Employee Summary, and Check Amount, just to make sure nothing is amiss.

4. When you are happy with how a check looks, click **Create**. If you have a sound card in your computer, you'll here the reassuring clangs of a cash register, letting you know that a check has been processed, awaiting printing.

5. When you've finished this process for all checks, all that remains is viewing the actual facsimile of each check if you so desire, and printing them out.

Notice you can also associate each payroll item in the Earnings section with a particular job and customer. Use this option when applicable because the reports you generate later will be better able to indicate which jobs are more profitable.

Viewing the Checks

Retrieving and viewing the paychecks

1. With Intuit's checks loaded into your printer, select **Reminders** from the **List** menu.

2. Click **Paychecks to Print**, as shown in Figure 18.15.

3. Double-click **Paychecks**, and you see a list of each paycheck you processed earlier, as well as any other paychecks that had not previously made it this far.

Warning: Don't press enter to move between fields

As you click in fields and make changes to any of these totals, don't press enter until you are entirely finished with this paycheck. Pressing **Enter** confirms your edits, and moves you on to the next employee. To see the result of your tinkering, just make an edit, click in another field, and watch the check amount at the lower right adjust itself.

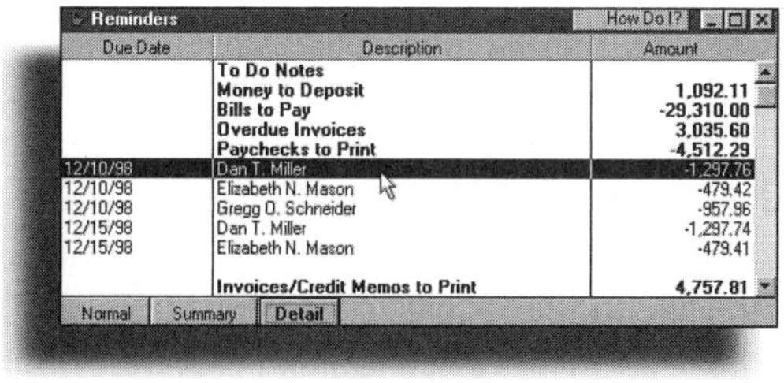

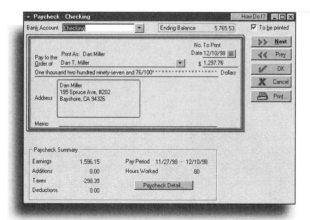

FIGURE 18.15

The Reminder List is the fastest way to retrieve paychecks ready to print.

4. Double-click the check at the top of the list, and you see a check facsimile, as shown in Figure 18.16.

5. If you want to make any changes, click the **Check Detail** button, at the bottom of this dialog box. You'll notice that it returns you to the Preview Paycheck area you had just been working with.

FIGURE 18.16

Previewing a check facsimile before you actually print it.

6. By default, the **To Be Printed** check box at the upper right of each check is selected. However, if this is a direct deposit check that you are making a record of, or recording a paycheck that got paid in some other way, you can uncheck the **To Be Printed** check box.

7. You may have to void a paycheck. Perhaps it didn't print correctly, or an error was discovered. To do so while the check is displayed on your screen, click the **Edit** menu (at the top left, as shown in Figure 18.17), and choose **Void Paycheck**. The paycheck still shows up in your chart of accounts, and it appears voided.

8. You can also delete the paycheck from the same menu. This entirely removes the transaction. To void and delete paychecks at some other time, select the **Chart of Accounts** from the **List** menu, and click the account responsible for this check. Scroll down and locate the check you want to void or delete. Select either command from the **Edit** menu, as described.

FIGURE 18.17

Use the Edit menu to void a paycheck.

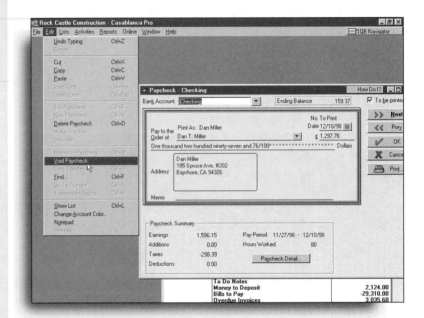

Obtaining Intuit paychecks

You can purchase checks from Intuit that work with most commercial printers. They come in a variety of formats and styles, and can be ordered from www.intuitmarket.com.

Printing Paychecks

To print your paychecks, click the **Print** button next to the check facsimile and make any adjustments to Check Style (See Figure 18.18). Check the **Print Company Address** button if you want such information on the paycheck.

Printing a Logo

If you are interested in using a logo on your check, click the **Logo** button on the right side of the Print Checks dialog box, and choose a .BMP file for your logo by clicking the **File** button (Figure 18.19) and locating an applicable file.

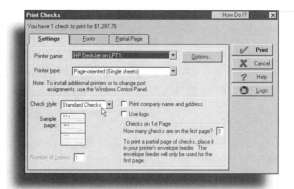

FIGURE 18.18
By adjusting Check Style, you can accommodate several different check sizes and shapes.

You need not move the bitmap image to the same folder as QuickBooks, but if you do move the file, you'll have to pinpoint its location again, using this same dialog box.

Printing a Partial Page of Checks

Checks are not cheap, and if you only want to print one or two right now (or if you printed a partial page of checks previously, and don't want to waste the rest of the page), click the **Partial Page** tab of the Print Checks dialog box. Using the Print Envelope feature of your printer, you can get QuickBooks to print a single check. The dialog box makes it clear how to position your check in the printer.

FIGURE 18.19
Click **File** to search your hard drive for a .BMP logo for your check.

Special Payroll Reports

You can generate lots of reports associated with Payroll, such as QuickReports on each employee, reports that summarize deductions, types of pay, various company contributions and YTD liabilities that summarize how much you owe to various tax agencies and health insurance firms.

Controlling Overtime

Reports are helpful for controlling overtime. Rather than find
out long after the fact that a job has not been profitable because
of overtime, use reports to regularly keep track of overtime by
choosing **Reports** on all payroll items from the **Reports** menu
of the Payroll Item List, and select **Summary by Item**, as shown
in Figure 18.20. (In the Standard Edition of QuickBooks, your
Reports may appear in a different order.)

FIGURE 18.20

Use this report to view payroll
items, either as totals, by
employee, or with many
details.

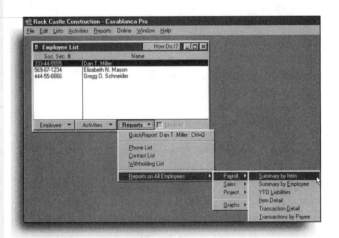

The third report item from the top shows overtime use for each
employee (Figure 18.21). You have to scroll to the right to see
each employee.

It's possible to create a specific report detailing only overtime
usage.

Creating an overtime report

1. Click **Filters** from that same report as shown in Figure
   18.21. The Report Filters dialog box appears (see Figure
   18.22).

2. Scroll down the Filter list, and click **Payroll Item**.

3. In the field to the right, scroll down and select **Overtime**.

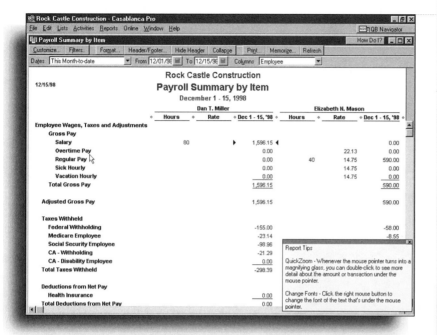

4. Click **OK**, and a report appears that shows only overtime use for each employee.

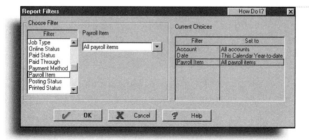

Viewing Year-to-Date Payroll Liabilities

QuickBooks can generate a helpful report showing your company's year-to-date payroll liabilities as a summarized dollar amount (see Figure 18.23). Select **Reports on all Items** from the Reports drop-down menu of the Payroll list as shown, and choose **YTD Liabilities**, as shown. You can click any item in the list (click any individual sum, not its item name) to see more specific information about any particular deduction or owed amount. (The Standard Edition refers to the report as **Liabilities**, not **YTD Liabilities**.)

FIGURE 18.23
Quickly view all your payroll liabilities in a single report.

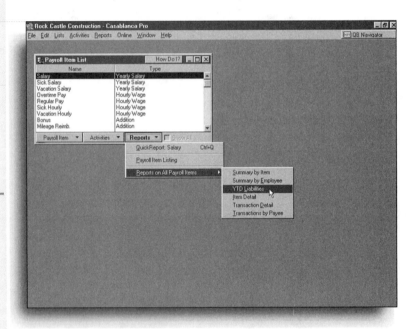

Ordering and printing onto blank W-2 forms

Although QuickBooks prepares and prints W-2 data for each employee, you cannot print W-2s on standard paper. Also, the blank W-2 forms you can order from the IRS are set up for multifeed printers (tractor printers) and typewriters. These forms are designed to make triplicate copies all at once, and you can't use them on laser or inkjet printers. You can order blank computer-friendly W-2 forms from Intuit by calling 1-800-433-8810 or buy them from most office supply stores.

Because you need to print out several copies of each form, the question arises, "do I collate?" The answer is no. QuickBooks prints out all the Copy A forms, then all the Copy B forms, and so forth. Therefore, when loading blank W-2 forms into your printer, load as many copies of each form as you have employees, and then load the next form.

Working with W-2s

At the end of the year, an employer must submit a record of all wages paid and taxes deducted from each employee. One copy goes to the federal, state, and local tax agencies. One copy goes to the employee, and one copy is saved for your records. Additionally, an employer must submit a W-3 form to the tax agencies, summarizing all W-2 information.

QuickBooks makes dealing with W-2 and W-3 forms very easy. If you made all your year-to-date adjustments to your payroll accounts, as specified earlier in this chapter, then all the W-2 data generated by QuickBooks should be accurate. Here's how QuickBooks handles W-2s:

- Gathers all tax and wage information on each employee and generates a W-2.

- Displays each employee's W-2 on the screen, allowing you to make adjustments to any field.

- Prints W-2s onto forms that you can order from Intuit. These forms work on any standard laser or inkjet printer.

- Assists you in reviewing and printing a W-3 form (a summary of all W-2s), which the government also expects to receive from you.

Reviewing and Editing Your W-2s

Start reviewing W-2s by selecting the **Payroll and Employees** tab on the Navigator and clicking the **Process W-2** icon. (You can also click **Process W-2s** from the **Activities** menu of the Employee List.) You see the dialog box shown in Figure 18.24.

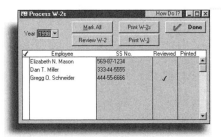

FIGURE 18.24

Click the **Process W-2** icon in the Navigator to see a list of all employees' W-2s.

You can do the following:

- To review all W-2s for the current year, click the **Mark All** and then the **Review W-2** buttons.

- To review select W-2s, rather than all of them, place a check at the left of each name who's form you want to look at, and then click the Review W-2 button.

In either case, you see the Employee W-2 screen, and here you can simply review the data, or make changes by hovering your mouse over any field until it turns into a magnifying glass and double-clicking. When you use this zoom feature to see a close up of one field (as shown in Figure 18.25), you can type an adjustment in the **Amount** field. Any number you include here is added to the previous amount shown.

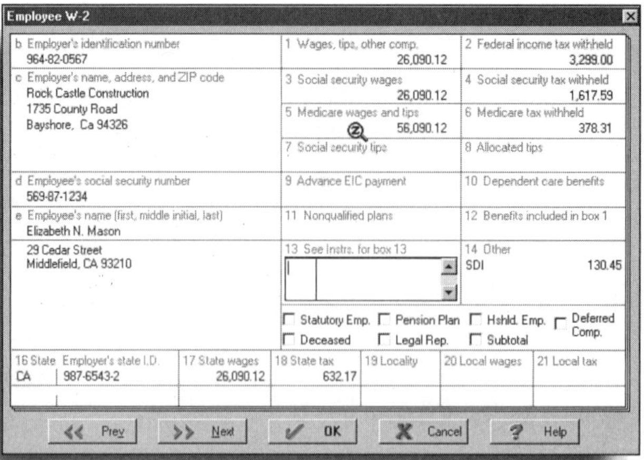

FIGURE 18.25

Click any W-2 field to make an adjustment.

Please note that this is your last chance to gracefully make changes in an employee's W-2. There are some instances in which you may really need to. For example, if you've provided a day-care service for your employees and want to obtain the dependent care tax credit for it, this is your last chance to put the fair market value of this service on an employee's W-2. Or, if you've provided scholarships or relocation assistance to employees and want to take tax credit for its fair market value, you can make such a change here.

After finishing with one employee's W-2, click **Next** to move on. When finished reviewing each, click **OK**. The Process W-2s dialog box reappears. If you've reviewed an employee's W-2, a Reviewed check appears near their name.

Printing W-2s

QuickBooks will not let you print W-2s until you've reviewed all of them. After you've done so, click the **Print** button. QuickBooks prepares to print any employee's W-2 who has a check to the left of their name in the Process W-2s dialog box. Because government regulations require a certain appearance to W-2s, there are very few alternate options available when printing out these forms.

Help with W-2 forms

If you are not sure of the significance of any W-2 field, press **F1** while the W-2 is onscreen, and QuickBooks' help system displays a clickable representation of the W-2 form. Click any field for a very helpful description and instructions on how to change or add data to that field.

Make sure the correct printer and printer type are selected, and do take the time to run a test print before loading up all your blank W-2s, pressing **Print** and running to get coffee. You might want to read the preceding sidenote, "Ordering and printing onto blank W-2 forms," before continuing.

Printing W-3s

The W-3 form is a single summary of all data from your W-2s, and QuickBooks only lets you print them out after you've properly reviewed (and ideally, printed) all your W-2s. To print one or more copies of your W-3 (all tax agencies would like to see a copy), open the Process W-2s dialog box and click the Print W-3 button.

Paying Independent Contractors

Contractors are people you pay to work for you who are not your employees. They should be tracked as vendors, and are not paid from your payroll accounts. Independent Contractors have special tax issues that need to be looked at. Each contractor that you pay over a certain dollar amount (currently $600 per year) needs to receive from you a 1099 form. (You'll also send a copy to the IRS.) Because you may not know at the year's outset which contractors will reach this $600 threshold, QuickBooks helps you keep track of how much contractors are paid, as well as manage the compiling and printing of 1099 forms at the end of the year.

You must supply each Form 1099 recipient with a copy of the 1099 form by January 31 of the following year. State government agencies and the IRS require copies of the forms be filed by February 28 of the following year.

Paying independent contractors

  1. First, you must turn on tracking for 1099 forms in the **Preferences** menu, and specify a 1099 category.

Previous year W-2 data

If you'd like to see W-2 data from previous years, select **Process W-2s** from the **Payroll and Employees** tab of the Navigator, and use the **Year** drop-down menu to dial in the year you'd like to review. You can also print out previous year's forms as well.

Penalties for not filing 1099 forms

It may seem like a lot of trouble to prepare and file 1099 forms, and you may even have some people who work for your company who would prefer that you just don't bother with the form.

Be aware that there are penalties that the taxing authorities will gladly charge if you don't comply with the law in this area. There is a $50 per form penalty for not providing 1099 forms to payees. Other penalties can apply for not filing the required copies of these forms with federal and state government agencies.

It is definitely in the interest of your company to file all required forms in a timely manner.

2. Then you must create or choose an account to use for paying 1099-eligible vendors. Having this special account makes it easier at the end of the year to track all contractors who've reached that payment threshold and need to receive the 1099 form.

3. As you add vendors that you want to track as independent contractors, make sure you select **Eligible for 1099** when setting up their information.

4. If you create a Service Item performed by a subcontractor, (For Example "Brickwork" or "Proofreading,") check **This Service is Performed by a Subcontractor** in the New Item dialog box.

5. Finally, at the end of the year, you can run 1099 reports, check and verify totals, and print out your 1099 forms.

Let's look at how to collect and print out all the 1099 data you need. First, we'll turn on 1099 Tracking.

Turning on 1099 tracking

1. Select **Preferences** from the **File** menu, and click the **Tax 1099** button on the left (see Figure 18.26). Make sure the **Company Preferences** Tab is showing. Answer **Yes** to "Do you file 1099-MISC forms?"

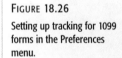

FIGURE 18.26

Setting up tracking for 1099 forms in the Preferences menu.

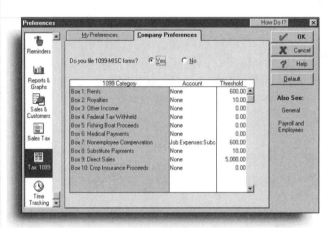

2. Although many category options are available, Box 7 is the one used in tracking nonemployees being paid for services. Move your mouse down to the Box 7 line.

3. In the **Account** field, choose an account for following payments made to independent contractors. By default, QuickBooks sets up a subaccount called Subcontractors (under Job Expenses) for this purpose. You may choose this account, or create a new one, if you want.

4. In the **Amount** field, type a threshold amount. This amount is currently $600. To find out if it's changed, call Intuit at 1-800-771-7248.

Now we'll go over how to set up an Independent Contractor, and retrieve 1099 information at the year's end.

Setting up and tracking independent contractors

1. Create a **Vendor Item** as usual, selecting **New** from the **Vendor** menu of the Vendor List.

2. Click the **Additional Info** tab (see Figure 18.27).

3. Check the **Vendor Eligible for 1099** box. After doing this, QuickBooks tracks how much money you pay this vendor throughout the year, and makes such information available for reports and creating 1099 forms.

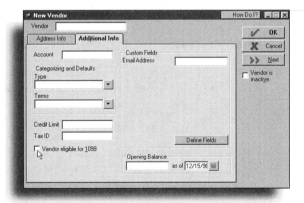

FIGURE 18.27
Setting up a Vendor for 1099 eligibility tracking.

4. At the end of the year, open the **Vendors List**, and select the **Reports** drop-down menu.

5. Choose **Reports on all Vendors**, then **A/P report**, and finally, 1099 Report (see Figure 18.28).

6. You see a list of all vendors that are eligible for 1099 reports. Printing the actual 1099 forms is covered in the very last section of this chapter, curiously titled "Printing 1099 Forms."

FIGURE 18.28

Choosing a report that prepares you for mailing 1099 forms to vendors.

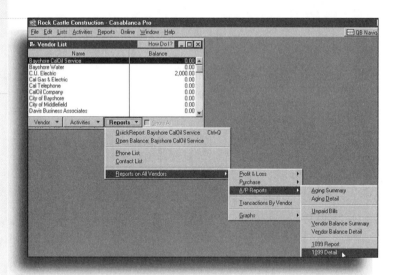

SEE ALSO

➤ *For information about obtaining tax forms from the IRS and state governments, see Chapter 23, "Going Online with QuickBooks", page 451*

Checking Your 1099 List for Missing Vendors

Sometimes a Vendor can be missing from the list. The following are some steps for making sure every eligible vendor is on it.

Checking for missing vendors

1. Open the 1099 report, as outlined in the preceding section

2. Use the three drop-down menus at the top (see Figure 18.29) to view all vendors, and then view all vendors eligible for 1099.

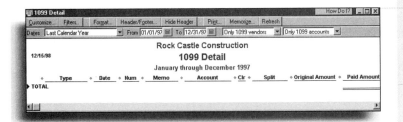

FIGURE 18.29

The drop-down menus to the right help track down vendors missing from the 1099 reports.

3. If you notice someone who should have been set up for 1099 forms, but wasn't, double-click that vendor's name, which brings up the Edit Vendor dialog box.

4. Click the **Additional Info** tab and place a check by "Eligible for 1099." You now see that vendor's name among others who are eligible for 1099s.

5. If you think someone is still missing, use the Use Threshold drop-down menu at the upper right of the 1099 report to view all qualifying vendors regardless of their threshold amount. Perhaps someone just "squeaked under" the qualifying amount.

Printing 1099 Forms

After verifying that every vendor is on the 1099 report who should be, open the **Vendor List** (From the **List** menu, select **Vendor**. Select the Vendor drop-down menu on the bottom left of the list, and choose **Print 1099**.

QuickBooks and Taxes

Understand what an employer's responsibilities are regarding taxes

Generate checks for paying tax liabilities

Set up tax withholdings, deductions, and statuses for employees

Create new payroll items for taxes

Fill out and troubleshoot tax forms 941 and 940

Locate and fix common Liability Amount Due mistakes, and make adjustments in the Liability Adjustments window

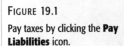

Make YTD amount adjustments first

For QuickBooks to have an accurate picture of all your tax liabilities, make necessary adjustments using the YTD Amounts feature (see the preceding chapter).

As an employer and business owner, your basic responsibilities regarding taxes are as follows:

- Make sure you've set up each employee to have taxes deducted from his paycheck. QuickBooks does not create state disability or state unemployment tax items, so you have to create those yourself. See the previous chapter for instructions on how to create payroll tax items.

- Send Federal taxes you deducted to Federal tax agencies such as the IRS and Social Security.

- Send state taxes you deducted to state tax agencies. To do this, you may have to calculate a wage base, which QuickBooks does for you. A Wage Base actually helps insure that you do not pay too much. We explore this in detail.

- Create and send quarterly 941 forms stating your tax liabilities.

- Create and send a yearly 940 form, which reports your federal unemployment tax (FUTA) liability.

The following are your tools for managing these tasks:

- Use the **Employee List** to set up tax status, withholding, and allowances for each employee.

- Create checks for mailing in your taxes by clicking the **Pay Liabilities** icon on the **Payroll and Time** tab of the Navigator (see Figure 19.1).

FIGURE 19.1

Pay taxes by clicking the **Pay Liabilities** icon.

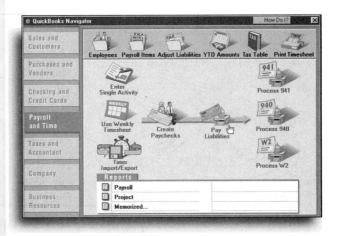

- Double-check the amounts you owe by looking over the three main Payroll reports—Summary by Employee, Employee Journal, and Liabilities by Item. (The names of these reports may vary slightly for QuickBooks standard version users.)

- Create 941 forms by clicking the **Process 941** icon on the **Payroll and Time** tab of the Navigator. (Figure 19.2 shows a complete 941 form.)

- Create 940 forms by clicking the **Process 940** icon on the same tab.

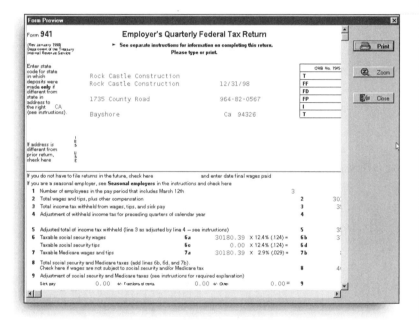

FIGURE 19.2
A completed form 941.

Creating Checks to Pay Your Taxes

Regarding Federal taxes, when you obtain your Employer ID number, you should have also received a booklet of coupons for mailing in your tax payments. These tax payments are all the monies you've been collecting from employee's paychecks for various Federal taxes, and they need to be mailed regularly. Mailing these coupons with your payment assures that you receive credit for your payment.

To pay all tax-related liabilities that have been set up as payroll items (see the preceding chapter), click the **Payroll and Time** tab on the Navigator, and select the **Pay Liabilities** icon. You see the Pay Liabilities dialog box. (See Figure 19.3. Standard Edition users: The tab may be called Payroll and Employees.)

FIGURE 19.3

The Pay Liabilities dialog box. Here you can choose what taxes to pay at the moment, or pay them all with one click.

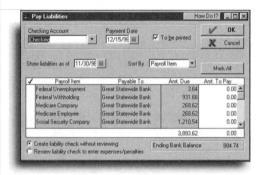

Among other things, the choices you make here determine how much you pay on each payroll item and what account to use in payment.

Making a liability payment

1. When you're ready to pay taxes, click the **Pay Liabilities** icon on the **Payroll and Time** tab of the Navigator, which opens the Pay Liabilities dialog box.

2. By default, payment is made from your checking account. Choose a different account if you'd like.

3. The **Show Liabilities As Of** field shows all taxes not yet paid, up to the end of the previous month. If you pay more often than once a month, choose a more recent date.

4. To create a check to be mailed at a later date, change the **Payment Date** field. QuickBooks reminds you of this date when the time to mail the check draws near.

5. To use QuickBooks' checks for these payments, check the **To Be Printed** box. If you're writing them by hand, remove the check.

6. Check the far left area of the liabilities you intend to pay now, or click the **Mark All** button.

A note to QuickBooks standard edition users

The tab discussed here may be called **Payroll and Employees**, rather than **Payroll and Time**.

Choosing who should receive the check

When setting up each liability payroll item, you also named a tax agency or a bank as a vendor to receive the check. If, however, one of the payroll items you've set up is not associated with a vendor (you've not yet determined which bank or agency to send it to), you receive a warning, and that item's edit dialog box opens, prompting you to select one. The vendor you choose should be a bank empowered to handle your tax disbursements, or the tax agency itself.

7. Review the payroll items and the amount, making sure the amounts seem right to you. (Later in this chapter, you learn how to find errors in the Amount Due, and make adjustments.)

8. By default, QuickBooks creates checks for the entire amount due. If you want to pay a different amount, click any line in the **Amount to Pay** field and type a new amount. The Amount Due total at the bottom of the dialog box decreases by the amount you choose to pay.

9. Using the options at the bottom left, indicate whether you want QuickBooks to create the checks without your review or whether you need an opportunity to make adjustments.

10. Click **OK**, and your accounts are appropriately updated. If you've indicated that you want to review the check before sending it, a check appears on the screen. Make manual adjustments as needed. Click **OK** to add the check to the printing queue.

Although you can certainly make manual adjustments in your checks to tax agencies, it's best to try tracking down the actual mistakes in your Liability accounts. Later in this chapter, we describe making liability adjustments and reports that help you find the errors.

Writing Two Liability Checks to the Same Vendor

Most employers establish a relationship with a single bank, empowering it to do the actual check distribution to the various tax agencies. When QuickBooks sees a single vendor name to receive tax liability payments (see Figure 19.4), it simply issues one check to that vendor.

Sending two liability checks to a single vendor

1. Create a new vendor item using a dummy name.

2. Assign one of the amounts to that new vendor. That way, you get two checks printed.

3. When you are finally reviewing the checks before you print them, change the vendor name of the dummy vendor back to the real vendor.

4. You still get two checks printed, both to the same vendor.

Don't press Enter after typing an amount

After typing in a new amount number in the **Amt to Pay** window, view your change by clicking any other line. Pressing **Enter** has the same effect as clicking the **OK** button. The Pay Liabilities box disappears, and QuickBooks records your transaction as complete.

How tax credits are shown

If you are eligible for tax credits, such as the Advanced Earned Income Credit, these appear in the Pay Liabilities dialog box as negative numbers.

FIGURE 19.4

Although this check is payment for many taxes, there is one payee.

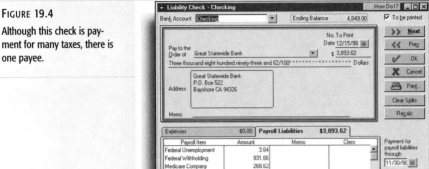

Setting Up Employee Tax Status, Withholding, and Allowances

When you create an employee item, you notice three tabs. One of them is **Payroll Info**. In the previous chapter, we described using **Payroll Info** to set up earnings and specific tax items for each employee, but we've yet to discuss how to make QuickBooks aware of standard tax information that every new employee specifies when hired.

Setting up an employee's tax status

1. Select **Employees** from the **Lists** menu, and click **New** from the **Employee** drop-down menu.

2. Select the **Payroll Info** tab (see Figure 19.5).

FIGURE 19.5

The **Payroll Info** tab, for storing payroll information on an employee.

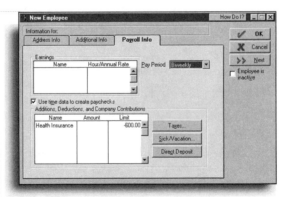

3. Select the **Taxes** button, and you will see the Taxes dialog box (see Figure 19.6).

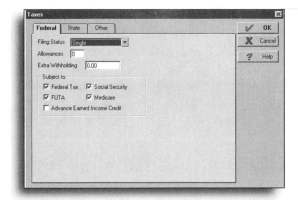

FIGURE 19.6

Use the Taxes dialog box to keep a record of tax status on an employee.

The Taxes dialog box is divided into three tabs: **Federal**, **State**, and **Other**.

Federal Taxes

Select the **Federal taxes** tab to choose **employee federal tax options**.

Setting up federal tax options for an employee

1. Use the drop-down menu at the top to select a **Filing Status** for this employee. Choose **Single**, **Married**, or **Head of Household**.

2. In the indicated boxes, type the number of allowances and dollar amount for **Extra Withholding**.

3. In the **Subject To** panel, indicate whether there are any taxes that this employee is not subject to. By default, every check box is selected, except for **Advanced Earned Income Credit**. (We discuss AEIC later in this chapter.) If you know an employee is going to be earning an amount below the threshold for paying federal income tax, you can deselect that option, but saying it doesn't make it so. It's probably better to let QuickBooks determine that status based on the Tax Table.

4. Click the **State** tab to set up state tax information for this employee.

State Taxes

Select the **State taxes** tab (see Figure 19.7) to choose options for this employee's state tax status.

FIGURE 19.7

Click the **State** taxes tab to maintain state tax status on an employee.

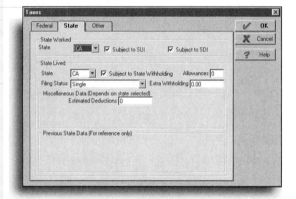

No SDI option?

If you do not see an SDI option, don't worry. Your state may not deduct for state disability insurance.

Setting up state tax deductions

1. Use the drop-down menus to choose a state where this employee works, and if different, a state where he lives.

Indicate with the check boxes whether this employee is subject to **State Disability Insurance** (SDI) and **State Unemployment Insurance**. Check with your accountant or your state tax board for more information about this choice.

2. Most states require that an employee specify filing status (single, married, head of household), allowances, and extra withholding amounts. If your state is among those that want this information, fill in the various windows in the **State Lived** panel.

3. QuickBooks includes a Miscellaneous Data area for some states. For example, California requires employees to include estimated deductions, if applicable. Type something in this area if the employee requires it.

4. Click **OK** if you are done, or if a special tax needs to be applied (perhaps a local or unique state tax) select the **Other** tab.

Other Tax

If a tax was created that does not fall neatly into the categories of state or federal, click the **Other Tax** tab (see Figure 19.8) to apply it to this employee.

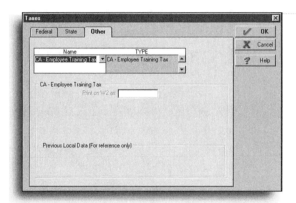

FIGURE 19.8

For city or county taxes, click the Other Tab. QuickBooks has predefined taxes for a number of U.S. municipalities.

Applying an Other Tax to an employee

1. Use the drop-down menu in the **Name** field to choose an **Other Tax** to apply to this employee. If it suddenly occurs to you that you need to create this new tax item, just click **Add New**.

2. If you choose **Add New**, you see the New Payroll Item dialog box (discussed later in this chapter in the section "Creating a New Tax Payroll Item").

3. An option or two may appear below the **Name** field. If so, type the appropriate information.

4. Click **OK**, and you're finished setting up tax information for this employee.

Supplying Wage Base Information for State Taxes

QuickBooks does not print state tax forms but can help you in preparing the information you need, making it much easier to fill them out.

Some states calculate state taxes on a wage base. A wage base is an employee's taxable salary, and can be defined as follows:

- If an employee has pretax deductions such as 401K and flexible spending accounts, these sums are subtracted from the total wages, and the remainder is the Wage Base.

- In some instances, a wage base excludes employee overtime hours, and shift differential payment.

- The wage base also refers to annual limits on certain taxes. For example, only the first $7,000 dollars of an employee's annual salary is subject to federal unemployment tax. Likewise, employees do not pay Social Security tax on earnings above $68,000 annually.

You can locate every employee's wage base by opening the Payroll Item Detail report, as follows.

Locating employee wage base info

1. Click the **Reports** drop-down menu from the **Employee List**.

2. Choose **Reports On All Employees**, followed by **Payroll**, and **Item Detail** (see Figure 19.9).

3. Every employee is represented in this report, and it shows the following detail:

   - Each row represents a salary type paid to each employee.

   - Near the bottom of the report, other payroll items such as deductions and contributions are reported, row by row.

   - If you've not customized the report, then the sixth column from the right should list the wage base for each employee's salary.

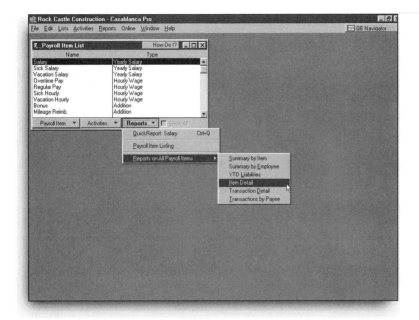

FIGURE 19.9
The Item Detail report lists
wage base information.

4. Note every employee's wage base, and include those numbers as needed in your state tax forms.

Setting Up Payroll Items to Collect State Taxes

In the previous chapter, we discussed how to set up new payroll items. You can create payroll items to collect taxes at a certain rate or dollar amount, and they can be applied to each employee's paycheck. (If you have employees that work in other states, see the Out of State Employees sidebar.) However, you may not have to create new payroll items for state taxes because when you conduct the EasyStep Interview, you make QuickBooks aware of your company's location. As part of the setup process, QuickBooks, in turn, uses the current tax table data to set up state-related payroll items for your state. Therefore, in order to collect adequate state taxes from each employee, you might not need to set up any additional payroll items. (You still have to set up each employee's state tax status, withholdings, and so on, as outlined in the previous section.)

Below is a list of state tax items that are likely to appear in your **Payroll Items List**:

- Withholding
- Disability
- Unemployment
- Employee training

Creating a New Tax Payroll Item

To create a new payroll item for deducting taxes from employee's paychecks, select **New Item** from the **Payroll Item List's** drop-down Payroll menu. You see the Add New Payroll Item dialog box (see Figure 19.10). Check the type of item you want to create. If you try to create a payroll item for a tax for which QuickBooks has already set you up, you are not allowed to proceed. In fact, you find that most of them already are in place. If you do need to set up an additional state or local city tax, follow the steps below.

FIGURE 19.10

Create a new Tax Payroll item just as you would any other payroll item.

Setting up a New Payroll Item

1. Select **New Item** from the **Payroll Item List's** drop-down Payroll menu.

2. The Add New Payroll Item dialog box appears. Select a payroll item type and click **Next**.

3. If you selected **Other Payroll Item**, indicate whether this tax is to be paid by the company (that would be you), or the

employee. Click the **Other Tax** drop-down list (see Figure 19.11) to see whether QuickBooks has created a predefined tax that suits your needs. If you select a **State Tax Item**, your options depend greatly on what state you chose.

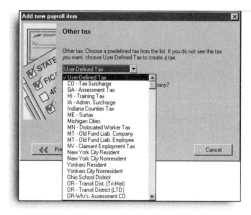

FIGURE 19.11
Review one of QuickBooks Other Tax options, to see whether a predefined tax suits your needs.

4. Whether you select **Other Tax** or **State Tax**, you're prompted by a series of dialog boxes to do the following:
   * Type the name of the tax item you are creating.
   * Assign an account to the item.
   * Indicate the agency to be paid.
   * Provide an identifying employer number that you set up with the agency.
   * Select an option describing how this tax item will be tracked on tax forms.

5. If applicable, you're then asked to indicate a **Calculation Type** (see Figure 19.12; your Calculation Type screen might have fewer options). Your tax item could appear as
   * A dollar amount.
   * A percentage of total pay.
   * A dollar amount times a quantity.

6. You have to fill in a default tax rate (a percentage that applies equally to all employees) and a ceiling amount for this tax.

FIGURE 19.12

QuickBooks asks how your
new tax item should be calculated.

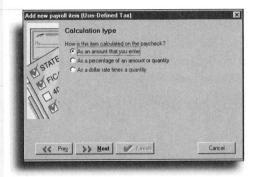

FIGURE 19.12

QuickBooks asks how your
new tax item should be calculated.

7. Finally, in the Taxable Compensation dialog box, check all
wage types that have an affect on this tax (see Figure 19.13),
and click the **Finish** button. Removing a check from a wage
type means that money earned via that particular wage type
is not taxed.

FIGURE 19.13

If you want certain income
types to not be affected by this
new tax, remove the check by
its name.

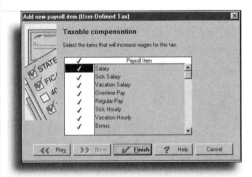

8. Your new tax item appears on the **Payroll Item List** with
all the others and can be applied to any employee's paycheck who lives in the state or city in question.

Creating a Report of State Payroll Taxes

Out-of-state employees

If you have an employee who lives
out of your state, do not collect
state taxes for your state from her
paycheck. Ask your accountant
whether that employee's state
requires that you collect and submit
taxes on her behalf. It may be that
her state simply requires that she
report the additional income herself.

Sometimes it's helpful to see various breakdowns of state taxes
you deducted, either by Payroll Item, or by Employee. The
difference is as follows:

- Viewing a state tax report **By Employee** enables you to
  see in a simple list how much state tax was deducted from
  each employee.

■ Viewing a report **By Item** enables you to see each state tax deduction paycheck by paycheck.

For our example, let's look at **By Employee**.

Creating a state tax report for each employee

1. Open the **Employee List**, and click the **Reports** drop-down menu.

2. Click **Reports on All Employees, Payroll**, and **Summary by Employee**. (Figure 19.14 shows the report. The Standard Edition may title the report Summary by Employee Earnings.)

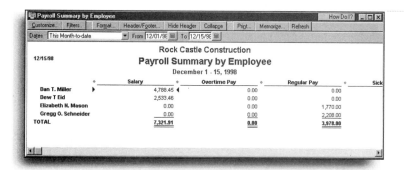

FIGURE 19.14

The Summary by Employee report can generate a report of state taxes. Standard Edition users may find that the report has a slightly different title.

3. Adjust the time (From and To date range) frame of the report to suit your needs, perhaps locating some anomaly in a deduction you are trying to track down.

4. On the upper-left of the Report, click the Filters button.

5. In the Filters window, scroll down and click **Payroll Item** (see Figure 19.15). You notice the drop-down menu next to it changes to read Payroll Item.

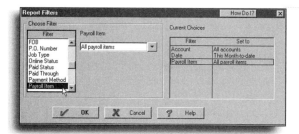

FIGURE 19.15

Creating a filter to track a certain payroll item in a report.

6. Click the drop-down menu, and click **Selected Payroll Items**, near the top of the menu. A new window appears, called Select Payroll Items.

7. Scroll down and locate the State Withholding item created for your state. In this example, CA-Withholding is selected (see Figure 19.16).

FIGURE 19.16

Locating a state tax item in a list of Payroll Items.

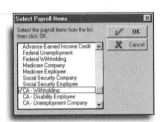

8. Notice that the Current Choices window on the Filters dialog box now includes an entry: Selected Payroll Items. (It may be simply titled Payroll Items.) Click **OK**, and view the Report.

9. The report now shows a list of employees and the amounts deducted for state tax withholding.

10. To view paycheck-by-paycheck detail, double-click a deduction amount next to any employee's name (shown in Figure 19.17).

FIGURE 19.17

In a report, you can select a specific transaction by clicking it.

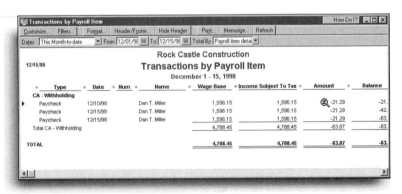

Preparing, Reviewing, and Printing Form 941

Form 941 is a quarterly tax form on which you report federal income tax withheld, as well as Social Security and Medicare tax. Because these taxes are based on total wages you paid your employees, QuickBooks makes creating this form very easy.

You should create and mail form 941 at the end of every quarter, and creating one is as easy as clicking the **Process Form 941** icon on the **Payroll and Time** tab of the QuickBooks navigator. After clicking that icon, QuickBooks steps you through a Wizard that creates form 941 information line by line, just as if you were filling out the paper version. You're asked to provide the following figures:

- Number of employees whom you paid
- Wages paid and income withheld from wages
- Social Security and Medicare tax withholding
- Withholding adjustments you need to make carried over from last quarter

The good news is that as you click Next and move through each set of questions, QuickBooks has already filled in the answers. Most often, you just salute the numbers as they sail by. In the final screens, you see the following:

- You're asked whether you want to apply an overpayment (if there is one) to the following quarter, or be mailed a refund (see Figure 19.18).

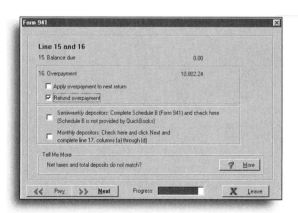

FIGURE 19.18

In creating form 941, QuickBooks asks you how to apply an overpayment.

- You receive a last chance to make final adjustments to each month in the quarter.

- Finally, you can print or preview the form as it will appear when it's printed. (Form 941 can be printed on a blank, 8 1/2 x 11 inches piece of paper.)

Making Adjustments

You can make adjustments if you need to, typing in new numbers as you go along. Figure 19.19 shows a typical dialog box from the Form 941 Wizard.

FIGURE 19.19

In this typical 941 Wizard dialog box, you can simply approve the numbers or click Yes to edit them.

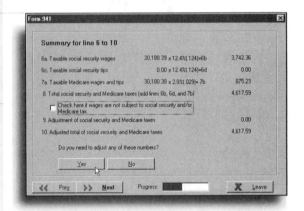

Notice that numbers are provided, and you can adjust the numbers simply by clicking the Yes button. The question arises, though: Where do I get the information to make these adjustments? How do I know whether the numbers are right or wrong? We discuss that issue momentarily.

Beyond simply stepping through the Form 941 Wizard and double-checking the salary and deduction dollar amounts QuickBooks uses to create the final form, not much is here that can throw you. You are, however, asked these three questions while completing the form, and you might want to have the information handy:

- Are you obligated to file 941 Forms in the future? What date will you be issuing your final paychecks?

- Are you a seasonal employer? (Special rules apply to them.)
- If your monthly tax liability is particularly high, isn't it better to pay biweekly instead?

Creating Form 940

Form 940 is an annual tax form on which you report your federal unemployment tax (FUTA) liability (see Figure 19.20).

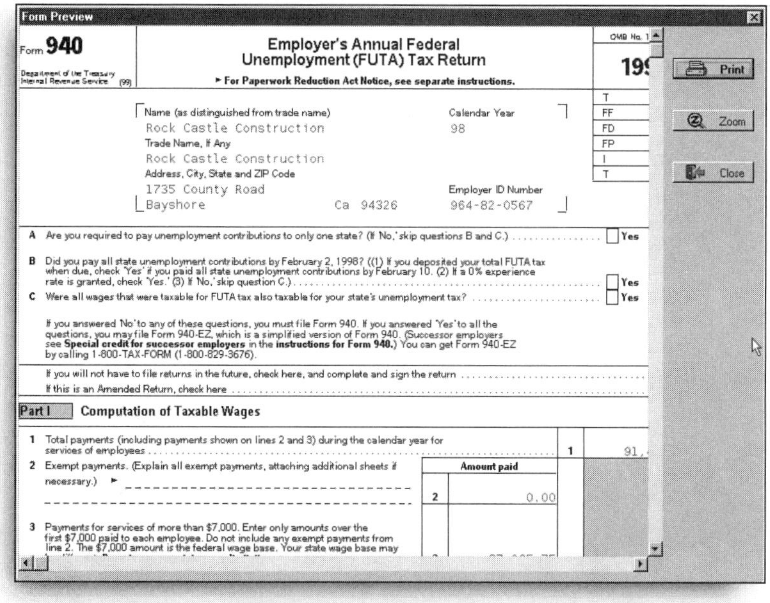

FIGURE 19.20

A QuickBooks-generated Federal Income Tax Report, which you file yearly.

Organizing your FUTA information and creating form 490

1. Click the **Payroll and Time** tab of the Navigator and select the **Process 940** icon. The Form 940 Wizard appears.

2. Fill out form 940 by stepping through a series of dialog boxes, acknowledging the information that QuickBooks has already provided in each of the windows (see Figure 19.21).

3. Like form 941, you can edit the information at any time, simply by clicking the **Yes** button, as shown in the preceding figure, or later, you may reopen the Form 940 Wizard and choose to edit the form, rather than create a new one.

FIGURE 19.21
Step through the form 940 dialog boxes to fill out the form.

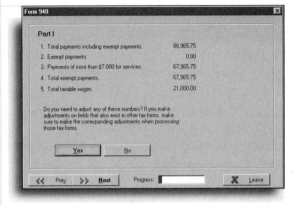

$7,000 limit on FUTA tax

You must only collect federal unemployment taxes on the first $7,000 of an employee's income. So expect to find that your FUTA taxable income is equal to the number of employees you have, times $7,000. You may, however, owe more than that if there were payments not made in the previous year, and you may owe less than that if you made contributions to a state unemployment tax.

4. The following are some of the questions you have to be prepared to answer and numbers that need your approval:

- Indicate whether you are required to pay unemployment contributions in only one state.

- Indicate whether you paid all the previous year's unemployment contributions by January of this year.

- Specify whether all wages that were taxable for federal unemployment tax were also taxable by your state unemployment tax.

- Verify total wages paid, and verify any prior FUTA payments during the current year. As QuickBooks fills out form 940, you notice that the income taxable by FUTA equals $7,000 times the number of employees you have. Notice in the preceding example in Figure 19.21, the QuickBooks sample company has three employees, thus the total FUTA taxable income is $21,000.

- Verify any carryover unpaid FUTA tax from the previous year.

5. If you are to receive a refund, you're asked whether you want to apply it to the following tax year or be issued a refund check.

6. Finally, you're given an opportunity to make any adjustments to unemployment liability for each quarter of the year (see Figure 19.22) and asked whether you want to print or preview your form 940.

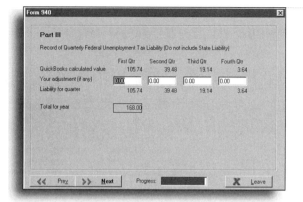

FIGURE 19.22

Before final approval and printing of your form 940, you can make adjustments to any quarter of the year.

Reports That Help with Tax Corrections

As mentioned earlier, when paying taxes with QuickBooks, the process is mostly a matter of stepping through dialog boxes, clicking Next, and verifying the numbers used to generate the payments. The same goes for creating tax forms. You answer a few questions about special circumstances, previous payments and such, and just approve the figures as they sail by. The trouble is, what if you sense something is amiss? How do you track down the error? Do you have reports that break down the figures for you, perhaps paycheck by paycheck? Yes, you do.

You have essentially three reports that break down amounts you've deducted from each employee's paycheck, contributions, and prior payments, as well as reports that specify your company's total tax liability for any given period of time. They are listed as follows (Standard Edition users may find the reports have slightly different names):

- Summary by Employee
- Summary by Item
- Employee Quick Report

Summary by Employee

The payroll Summary by Employee report shows each employee's gross pay (which includes salary, hourly wages, commissions,

How QuickBooks names payroll tax items

When viewing a report that includes standard federal and state taxes, it's helpful to understand how they are named. Some taxes, such as Social Security, are contributed to by both the employer and employee. Some contributions are made only by the employer, and others–by the employee. In any tax generated by QuickBooks, look at the final word of its name, and you see who the contributor is. For example, the payroll item Medicare Company refers to the company's share of the Medicare tax. Social Security Employee refers to the employee's share of Social Security.

Some taxes, as you can see, are comprised of two items: one item collects the employee's share and the other collects the employer's share. Keep this in mind as you scroll through reports interpreting the items they refer to.

and any other additions), as well as sick and vacation pay. Employees are divided into rows, and each Payroll Item has its own column, as shown in Figure 19.23. (Standard Edition users may find that this report is titled Employee Earnings Summary.)

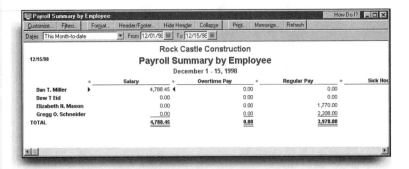

FIGURE 19.23

The Summary by Employee report.

The following information from this report is of particular interest during tax time:

- Deductions from gross pay
- Gross pay after deductions
- Taxes withheld
- Deductions from net pay
- Net Pay after deductions
- Employer-paid taxes and contributions

To access the Summary by Employee report, select Reports On All Employees from the Report drop-down menu of the Payroll Items list, and choose Summary by Employee. Please note that this report is wider than your computer screen, and you have to scroll to the right to see additional columns.

Summary by Item

The Summary by Item report is similar to Summary by Employee, except each employee has his own column, and Payroll Items are broken into rows. Access it by clicking the drop-down Report Menu on the Payroll list, choosing Reports on all Employees, and then Summary by Item.

Searching for More Specific Information

Using the Employee Quick Reports mentioned above, you have three ways to quickly drill down to find the information you may be looking for.

Change the Date Range

At the top of every report are Date fields. Use the drop-down Dates menu to select a new time scope for your report. When searching for the source of an error, it helps to be able to quickly include or exclude more dates from your report. To choose a very specific date range, use the From and To windows at the top of the report, specifying only the dates you have in mind.

Use Filters To Isolate Specific Payroll Items

Suppose that you have a strong suspicion that an error is occurring because somebody is being taxed twice for sick hours. You could check to see whether sick hours were double-reported (stranger things have happened). The following steps show how a report could help.

Isolate a specific payroll item with a report

1. Open the report you want to filter.

2. Click the Filters button at the upper left of the report. The Report Filters dialog box opens.

3. In the Filters window, scroll down and click **Payroll Items**.

4. The drop-down menu to the right of the Filters window is now labeled Payroll Items. Click that drop-down menu.

5. Click **Selected Payroll Items**. The Selected Payroll Items dialog box appears.

6. This dialog box shows all payroll items. Scroll down and click the item you want specifically to see.

7. On the Report Filters dialog box, the Current Choices Window now includes the filter you selected.

8. You can actually go back to the Filters drop-down menu and add more filters if you want—for example, narrowing your search to a specific Job Type.

9. When you are happy with your choices, click **OK**, and a new report is generated, showing only the items you want to see.

You may drill down further, clicking a specific line to see the check in question, as outlined in the section below.

Double-Click a Specific Transaction

When you find a line in a report referring to some transaction that might be the source of your problem, double-click it, and drill down even further to see the source document from which a particular line from a report is taken.

Locating a paycheck deduction that might be in error

1. Open the Summary by Item or Summary by Employee report, and locate a line showing a figure that is perhaps too high or too low.

2. Double-click that line. Figure 19.24 shows the user clicking the Medicare Employee line for a particular employee.

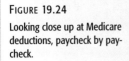

FIGURE 19.24

Looking close up at Medicare deductions, paycheck by paycheck.

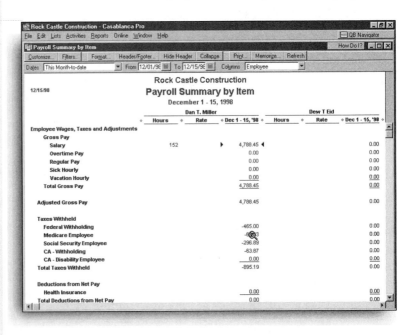

3. You see a brief report open that breaks down that employee's check-by-check contribution to Medicare.

4. Click a specific line in that new report. That line refers to a specific check paid out on a specific date.

5. An actual check appears on the screen. View the numbers here to see whether something is amiss.

6. Return to the first report you opened and view any other check that seems questionable.

Common Problems with Tax Figures

Let's look at a few typical situations that cause your liability account to report inaccurate numbers.

Federal Unemployment Tax Seems High

If the amount you owe for Federal Unemployment tax seems higher than you expected (you see how much your FUTA tax is when creating a Form 940), you probably forgot to treat yourself to the state contributions tax credit.

Getting QuickBooks to acknowledge FUTA tax credit

1. First, check with your accountant to make sure you can take this credit. If you pay state unemployment, then you probably can.

2. Locate the payroll item called **Federal Unemployment** in the Payroll Item List.

3. Double-click it to edit it.

4. Click the **Next** button twice, and you see the Federal Unemployment Tax Credit dialog box (shown in Figure 19.25).

5. Select **%0.8**, rather than %6.2.

6. Continue to click **Next** until you arrive at the final screen, and then click **Finish**.

7. Click the **Process 940** icon on the **Payroll and Time** tab. One of the final screens shows how much you owe for federal. The amount should be much lower now.

FIGURE 19.25

Make sure you are getting credited for your state unemployment payments by editing the Federal Unemployment tax Payroll Item.

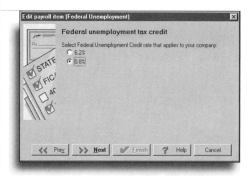

Liability Amounts Seem Incorrect

The following are a few things to check when you select **Pay Liabilities** from the **Payroll and Time** tab of the Navigator and the amount you owe seems wrong.

Checking for tax liability errors

1. Check the Show Liabilities As Of date.

    By default, the Pay Liabilities window shows amounts due as of the last day of the previous month. If you made a payment during the current calendar month, the Pay Liabilities dialog boxes do not show correct amounts. To be credited for this most recent payment, move the Show Liabilities As Of date forward to include the date of that payment.

2. If you used the Write Checks window to make payments on any tax liability, the Pay Liabilities window does not credit these payments. To receive credit, you have to make a manual adjustment using the Adjust Liabilities window (see next section). For proper accounting, you have to use the Pay Liabilities feature to make tax payments of any type.

3. Pay attention to Tax Tracking. Perhaps the payroll item itself was applied on an employee's paycheck incorrectly. When you add a new deduction or contribution to an employee's paycheck, you use the Payroll info tab of the New Employee dialog box to specify how deductions and additions should affect salary and taxable income. (See the sidebar "How tax tracking affects deductions.")

4. The Tax Tracking window of the Add New Payroll Item dialog box enables you to determine exactly how this item affects the employee's taxes. When you select a Tax Tracking option from the drop-down list, QuickBooks shows a paragraph or two explaining how that particular item affects taxable income.

Correcting Liability Amount Errors

The following are two examples of potential errors in your QuickBooks liability account records:

- You once paid an employee from an account not associated with QuickBooks.
- You used the Write Check Window to pay last month's liabilities, and QuickBooks did not credit your payment.

Now that you've figured out why your numbers were off, what do you do about it? How do you make QuickBooks aware of the additional income or deductions you need to apply?

Fixing tax liability errors

1. Note the amount of the adjustment you need to make, and the type of payroll items you want to adjust (for example, if you made a company-contributed health insurance payment last week from your paper checkbook, you need to update the payroll item Health Insurance Company.)

2. Select the **Payroll and Time** tab from the QuickBooks Navigator and click the **Adjust Liabilities** icon. The Liability Adjustment dialog box opens (shown in Figure 19.26).

3. The current date appears in the Date window at the upper left. Make sure the For Period Ending window shows the pay period that is affected by this adjustment.

4. Specify whether this adjustment affects a particular employee or a company payment or contribution.

5. In the **Item Name** field, use the drop-down menu to choose a Payroll Item to adjust.

How tax tracking affects deductions

Payroll additions or deductions all affect tax liability, but you often need to specify whether this payroll item should tax gross pay or net pay. Also, the sequence of payroll items as they appear on an employee's Paycheck Detail can make a difference. For example, if you set up a payroll item that pays an employee extra for working weekends, that item needs to appear above any company's contribution that is a percentage of gross pay.

FIGURE **19.26**
The Liability Adjustment dialog box.

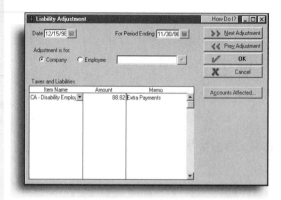

6. Type a dollar amount in the **Amount** field.

7. Include a memo to later jog your memory regarding this adjustment.

8. In the **Item Name** field, click additional lines to make adjustments to other items, if needed.

9. If you really did use a QuickBooks account to make this payment but just used the Write Checks window to write the liability check, then click **Affected Accounts**, and check **Do Not Affect Accounts**.

10. If you are making QuickBooks aware of a payment made from a source that had nothing to do with QuickBooks (for example, a paper checking account you don't normally use for this purpose), then click **Affected Accounts**, and check **Affect Liability and Expense Accounts**.

11. If your adjustment requires you to calculate from a Base Wage, click the **Show Wage Base** button to view it momentarily.

12. If you are making adjustments for several pay periods, **Click Next Adjustment** or **Prev Adjustment** to move on.

13. After making your final adjustment, click **OK**.

Setting Up Advanced Earned Income Credit

If an employee of yours makes below a certain income threshold and has a qualifying child, he can be eligible for Advanced Earned Income Credit. Currently, the total credit you must pay to a qualifying employee can be as much as $1326.00 for the year. The following are some facts about how this process works:

- AEIC is a way for low-income individuals who expect to pay little or no federal income tax to avoid having to wait until the end of the year to file for a return refund.

- To establish eligibility for AEIC payments, your employee must fill out and return to you a W-5 form (also known as an Earned Income Credit Advance Payment Certificate). Call 1-800-829-3676 to obtain one.

- QuickBooks has created a payroll item called Advanced Earned Income Credit, which you can quickly apply to any qualifying employee's paycheck, and the payments can be generated automatically.

- You, the employer, actually make this payment to the employee as part of the regular paycheck process, and in turn, deduct what you paid the employee from your tax burden at the end of the year.

- At the end of the year, when you create a Form 941, you notice a provision exists (summary for Line 11 to 14) for claiming your AEIC payments.

- Finally, in order to feed the right AEIC figures to your Form 941, you need to generate a report showing how much you paid out. Simply use the Payroll Summary by Item report, creating a filter as previously outlined. QuickBooks includes an AEIC payroll item for which you can easily create a report.

Making QuickBooks Work for You

Customizing QuickBook Forms

Select which form would be the easiest to customize for your needs

Edit a form's text and fonts, changing font size, color, and appearance

Personalize your forms by turning fields and columns on and off

Edit a form's layout, rearranging where the title, address, and other fields appear

Change a field's label and default text

Add a customized form to the icon bar

There are many reasons why you might want to customize a form. You could:

- Add your name, address, or color logo at the top of the form.
- Create unique invoices for each type of customer you have.
- Add fields for customer-specific information, such as shipping and handling charges.
- Specify that certain information should be seen on the onscreen version of your form, but not be printed.
- Customize your sales slips, adding fields for new information to one version, while removing them from another.
- Use the **Layout Designer** to move and resize fields and columns. This is helpful if you create a large logo that you want to appear prominently on your form.
- Create a special packing slip for checking the total of ordered goods versus the number that actually arrives in a particular shipment.
- Add fields that allow you to keep track of specific aspects of your client base, such as a special distinction for those who have placed especially large orders in the last year, or those who are more than three months behind in their payments.

Create a field that tracks clients by industry. Then you could have one form available for customers from the entertainment business and another for publishers and journalists, for example. After you have this industry-specific information on hand, you could create a direct mailing tailored for each type of client, and, most importantly, note which type of industry is most highly represented among your newer clients.

Customizing a Form

In QuickBooks, you can quickly customize a form by adding and removing fields. For more substantive changes, you can alter the form's layout, moving fields around the form and resizing them. Let's learn how to customize various types of forms.

Onscreen versus printing

QuickBooks enables you to quickly specify which fields of a form you want to see onscreen and which should be printed. For example, the customer's birthday might be handy to know, but you probably don't want it printed on an invoice or purchase order.

When to create a new field

If you find yourself scribbling important numbers or memos in the margins of your purchase orders, invoices, or credit slips, consider creating a new field specifically for that data. Also, check out QuickBooks and your industry (choose **QuickBooks** and your industry from the **Help** menu) to see how others in your field have customized QuickBooks forms to suit their needs.

Most of the examples in this chapter are invoices, although the methods used for customizing any sales form or statement are identical. These include credit memos, cash sales slips, and even purchase orders. Because we're using an invoice as our example, I'll point out that you might customize an invoice when you have a particular set of vendors or customers in mind. For example, if one set of customers always requires overnight shipping, create an invoice with special UPS or Federal Express fields; if certain customers always order large quantities from you at a discount, design a form with unique quantity fields.

Determining Which Template to Change

Customizing an invoice

1. From the **Activities** menu, choose **Create Invoices**.

2. From the Custom Template drop-down list at the upper right, choose the type of invoice you want to customize. This can be your starting point for customizing. You'll see the fields of the invoice change to reflect the type of template you choose for customizing.

3. Again, click the drop-down menu. You'll notice a check appears by the name of the template you are customizing.

4. Select **Customize**, and you'll see the Customize Template screen pictured in Figure 20.1.

5. Select **Customize** to display the Customize Template dialog box. When it appears, click **Edit** to make changes to the current template, **New** to start from scratch, and **Go to List** to open the Templates window.

Turn off Qcards

Sometimes the Qcards, as helpful as they are, position themselves right over a menu category you want to access. To remove Qcards, press Ctrl+F1. Press Ctrl+F1 again to bring them back.

FIGURE 20.1

Customize a template to create a reusable form.

Customizing a predefined template

If you choose a template for customizing that has the word Intuit in front of it, you'll be prompted to duplicate this template before proceeding. QuickBooks protects these default templates from being edited by prompting you to create a duplicate first. First, close the two dialog boxes that just opened and, from the **Lists** menu, choose **Templates**. The Templates window appears. Highlight the template you want to duplicate and click the **Templates** drop-down menu. Choose **Duplicate**. You'll be asked to specify the type of template you want to make. A new version of this template appears along with the others. The word DUP appears in front of the name of the template copy. You can now edit this duplicate knowing that you have a backup of the original, should you ever want to use that form.

FIGURE 20.2

The Templates drop-down menu lets you duplicate, delete, and import templates.

Create a form for repeated use

You might notice the form you are working with now is being referred to as a template. This means you are creating a document that you can open and reuse later in many instances, applying it in more than one circumstance.

From the Templates window, you can duplicate, delete, and import templates, as well as make them inactive and find templates used in specific transactions (see Figure 20.2). The Select a Template panel on the left is one other way to choose which template you want to edit.

Adding and Removing Fields

Click **Edit** to open the Customize Invoice dialog box (see Figure 20.3). You'll see five or six tabs. Each tab controls a specific area of the form. For example, to specify if a date or invoice number should appear at the top of your form, click the **Header** tab. To include a special message, memo, or grand total figure at the bottom of your form, click the **Footer** tab. To turn fields on and off or change their titles, click the **Fields** tab.

Change the name of your template by typing in something new in the Template Name area at the top of the template. After renaming, this new template appears with the others in the Templates window. If you save without renaming, the template you based your new invoice on will be changed.

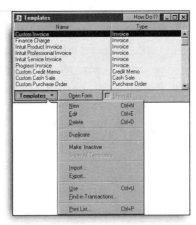

All the tabs in this dialog box merely allow you to specify if a certain field or data area should appear or not. You can determine, for example, that the shipping number or customer's email address should appear on your computer screen, but not be printed out on the paper form itself. You can change the title of the form or any field. For example, you can change REP to a more explanatory Sales Rep, or change FOB to Goods Liability. Or perhaps the form title Invoice is too generic for you. It can be personalized.

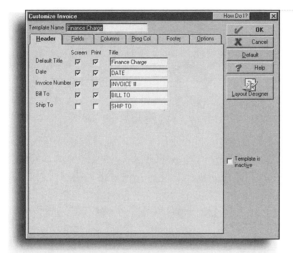

FIGURE 20.3

Click a check box to view any field onscreen or printed.

Customizing a Form Header

The **Header** tab is where you can name the invoice. This is the title that appears on the invoice itself. It can contain up to 41 characters, so if you'd like, you can be much more descriptive than "Invoice."

As with all fields, you can specify if the Invoice Number should appear onscreen, printed, both, or neither. Although you can change the title "Invoice #," the invoice number itself is generated by the number of invoices created since the beginning of your fiscal period. If you try to type in a new invoice number, resetting it, you'll find the number returns to the proper sequence as soon as you press **OK**. Invoices are records and should not easily be altered. Most often, invoice fields receive data from a corresponding estimate (Lists, Create Estimates, Create Invoice), but data can easily be added that does not appear on the estimate.

Use the Find feature

If you are trying to find a form that closely resembles something you are trying to create, use the Find feature (**Edit**, **Find**). With it, you can scroll through every type of QuickBooks form, searching for a certain transaction type or payment method, or even for a particular template. When the form you want appears in the **Find** list, click **Go To**, and the form appears, ready for editing.

Use Rename a field

You cannot change a field's basic type by simply renaming it. For example, if you change the Shipping Date field title to Estimated Arrival Date, it will still appear with the shipping date. Likewise, changing the title of a column or header area does not cause that field to suddenly appear with different data. Data in an invoice is populated from the Customer: Jobs List, and any numbers you type in by hand. To change the type of data available to Invoice fields, work with the Customer: Jobs List.

Customizing Individual Fields

As an example of editing field titles and visibility, let's take a close look at the **Fields** tab (see Figure 20.4):

- Each line of this tab represents a field. The type of data that appears in the field appears at the left.
- To make any field visible on your screen, place a check in the Screen column next to that field's title.
- To make any field visible only on your printed form, place a check in the Print column next to that field's name.
- For visibility both onscreen and in print, check both the Print and Screen boxes.
- To the right of each field is the Title. You can change the title simply by typing in this area. Click **OK**, and your changes appear in the invoice.

FIGURE 20.4

Use the **Fields** tab to add or remove any field from your form.

Adding, Removing, and Reordering Columns

The **Columns** tab introduces another control (see Figure 20.5).

The Order box allows you to sequence the order your columns should appear in. Type 1 in the Order box to make a column appear farthest to the left, type 2 for a column to appear to the right of column 1, and so forth.

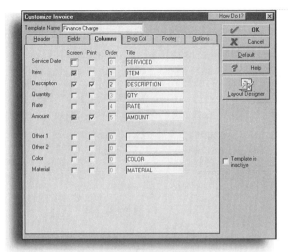

FIGURE 20.5

Change the columns sequence by using the **Columns** tab.

Remove a field

If you remove a field or column that has data in it, the data is not gone. By using the controls found here, you've merely chosen not to view it at this time. QuickBooks continues to save it. If you make that field or column visible again, the data it contained will be visible as well.

Customizing a Progressive Estimate Invoice

Earlier I mentioned that the Customize Template dialog box might show five or six tabs. Not all invoice templates show the **Prog Col** (Progressive Invoice Columns) tab (see Figure 20.6).

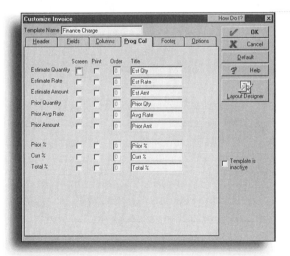

FIGURE 20.6

The **Progressive Invoice Columns** tab.

This tab appears if Progress Invoicing is turned on. Progress Invoicing is important if you bill customers for partially completed work. Here are two examples of when partial billing is important:

Restore the template

If your experimentation takes a turn for the worst, restore the template to its original state by clicking **Default** on the far right of the Customize Invoice dialog box.

- Contracting or construction jobs that require partial payment at the 25, 50, and 75 percent points
- Monthly client billing for legal work that is underway

If you think you might want to use Progressive Estimate Invoices, from the File menu, select **Preferences, Jobs & Estimates**, and answer **Yes** to **Do You Do Progress Invoicing**? (see Figure 20.7). If you answer **Yes**, then you will see the **Prog Col** tab when customizing invoices.

SEE ALSO

➤ *For more information about progress billing and billing from estimates, see Chapter 10, "Job-Cost Estimating and Tracking," page 185*

FIGURE 20.7

Set Progress Invoicing in the Preferences window.

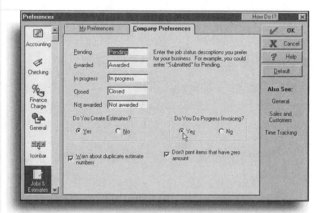

Why use Progress Invoicing?

Together with Progress Invoicing, Job Status Descriptions help you keep track of how far along you are in any work you are doing. You can, for example, use the Customer: Jobs List to call up all jobs with pending contracts, or all jobs that were eventually awarded to other businesses. Job Status Descriptions are covered in Chapter 10.

The **Prog Col** tab creates a special set of columns for Progressive Estimate Invoices. This tab creates fields for specifying the percentage of work completed, and comparisons between prior estimates and actual dollar amounts, billed as labor or supplies.

Like the **Columns** tab, the number in the Order box determines the sequence of columns. Type 1 to make a column appear first from the left, with each number moving progressively to the right.

Customizing a Form Footer

The **Footer** tab contains two special text areas. In the message area, type in a message 41 characters or less (long enough for

"Your bill is 3 months overdue," or "For 10$ off, re-order this month," for example). You can type beyond the visible field, if you want.

Below is an area for a long text, up to 960 characters. This is ideal for warranty information and legal disclaimers. This text block does not show up on your screen, only on your printed invoice.

Customizing Company Info and Adding a Logo

To place the company name and address on your form, select the **Options** tab (see Figure 20.8). Place a check by Print Company Name, Print Company Address, or both. The invoice prints the company name and address as it is found in Company Info (**File**, **Company Info**).

To include a company logo, click **Use logo**, and the Logo dialog box appears. Click **File** to open a **Browse** menu to search your hard drive for a logo. It must be a .BMP file. After the file is located and selected, QuickBooks automatically resizes it appropriately and relocates the logo to the QuickBooks folder.

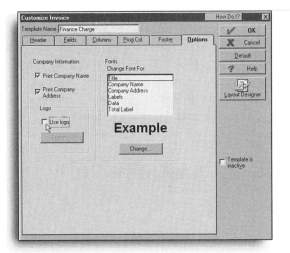

Excluding non-billable fields

Some invoices are set up to bill for various items, and not all items are applicable each time you bill. For example, at times, you'll perform labor, but not use billable parts. By default, though, QuickBooks includes that non-billable item on the invoice, showing a charge of $0.00. To make this non-billable item not appear on your invoice, choose **File**, **Preferences**, **Jobs & Estimates**, and select the **Don't Print Items That Have a Zero Amount** check box.

FIGURE 20.8

To place a logo on your form, from the **Options** tab, check **Use logo**.

Printing a logo on checks and paychecks

You can use a logo for checks and paychecks by choosing **Printer Setup** from the **File** menu. From the **Form name** drop-down menu, choose **Checks/Paychecks**. You'll notice a Logo button off to the right. Click it to choose a logo for your company's checks and paychecks. The logo you choose need not be the same as the one used on invoices, or sale or purchase forms.

Convert logos

If the artwork you want to use for your logo is not saved as a .BMP file, use any photo editing program such as Paint Shop Pro to convert the logo to the .BMP format.

FIGURE 20.9

Changing the form's fonts.

Changing fonts

1. In the **Fonts** section of the Options tab, click any item in the **Change Font For** box, and see the font size and type QuickBooks has selected (see Figure 20.9). The word Example is displayed. You might notice that the font size for Title is very large, while that for Labels is quite small.

2. While any Company Information item is selected, click the **Change…** button. A Font dialog box appears, allowing you to choose a new font, font style, and size for each item. Click **OK** to finalize your choice.

Font settings you change here apply to all items of that same type of business form. (Change the font for Labels, and every label printed from that type of form uses that same font setting.) If you want to use a unique font style to set a particular word or two apart from the rest of the items (for example, have the company name utilize two types of fonts), you have to use QuickBooks' **Layout Designer**, which provides many more customization options for your forms.

Making a Template Inactive

Making a template active again

If you have made a number of templates inactive, you might want to locate them again for editing or use. To view all your templates, inactive or not, select **Templates** from the **Lists** menu and place a check in the **Show All** box. Inactive templates appear with a very small "ghost" symbol, to their left. To make a template active, select it, click the **Template** drop-down menu, and choose **Make Active**.

You can also open the original template and uncheck the **Template Is Inactive** check box.

To make a template inactive, click the **Template is inactive** check box, near the bottom right of the Customize Invoice dialog box. There are several reasons why you might want to make a template inactive. For example, if you decide that only one version of a particular invoice should be used, you might want to deactivate a particular template with the same or a similar name.

An inactive template does not appear in the list of available templates. Deactivating a template places it off limits to employees, until you activate it again.

Moving and Resizing Fields

Moving and resizing fields

1. Open any form from the **Activities** menu (Estimates, Invoices, Cash Sales, Credit Memos or Statements), then click the **Custom Template** drop-down menu, just as if you were simply going to edit the template.

2. Next, select **Edit** or **New**.

3. Click the **Layout Designer** button. You'll see the Layout Designer, as shown in Figure 20.10.

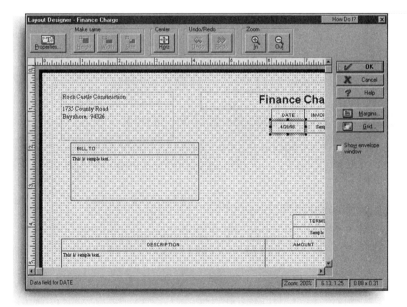

FIGURE 20.10
The Layout Designer.

The Layout Designer is where you can rearrange form elements, aligning them horizontally or vertically, either giving your form a whole new look or perhaps just making key elements stand out a bit more.

In Layout Designer, your form appears as clusters of rectangular boxes. Each box is an element of your form, for example, the Address data field or the Due Date label. Click any box and look at the bottom left of the screen. The form element you've clicked on is identified. They appear as rectangles simply to make it easy for you to resize or move them. The rectangles are not printed on the final form.

Here's how to work with form elements in Layout Designer. When you click any form element, eight black handles appear on the sides of the rectangle. Try the following:

- To move a form element anywhere on the page, click inside its rectangle and drag it to a new location.

- To center an object or group of objects horizontally, make your selection, then click the **Center Horizontal** button at the top of the screen.

- To select multiple fields, use the mouse to lasso the fields or hold **Shift** while clicking the fields.

- To resize a form element, click and drag the handles inward or outward.

Creating a Common Height or Width

In Layout Designer, you can select two or more elements, then instantly make them the same height or width (see Figure 20.11).

Modifying form elements uniformly

1. Select the form element whose size you want the others to shrink or grow to.

2. Press the **Shift** key and click one or more additional form elements. All selected elements change to match the first element selected. (Notice that when you press the **Shift** key, handles appear around all the form elements you click on.)

3. To make your selected objects have a common height, click the **Make Same—Height** button.

4. To make your selected objects have a common width, click the **Make Same—Width** button.

Create a new field

If you want to create a new field, you need to return to the Customize dialog box. Click **OK**, select the **Fields** tab, and choose **Other**. Create a title for this field, and it appears on the form. You can then return to the Layout Designer where you can resize and move your field as you like.

5. To make them all the same height and width, click the
Make Same—Size button.

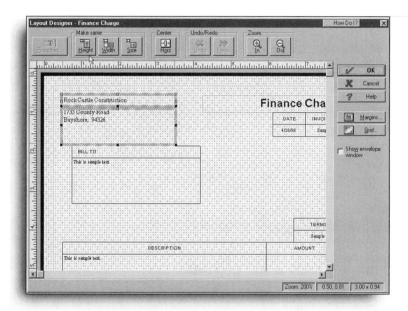

FIGURE 20.11
Making form elements of equal
height or width.

Resizing and Changing Text in a Form

If you want to make a form element larger, drag the handles to
increase its size, then make the font inside it larger. To change
the font, font style, or size of any form element, double-click it,
which opens the Text Properties dialog box, and then select the
Font button.

The Text Properties dialog box lets you justify text, as well as
create a border or partial border, around your form elements.
There are two tabs on the Text Properties dialog box. To justify
text horizontally or vertically, click the appropriate button in
either the Horizontal or Vertical Justification panel.

You can also edit text by selecting a field and clicking the
Properties button on the upper left of the **Layout Designer**
toolbar.

Change the text message

You might have discovered that,
in Layout Manager, you cannot
change the text message inside
any form element. You can
change the size, font style, and
font, but not the content. To
change content, return to the
Customize screen by clicking
OK and make your changes
using the tabbed menus, as
described previously. Then
return to Layout Manager to
rearrange and resize your
objects.

Adding a Border to a Form Element

Click the **Border** tab to perform these tasks:

- Add a visible rectangular border around a form element.
- Add a partial border, or half a rectangle, as shown in Figure 20.12.
- Add a single underline.

For example, click **Left** to add a visible line on the left side of the form element, click **Bottom** to add an underline, and so forth.

FIGURE 20.12

Creating a half-rectangle border around a form element.

Changing Your View of Your Form

Layout Designer provides **Zoom In** and **Zoom Out** buttons at the top of the screen to view your form close up or farther away. You can do the following:

- Click the **Zoom In** button to make form elements appear larger on the screen. You might have to use the scrolling buttons at the right and bottom of the screen to see the element.
- Click the **Zoom Out** button to see more of your form at once.

The Layout Designer Grid

The Layout Designer shows your form against a grid. For some people, this series of dots makes it easier to visualize how to evenly align and position form elements. You can do the following:

- To change grid settings, or turn the grid off entirely, click the **Grid** button on the middle left of the Layout Designer. The Grid and Snap Settings dialog box appears (see Figure 20.13).

- To turn the grid off, remove the check from **Show Grid**.

- If you prefer the grid dots closer together or farther apart, change the **Grid Spacing** drop-down list box.

- If you are repositioning form elements and want them in just the right position, turn on the **Snap to Grid** feature. With **Snap to Grid** on, your elements will snap into place, aligning with a common grid boundary.

FIGURE 20.13
Changing grid settings and visibility with the Grid and Snap Settings dialog box.

Layout Designer Margins

Layout Designer provides a lightly dashed margin around your form. The dashes do not print. Layout Designer's margin does not correspond to your printer's set margin. It's merely a visual reminder to help you keep all your form elements inside a boundary you specify.

You can change the margin by clicking the **Margins** button on the right side of the Layout Designer. The Margins dialog box appears (see Figure 20.14). Notice that you can set separate measurements for each margin, allowing a bigger margin at the bottom than at the top, for example. However, you might never need to alter these margins at all, because they default to fairly universal settings that work well with most printers and conventional form sizes.

FIGURE 20.14
Changing margins in Layout Designer.

You can do the following:

- The unit of measurment used by the Margin controls defaults to inches, but several other units of measurement can be employed, including millimeters and picas.

More allowable abbreviations

A more comprehensive list of allowable abbreviations is available by clicking the **Help** button and selecting the **Changing the Unit of Measure** topic.

- To change the unit of measurement, type a new abbreviation into the margin data area. For example, rather than the default 0.5 in., type 13 mm., or 3 pi.

- Click inside the **Top** margin data area, and the QuickBooks Qcard reminds you of the allowable measurement abbreviations.

Show Envelope Window

Intuit sells envelopes with viewing windows. Office supply stores sell these as well. These allow you to put a form in the envelope with a pre-written address and return address area, which shows through the window. If you use window envelopes, turn on **Show Envelope Window**, and a gray area appears where the windowed area of the envelope would be. Then you can position a form's return address and address to be viewed in the window.

Previewing Your Form

Previewing a form

1. Click **OK** to close the Layout Preview dialog box.
2. Click **OK** to close the Customize dialog box.
3. Click **Preview** on the Create dialog box to see a full-screen version of your form as it would appear printed out.

To do further editing, you must return the way you came, back to the Layout Designer. There are apparently no shortcuts for obtaining a quick preview while the Layout Designer is still open. For this reason, I'd try to do most of my editing all at once, and then preview it.

Creating Custom Fields

You can create custom fields that can appear in invoices, job orders, sales receipts, statements, and credit memos. These can be prefilled with your information from an estimate or other source from a QuickBook file. Custom fields can appear onscreen, be printed, or both, just like all other fields. Curiously though, when you use the Create dialog box to add these custom

fields to your forms (as described earlier), they appear in the
Columns tab, not the **Fields** tab, as you might expect.

When to Use Custom Fields

The process described here is rather complex and is significant if
you are creating a new field that you want to apply to many
receipts or invoices, or setting up criteria for tracking or billing
many customers or clients. Short of this, you might find it easier
to use one of the extra fields provided by QuickBooks in the
Fields tab (called Other), and title it anything you want. Adding
a field using the method described in this section is valuable if
you are planning to add a data source to go along with it.

Reviewing a Custom Field Example

Let's use an example creating two fields, one called Referred By
and the other 10% Discount. These two fields allow you to track
how a particular client was referred to you and those who are
eligible for a 10 percent discount that you are offering to repeat
customers. After these fields are added, you can add them to
your invoices and other forms and use the Find in Transactions
feature to look at all customers who fit these new categories.

Creating custom fields

1. Select **Items** from the **List** menu.
2. Click the **Item** drop-down menu.
3. Select **New**, and the New Item dialog box appears (see
   Figure 20.15).
4. Click the **Custom Fields** button and click past the warning
   that no custom fields have been created yet.

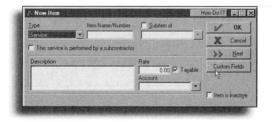

FIGURE 20.15
The New Item dialog box,
where Custom Fields are
created.

5. Select **Define Fields**. You'll notice Color and Materials are two fields that have already been created. As you can tell, you are allowed to create up to five custom fields. We are going to create two.

6. Below Color and Materials, type `Referred By` and `10%` `Discount` (see Figure 20.16). If you intend to make these fields available to forms, check the **Use** box.

FIGURE 20.16
Creating two new fields.

7. You'll see these new fields appear in a dialog box called **Custom Fields for Unnamed Item**. They are now available for use, but have not been applied or assigned to any existing forms yet. Click **OK** to close that dialog box and click **OK** to close the New Item dialog box as well.

Applying Your New Fields

Adding new custom fields

1. Select **Create Invoice** from the **Activities** menu.

2. Select **Custom Template** from the **Template** drop-down menu.

3. Return and choose **Customize** from the same drop-down menu. The Customize Template dialog box appears.

4. Click **E**dit and select the **C**olumns tab.

5. You'll see your two new categories: Referred By and 10% Discount (see Figure 20.17).

6. In the Referred By field, place a check under **Screen** but not **Print**, because it's not important for the customer to see who he was referred by; it's just good information for you.

7. In the 10% Discount field, place a check by both **Screen**
   and **Print** because you do want your customer to know he's
   getting special treatment for his repeat business.

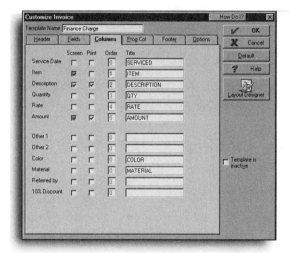

FIGURE 20.17

The two newly created fields appear in the **Columns** tab of the Customize Template dialog box.

Locating Forms That Use Your New Field

After you've added these new fields to a number of customers'
documents, you might want to see where your referrals are coming from and how much repeat business your 10 percent discount offer is generating. Using the Find in Transactions
command, you can view all the invoices, sales receipts, credit
slips, and estimates that use these fields and, thus, compare your
data.

Determining if your fields are being used

1. Select **Items** from the **Lists** menu and choose the **Items**
   drop-down menu.

2. Select **Find in Transactions**. You'll see the dialog box
   shown in Figure 20.18.

3. Select which filter you'd like to use as a search criterion.

4. Click the **Find** button, and you'll see all the transactions
   that have used this field at the bottom of the dialog box.
   The Number of Matches are noted on the bottom right of
   the dialog box.

FIGURE 20.18

Click **Fin̲d in Transactions** to open the Find dialog box.

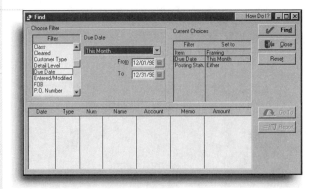

Customizing Tips

Although we've used invoices as our customizing forms example, all sales forms, such as cash receipts, credit memos, and statements, are customized the same way. Let's look briefly at a few examples of how and why you might customize specific types of forms.

For credit memos, it might be helpful to have a field indicating if an item was returned because of customer dissatisfaction, was exchanged as defective merchandise, or if there was an overpayment. If an item was returned, did the customer accept credit towards another purchase or demand a refund? These are things you might want to know at a glance, just by looking at the credit memo. Also, with such data, you could use Find in Transactions to view trends in your customers' satisfaction, or generate reports from these fields.

Use a Cash Sales form to create a quick record of all sales over a given period, perhaps a Weekly Sales Summary or something similar. A Cash Sales form is used to receive payment for any item that is not ordered on a regular basis. It can be used to record payments with checks and credit cards as well.

Creating a summary of sales activities

1. Select **Enter Cash Sales** from the **Activities** menu, at the top of the screen.

2. Select a payment method.

3. In the Item area, use the drop-down menus to make a list of items you sell most regularly. You can always add more on-the-fly.

4. Don't type anything in the Quantity column, because you'll be using this form on a regular basis to summarize sales activity. Also, don't type anything in the Customer:Job area.

5. Select **Edit**, **Memorize Cash Sale**. This adds your custom form to the Memorized Transactions List.

6. In the Name area, type in a descriptive title for this form.

7. Click **OK**, and when you are back at the Enter Cash Sales dialog box, click the **Cancel** button. Do not click **OK**, because you don't want to record the transaction.

Summarizing your sales activities

1. Click the **Mem Tx** icon or select **Memorized Transactions** from the **List** menu.

2. From the **Memorized Transaction List** that appears, double-click on the transaction you saved, type in Quantities for the period in question, and fill in any sale items that did not get included in the item list you originally saved with this file.

3. Click **OK** to save the new file for that particular month or week with a new name. That way, you won't overwrite the form you created for regular use.

Another reason to customize a sales form is, if you plan to sell on consignment, you need a form with a service item that debits your account with your percentage of each sale and a standard sales item that pays the remainder to the consignor.

Special Considerations for Statements

For statements, you might want to have a Bounced Check, Stop Payment, and Bank Fee fields, or a field that indicates if a particular statement has been printed or mailed yet. This information is available from reports, but it could be convenient to have it right on the statement itself.

Don't forget that many charges can be applied to a statement automatically, such as regular membership fees or monthly rents. Consider automating any recurring charges.

Additionally, you might want to bypass entering charges to each customer's register and, instead, enter statement charges all at once directly into your Accounts Receivable Register. This could save you lots of time. Furthermore, you can create a Memorized Transaction for an entire group of regular statements—for example, if you bill all regular customers at the same time of the month.

Adding a Form to the Icon Bar

Placing a form on the icon bar

1. Open the form you want fast access to and then select **Window, Add Window to Icon bar**.

2. You'll see a dialog box prompting you to name your icon as it will appear on the bar and add a brief description, which will not appear. Type in a name and a description.

3. On the left side of the dialog box, scroll through the list of icon possibilities, picking one that jogs your memory, reminding you what the icon is for.

4. Click **OK** to close the dialog box and the button is included with the others on the toolbar. Clicking the icon once opens that form.

5. If your icon toolbar is not yet visible, do this:

   - Select **Preferences** from the **File** menu.

   - On the far left, scroll down to click the **Icon bar** button.

   - On the **My Preferences** tab, click which version of the icon bar you want to view (icons and text, icons only, or text only).

   - Click **OK** to close the Preferences dialog box and save your changes. The icon bar will remain on your screen until you change your preferences.

The **My Preferences** tab reveals options to make your icon bar visible, showing only the pictures, only text, or both. To choose icon visibility, click one of the radio buttons.

Notice here that you can also add, remove, and edit icons, as well as place a space between them if you want your icons to appear in logical groupings.

Click **OK** to save your customized settings. To change the icon bar back to the way it was before you altered it, click **Default**.

QuickBooks' Reports and Graphs

Customize reports so they produce exactly the information you need

Memorize reports you have customized so you don't have to create them from scratch the next time you need them

Print hard copies of your graphs and print to files on your disk

Get visual with QuickBooks' graphs

After you have taken the time to enter all your business transactions in QuickBooks, it would be a shame not to reap the benefits of that work by producing reports that summarize your business activity.

You can produce many types of reports in QuickBooks. You can create, for example:

- Profit and loss reports that show you how much revenue your company is producing

- Balance sheet reports that show you how much your company is worth

- Comparative reports that display current year numbers with prior year numbers so you can see how performance has changed

- Forecast reports that help you predict the financial future

- Trial balance reports that show the balance in every account

- Transaction reports that display every transaction in every account for a specified time period

- Audit trail reports that show all changes and adjustments that have been made

- Budget reports that let you know how close you're coming to meeting your goals

- Accounts receivable reports that provide you with information on how much is owed to your company

- Sales reports that tell you how sales of particular items are going, or how much business particular customers give you

- Job costing reports (available in QuickBooks Pro) that give you the details on how each job is doing and how estimates compare to actual performance

- Accounts payable reports that tell you how much your company owes others

- Purchase reports that give you breakdowns of how your money is being spent

- Inventory reports that tell you what items are in stock and what items are on order

- Tax reports that help you prepare your tax forms
- Payroll reports that give you updates on how much you are spending on payroll and payroll taxes

Many of the reports that QuickBooks prepares are discussed throughout this book in the appropriate chapters. Payroll reports, for example, are described in the chapters on payroll and payroll taxes; inventory reports are described in the inventory chapters.

In this chapter you'll find an overview of QuickBooks reports, information on how to find and request them, and instructions on customizing and memorizing reports.

Standard Reports

QuickBooks comes with many standard reports that you can display and print. You can access the **Reports** menu in QuickBooks and examine the list of standard reports, which you'll see are organized by topic (see Figure 21.1).

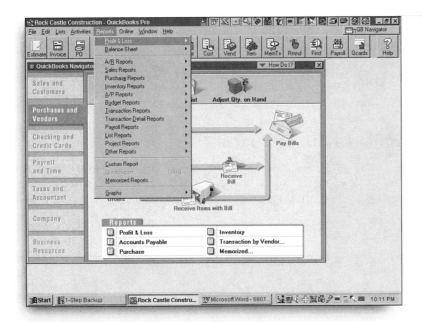

FIGURE 21.1

The main **Reports** menu. Clicking a topic provides a side menu of additional reports.

You can create any of the standard reports by selecting the report you want from the **Reports** menu. Choose **Reports**, then click the general type of report you wish to view. When a side menu appears, click the report you want and QuickBooks will display the report onscreen.

Many reports are also available from the List window and the Items window. For example, choose **Lists**, **Chart of Accounts**. Click the **Reports** button in the **Chart of Accounts** list window, choose **Reports on All Accounts**, and a menu of standard reports appears.

Commonly Used QuickBooks Reports

You'll find, as you experiment with the QuickBooks reports, that some reports don't provide you with information you find useful to your business, but other reports are so useful you can't function without them.

In this section, you'll get an introduction to some of the most commonly used reports. Later on in this chapter (see the section "Customizing Reports") you'll learn how to customize your reports so that if the standard report is close to providing what you need, but needs a little tweaking, you can alter the report to conform to your needs. Maybe you need to have things sorted differently, for example, or maybe one of the columns on the report is not of use to you.

Profit and Loss Statement

The Profit and Loss Statement lists all your income and expense accounts and shows the current total in each account, resulting in a net income figure derived from reducing your total income by the total of your expenses. Individual transactions are not shown on this report—only the balance for each account.

From the Chart of Accounts list window, select the **Reports** drop-down menu. Then click **Reports on all Accounts**, **Profit & Loss** and choose from a variety of ways to view Profit and Loss Reports. Each report allows you to choose which time frame to view, from an entire year to a single day. Choose **Standard Report, Year to Date Comparison, Previous Year Comparison,** or an itemized, highly detailed look.

Creating a standard Profit and Loss statement

1. Choose **Reports, Profit & Loss**. The Profit & Loss side menu appears.

2. Choose **Standard**. The Profit and Loss report appears onscreen and displays a balance for each income and expense account (see Figure 21.2).

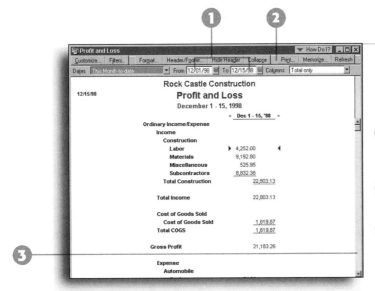

FIGURE 21.2

The standard Profit and Loss statement summarizes your company's net income (or loss) for the designated period.

① Click here to change the period of time covered by this report.

② Click here to print a hard copy of the report.

③ Scroll to see the entire report.

3. QuickBooks has selected a period of time which this report covers. The period of time is shown in the **Dates** area at the top of the report. Click the arrow to the right of the **Dates** area to choose a different time period, or indicate specific dates in the **From** and **To** areas at the top of the report.

4. Print a hard copy of the report by clicking the **Print** button, then clicking the **Print** button located on the Print Reports window that appears.

The Profit and Loss statement

The Profit and Loss statement is one of the most commonly produced reports—and one of the most useful. The report gives you an up-to-the-minute view of the income and expenses of the company. Potential lenders and investors will want to see this statement. Produce this statement at least monthly and keep the reports on file so you can refer back to them for budgeting and forecasting purposes.

With the Profit and Loss Statement displayed, you can double-click any dollar amount to display a secondary report showing the detail of all transactions that make up that amount on the Profit and Loss Statement. On the secondary report, double-click any item to open and view the original document from which the amount was created.

Balance Sheet

The Balance Sheet goes hand in hand with the Profit and Loss Statement; together, they give a clear view of how a business is performing. The Profit and Loss Statement shows how much money a company has made for a selected period of time, and the Balance Sheet shows what the company is worth at a particular point in time.

Like the Profit and Loss reports described above, QuickBooks' Balance Sheet reports show a global view of their topic and enable you to double-click any amount to open a supporting report that shows the details behind the amount.

The Standard and Summary balance sheet reports provide simple balance information, and the Comparison report compares the current year with the previous, showing the percentage of difference between the two. The Itemized report includes Memo, Split Transaction information, and the amount of individual transactions.

Creating a standard Balance Sheet report

1. Choose **Reports**, **Balance Sheet**. The Balance Sheet side menu will appear.

2. Choose **Standard**. The Balance Sheet appears onscreen, displaying a value for each of your company's asset, liability, and equity accounts (see Figure 21.3).

3. Typically, the Balance Sheet is displayed as of today's date. You can change the date, however, by clicking the arrow next to the **Dates** area and choosing the date that you want.

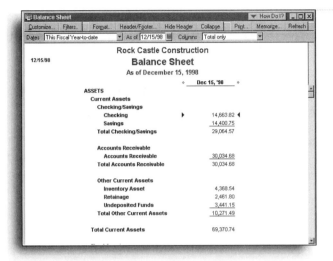

FIGURE 21.3
The standard Balance Sheet displays your company's net worth (assets minus liabilities) as of the specified date.

Accounts Receivable Aging Reports

The Accounts Receivable Aging Reports will give you insight about the timeliness of your customers' payments. The Aging Summary report shows outstanding balances arranged by customer name and divided into time periods: amounts due currently, 1-30 days overdue, 31-60 days overdue, 61-90 days overdue, and over 90 days overdue. The Aging Detail report provides the same information for each invoice that is overdue.

Creating an Aging Summary report

1. Choose **Reports**, **A/R Reports**. The Accounts Receivable side menu will appear.

2. Choose **Aging Summary**. The A/R Aging Summary appears onscreen, displaying all customers with outstanding balances and the time period into which each balance falls (see Figure 21.4).

The Aging Report is an essential tool of good business management. Use this report to discover which accounts require special attention due to the age of the overdue accounts. This report is also useful in exploring the effectiveness of the credit terms you assign to your customers. Customers who are notoriously past due may need to be placed on a prepayment or COD status. Or an incentive, such as a discount for timely payments, may stimulate customers to pay on time.

Collections Report

Another useful report, the Collection Report, lists all customers with balances over 30 days overdue, along with phone number information so you can easily follow up on the collection with phone calls.

Producing the Collections report

1. Choose **Reports**, **A/R Reports**. The Accounts Receivable side menu will appear.

2. Choose **Collections Report**. The report appears, displaying customer and outstanding balance information. This report includes information as of today's date (see Figure 21.5).

General Ledger

Use the General Ledger as a guide to finding any transaction that has occurred in your company. The General Ledger is a collection of all company accounts—asset, liability, equity, income, and expense accounts—and the transactions that occur in those accounts.

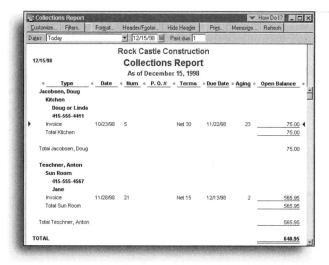

FIGURE 21.5
Use the Collections Report as a guide for tracking customers with overdue balances.

Many companies print a General Ledger report monthly to provide a hard copy reference for activity in all the company accounts.

Creating a General Ledger report

1. Choose **Reports**, **Other Reports**. The Other Reports side menu will appear.

2. Choose **General Ledger**. The General Ledger report will appear (see Figure 21.6). The report lists each account alphabetically within these groups and in this order: assets, liabilities, equity, income, and expense. If you use account numbers, the accounts will appear in numerical order within each group.

3. By default, the report displays the transactions for the current month up to today's date. You can change the date (you may want to display the prior month's activity, for example, or the current year to date rather than month to date) by clicking the arrow in the **Dates** area and choosing the appropriate time period.

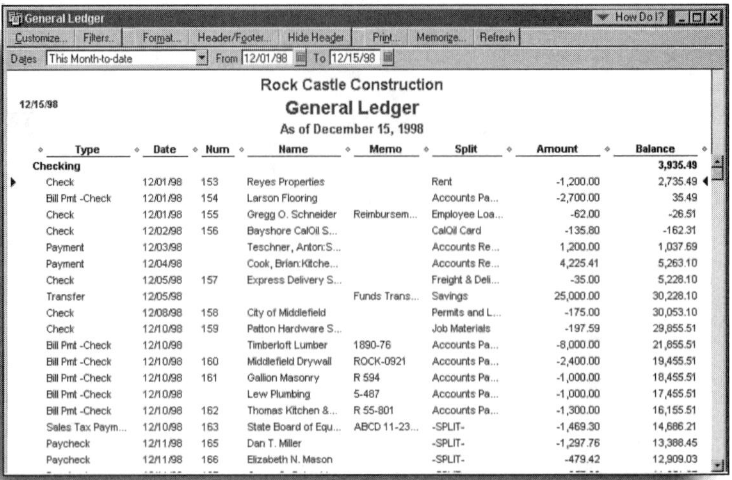

Type	Date	Num	Name	Memo	Split	Amount	Balance
Checking							**3,935.49**
Check	12/01/98	153	Reyes Properties		Rent	-1,200.00	2,735.49
Bill Pmt -Check	12/01/98	154	Larson Flooring		Accounts Pa...	-2,700.00	35.49
Check	12/01/98	155	Gregg O. Schneider	Reimbursem...	Employee Loa...	-62.00	-26.51
Check	12/02/98	156	Bayshore CalOil S...		CalOil Card	-135.80	-162.31
Payment	12/03/98		Teschner, Anton:S...		Accounts Re...	1,200.00	1,037.69
Payment	12/04/98		Cook, Brian:Kitche...		Accounts Re...	4,225.41	5,263.10
Check	12/05/98	157	Express Delivery S...		Freight & Deli...	-35.00	5,228.10
Transfer	12/05/98			Funds Trans...	Savings	25,000.00	30,228.10
Check	12/08/98	158	City of Middlefield		Permits and L...	-175.00	30,053.10
Check	12/10/98	159	Patton Hardware S...		Job Materials	-197.59	29,855.51
Bill Pmt -Check	12/10/98		Timberloft Lumber	1890-76	Accounts Pa...	-8,000.00	21,855.51
Bill Pmt -Check	12/10/98	160	Middlefield Drywall	ROCK-0921	Accounts Pa...	-2,400.00	19,455.51
Bill Pmt -Check	12/10/98	161	Gallion Masonry	R 594	Accounts Pa...	-1,000.00	18,455.51
Bill Pmt -Check	12/10/98		Lew Plumbing	5-487	Accounts Pa...	-1,000.00	17,455.51
Bill Pmt -Check	12/10/98	162	Thomas Kitchen &...	R 55-801	Accounts Pa...	-1,300.00	16,155.51
Sales Tax Paym...	12/10/98	163	State Board of Equ...	ABCD 11-23...	-SPLIT-	-1,469.30	14,686.21
Paycheck	12/11/98	165	Dan T. Miller		-SPLIT-	-1,297.76	13,388.45
Paycheck	12/11/98	166	Elizabeth N. Mason		-SPLIT-	-479.42	12,909.03

FIGURE 21.6
Use the General Ledger as a master reference to all company transactions.

Customizing Reports

You have learned that QuickBooks provides many standard reports that can help you understand the progress and performance of your business. Sometimes, however, the standard reports don't give you exactly the information that you need. You may need to display information for different dates than those shown on the standard report, for example, or perhaps you want to display a report of receivables, but only those receivable over a certain dollar amount.

You can customize reports to display the exact information that you need. The buttons at the top of the report window provide you with options for customizing. You can also click the **Customize** or the **Filters** buttons at the top of the window to provide even more fine-tuning for your report.

Changing the Report Date

Each report you create is either for a specified period (such as a Profit and Loss Statement for the year to date) or as of a specific date (such as a Balance Sheet showing balances as of today).

You can change the dates on reports by either clicking the **Dates** button and choosing a specific time period, or by entering exact dates in the **From** and **To** areas (see Figure 21.7).

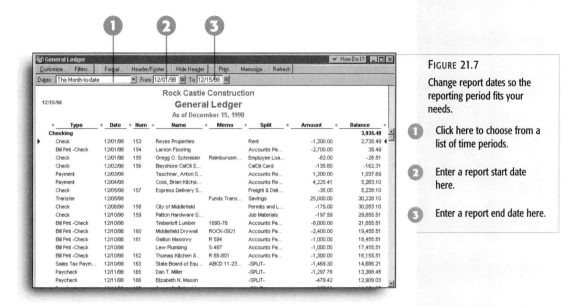

FIGURE 21.7

Change report dates so the reporting period fits your needs.

① Click here to choose from a list of time periods.

② Enter a report start date here.

③ Enter a report end date here.

Changing the Report Columns

Some reports include a **Columns** area at the top of the report. You can use this feature to determine how a report is subtotaled. If you use class tracking, for example, you can choose to subtotal a report, such as the Profit and Loss report, by class and see the income and expense activity for each division of your company (see Figure 21.8).

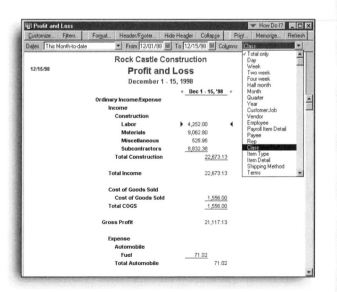

FIGURE 21.8

Click here to display a drop-down list of choices for subtotaling your report.

Changing Report Headers and Footers

Click the **Header/Footer** button at the top of a report to customize the header information (see Figure 21.9), including the wording of the **Company Name**, the **Report Title** and **Subtitle**, and the **Date Prepared** (which appears in the upper-left corner of the report). You can select from a group of date styles by clicking the arrow in the **Date Prepared** area. In addition, you can choose to exclude any of these header features.

FIGURE 21.9

Click **Header/Footer** to choose your own header and footer information, or choose to exclude this information by unchecking the boxes.

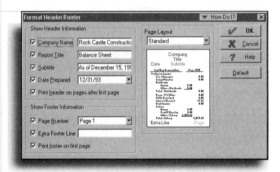

Indicate if you want to display a **Page Number** in a footer at the bottom of each page of a report or **an Extra Footer Line**.

You can choose to exclude the header in all but the first page of your report, and you can choose to exclude the footer from the first page. You can also select an alignment option for the header and footer information on your report by clicking the **Page Layout** button and making a selection from the drop-down menu.

A **Hide Header** button on the report screen enables you to turn off the display of the header altogether. On reports for internal use, you may not need to display the header because you already know what company this report is for, and you can thereby save space on your report page.

Collapsing Subaccounts

When you click the **Collapse** button on the report screen, the balances of any subaccounts are combined with their parent accounts and are removed from the report.

The **Collapse** button becomes an **Expand** button when you click it. Clicking the **Expand** button returns the subaccounts to the report.

Using the Customize Button

Click **Customize** to determine what information should be included with the report, as shown in Figure 21.10. Each parameter you include (**Previous Period**, and **% of Column,** for example) requires a column, so keep space limitations in mind as you add these fields.

FIGURE 21.10

Customize, one of the options available at the top of every report, enables you to determine the scope and content of your report.

❶ Click here to select additional parameters to include on your report.

You can indicate if this report should be prepared on the **Cash** or **Accrual** basis. Typically, you won't have to change this field because you have already told QuickBooks whether your company is a cash basis or an accrual basis company.

SEE ALSO

➤ *For more information about the selection of cash or accrual basis, see page 422*

Click the **Advanced** button and indicate if you want rows and columns to appear on your report only if they are active (have had transactions), and if you want to display accounts that have zero balances. Also, choose the reporting year if you use different years for your fiscal year and your tax year (the years are entered when you set up your QuickBooks company).

Applying Filters

Click **Filters**, either from the Customize window or from the main report screen, to narrow the scope of each parameter you've selected to view. You can create a report that displays merchandise shipped on a specific date, for example, or you can choose to display accounts only if the balance exceeds a certain amount.

Setting filtering options

1. Click the **Filters** button from either the main report screen or from within the Customize window. The Report Filters window will appear (see Figure 21.11).

FIGURE 21.11

Set filters to limit the information in your report to meet specific criteria.

2. From the choices in the **Filter** list, click the type of item you want to filter. You can choose more than one item, but choose one item at a time. To limit the accounts that appear on your report to those with a balance of over $1,000, for example, choose the **Amount** filter.

Filter options change

Depending on the filter choice you make at the left side of the Filter window, the options available to you for setting the filter criteria will change.

3. In the area to the right of the filter list, set your filter criteria. To limit the accounts that appear on your report to those with a balance of over $1,000, for example, click the >symbol, then enter "1000" in the box provided. After you click another item to filter or click the **Amount** filter in the **Current Choices** list at the right of the window, your filter will be added to the list and applied to the report the next time you view it.

4. Click **OK** to save your filtering choices and close this window.

Change your mind? You can delete a filter by clicking the **Filter** button. In the Report Filters window that appears, all filters pertaining to the current report are listed at the right side of the window in the **Current Choices** column. Click a filter you want to remove and press the Delete key on your keyboard. Click **OK** to save your changes and close the Report Filters window. Your report will be rewritten to include the change.

Formatting a Report

Click the **Format** button at the top of your report window to choose how negative numbers are shown, the font for column labels, and whether numbers should be shown divided by 1000 or without cents.

Memorizing the Report Format and Setting

Now that you've customized your report, you may want to be able to use this report again without having to start from scratch with customizing.

Updated data on memorized reports will be displayed the way in which the form is saved. Memorizing a report is important—if you go to all the trouble to customize a form to make it look just so, you'll probably want to use this same report format at a later date, as well.

To save your report for future uses, click the **Memorize** button at the top of the Report window. You will be asked to give this report a name (see Figure 21.12).

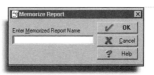

FIGURE 21.12

Give your memorized report a unique name so you can use the report in the future without having to re-create it.

The next time you want to use this report, choose **Reports**, **Memorized Reports**, and this report will appear on the list of memorized reports. From the names on the list, click the report you want to view and click the **Generate Report** button. The report will appear as you created it, with updated information.

Editing and Deleting Memorized Reports

You change the name of a memorized report or delete it if you no longer plan to use the report.

To change the name of a memorized report, choose **Reports**, **Memorized Reports**. The Memorized Reports List window will appear. Click the name of the report you want to change, then click the **Memorized Report** button at the bottom of the window. Click **Edit**. Enter a new name in the box that appears, then click **OK**.

To delete an existing memorized report, choose **Reports**, **Memorized Reports**. Click the name of the report you want to delete, then click the **Memorized Report** button at the bottom of the window. Click **Delete**. You will be asked to confirm that you want to delete this report.

Printing Reports

Viewing a report on the screen is helpful, but often you'll want to have a copy of the report to file, pore over, or give to someone else. QuickBooks lets you print reports to your printer or to a file, so that you can open the report in a word processing or spreadsheet program.

Printing reports to your printer

1. Create the report you want to print.

2. Click the **Print** button at the top of the report window (or choose **File**, **Print Report**). The Print Reports window will appear (see Figure 21.13).

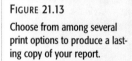

FIGURE 21.13

Choose from among several print options to produce a lasting copy of your report.

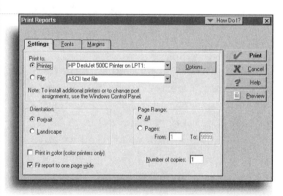

3. Choose either **Printer** or **File** for your output. Then click the down arrow across from your selection, if necessary, to choose the printer you plan to use or to choose the type of file to which you plan to print.

4. Choose **Portrait** or **Landscape** orientation. If you're not sure which orientation works better for this report, click the **Preview** button to display your report onscreen.

5. If you need to print only a portion of your report, enter the page numbers you need to print in the **Page Range** area. Otherwise, leave the page range set to **A̲ll**.

6. Check the **Print in color** box if you want this report printed in color. (You must have a color printer to take advantage of this option.)

7. Check the **Fit report to one page wide** box if you want to force QuickBooks to print this report on a single page width. This may result in a smaller typeface for your report.

8. Indicate the **Number of copies** you wish to print.

9. If you wish to change the typeface or other formatting options used in the report, click the **F̲onts** tab at the top of the screen, then click the **Fonts** button. The Format Report window will appear (see Figure 21.14). Select from various methods of displaying negative numbers and choose whether you want your report numbers divided by 1,000 and displayed with or without cents. Choose one of the report labels in the **Change Font For** list, then click the **Change Font** button to open the Column Labels window. Choose from lists of fonts, font styles, and font sizes, and indicate whether you want to print these labels in color. Click **OK** to return to the Report Format window, then click **OK** to save your changes and return to the Print Reports window.

Printing to a file

If you choose to print your report to a file, you can easily retrieve the file into a spreadsheet or word processing program for further calculations or enhancements. When you print to a file you can choose from three options: ASCII text file, which can be read by word processing programs; Excel/Lotus 123 spreadsheet, which can be read by spreadsheet programs; and Tab delimited file, which can be read by either word processing or spreadsheet programs.

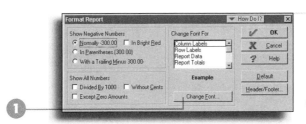

FIGURE 21.14

Set specific report formatting options, including changing the typeface of headings in the Format Report window.

❶ Click here to change the typeface.

10. If you want to change font settings for all future reports, click the **Default Fonts** button. The Report Format Preferences window will appear (this window contains the same information as the Format Report window discussed in step 9) in which you can set report appearance choices that will carry forward to future reports.

11. You can set specific margins for your report by clicking the **Margins** tab in the Print Reports window (see Figure 21.15). Enter the measurement for each margin—the default is _" on each side—keeping in mind that the smaller your margin, the more difficulty your printer may have in printing the information close to the edge of the paper.

FIGURE 21.15
Enter new report margins on this screen.

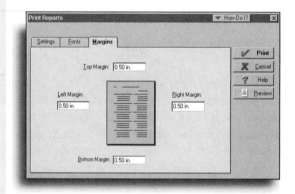

12. Click the **Preview** button to verify that the report looks the way you intended. Click **Close** to close the preview.

13. Click **Print** when you have finished making your changes, or click **Cancel** if you decide you don't want to print at this time.

QuickBooks' Graphs

You can create graphical representations of the information in your reports. The graphs provide illustrations that are often easier to understand and embrace than all those gray numbers on the reports.

QuickBooks offers six standard graphs, which are found nested at the bottom of the **Reports** menu. Each time you choose a graph, you actually get two graphs for the price of one. You can double-click any piece of either graph to see an additional graph of just that item. Then double-click the secondary graph to see a report of all the transactions that make up that graph piece.

You can change the period of time represented by the graphs by changing the dates at the top of the screen. You can also right-click any bar or pie piece to see the actual dollar amount represented by the graph.

The graphs from which you can choose are

- **Income and Expenses.** The Income and Expense Graphs (see Figure 21.16) show how much income your company has earned and how much you have spent for a selected period of time. The bar graph displays total income and total expenses, and the accompanying pie graph shows a piece of the pie for each income or expense account (your choice).

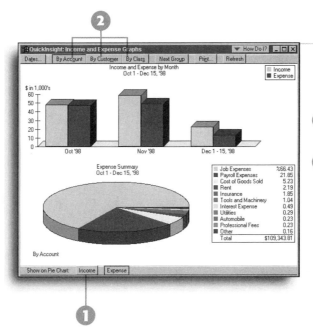

FIGURE 21.16

The Income and Expense Graphs show your company's earnings and expenditures.

1. Click here to switch the pie graph to income accounts.

2. Choose to display income and expenses by account, customer, or class.

■ **Sales.** The Sales Graphs (see Figure 21.17) show sales income for the selected period of time. The bar graph shows sales by month; the pie graph shows sales by item, customer, or sales rep (click your choice from the buttons at the top of the graph).

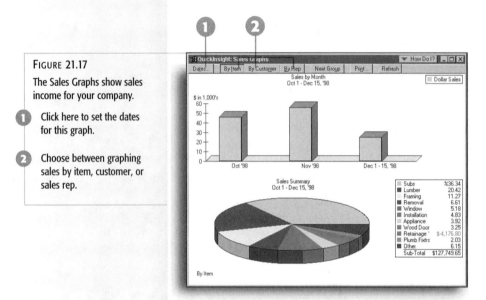

FIGURE 21.17

The Sales Graphs show sales income for your company.

1 Click here to set the dates for this graph.

2 Choose between graphing sales by item, customer, or sales rep.

■ **Accounts Receivable.** The Accounts Receivable Graphs (see Figure 21.18) show how much your customers owe. The bar graph is an aging graph, showing how much is overdue in 30 day intervals. The pie graph shows a piece of the pie for each customer who owes you money. This graph is incredibly useful for giving you a complete image of your outstanding receivables by showing which customers make up the bulk of the outstanding amounts and how overdue your receivables really are.

■ **Accounts Payable.** The Accounts Payable Graphs (see Figure 21.19) are much like the accounts receivable graphs, but they show how much you owe rather than how much is owed to you. The bar graph shows an aging schedule of how overdue your bills are. The pie graph breaks out a piece of the pie for each creditor so you can easily see to whom you owe the most money.

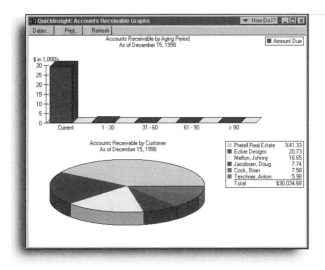

FIGURE 21.18

The Accounts Receivable Graphs present an A/R aging schedule and a breakdown of receivables per customer.

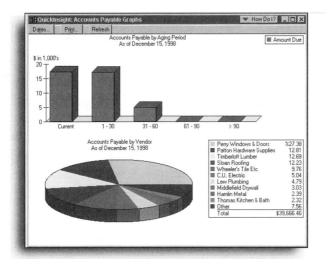

FIGURE 21.19

The Accounts Payable Graphs show how much your company owes and to whom.

■ **Net Worth.** The New Worth Graph (see Figure 21.20) is a little different from the others. It is a bar graph with a bar for each month, and it shows assets above the zero line and liabilities below the zero line. A line graph connecting each bar shows your actual net worth for each month (assets minus liabilities). Double-click any asset or liability part of the graph to see a pie graph that details the accounts that make up the bar. Double-click any net worth point (shown as small squares within the bars) to see a pie depicting the breakdown of assets, liabilities, and net worth.

FIGURE 21.20

Use Net Worth Graphs to visualize the value of your company.

1 Double-click a bar to view the components of the graphed item.

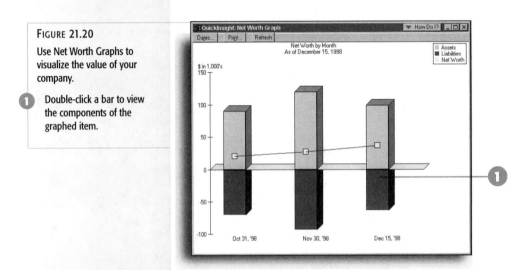

- **Budget vs. Actual.** Two bar graphs (see Figure 21.21) display the difference between your budget and your company's actual performance. The top graph shows actual net income compared to budgeted net income for the month. The bottom graph shows the individual accounts and how far they are off the budget.

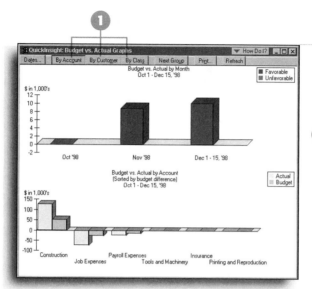

FIGURE 21.21

Use the Budget vs. Actual
Graphs to visualize how close
you are coming to meeting
your budget.

1 Click here to change the view
of budgeted amounts to
account, customer, or class.

Setting Preferences

Enter preferences that help QuickBooks decide
what to display on invoices, reports, checks, and other
forms and statements

Customize reports and forms by setting standards in
these screens

When you begin using QuickBooks, there are procedures and options already in place that control the way you enter information and the way QuickBooks performs.

You can change many of the program options so that QuickBooks behaves the way you want it to and offers the options that suit the needs of your company.

Many of the preferences can only be changed by your QuickBooks program administrator. If you have established security and password settings, as described in Chapter 28, "Security," you may need to rely on your administrator to adjust the settings as described in this chapter.

The sections in this chapter provide guidance for changing and setting all the performance options in QuickBooks. All these options are accessed by choosing **Preferences** from the **File** menu.

Accounting Preferences

When you click the Accounting icon in the Preferences window, you see there are no options available on the **My Preferences** tab. On the **Company Preferences** tab (see Figure 22.1) you can turn on or off the following preferences:

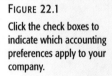

FIGURE 22.1

Click the check boxes to indicate which accounting preferences apply to your company.

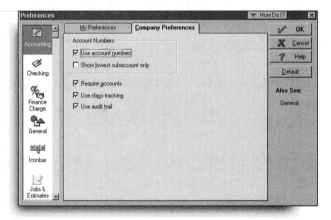

- **Use account <u>n</u>umbers.** You can turn the account numbers preference on and QuickBooks automatically assigns account numbers to all existing accounts. In the future, when you create new accounts, an account number field appears so that you can assign account numbers to your accounts. The account number becomes part of the account name so that reports sorted by account name will be listed in account number order. To override the QuickBooks automatic account numbers, you have to edit each account individually by choosing **Accounts**, **Edit** from the Chart of Accounts List window.

- **Show <u>l</u>owest subaccount only.** If you don't use account numbers, choosing this option has no effect. If you use account numbers, and you choose an account on a form or register transaction, the parent account name is displayed with the subaccount name unless you turn on this feature. Check this box and a subaccount name that you choose appears without its parent's name.

- **Require <u>a</u>ccounts.** If this box is checked, you won't be able to exit a transaction if an account hasn't been indicated in any area requesting an account. This box is checked by default when you start using QuickBooks and I recommend you keep it checked. Having the ability to enter transactions without account numbers causes QuickBooks to assign transactions to accounts with names such as "Uncategorized Expense" and that may cause confusion on your financial statements.

- **Use cla<u>s</u>s tracking.** If you want to use the class tracking feature offered by QuickBooks, you must check this box. QuickBooks then provides a field for entering a class on all your transactions. See Chapter 9, "Separating Your Company into Logical Divisions," for more information about class tracking.

- **Use audit <u>t</u>rail.** The audit trail is a record of all transactions and changes made to transactions in QuickBooks. Although you may find using the audit trail slows the performance of your QuickBooks program, this is a beneficial

Using account numbers

The choice to use account numbers is yours. QuickBooks doesn't require the numbers and, in fact, won't assign account numbers unless you request it in this preference window. For companies with a small quantity of accounts (under 50, for example), account numbers may not be necessary. A company that has many accounts may appreciate the fact that using account numbers enables you to control the organization of accounts as they appear in reports. Accounts that are numbered are grouped in order of their numbers. Without account numbers, QuickBooks groups accounts in alphabetical order on reports.

feature for tracing activity and changes that have been entered in the program. The audit trail is particularly useful if more than one person has access to your QuickBooks file.

If you are finished entering or changing preferences, be sure to click the **OK** button, so your selections will be saved and implemented.

Checking Preferences

Consider changing checking preferences if you use the check-writing feature of QuickBooks. When you click the **Checking** icon in the Preferences window, you see that the only options available are on the **Company Preferences** tab (see Figure 22.2). On this tab you can turn on or off the following preferences:

FIGURE 22.2

Customize some of the checking preferences if you use the check-writing feature in QuickBooks.

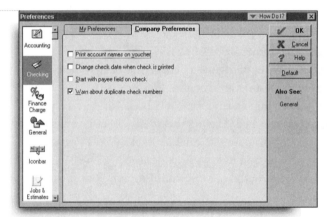

- **Print account names on voucher**. If this selection is turned on, QuickBooks includes the name of the account with the detailed information that prints on the voucher that accompanies your check.

- **Change check date when check is printed**. When you create a check, a date appears on the check form. If you want to use the date from the check form on your printed check, leave this option unchecked. Check this box if you want QuickBooks to use today's date when it prints checks.

- **Start with payee field on check**. Rather than positioning your cursor at the top of a check, bill, or credit card charge form, checking this option forces QuickBooks to position your cursor in the **Payee** or **Vendor** field as soon as you open one of these forms.

- **Warn about duplicate check numbers**. As a reminder to you, QuickBooks issues an audible warning if you are about to write a check with a number that duplicates a check previously written. If this box is unchecked (it is checked by default), you get no warning when a check number is about to be duplicated.

SEE ALSO

➤ *For more information about using QuickBooks to write checks, see page 257*

Finance Charge Preferences

If your company regularly assesses finance charges and does so in a consistent manner, it may be useful to you to set standard finance charges that apply to all customers. This way you won't have to determine a separate charge for each customer—you can rely on QuickBooks to assess finance charges for you.

Click the **Finance Charge** icon on the left side of the Preferences window to access these options that appear on the **Company Preferences** tab (see Figure 22.3). On this tab you can see the following preferences:

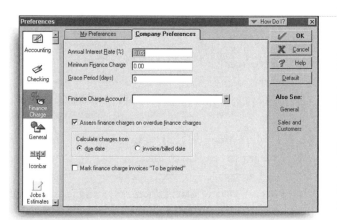

FIGURE 22.3

Does your company apply finance charges when customers don't pay on time? If so, set your standard rate and minimum amount of charge on this screen.

- **Annual Interest Rate (%).** The annual interest rate is the standard rate that applies to all or most of your customers. The rate should be entered here as an annual rate (enter 12 for 12 percent, 9.5 for 9.5 percent, and so on)—QuickBooks calculates the rate as a monthly charge on outstanding balances.

- **Minimum Finance Charge.** This is an amount—the smallest amount you want QuickBooks to charge to a customer. For example, you may want QuickBooks to round a small finance charge up to $1 if the assessed charge is less than $1. If that is the case, you would enter 1.00 for the minimum finance charge.

- **Grace Period (days).** You can designate a grace period before finance charges are assessed. Giving customers a few extra days after a payment is due allows for delays in mail delivery or delays due to customer emergencies.

- **Finance Charge Account.** Indicate the income account to which finance charges should be added. This might be an account called Finance Charges, Late Payment Fees, or Interest Income.

- **Assess finance charges on overdue finance charges.** If a customer owes you $1,000 and has already been assessed a finance charge of $12, is the next month's finance charge based on $1,000 or the full balance due of $1,012? Check this box if you want to include the finance charge already due (in this case, $12) when calculating the next month's finance charge.

- **Calculate charges from: due date or invoice/billed date.** If your finance charge is to be assessed if payment is not received within 30 days, does the 30 days start with the date the invoice is due or the date the invoice is issued? After you have established this company policy, check the appropriate box.

- **Mark finance charge invoices "To be is printed."** If you want to send an invoice to your customers when finance charges are assessed, QuickBooks automatically generates invoices and places them in your list of statements that are waiting to be printed. Check this box if you want QuickBooks to set up these forms for printing.

General Preferences

When you click the **General** icon on the left side of the Preferences window you see that you have both personal preferences (**My Preferences**) and **Company Preferences** available to you.

The general preferences include options for changing the way that your QuickBooks program performs and responds to you. The preferences are listed as follows:

- **Hide Qcards for all windows.** If the pop-up Qcards seem to frequently get in your way, or if you are familiar enough with the program that you don't need constant reminders about how each feature works, you can uncheck this box and the Qcards leave you alone. Check the box again and Qcards come running back to greet you.

- **Pressing Enter moves between fields.** When entering transactions on forms or in a register, pressing **Enter** normally finishes the transaction and moves you to the next form or the next register entry. If you would prefer to have **Enter** move you from field to field, check this box. Then, instead of pressing **Enter** to complete the transaction, press Ctrl+Enter, or click the **OK** or **Next** button.

- **Beep when recording a transaction.** Each time you finish a transaction and either close the window or move to the next transaction, a "beep" sounds if this box is checked.

- **Automatically place decimal point.** If most of the entries you make include numbers that have two decimal places (such as 12.75 or 1978.55), you may want to consider having QuickBooks type the decimal place for you. You enter all the digits of the number (197855, for example), and QuickBooks inserts the decimal place before the last two digits (1978.55). Be careful, if you check this option, that when you enter a number with zeros in the decimal places (345.00, for example), you type the zeros.

- **Warn when editing a transaction.** If this option is checked, and you have made changes to a previously-saved transaction, QuickBooks presents you with a pop-up warning if you try to close the transaction without saving it.

- **Warn when deleting a transaction or unused list item.** If this option is checked and you attempt to delete a transaction, or if you attempt to delete an item that hasn't been used, QuickBooks presents you with a pop-up warning, asking you to verify that you want to continue with the deletion.

- **Bring back all one time messages.** Sometimes you see messages in QuickBooks that are accompanied by a check box enabling you to request that the message not be viewed again. If you checked all those boxes and now the one-time-only messages are only a fond memory, you can check this box and bring them all back.

- **Automatically recall last transaction for this name.** If this option is turned on, QuickBooks automatically fills in a bill, check, or credit card with the same information you used the last time you issued such a form with the same vendor name. For example, if you wrote a check last month to Electric Power Co. for $212.50 for utilities expense, and this month you begin writing another check to Electric Power Co., QuickBooks fills in the rest of the check with the same amount and account as you used the last time. You always have the option of overriding this information.

- **Desktop options.** Choose one of the desktop options (as shown in Figure 22.4). If you select **Save when closing company**, all the windows you were displaying when you closed the company file appear the next time you open QuickBooks. If you pick **Save current desktop**, all the windows that are visible on the desktop at the moment you choose this option (with the exception of the Preferences window), appear each time you open QuickBooks. (Note that if you choose **Save current desktop**, the next time you open this screen in the preferences window, a fourth choice appears—**Keep previously saved desktop**. You should choose this setting if you want to return to the desktop you saved the last time you set this preference.) If you pick **Don't save the desktop**, your desktop is always cleared each time you open the program.

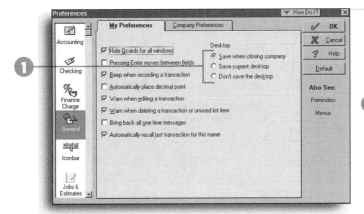

FIGURE 22.4

The **General** preferences include several miscellaneous items that control how your QuickBooks program performs.

① Choose which desktop option you prefer.

- **Time format.** On the **Company Preferences** tab (see Figure 22.5), choose a format for displaying time, either with a period or a colon separating hours and minutes. The time format is used when tracking time for payroll or billing time to customers.

- **Never update name information when saving transactions.** If you change the address or other information about a vendor or customer while creating a form such as an invoice or purchase order, a box pops up onscreen asking you whether you want to update the name information in your customer or vendor list. Checking this box in the **Company Preferences** prevents QuickBooks from asking whether you want to update the name information.

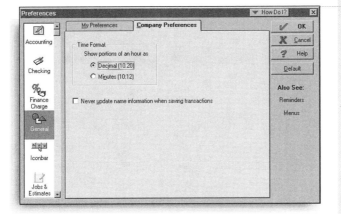

FIGURE 22.5

Click in the check box to have QuickBooks update your vendor and customer lists whenever there is a change of address or similar change.

Quickly add button to iconbar

If you find there is a particular window, such as a favorite report, that you display frequently, turn that window into a button on your iconbar and save yourself the time of searching through the menus every time you want to open the window. To add a button to the iconbar that displays a window, open the window on your screen, then choose **Window**, **Add Window to Iconbar**. In the window that appears (see Figure 22.7), choose an image for the button by clicking a picture in the available list, then add a name that will appear as text on the button, and a description that will appear when your mouse hovers over the button. Click **OK** to add the button to your iconbar.

Iconbar Preferences

Wondering where the iconbar is hiding in QuickBooks? If you want to see the iconbar, you have to ask for it in the Preferences window. In addition to choosing whether to display the iconbar, there are some steps you can take to customize the bar. Click the **Iconbar** icon on the left of the Preferences window to explore these options:

- **Displaying the iconbar.** Choose from one of four display options (see Figure 22.6). **Show icons and text** displays the iconbar with both pictures and text on the buttons. **Show icons only** displays the iconbar with only the pictures. **Show text only** displays the iconbar with words but no pictures. **Don't show iconbar** turns off the display of the iconbar.

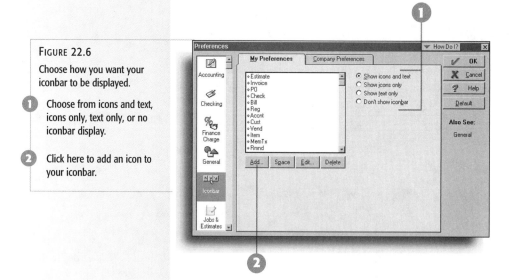

FIGURE 22.6

Choose how you want your iconbar to be displayed.

1 Choose from icons and text, icons only, text only, or no iconbar display.

2 Click here to add an icon to your iconbar.

- **Add.** Add a button to the iconbar by clicking **Add** and choosing from a limited list of additional buttons available through QuickBooks. The Add Iconbar Item window appears and you are expected to click the name of a button you want to add, click an image for the button from a list of available pictures, enter a name that will appear on the button, and enter a description that will appear if you hover your mouse over the button. Personally, I like adding the **Calculator** button to the Iconbar so that I can pop up a calculator onscreen just by clicking a button.

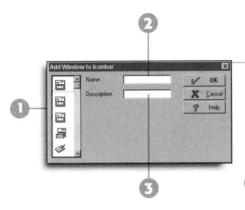

FIGURE 22.7

It's a quick process to add a button to your iconbar that displays a favorite window. Display the window, then choose **Window, Add Window to Iconbar**.

❶ Scroll through this image list until you find the image you want on your new button, then click once on that image.

❷ Enter the name that will appear as text on your new button.

❸ Enter a description that will appear as fly-over information when your mouse passes over the button.

- **Space.** To place a separating space between buttons on your iconbar, click the name of the button *after which* you want to place a space, then click the **Space** button. When you close the Preferences window, a space appears after the button you indicated on your iconbar.

- **Edit.** To change the picture that appears on an iconbar button, or the accompanying text, click the name of the malfeasant button on the list of iconbar buttons, and then click **Edit**. In the window that appears, make your choices for a fresh face for this button. Click **OK** to save your changes.

- **Delete.** One problem with the QuickBooks iconbar is that the buttons seem awfully large and it's hard to fit additional buttons on the bar. But maybe there are some buttons you don't ever use and you would like to bump them off the bar to make room for other, more useful buttons. Click the name of a button you don't want, and then click the **Delete** button. Presto! The button is off the list.

Jobs & Estimates Preferences

If you use QuickBooks Pro, you have a **Jobs & Estimates** icon in your Preferences window. The options presented in this category include the right to reword the choices for job status, and some general questions about whether your company prepares estimates and does progress billing. You can skip this section if you use the regular QuickBooks program.

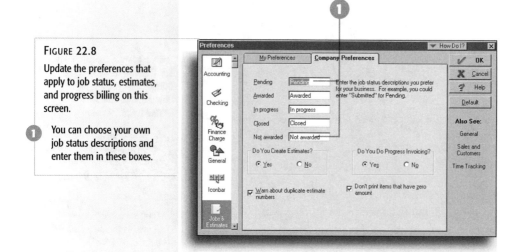

The preferences are listed as follows:

- **Job status descriptions.** QuickBooks uses the descriptions of **P**ending, **A**warded, **I**n progress, **C**losed, and **No**t **awarded** to describe the status of jobs you perform. If other descriptions fit your business better (a freelance writer, for example, might use descriptions such as Proposal, Outline, Manuscript, Edit, and Completed to describe the stages of his work), you can enter your own descriptions in the spaces provided on the **Company Preferences** tab.

- **Do You Create Estimates?** Indicate whether your company uses QuickBooks to create estimates. Choose **No** if you create estimates on paper, but don't record them in QuickBooks.

- **Do You Do Progress Invoicing?** Indicate whether you want to use the progress billing option for partial billing of jobs in progress. Choosing **Yes** doesn't mean you have to bill a job in pieces; choosing **No** prevents you from ever doing so— you probably want to choose **Yes** just so you have the option.

- **Warn about duplicate estimates numbers.** Leave this question blank if you do not create estimates in QuickBooks. Check this box if you want QuickBooks to give you a reminder that you're about to issue the same estimate number to a second estimate.

- **Don't print items that have zero amount.** Leave this question blank if you chose **No** for the progress invoicing question. If you plan to use progress invoicing and some items on your invoice have been paid, thus leaving a zero balance, check this box if you want to leave the zero-balance items off of future invoices.

Menus Preferences

After you get used to finding your way around QuickBooks, you may find that some of the menu choices you use frequently are hidden away on side menus such as **Other Activities** and **Other Lists**. To bring those shy items into the spotlight of the main **Activities** and **Lists** menus, click the **Menus** icon in your Preferences window and check off the items you want to free from the **Other** side menus.

The items listed under **Activities Menu** (see Figure 22.9) normally appear on the **Activities, Other Activities** menu. Check the box next to any item you want to move to the main **Activities** menu.

FIGURE 22.9

Check off all the items that should appear on your main **Activities** and **Lists** menus.

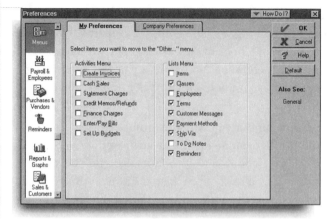

Likewise, the items shown under **Lists Menu** normally hide out on the **Lists**, **Other Lists** side menu. Check any of these boxes and these lists are more prominently displayed on the main **Lists** menu.

Payroll and Employees Preferences

If you use QuickBooks to track your payroll, you may be interested in the preferences that apply specifically to employees and payroll. Only available on the **Company Preferences** tab, choose from several options to help customize the performance of QuickBooks in this area (see Figure 22.10). The preferences are listed as follows:

FIGURE 22.10

Choose from several preferences relating to your QuickBooks payroll.

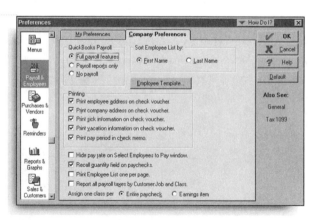

- **QuickBooks Payroll.** Tell QuickBooks whether you plan to use the program to track all your payroll, only to produce payroll reports, or if you don't use QuickBooks at all for payroll.

- **Sort Employees List.** You can sort your employees list (available on the **Lists** menu) by first name or last name.

- **Printing options.** If you plan to use QuickBooks to print paychecks, choose which items you would like to have print on the check voucher form. See Chapter 18, "Paying Employees and Contractors," for more information about using QuickBooks for processing your payroll.

- **Hide pay rate on Select Employees to Pay window.** Depending on who has access to your QuickBooks file, you may want to make the Select Employees to Pay window available to other users, but without the pay rate displayed. Check this box to prevent display of the pay rate.

- **Recall quantity field on paychecks.** Check this box if you want to have QuickBooks carry forward information from prior paychecks relating to amounts based on quantities. For example, amounts based on the number of hours an employee works, where the employee works the same number of hours in each pay period, can be repeated on future pay checks without having to enter the information over again.

- **Print Employee List one per page.** When you print an employee list in QuickBooks, you have the option of printing one employee per page with all that employee's related information. That option, however, is available only if you check this box in the Preferences window.

- **Report all payroll taxes by Customer: Job, Service Item, and Class.** Some, none, or all the options may be presented to you, depending on what QuickBooks features your company uses. Checking this item enables you to print reports that break down payroll taxes by the features listed (job, item, class).

- **Assign one class per paycheck/earnings item.** This item is available only if you use the QuickBooks class tracking feature. Choose to assign a class to an entire paycheck or break out separate service items and assign each item to a class.

In addition to the preceding preferences, you can click the **Employee Template** button (see Figure 22.11) to open a window that enables you to set payroll information that all employees have in common. The information you enter in the employee template window appears on the payroll record for each employee. Then, when you create a paycheck for an employee, you can use this information. You can also remove or overwrite this information for individual employees.

The following payroll information can be entered on the employee template:

- **Type of earnings.** Enter regular pay, vacation pay, overtime pay, and so on, and a standard rate for these earnings. This option is particularly useful for a company that employs a lot of hourly employees who all work at the same pay rate.

- **Pay period.** Choose the frequency with which you issue paychecks.

- **Use time data to create paychecks.** If you use the QuickBooks **Timer**, check this box to instruct QuickBooks to use data from the **Timer** program when creating paychecks.

- **Additions, deductions, and company contributions.** Indicate items that appear on all or most paychecks, such as deductions for health insurance, expense reimbursements, or bonuses. If the amount is the same for all employees, include an amount here in addition to the item name. If there is a maximum amount that applies to all or most employees (for example, bonuses cannot exceed $500), enter that maximum amount in the **Limit** column.

- **Taxes.** Click the **Taxes** button to indicate which taxes apply to all or most employees (such as federal withholding, social security, state income tax, and so on).

■ **Sick/Vacation Pay.** Click the **Sick/Vacation** button to set company standards for issuing and tracking sick time and vacation pay. Indicate the total number of hours per year or pay period that should be issued to employees, and whether sick and vacation hours start over with zero at the beginning of each year (check the **Reset hours each new year** box to start over again).

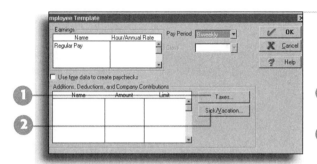

FIGURE 22.11

Choose payroll preferences that appear on each employee's payroll record.

❶ Click here to indicate which taxes apply to all employees.

❷ Click here to set standards for sick and vacation pay.

Purchases & Vendors Preferences

There are a few company preference items that affect the treatment of purchase orders and inventory. If you don't use the QuickBooks inventory feature and don't use purchase orders, these items won't apply to you. The preferences are listed as follows:

■ **Inventory and purchase orders are active.** Check this box if you use the inventory and purchase order features in QuickBooks. This box is automatically set if you indicated an interest in using these features during the EasyStep Interview.

■ **Warn if not enough inventory to sell.** QuickBooks keeps track of the quantity of inventory items you have on hand. If you prepare an invoice or a cash sale form for a quantity of inventory items that exceeds the amount you have on hand, QuickBooks pops up with a message letting you know about the potential problem. Uncheck this box and QuickBooks won't bother you with information about inventory shortages.

- **Warn about duplicate purchase order <u>n</u>umbers.** Check this box if you want QuickBooks to pester you with a warning that you are issuing a purchase order with a number that duplicates another order.

- **<u>B</u>ills are due.** When you enter bills in QuickBooks, a reminder appears in the **Reminders** list to indicate that the bill payment is due. Set the number of days here (see Figure 22.12) so that QuickBooks knows how long to wait before getting after you to pay your bills.

FIGURE 22.12

Set up preferences that apply to your inventory and other purchases.

1 How many days should pass after a bill's date before the bill is due?

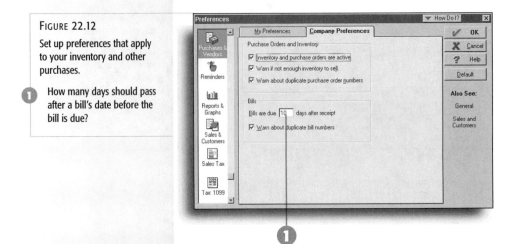

Not enough inventory on hand

When you issue an invoice, if you get a warning indicating there is not enough inventory on hand to fill the quantity shown on the invoice, you are not prevented from issuing the invoice for the quantity requested. When you see a warning that the quantity of inventory items you are selling exceeds the amount you have on hand, make a note to yourself to check inventory items on order, or to order more items so that you won't run short.

- **<u>W</u>arn about duplicate bill numbers.** This check box is quite handy. Suppose you get a bill from Acme Supply Company and you enter it in QuickBooks. Two weeks later you get another bill from Acme Supply Co. and you enter it in QuickBooks. If the second bill has the same number as the first, you've probably got a duplicate bill. Check this box and QuickBooks lets you know you've got a duplicate.

Reminders Preferences

The QuickBooks **Reminders** list gives you a summary of every-thing that needs to be done. It's your master to do list—with reminders about checks and forms that need to be printed, bills that need to be paid, invoice payments that are late, and money that is waiting to be deposited.

When you use the **Reminders** list, you can easily stay on top of all the day-to-day tasks that help keep your company running. Click the **Reminders** icon in the Preferences window to access these options:

- **Show Reminders List when opening a Company file.**
  Check this box on the **My Preferences** tab and QuickBooks displays your **Reminders** list every time you open the pro-gram (see Figure 22.13).

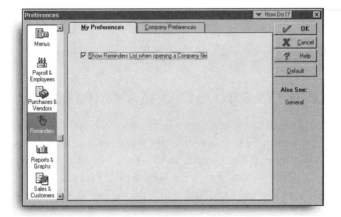

FIGURE 22.13
Check this box and you see your **Reminders** list each time you open QuickBooks.

- **Reminders: Company Preferences.** Click the **Company Preferences** tab and choose which items you want to see displayed on your **Reminders** list. The **Show Summary** option displays a total amount without any detail of the actual items. Click **Show List** next to any item on the list and the **Reminders** list displays the detail of what makes up the total amount. Click **Don't Remind Me** and the item won't appear on your **Reminders** list. For all items that include a **Remind Me** option, indicate the number of days before the item is due that you want to start seeing this type of item in your **Reminders** list. For example, in Figure 22.14, a reminder to print paychecks appears in the **Reminders** list five days before the paychecks are due.

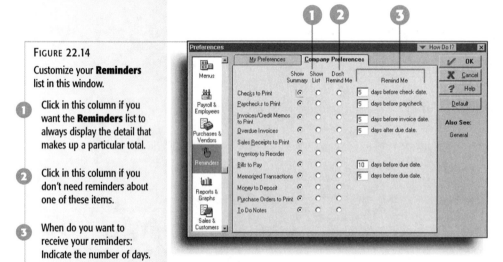

FIGURE 22.14

Customize your **Reminders** list in this window.

1. Click in this column if you want the **Reminders** list to always display the detail that makes up a particular total.

2. Click in this column if you don't need reminders about one of these items.

3. When do you want to receive your reminders: Indicate the number of days.

Reports and Graphs Preferences

Make some basic decisions about how you want your reports to print and you save lots of time when you actually create the reports. The options in this section apply to all reports in QuickBooks. Click the **Reports & Graphs** icon in the Preferences window, and then choose the options that will be helpful to you:

- **Refreshing Reports and Graphs.** If you make changes to a report or to the underlying data that makes up a report, you may want QuickBooks to update the report immediately, or perhaps you don't. On the **My Preferences** tab (see Figure 22.15), Choose **Prompt me to refresh** if you want QuickBooks to ask you whether you want a report refreshed to reflect your changes. Choose **Refresh automatically** to have QuickBooks take care of refreshing your reports every time you make a change. Choose **Don't refresh** if you want to take charge of refreshing your reports yourself (by clicking the **Refresh** button that appears on each report).

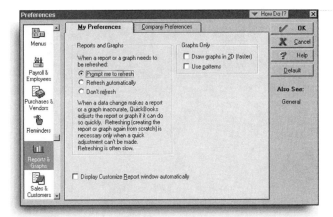

FIGURE 22.15
Enter report preferences on this screen.

- **Draw graphs in 2D (faster).** Two dimensional graphs work just as well as the fancy 3D kind, and QuickBooks can create them a bit faster as well. Click this check box if you find your 3D graphs are taking too long to create, or if you simply prefer the 2D style.

- **Use patterns.** Click this box if you want QuickBooks to display your graphs in designs made up entirely of black, gray, and white. The color graphs are nice, but the effect can be lost if you don't have a color printer.

- **Display Customize Report window automatically.** If you spend a lot of time customizing your reports, and are a regular customer of the Customize Reports window, you can check this box and QuickBooks automatically displays that window each time you open a report.

- **Summary Reports Basis.** Is your company a cash-basis company or an accrual-basis company? Do you typically like to see your company reports on the cash basis or the accrual basis? Generally, the answer is the same to both of these questions. If your company tracks accounts receivable and accounts payable, you want accrual-basis reports. If you report income when you receive it rather than when it is earned, and expenses when they are paid rather than when they are incurred, it sounds like you are a cash basis company. On the **Company Preferences** tab indicate which basis applies to your company (see Figure 22.16).

FIGURE 22.16

Choose from several options that determine how your reports are prepared and displayed.

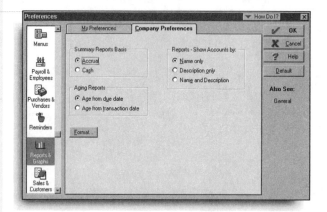

- **Reports—Show Accounts by.** Another option for displaying information on reports. Choose **Name only** if you need to see only the name of your accounts on your company reports. Remember that if you use account numbers, the account number is part of the name and is displayed along with the name. Choose **Description only** if you prefer to show account descriptions rather than names. If you display your reports with account descriptions, be sure to fill in the description field every time you create a new account. Choose **Name and Description** if you want your reports to display both types of information for your accounts.

- **Aging Reports.** Accounts Receivable Aging Reports show how much is owed to your company and for how long the amounts have been owed. Choose whether aging is determined from the due date of the invoice or the date of the actual transaction. If you create invoices on the same day of your transactions, it doesn't matter which option you choose here.

■ **Format.** Click the **Format** button to display the Report Format Preferences window (see Figure 22.17). Choose items in this window that apply to all reports you create. Choose whether negative numbers should be displayed with a minus sign to the left of the number, in red, in parentheses, or with a minus sign to the right of the number. Choose to display all numbers divided by 1000 (1,000,000 would then be displayed as 1,000), not to display accounts with zero amounts, and whether to display cents. Choose font options, and choose a standard header and/or footer for your reports. Click **OK** to close the format window when you have made all your choices.

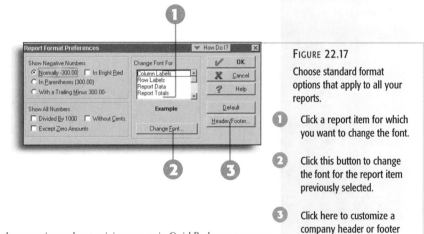

FIGURE 22.17

Choose standard format options that apply to all your reports.

❶ Click a report item for which you want to change the font.

❷ Click this button to change the font for the report item previously selected.

❸ Click here to customize a company header or footer that appears on all your reports.

SEE ALSO

➤ *For more information about creating and customizing reports in QuickBooks, see page 397*

Sales & Customers Preferences

Click the **Sales & Customers** icon in the Preferences window to set some standard sales options that apply to all your invoices. You can always override these options on the actual invoice form. The preferences are listed as follows:

■ **Usual Shipping Method.** Is there one method of shipping you use time and again? Choose the carrier you prefer and your entry appears on all your sales forms (see Figure 22.18).

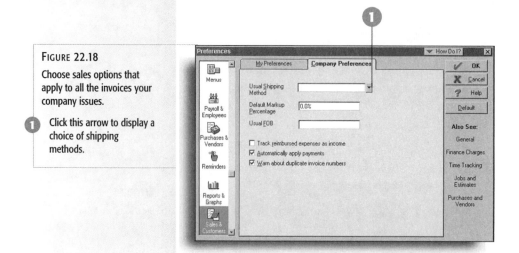

■ **Default Markup Percentage.** Enter an amount for standard markup. Any items you purchase and resell are affected by this amount. To enter a 20 percent markup, enter 20 in the space provided. A 10.5 percent markup should be entered as 10.5. QuickBooks fills in the "%" sign.

■ **Usual FOB.** Choose the normal FOB status that applies on your sales. You would enter Destination if your company pays to ship the order to its destination and retains ownership of the item until it reaches its final destination. Enter Our warehouse if the customer pays to ship the item from your warehouse and takes over ownership at the time of shipment. This status is for your information only, can be over-ridden on the actual invoice, and has no accounting implications.

■ **Track reimbursed expenses as income.** When you make a purchase and expect reimbursement from your customer, does that reimbursement offset the purchase price, or do you report it as income? If you report reimbursements as income, check this box. If you don't use this option, QuickBooks relieves the expense account by the amount of the reimbursement and the result on your income statement is as if no transaction had occurred.

- **Automatically apply payments.** If this box is checked, payments you receive are applied to outstanding invoices, the oldest invoice first. If you leave this box unchecked, when you receive a payment and open the Receive Payments window, QuickBooks lists the outstanding invoices for the customer, but makes no attempt to apply the payment to any particular invoices.

- **Warn about duplicate invoice numbers.** Check this box if you want QuickBooks to indicate that you are about to issue an invoice with a number that has already been used.

SEE ALSO

➤ *For more information on the meaning of FOB (Free on Board) and its importance to your company, see page 205*

Sales Tax Preferences

If your company doesn't charge sales tax, you can skip this section. If you do charge sales tax, click the **Sales Tax** icon in the Preferences window, and choose **Yes** as an answer to the **Do You Charge Sales Tax?** question on the **Company Preferences** tab (see Figure 22.19). The other options on this tab are only available if the first question is answered **Yes**.

The preferences are listed as follows:

- **Owe Sales Tax.** When do you charge sales tax to your customers? At the time you issue the invoice or when you receive payments? Cash basis taxpayers don't charge sales tax until they actually receive money from the customer. Accrual basis taxpayers charge sales tax on their invoices and owe sales tax to authorities based on invoiced sales rather than cash received.

FIGURE 22.19

These sales tax preferences automate the process of charging sales tax to customers.

❶ Click here to display the sales tax items.

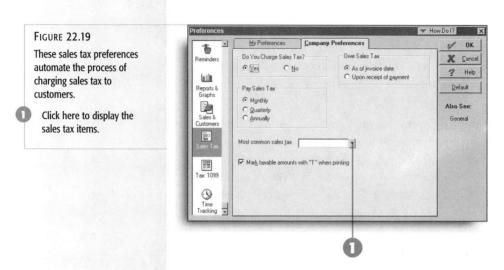

- **Pay Sales Tax.** Do you report and pay your sales tax monthly, every three months (quarterly), or once a year (annually)? Choose the option that applies to your company.

- **Most common sales tax.** Click the arrow and choose the sales tax item that you most frequently charge to customers. You should have already set up items for your sales tax rates, but if you haven't, choose **<Add New>** from the list that appears when you click the arrow. If you only charge one type of sales tax, that is what will appear in this area. Some companies charge both a state and local sales tax. Only one item can appear here. The sales tax you indicate here will automatically appear on your invoices. You can override that amount on the invoice form, or add another sales tax, if necessary.

- **Mark taxable amounts with "T" when printing.** If you sell both taxable and nontaxable items (you may charge sales tax on sales of merchandise, but not on services you provide), QuickBooks marks the taxable items with a capital letter "T" if you check this box. You probably don't need to bother with this if the items you sell are either all taxable or all nontaxable.

Tax 1099 Preferences

There are guidelines set out by the IRS indicating when a 1099 form must be issued. For example, if you pay a contractor more than $600 in a calendar year, you are supposed to present him with a 1099 form showing his earnings for the year.

You probably won't need to change the threshold amounts that are already listed in the Tax 1099 Company Preferences window (see Figure 22.20) because these amounts comply with the federal guidelines.

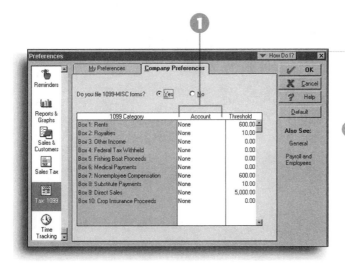

FIGURE 22.20
You probably won't need to change the thresholds listed in this window.

① Enter the account where the 1099 category items are recorded.

You do, however, need to indicate the accounts in which these types of amounts are tracked. For example, if you pay rent, you probably have a Rent Expense account. That is the account you would choose for the 1099 category of Rents. If you pay subcontractors, you probably have an account called Contract Labor or Subcontractors. That is the account you would choose for the 1099 category of Nonemployee Compensation.

SEE ALSO
➤ *For more information about 1099 filing requirements, see page 335*

Time Tracking Preferences

If you don't use the QuickBooks **Time Tracking** feature, you can skip this section. If you do use this feature, your preference choices here are simple.

Click the **Time Tracking** icon in the Preferences window, then choose **Yes** on the **Company Preferences** tab to indicate that you use the time tracking feature (see Figure 22.21).

Indicate the day that represents the first day of your work week. This is the day on which your company time sheets begin.

FIGURE 22.21

Click Yes if you use the QuickBooks **Time Tracking** feature.

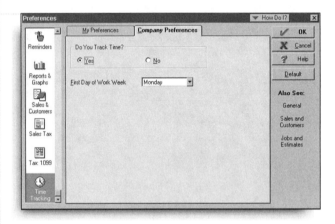

PART

V

QuickBooks Meets the 21ˢᵗ Century

Going Online with QuickBooks

Review common questions about online banking, and get a quick overview of what's involved

Setting up your Internet connection so that QuickBooks recognizes it

Exploring online banking options and applying for an account

Setting up and initially reconciling your online account

Making deposits and payments; transferring funds online

Sending email messages and online payment inquiries to your bank

QuickBooks' online payroll service and QuickBooks-sponsored educational resources on the Internet

Some business owners love online banking and swear by its convenience. Others question the safety of its transactions, and prefer to stick to paper checks. In this chapter, we explore online banking, online payments, and look at some of the online resources QuickBooks provides. Even if you decide not to do your banking or bill-paying online, there's a wealth of relevant and frequently updated information on the Web to which QuickBooks provides links.

Common Questions About QuickBooks and Online Banking

For the moment, let me cut to the chase and answer a handful of questions many people have about online banking and bill payment.

- To begin with, QuickBooks does not conduct financial transactions over the Internet. A private secure line is used. If you log on through and fill out any bank's online application, it's highly doubtful that anyone can see what you are doing.

- Most of the complaints people have with online banking are not issues of security, but of convenience never realized. Although it's true that with online banking you visit your lending institution much less frequently, the time spent handling initial glitches can add up to a good deal of frustration. Others point out that after you take the time to work out the kinks, you truly save time and money. Most complaints do not revolve around money unaccounted for or payments made late; rather, they concern the usual technological muddle of PIN code errors and the occasional inability to properly access your account because of some software problem.

- Even if your bank does not support online banking, you can sign up through Intuit for online bill payment.

- Online bill payment is almost never instantaneous. Very few institutions are set up to receive online regular customer remittance. Most often, when you pay bills online, you are

Where to learn more

To read some articles about what others think of online banking, check out these Web sites:

http://techweb.cmp.com/
hpc/Jan97/31BANK01.HTM

http://www.investor-
links.com/service-bank-
us.html

http://www.idg.net/idg_
frames/english/content.
cgi?vc=docid_
9-39612.html

http://www.exis.net/
umbrella/onlinbnk.htm

simply empowering a company to write checks on your behalf, which are sent through standard mail to your designated payee. The entire process for a bill to be noted as paid and the check to clear your account takes longer than if you mailed it yourself. Online bill payment does not mean saying goodbye to paper. It means you are paying someone else to manage the paper for you.

- Transferring money between your own accounts is somewhat instantaneous. If you are the type to snoop around your accounts and transfer extra dollars to those earning the highest interest, you can transfer these funds with a click of the mouse.

- When we go to the bank, most of us take the opportunity to ask questions about our accounts while we conduct regular bank business. It's true though, when you do online banking, you can send an email along with your transaction, and perhaps someone gets back to you. You should understand, however, that the ability to raise a real response from your bank via email truly varies from institution to institution. Some banks are simply going to be more in tune with their online client's needs than others.

Preliminary and Precautionary Steps

You find that the nuts and bolts of carrying out online banking are pretty easy. Before we go into detail about setting up accounts and conducting online transactions, the following are some preliminary and precautionary steps to keep in mind. This bird's-eye view is just to show you, at a glance, what's involved.

Following the process

1. First, you should determine whether your existing bank provides online services. You can do this by calling them, or viewing QuickBooks' list of QuickBooks-friendly online institutions.

2. To see what your options are, begin walking through the QuickBooks Online Banking Interview (from the QuickBooks Navigator, select **Online Banking** from the **Checking and Credit Card** tab). Be prepared to deal with the following choices:

   - If your bank is one of the couple dozen that provides online services directly through QuickBooks, then you've won half the battle. You can simply continue the interview, make your lending institution aware that you will now be taking advantage of its online service, and begin banking and bill-paying through QuickBooks.

   - If your bank provides online services, but is not familiar with QuickBooks, you can still use the software your bank provides for an online connection to pay bills through QuickBooks, but you cannot do full online banking through QuickBooks. Stop the Interview, consult your lending institution, and get them to send you their software package for going online. It may not be difficult, however, to convince them to begin working with Intuit to provide online service through QuickBooks.

   - If your bank does not provide online banking, you can change your bank to a QuickBooks-friendly lending institution or simply sign up for Intuit's online bill paying service. You may continue the interview, exploring the options offered.

   - If you decide to switch banks to one that works online with QuickBooks, submit your online application as mentioned above and wait for account information to appear in the mail. (Check out the sidebar "Are online banking privileges a good enough reason to change banks?")

3. After you've received your bank info through the mail, return to the QuickBooks Online Banking Interview. You can then set up online accounts.

More online banks

The following are Web page links to other banks that do online banking, but may not yet set up to bank directly through QuickBooks. This can change quickly, though.

http://www.netbanker.com/index.shtml

http://www.keybank.com/educate/

As with many Internet links, content gets rearranged, and sent to different pages within a site. If you find one of the links above to be invalid, simply lop off the final segment of the URL. For example, remove the /educate segment from the www.keybank.com address.

After Your Account Is Activated

What follows is a synopsis of what you must do after your account is activated and before you can really start making online transactions. This may help you decide whether online banking is really for you or not.

After you establish online bank accounts, go online and download the most recent transactions that have cleared at your financial institution. It's important to know what transactions are outstanding before you generate new transactions. If you find discrepancies between the downloaded account information, and what you think is correct, call your bank and clarify. If you have to perform a reconciliation adjustment, do so before you do any transacting. Before you move on, your information in QuickBooks must match what your lending institution says about your account.

Finally, from the Chart of Account list, click your online account and choose **Edit**. You see an Online Account Info tab. Make sure this account information (routing number, account number, federal tax ID) matches what your bank sends you on paper. These precautions cut down on missing transactions. You can then begin transferring money between accounts online, paying bills, as well as occasionally matching transactions and reconciling accounts.

Let's roll to the beginning and take a close look at what's involved with QuickBooks online banking and bill-paying. At the end of the chapter, we look at QuickBooks online information resources that are valuable for any small business, even if you decide online banking is not for you at all.

Setting Up QuickBooks' Internet Connection

When QuickBooks takes you online, it does so using an Internet connection that you must specify in advance. QuickBooks does not walk you through setting up Internet access as part of the

---

Are online banking privileges a good enough reason to change banks?

If you are considering changing banks simply for online access, think twice. Even in this electronic age, some important banking and lending decisions are still based on rapport. If you've taken the time to get to know your banking officer, loan managers, and such, give a little thought to severing those relationships just to do things electronically. If, however, month after month, you simply dread the process of licking those stamps and envelopes and filling out all those checks yourself, then it's very true, online banking can diminish a lot of that drudgery.

Online Banking Interview. You may have taken the time to set this up when you first installed QuickBooks, but if not, you have to do it now before you can even begin investigating online banking. Before you start the Online Banking Interview, choose your Internet connection as follows. From the **Online** menu (at the top of the QuickBooks screen), select **Internet Connection Setup**, and the dialog box shown in Figure 23.1 appears. You have the three following choices:

- If you use a dial-up connection through an Internet Service Provider, or have AOL 4.0 for Windows 95 (or higher), check the first option: **I have an existing dial-up Internet connection**. Click **Next**, and you then see a list of the valid Internet dial-up connections on your computer. Select one, and each time you begin a QuickBooks online session, QuickBooks dials this connection for you. If you are already online when you start your next QuickBooks online session, QuickBooks simply uses the existing connection. If you change your Internet connection, QuickBooks tries to dial it up the old way, and your connection won't work (see the sidebar "If you change the way you log on to the Internet").

- If you connect to the Internet through a LAN, or some other continuous access that does not require a dial-up, check the **I have a direct Internet connection** option.

You're then asked to identify your HTTP Proxy, Security Proxy, and Browser. Use the Next button to click through the rest of the setup windows to provide this information.

- If you have no Internet access and want to give Intuit's preferred Internet service provider a spin, check **Sign me up for a Concentric Internet account.** QuickBooks then asks you to choose a user name and a password and provide billing information. It tries to automatically identify your modem as well. If you choose to sign up for Concentric, be prepared to log on to the Internet now, to complete the setup process.

After you have made your choice, click **Next** to continue.

Using QuickBooks Online Interview

Start learning about online banking and bill paying by walking through the Online Interview.

Starting the Setup Interview

1. Select the **Online Banking** icon from the **Checking and Credit Card** tab of the QuickBooks Navigator. You're informed that no accounts are set up for online service, and you're prompted to set them up (see Figure 23.2).

2. Click past the prompts, and the Online Banking Setup Interview appears. You notice three tabs: **Find Out More**, **Apply Now**, and **Enable Accounts**.

3. To see what QuickBooks has to say about online banking, click through the windows of the **Find Out More** tab of the Online Banking Setup Interview. You're then ready to explore your online banking account options at the **Apply Now** tab.

Going online with QuickBooks through AOL

Only the most recent version of AOL provides the type of Internet access that QuickBooks can use. Unless you have AOL 4, you have to invest in an Internet service provider that can set up a more standard type dial-up connection.

Investigating QuickBooks banking online with your own browser

If you want to use your browser to learn more about banks that offer online banking through QuickBooks, point your browser to this URL:

`hhtp://www.intuit.com /banking/filist.html`. Please note that this page includes banks that use Quicken files, as well as QuickBooks.

Figure 23.2

When exploring online banking, QuickBooks wants to sign you up with accounts first.

4. You're asked whether you want to apply now over the Internet, or have already received online banking information from a lending institution (see Figure 23.3). What follows are two sets of instructions depending on how you answer this question.

FIGURE 23.3

Here you can continue to set up your account from paperwork you've received, or you can apply online.

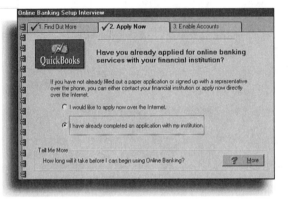

If You've Received Your Bank Info Through the Mail

If you've received a start-up kit from your online banking service, you are ready to make your account active. If you've been following along from the previous section and have not closed any dialog boxes, then proceed to the step-by-step that follows. If you haven't been following along from the previous section, then select the **Online Banking** icon of the **Checking and Credit Card** tab of the QuickBooks Navigator.

Activating your account

1. Select the **Apply Now** tab, and click the **Next** button. You're prompted with this question: **Have you already applied for online banking services with your financial institution?**

2. Choose the second option, **I have already completed an application with my institution**, and be prepared to enter your federal tax ID and a routing number provided by your bank.

3. You can either create a totally new QuickBooks account for your online banking or select an existing one.

4. Complete the account setup options, just as you would when creating any other QuickBooks account, providing an account number, opening balance, and name (see Figure 23.4).

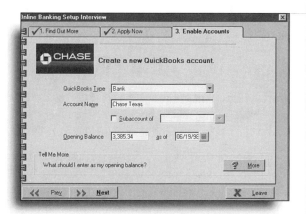

FIGURE 23.4

After choosing a bank and entering an account routing number, set up a QuickBooks account for that bank account.

5. Click **Next** to move through each window, as usual. Pay special attention to the distinction between online access, which simply enables you to check balances and transfer funds online, and online bill payment. Check both, if you want both enabled.

6. You can set up many online accounts at this time, or only one, returning later to set up others.

If You Are Still Exploring Your Options

If you are just now gathering information about applying over the Internet, do the following while viewing the screen (refer to Figure 23.3).

Exploring online banking options

1. Check **I would like to apply now over the Internet**, and click **Next**.

2. A new window appears. Select **Apply Now** (see Figure 23.5).

FIGURE 23.5

Click **Apply Now** to look at a
list of available online banks.

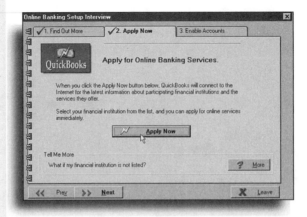

FIGURE 23.5

Click **Apply Now** to look at a
list of available online banks.

3. You see the Financial Institutions Directory dialog box.
It takes a moment for this screen to appear, because an
open Internet connection is required. If you are not currently online, QuickBooks logs on and opens the page (see
Figure 23.6).

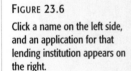

FIGURE 23.6

Click a name on the left side,
and an application for that
lending institution appears on
the right.

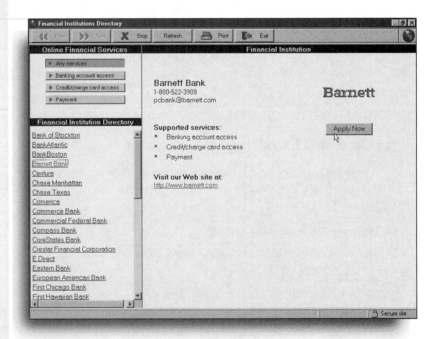

4. The left side of the screen is a scrolling menu listing banks that offer online services through QuickBooks. Click one, and the right side of the screen fills with information about that particular bank. Most banks offer online applications right there on the spot. Determine the following:

   • If you want to apply, fill out an application and click the **Submit** button. After you've filled out an application, or perhaps found a bank that requires you to call first, back out of the Financial Institutions Directory by clicking the **Exit** button, at the upper right.

   • If you did not apply, feel free to jump back into this lion's den at some later time and explore some more. Back out now by selecting the **Exit** button. Later, just click the **Apply Now** tab of the Online Banking Interview, and you can search through more banking selections. When you return to the Online Banking Interview, you find yourself just where you left off. QuickBooks does not make you go back to step 1 again.

5. Before closing the private connection, QuickBooks automatically searches each bank's data for updates (see Figure 23.7). Be patient while QuickBooks downloads newer info, and returns you to the opening Apply Now screen.

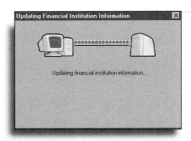

FIGURE 23.7
When you log off QuickBooks' connection, it retrieves new data from all lending institutions.

6. After submitting your application, wait a few days for a packet to arrive in the mail with your account information. This usually includes a PIN number, routing number, clarifying provisos, and other legalese that you'd better take the time to read (see the sidebar "What am I getting into?").

What am I getting into?

What sort of guarantees do banks make regarding online transactions? When you fill out an online application, each bank spells out how much responsibility it assumes regarding your online transactions. Sometimes, a bank views an online transaction similarly to an ATM withdrawal. Read very carefully what kind of recourse you have if there's a disagreement.

If you are going to use this account to pay bills online, get a clear picture how much responsibility the bank takes if a payment arrives late to the payee, even though you sent it online in plenty of time. Please keep in mind that most banks do not consider an email notice of a disagreement as binding as a written letter.

Using QuickBooks' private online connection

When you conduct the QuickBooks Online Interview, you have to go online through QuickBooks. You can't simply log on as normal and begin selecting QuickBooks online options. That's because QuickBooks conducts online business through a secure connection.

How to spot an online account in your account list

If you create a new online account, or convert an existing account to an online one, a small lightning bolt appears next to its name in your Chart of Accounts.

7. With your account number, routing number, and additional online info handy, read the preceding section and move on to "Going Online with a New Account."

Going Online with a New Account

After setting up your account, leave the interview and click the **Online Banking** icon again (from the **Checking and Credit Card** tab of the Navigator). You see the Online Banking Center window. Click here to send and receive online transactions. The top panel shows your pending outgoing transactions, and the bottom panel shows incoming notices from your bank. Let's look a bit closer.

Retrieving Your QuickStatements

You have a handful of chores to take care of when your account is finally active.

Retrieving and verifying account balances online

1. Your first order of business is to retrieve your statement from your bank. In the Items to Send panel, highlight the entry Get New QuickStatement for your account and select **Send**. You've just sent a request to your bank to receive a statement on your most recent transactions. Electronic statements usually cover the last three months of transactions. If you've set up more than one account, you notice two Get New Statement entries. Before you can do much else, you should view these.

2. When your QuickStatement for that particular account arrives, it appears in the Items Received from Financial Institution panel, the lower half of the Online Banking Center. A QuickStatement tells you about transactions that have cleared the bank, not only those that have been conducted online.

3. Click **View** and you can compare this downloaded statement with what QuickBooks says about your accounts. What appears is the Match QuickStatements dialog box, which we cover next.

Matching QuickBooks Accounts with Online Bank Statements

To match your bank's QuickStatement with your QuickBooks numbers, select a QuickStatement from the Items Received From Financial Institution window of the Online Banking Center and click **View**. The Match QuickStatements dialog box appears (see Figure 23.8).

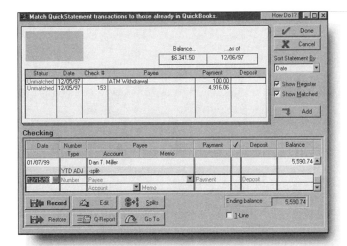

FIGURE 23.8

You must regularly match your downloaded statements with your QuickBooks account records.

Matching QuickBooks numbers with your online statement

1. Your account balance is located at the top of the Match QuickStatements dialog box, as of a particular date. Please note this date may not be as recent as you think. Some transactions may be missing.

2. At the bottom is your Checking Register for that account. Scroll through to see the most current QuickBooks data on this account.

3. In the middle is the Matching window. You see a list of all transactions since the previous QuickStatement was sent to you. Determine the following:

   • If a transaction appears in your bank's records and in QuickBooks, it is said to be matched.

I still want to see what other banks have to offer

After you've chosen a bank through QuickBooks and have begun creating an account, QuickBooks does not make it that easy to explore other banks. When you click the Online Banking icon, you're opening your own account. You won't see that screen from earlier that enabled you to tour through all the different available banks.

If you want to get your feet wet again and look at what other banks have to offer, select **Online Banking** from the **Online** menu (at the top of the QuickBooks screen), and choose **Getting Started**. When the Getting Started with Online Banking screen appears, select **Apply Now**. Click **Next** a couple times, and you will be able to review other banks' options again.

I clicked a QuickStatement, and I was told I could not view it. What's up?

The QuickStatement items in the upper window of the Online Banking Center are *requests* for QuickStatements. To view and match your account balance numbers, click the QuickStatement itself in the lower window, then the Items Received From Financial Institution.

What if a transaction appears unmatched?

A transaction can be unmatched because you have yet to record it in QuickBooks, or because it is made out to a slightly different name, or the check number is different. To match QuickBooks with the QuickStatement, scroll through the check register and try to find an entry that records the same dollar amount, but perhaps with a different payee or check number. This way, you can make an adjustment without the risk of creating a duplicate entry in QuickBooks representing the same transaction.

- If a transaction appears in your bank's records, but not in QuickBooks, then it is labeled unmatched.

4. If the transaction is unmatched, click **Add**, and QuickBooks creates a transaction in your check register that matches the one in your bank records. However, before you do that, read the sidebar "What if a transaction appears unmatched?"

5. When you are done matching transactions, click **Done**, and the Online Banking Center screen appears again. Remember that if you have more than one online account, you have to check each QuickStatement for unmatched entries. Highlight the other account's QuickStatement, select **View**, and repeat the matching process with each online account.

6. After matching QuickBooks with your online statement, you are ready to conduct banking business online.

Looking Up an Account's Identification

Sometimes you quickly want to track down an online account's routing and account number. This can be especially important for finding out what happened to a transaction that never appeared on a QuickStatement, and you want to find out what happened to it.

Each online account has an **Online Info** tab (shown in Figure 23.9). To locate this information, do the following steps.

FIGURE 23.9

When you make an account into an online account, it has a special tab for online information.

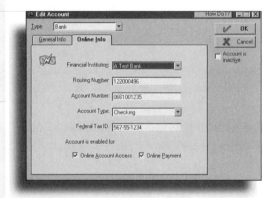

Locating vital account numbers

1. Open the **Chart of Accounts** from the QuickBooks **Lists** menu.

2. Click once on the account you want to view, and select **Edit** from the **Account** drop-down menu. An online account has a lightning bolt next to its name.

3. You see two tabs: **General Info** and **Online Info**. Click **Online Info** to view the account's routing number, account number, account type, and your federal tax ID number.

4. Please note that you cannot edit these numbers. Your financial institution or the IRS assigns them to you. You can, however, change the type of access for which your account is enabled.

Making an Online Payment

If you have online banking through QuickBooks, or have set up an online bill-paying service, such as Intuit's Online Payment Service, just make payments as you normally would with QuickBooks.

Let's look at what happens when you pay a bill or write a check in QuickBooks, and want to make that transaction online.

Check writing and paying online

To review, the following are three ways you can write checks or pay bills in QuickBooks. Also noted are those things you do differently to make this into an online transaction:

1. Click the **Checks** icon in the **Checking and Credit Card** tab of the Navigator. For online payment, fill out an amount, specify a payee, assign the payment to an account as you normally do, and check the **Online Payment** box (see Figure 23.10). Select **OK** to close the checkbook, or click **Next** to move on to another payment.

What counts as unmatched?

Transactions that appear in QuickBooks but have not yet cleared your bank (are not yet part of your downloaded statement) are not counted as unmatched. The Online Banker simply assumes that transaction has not yet cleared. Only transactions that are part of the bank's record but not found in QuickBooks are called unmatched.

Making an account into a bill-paying account

If you decide you want to pay bills from your online account and discover you are not allowed to, you simply have to enable your account to perform this task. To do so, open the Chart of Accounts and click once on the account from which you want to enable bill-paying. Select **Edit** from the drop-down Accounts menu. On the **Online Info** tab, check **Online Payment**.

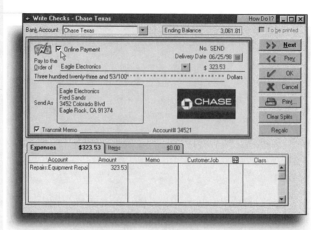

2. Select **Pay Bills** from the QuickBooks **Activities** menu. The Pay Bills dialog box appears. Check any upcoming bill that you want to pay, as you normally do, and if you want to see pending bills due by another date, rather than the date shown, select a new date using the calendar provided. To make this an online payment, check the **Online Payment** box in the **Pay By** panel.

3. Select the **Check Register** from the **Checking and Credit Card** tab. Specify which account you want to write a check from. Fill out a payment as you normally do in the register, using the drop-down menus to choose a vendor, and assign this expense to a particular account. To make this an online payment, type the word SEND in the **Number** field (see Figure 23.11).

Sending and Editing a Payment

After creating a payment, that payment item appears in the Items to Be Sent window of the Online Banking Center the next time you open it. The following happens next.

- To send the payment, highlight that item, making sure a check appears next to its name, and click **Send**.

- To edit the payment, highlight it and click the **Edit** button. The payment appears as a check, ready to edit. The following are the changes you can make:

  - The amount

  - The payee

  - The account to which the payment is assigned

  - The date on which you will send the payment out

All changes you make are noted in the QuickBooks register, and are not recorded as a second payment. Rather, QuickBooks understands that you mean to edit the first one. Please note that most online financial institutions recommend that you send your payment to them about 10 days before you actually want the payment to clear your account. Keep in mind that you are not sending your payment online to the payee, but rather, to your bank or online financial institution, which then assumes some responsibility for making sure that money gets where you intend it.

Highlighting Items You Want to Send

Many items at a time can appear in the Items To Be Sent window in the Online Banking Center. It is not assumed that you want to send every item simultaneously.

Sending the correct items

1. When you click the send button, only those items with a check by them are sent.

2. If a check does not appear next to an item's name, click it once, and the check appears. The next time you click the Send button, that item is sent.

3. To remove the check, click the item again.

Sending an Online Message

When you send an online message to your bank, it appears as an email on your online account manager's computer. To increase the odds that your message gets the attention it deserves, do the following:

- Send your message separately from your other transactions (fund transfers and bill payments). That way it appears as a separate item on your bank's list of incoming messages and transactions. Someone is more apt to see what is written in the **Subject** field, and perhaps take a moment to look at it.

- The **Subject** field is the first thing your online account manager sees when he views your message. Therefore, use the **Subject** field to your advantage, quickly summarizing the message contents and emphasizing its urgency.

- Keep in mind that, at times, an email is no substitute for a phone call. Do not assume that just because you've sent an email, a request has been acted upon. At least until you get acquainted with how your bank responds to email, and you've become a familiar face to your online banking people, you may have to follow up your initial inquiries with an old-fashioned trip to the phone.

Sending an email message to your bank

To send a message to your bank, do the following:

1. From the **Online** menu, select **Online Banking**, **Create Message**, and **Online Banking Message**. The Banking Message dialog box appears (see Figure 23.12).

FIGURE 23.12

Send a message to your bank separately from a payment.

2. If you have more than one bank you do online business with, select a bank in the **Message to** field. Also, in the **From** field, identify yourself in such a way that the reader most certainly knows who you are.

3. Include a subject, remembering that what you type here is seen first. Use the **Regarding Account** drop-down menu to choose the account to which this message pertains.

4. Finally, in the **Message** field, type in a message. Don't be fooled by the size of the message box. You can type in a message many times larger than the visible field. (Eighteen lines of 60 characters each.) Use the QuickBooks **Edit** menu to cut, copy, and paste message content as well.

5. Click **OK**, and the message appears ready to send in the Items to Send window of the Online Banking Center dialog box.

> **An email message may not be binding**
>
> Many banks still require complaints to be sent to them in writing. An email message may not be regarded as an official word from you. The liability a bank holds itself to regarding an email message varies from bank to bank.

Sending a Payment Inquiry

A payment inquiry is treated with more urgency than a message by the receiving financial institution. It is flagged differently.

Sending an inquiry about a payment you made

To send a payment inquiry, you must have already sent the payment to the bank in question and have the payment highlighted in the Online Banking Center. (That simply means opening the **Online Banking Cente**r by clicking the **Online Banking** icon and clicking once on the payment you are inquiring about). After the payment is highlighted, do the following:

1. From the **Online** menu (at the top of the QuickBooks screen), select **Create Message**.

2. From the fly-out menu that appears, select **Payment Inquiry**.

3. You're prompted to answer some questions about the payment.

4. When you are finished, click **OK** to close the dialog box and send your inquiry.

Transferring Money Between Accounts Online

To transfer money between accounts, both the source and destination account must have online access. Please note that transferring money between accounts online is somewhat instantaneous, but may still require the intervention of an account manager at the other end of the transaction. For this reason, do not assume that your transfer is immediately effective until you've experienced a track record with this particular institution. Do the following.

Transferring funds between two online accounts

1. Click the **Transfer** icon in the **Checking and Credit Card** tab of the Navigator. The Transfer Funds Between Accounts dialog box appears (see Figure 23.13).

FIGURE 23.13

You can transfer funds between any two online accounts at the same bank.

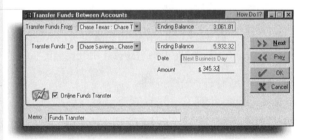

2. To select a source account, use the **Transfer Funds From** drop-down menu.

3. To select a destination account, use the **Transfer Funds To** drop-down menu.

4. Type in an amount.

5. Check the **Online Transfer** option.

6. Click **OK**, and your transfer is now waiting to be sent.

7. Click the **Online Banking** icon in the **Checking and Credit** tab of the Navigator, and your transfer appears as an **Item Waiting To Be Sent**.

8. At this time you can go back and edit your transfer transaction or click **Send** to really send the transfer instructions to your bank.

Obtaining a Report on Online Transactions

To create a report of any group of transactions you've conducted online, just use the right filter on any transaction report, and you can create any grouping you like.

Creating an online transactions report

1. From the **Reports** menu at the top of the QuickBooks screen, select **Transaction Detail Reports** and then **By Date**.

2. When the report appears, change the dates covered by the report, if you like.

3. Select **Filters,** scroll through the **Choose Filter** menu, and locate **Online Status** (see Figure 23.14).

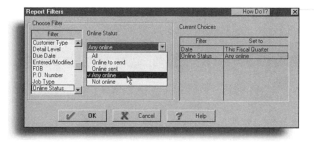

FIGURE 23.14

To create a report of online transactions, select **Online Status** as your filter.

4. The drop-down menu to the right of Choose Filters enables you to pick which online status to filter your reports by. You can, for example, view only those transactions you have yet to send, or those you've already sent.

5. When you are finished choosing filters for your report, click **OK**, and the report appears. (Figure 23.15 shows a report of all transactions conducted online during the previous quarter.)

FIGURE 23.15

A report based on online
transactions.

QuickBooks Online Payroll Service

QuickBooks provides an online payroll service. The type of service offered varies greatly depending on your business and payroll needs. To learn more, select **Payroll Service** from the **Online** menu (at the top of the QuickBooks screen), and click **About QuickBooks Online Payroll**. Select **Help** to view the video that provides a general overview of what's available. At the present time, QuickBooks Payroll Online Service cannot work with a number of businesses. Because this is a very new feature, however, expect more services to be added in QuickBooks' maintenance updates.

QuickBooks' Online Resources

QuickBooks has a number of online business resources, available from the **Business Resources** tab of the Navigator. These include product and technical support, including a very thorough FAQ site, as well as a site for locating a QuickBooks expert advisor in your community. A link is provided to Quicken's Small Business page, which provides frequently updated articles related to every aspect of running a small business, and to Cashfinder.com, which is a one-stop application center for obtaining a business loan. Let's briefly look at each of these.

QuickBooks.com

To access this site, click the `QuickBooks.com` icon in the **Business Resources** tab of the Navigator. This opens QuickBooks home Web site (see Figure 23.16). This site contains links to updated tax tables and maintenance upgrades, tax preparation software offers, and User-to-User forums, among other things. You can also order Intuit's checks from this site. The QuickBooks Frequently Asked Questions link, however, is worth a special look.

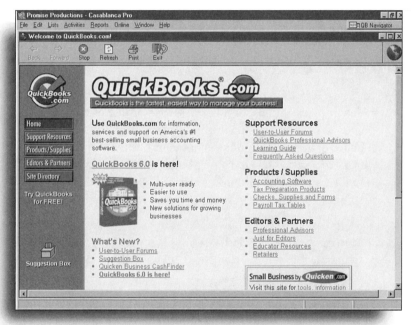

FIGURE 23.16
The QuickBooks Web site.

To reach this, click the **Frequently Asked Questions** link under the heading **Support Resources**, or if QuickBooks rearranges its page, point your browser to `www.intuit.com/support/quickbooks`. Here you can type in keywords regarding any QuickBooks topic and retrieve the most recent and thorough answers. Many points that are not really fleshed out in the manual, as well as highly specialized instructions for specific industries, can be found here. You can print out or save any information found here as well.

Find an Advisor

If you like the security of knowing a QuickBooks expert in your community, click the **Find an Advisor** icon in the **Business Resources** tab of the Navigator. When the page opens, type your city, state, and area code, and you see a list of accounts and consultants especially knowledgeable of QuickBooks in your community. This page can be especially helpful when choosing an accountant. If your accountant is set up to work with QuickBooks, her job and your job is much easier. If QuickBooks' internal browser can't access the site for some reason, just point your browser to www.quickbooks.com, and select **Professional Advisors**.

www.cashfinder.com

Cashfinder.com lets you apply through QuickBooks to a number of lending institutions for a business loan or line of credit. You do not send an online application. Rather, after answering a number of general questions about your business type, you can download a software wizard that builds a highly detailed application for you. This application is printed out and mailed. Cashfinder.com 's role is to help choose a lending institution that is likely to do business with you.

The major benefit you derive from this service is speed of response. Cashfinder.com claims you'll know about your loan in 48 hours from submission.

Cashfinder.com is free, but you must still pay loan application fees to the companies to which you ultimately end up applying. Currently, 10 lending institutions do business through Cashfinder.com although this number is likely to grow. If you have trouble with the internal QuickBooks link to Cashfinder, simply open your own Internet connection, and point your browser to www.cashfinder.com.

Small Business by *Quicken.com*

This Web site provides links to all types of information important to business owners (see Figure 23.17). It has general articles, and by following links, you can obtain very specific advice pertaining to your end of the marketplace. You find thousands of answers to many small business questions, as well as discussion boards where you can post questions and answers. At the top of the page is a drop-down menu that links you to a page dealing with your concerns. Some subjects covered are investments, taxes, insurance, banking and borrowing, and home and mortgage.

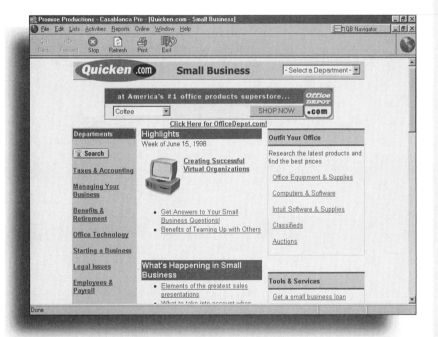

FIGURE 23.17

The Small Business by Quicken Web site.

Online Web Information

Use a search program to aid in your
Web wanderings

Use the QuickBooks Web site to link to many useful
locations

Search for loan and insurance information on the Web

Find tax forms for both the IRS and state governments

Where can I find more Internet information?

For more information on the Internet, refer to *Using the Internet, Fourth Edition* from Que Publishing, written by Barbara Kasser, or *Special Edition Using the Internet, Fourth Edition* from Que Publishing, written by Jerry Honeycutt.

A wealth of information is available on the Internet, including many links from the QuickBooks Web site and other financial resources. This chapter provides an introduction to finding financial and business information on the Internet.

Use these locations as a starting point when you begin your exploration. The Internet changes constantly, and some of the links provided in this chapter as well as the illustrations you see here may vanish into Internet obscurity before you get a chance to sample them. Rest assured that something comparable will take the place of the information that is retired. A little sleuthing will no doubt provide you with the information you seek.

This chapter assumes you have access to a modem and an Internet connection.

Poking Around on the Web

Several search engines are available for digging into the Internet. Here are some of the major search addresses:

Excite: `http://www.excite.com`

Yahoo!: `http://www.yahoo.com`

Lycos: `http://www.lycos.com`

Infoseek: `http://www.infoseek.com`

HotBot: `http://www.hotbot.com`

LookSmart: `http://www.looksmart.com/`

AltaVista: `http://www.altavista.digital.com`

When you search, enter a key word or a string of words. If you enter more than one word, type the words enclosed in quotation marks. Most search engines will also respond to Boolean searches using "AND" or "OR" in the search criteria. If you are searching for tax sites, for example, you might search for the word **tax**, or the phrase "income tax" (in quotes), or the combination tax AND property.

Visiting the QuickBooks Home Page on the Web

You can go to www.quickbooks.com and visit the QuickBooks home page, where you will find information about the program, technical support options, industry tips, an online store for ordering forms, an update service for payroll tax tables, and links to other Intuit sites.

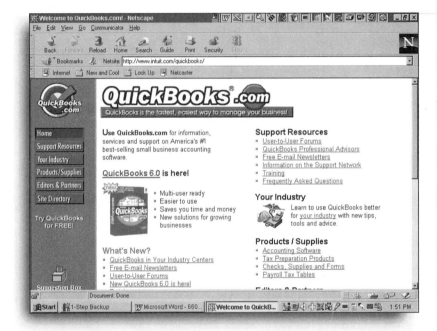

FIGURE 24.1

Find links to technical support and financial institutions among other things on the QuickBooks Web site.

SEE ALSO

➤ *For more information about QuickBooks' online resources, see Chapter 23, "Going Online with QuickBooks", page 451*

Useful Business Resources

The U.S. Small Business Administration has a Web site at www.sba.gov where you can find, among other things, information about starting a business and information about finding financing. You can download a business plan workbook, an application for an SBA loan, or you can browse it's online library for tax information and the text of the Small Business Act, and information about the Freedom of Information Act.

FIGURE 24.2

Starting a new business? The Small Business Administration at www.sba.com is a great place to start.

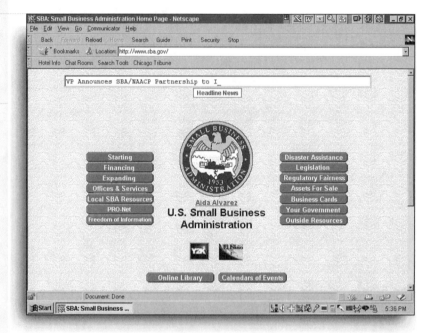

You can find links to insurance calculators for determining the cost versus benefit of your insurance, and insurance companies that provide services on the Web at www.insuremarket.com, sponsored by Intuit. Get price comparisons from major insurance companies at this site.

Follow up on the latest business news at the Business Week site, http://www.businessweek.com.

If you're looking for investment information and stock quotes, plenty of sites will provide you with the latest news and price information. Try CNN Financial Network at www.cnnfn.com/markets/quotes.html or www.stockpoint.com.

There are several online resources for stock trading at deep discounts, such as Charles Schwab at www.schwab.com, Datek at www.datek.com, and etrade at www.etrade.com. Or keep up with the financial gurus at Money Magazine by signing up for an online subscription at http://jcgi.pathfinder.com/money/plus/index.oft.

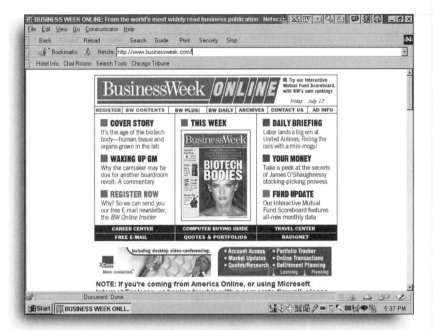

FIGURE 24.3

View the latest copy of
Business Week online at
`www.businessweek.com`.

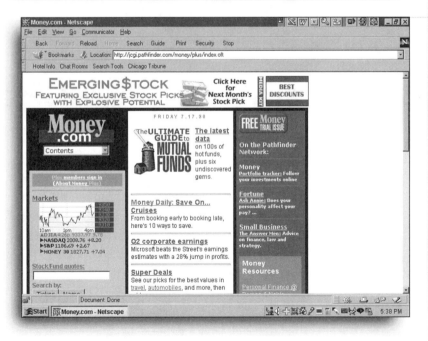

FIGURE 24.4

Subscribe to Money Magazine,
or use their free stock quote
service at `http://jcgi.path
finder.com/money/plus/
index.oft`.

Looking for a loan? Several Web sites provide you with loan calculators for determining potential loan payments, as well as links to financial institutions that provide online loan applications. Try www.financenter.com for personal finance advice, and online calculators for determining monthly payments, tax savings, and refinancing.

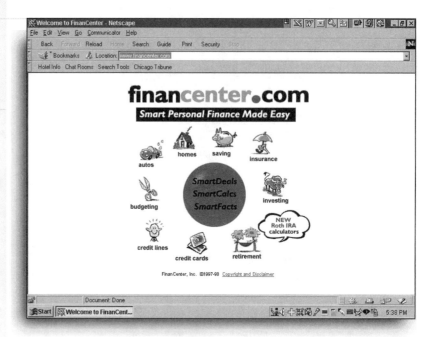

Taxes and Accounting

Nothing will clear up a tax headache faster than tax information at your fingertips. Visit the IRS's own Web site at `http://www.irs.ustreas.gov/cover.html`, where you can download federal tax forms and publications.

Visit the American Institute of Certified Public Accountants (AICPA) at `http://aicpa.org/` and find links to tax and accounting sites all over the Internet.

Confused about that new Roth IRA? The Roth has its own Web page, where you can get all your questions answered: `http://www.rothira.com/`.

PART **V**

What's in the News?   CHAPTER **24**   483

Check out the Tax and Accounting Sites Directory for links to all the state governments and a lot more: `http://www.taxsites.com/`. If that site doesn't get you where you want to go, another equally well-stocked Web page, called Tax Sites, contains links to income-tax related information on the Internet: `http://www.taxresources.com`.

Laws and Regulations

Search for the government document of your choice—the one that's sure to put you to sleep at night—at the U.S. House of Representatives' Internet Law Library, `http://law.house.gov/109.htm`. If you're still counting sheep after browsing the law library documents, try reading the full text of the U.S. Tax Code at `http://www.fourmilab.ch/ustax/ustax.html`. and `http://www.ed.gov/EdRes/EdFed/GenGuide.html`, the General Guides to Government Internet Resources, or the Federal Web Locator: `http://www.vcilp.org/Fed-Agency/fedwebloc.html#search`.

What's in the News?

Every good businessperson stays on top of the news. It's easy to keep up with current events with the aid of the Internet. Most metropolitan newspapers are available online either in full or in an excerpted form, and many offer "home delivery" right to your emailbox. Here's a sample of where you can go for the breaking stories:

The Boston Globe: `http://www.globe.com/globe/`

Cable News Network: `http://www.cnn.com/`

The Detroit Free Press: `http://www.freep.com/`

The Chicago Tribune: `http://www.chicago.tribune.com/`

The Economist: `http://www.economist.com/`

The New York Times: `http://www.nytimes.com/`

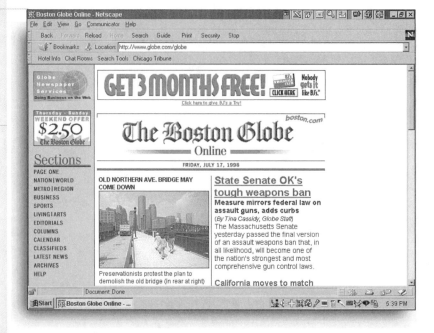

The Seattle Times: `http://www.seattletimes.com/`

The Washington Post: `http://www.washingtonpost.com/`

FIGURE 24.8

Stay on top of the next Watergate when you read The Washington Post.

The Baltimore Sun: `http://www.sunspot.net/`

Christian Science Monitor: `http://www.csmonitor.com/`

The Miami Herald: `http://www.herald.com`

The Philadelphia Enquirer: `http://www.phillynews.com/`

The St. Petersburg Times: `http://www.sptimes.com/`

USA Today: `http://www.usatoday.com/`

Odds and Ends

Test your financial knowledge at a fascinating Web site—the Financial Players Center—at `http://fpc.net66.com`. You can do loan calculations, learn about how the value of money changes over time, and take financial trivia quizzes.

FIGURE 24.9

The Financial Players Center delves into the meaning of money.

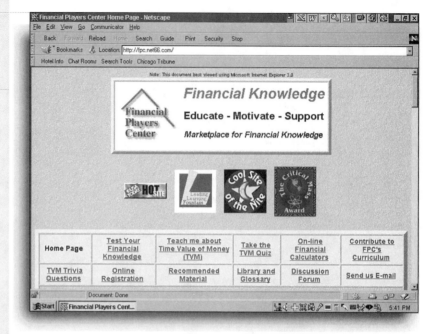

Check the ratings of mutual funds with the Morningstar service, or check up on the markets of the world at `http://www.quicken.com/investments/`.

This brief summary highlights only a few of the interesting business and financial sites available for you on the Internet. Start searching, and you'll find you have information coming out your ears!

Getting the Most from QuickBooks

QuickBooks and Time Tracking

Learn how to use the QuickBooks Pro Timer

Transfer files from QuickBooks to the Timer

Create install disks that enable your employees and vendors to install it on their computer

Learn how to install the Timer and import QuickBooks file lists

Create new activities, edit activities, and use the Activity Template

Condense and back up Timer files

We need to start out by saying that the QuickBooks Timer is a feature available only in QuickBooks Pro. Nothing in this chapter really applies to QuickBooks Standard Edition.

The QuickBooks Timer (see Figure 25.1) is a portable extension of QuickBooks. Employees, subcontractors, and vendors can install it on their own computer, where it runs as a digital stopwatch, tracking how much time is spent on a particular job.

FIGURE 25.1

This is how the Timer most often looks when you are working with it.

Following are some uses for the Timer:

- With the Timer, your employees can work offsite, and still have an accurate record of how much time is spent on a particular project. Timer data can be returned to you, and when entered into QuickBooks, each customer's account can be properly billed, and hours credited to the employee for payroll. A Timer user can type a memo. Later, QuickBooks imports this memo along with the other **Time**, **Employee** and **Customer: Job** data.

- Give the Timer to a vendor who does work for you, perhaps a graphics designer or proofreader. They can install the Timer in a couple of minutes. When they are finished, they can send you the data, and you have all the information QuickBooks needs to properly account for and pay the vendor.

- Give the Timer to several subcontractors who are working for you on a job. They can each keep track of their time, job type and customer, and when they are finished, QuickBooks instantly recognizes and processes the information just as if you had typed it into QuickBooks "the long way."

QuickBooks Timer Overview

Before we explore the Timer in detail, let's take a brief tour of how it works, and how data is shared between the Timer and QuickBooks:

- The QuickBooks Timer is more than just a stopwatch. What it does is track time on behalf of an employee or vendor, and notes what customer and job that time should be credited to. So before you really think about working with the Timer, your QuickBooks company needs to have a least one employee, as well as some customers and jobs that you are in the habit of billing.

- Save QuickBooks data in a form that the Timer can use (**File**, **Timed Activities**, **Export Lists for Timer**). This Timer data contains all your company's current employees, employee pay rates, vendors, customers, and jobs.

- Note the name of the file you save, because your employee or vendor will need to know it.

- Create Timer Install disks to give to your employee or vendor.

- Give the Timer Install disks to your employee or vendor, as well as the QuickBooks file you saved.

- Instruct your employee or vendor to install the Timer on their computer and copy the QuickBooks Timer data onto their hard drive.

- The employee or vendor is prompted to import a list from QuickBooks. They should locate the QuickBooks file you gave to them. The Timer is then set up to work with your company data.

- The employee or vendor then clicks the Timer's **New Activity** button, and uses the **Your Name** drop-down menu (see Figure 25.2) to select his name. (After all, you gave this Timer to one of your employees, or a vendor, so his name appears on the list, not yours.)

FIGURE 25.2

When using the Timer, **Your Name** refers to the employee or vendor's name, not the company owner or administrator.

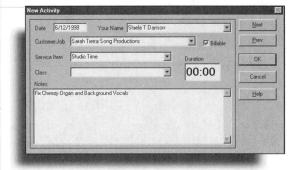

A lot of trouble?

If this seems like a lot of hullabaloo to put someone through, compare it to the amount of paperwork that would normally accompany someone working offsite on a project, and it doesn't sound so bad.

- The employee or vendor should use the other drop-down menus to choose a customer and job to charge for.

- Finally, after clicking **OK** and **Start**, the clock is ticking, and all time spent on a project is accounted for.

What You Need to Run the QuickBooks Timer

The QuickBooks Timer is a standalone program, and thus, does not have the same system requirements as QuickBooks does. Consequently, you can run it on Windows 3.1, as well as Windows 95, 98, and NT. You need only 8MB of RAM, although 16 is better, and 8MB of free disk space. Also, a user can get by with a VGA monitor. An SVGA is not necessary.

Really now! Who would use the Timer?

The idea might seem a bit odd at first, asking someone who works for you to let a computer clock run while they do a job for you. What if the work they do has nothing to do with a computer? One of the special benefits is how the Timer associates an employee's hours with specific customers and jobs. They can manually type the hours they've spent on a job, even if they do not use the actual "stopwatch" feature. Just the fact that they enter the hours for various jobs and save those as a single file makes it much easier for you to enter employee data into QuickBooks.

Getting Ready to Use the Timer

To understand what exactly the Timer does for you, let's take a look at what it imports from QuickBooks, and what it sends back to QuickBooks after an employee or vendor has used it.

The following list is data from QuickBooks that the Timer uses. When you export a file from QuickBooks to the Timer, this is what is exported:

- Employee Names
- Employee Payroll Items (Salary, hourly, overtime, and so forth)

- Customer: Job data
- Classes, if you have created any
- Memos

After an employee or vendor uses the Timer, this is the data imported back into QuickBooks:

- The number of hours an employee or vendor spends on a job. These hours are broken into regular time, salary, and overtime, depending on how you regularly pay that employee or vendor.
- The number of jobs an employee worked on.
- The number of timed sessions (called **Activities** by the Timer) on which an employee worked. These sessions could be on behalf of one customer, or many.
- Any memos generated by the employee or vendor, to help you keep track of where all this offsite time is being spent.

When Timer data is brought back into QuickBooks, QuickBooks accounts for the time in the following ways:

- Payroll keeps track of the hours spent by the employee and generates paychecks accordingly.
- The QuickBooks weekly timesheet shows the employee hours.
- Every timed activity in from the Timer appears as a single activity in QuickBooks' **Enter Single Activity** screen.
- When Timer data is imported, you can immediately view a detailed report of how much this offsite work has cost you.

Exporting a List for the Timer

Your first task in preparation for using the Timer does not involve the Timer at all. The Timer does not read QuickBooks files directly. QuickBooks converts necessary files in a few simple steps. After this is done, you can begin working with the Timer.

Exporting QuickBooks files for the Timer

1. Open QuickBooks and select **Timer Activities** from the **File** menu. Choose **Export Lists For Timer** (see Figure 25.3).

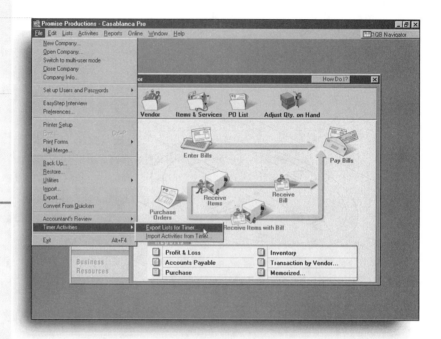

FIGURE 25.3

This is the only menu item in QuickBooks that deals with Timer data.

How QuickBooks and the Timer trade files

The link between QuickBooks and the Timer is the .IIF file type. QuickBooks exports its necessary files in this .IIF format, and they are read by the Timer. Likewise, when the Timer exports files for QuickBooks to use, they are converted to an .IIF file, which QuickBooks can read and import appropriately.

2. Click past the confirmation screen, and you see the Export dialog box (see Figure 25.4), which prompts you to type a file name and save it.

FIGURE 25.4

Exporting an .IIF file is the first step toward using the Timer.

3. Make a note of the save location, the folder you are saving in here, because you'll have to locate this file and copy it to a floppy disk shortly.

4. Type a name for this export file. It must end with a .IIF file extension. Do not simply overwrite one of the existing files, but rather, type a new name.

5. You see a confirmation that your file has been successfully exported.

6. Locate this .IIF file and copy it onto a floppy disk. This is done so that you can give it to your employees when you give them the Timer Install disks. It does them no good to have the Timer up and running unless you give them the company data as well.

7. Create as many copies of the .IIF file as you have employees or vendors who need to use it. The file size is not large, usually, so if they have email access, you can perhaps email them the file as an attachment.

Installing the Timer

Technically speaking, you don't even have to install the Timer on your own computer (unless you are an employee in your company, tracking your own time spent on a project). On a day-to-day basis, you are only working with data returned to you from your employees and vendors, not with the Timer itself.

However, if you're going to instruct your employees and vendors on how to use it, it's a good idea for you to be familiar with it, so let's explore how to install the Timer, and learn your way around the interface.

Installing the Timer

1. Insert the QuickBooks CD into your CD-ROM drive, and select **Install Timer** (see Figure 25.5).

FIGURE 25.5

Install the QuickBooks Timer
as a separate program.

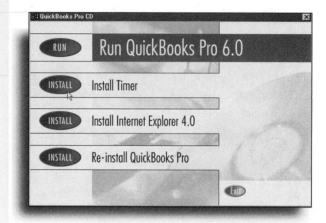

2. Follow the onscreen instructions, accepting the default choices for file location and options. There's nothing to customize here.

3. Make a note of name of the folder that the Timer is installed into, (the default is QBTIMER) because, to make the lives of your Timer users easier, you should tell them what folder to import and export Timer data to and from.

4. At the end of installation, QuickBooks Timer asks to restart your computer. Allow it to do so before proceeding.

Learning Your Way Around the Timer

When you first install the Timer, it tries to open a Timer data file, and can't find one, so you are prompted to create a Timer data file. Following are several points to clarify from the start:

- In the QuickBooks Timer program, you name a file at the time you create it, rather than saving and naming it later. This is confusing because the Timer shows you a screen that makes it look as if you are supposed to select an existing file and open it. But that is not the case.

- What you are supposed to do is type any name you like and *that* is your new file, *not* pick an existing file.

Getting started with the QuickBooks Timer

1. Start the Timer program by selecting the QuickBooks pro **Timer** icon from the QuickBooks Pro group of the Windows **Start** menu. The Timer is not started automatically when you open QuickBooks.

2. You are prompted to create a new Timer file (see Figure 25.6). To do so, click past the prompts and select **New Time File** from the **File** menu. In the dialog box provided, type a name similar to the name of your company. Click **OK**.

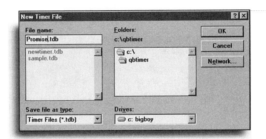

FIGURE 25.6

To create a new timer file, type a name and don't try to over-write an old one.

3. You are then prompted to import a QuickBooks list (see Figure 25.7). Import the .IFF file you created, as directed in the preceding section "Exporting A List for the Timer." Do this by selecting **Import QuickBooks Lists** from the **Timer File** menu.

FIGURE 25.7

Before you can start timing, you need to import your first .IIF file from QuickBooks.

• If, when you exported the list from QuickBooks, you saved the file in the QBTIMER folder, the file you need should be right there.

• If you saved the export file in the QuickBooks folder itself, change the folder to your QuickBooks folder and locate the .IFF file that has your QuickBooks company Timer data. (If this data was saved to a floppy disk, put the floppy in drive A, and locate the file there.)

4. After importing the QuickBooks lists, you are able to begin time tracking sessions. Whether you are simply experimenting right now, or explaining to employees and vendors how to use the Timer, the next step is to create a new activity to track time for. Proceed to the next section.

Creating a new activity

1. Click the **New Activity** button, and the dialog box shown in Figure 25.8 appears.

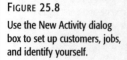

FIGURE 25.8

Use the New Activity dialog box to set up customers, jobs, and identify yourself.

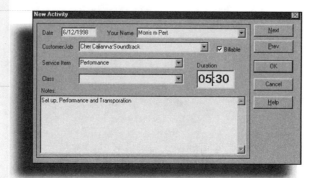

2. The **Your Name** drop-down menu contains the names of all employees and vendors. It doesn't have the company owner's name because the Timer is used for tracking employee and vendor hours spent on customer jobs, not the owner's time. Whoever is doing the work for this session should locate his name in the **Your Name** field.

3. Use the **Customer: Job** drop-down menu to select a job and customer associated with this activity. If the activity is going to be billed, check the **Billable** box.

4. Every employee or vendor has a type of task that they perform. You set these up as service items when you started your QuickBooks company. The employee or vendor selects a task from the **Service Item** drop-down menu.

5. The employee or vendor may type a memo helping identify this activity, after it's exported to QuickBooks later. This is highly recommended because offsite work can easily get expensive if untracked.

6. When the New Activity windows and fields have been filled out, click **OK**, and the Timer is ready to track activities. Please proceed to the next section.

Using the Timer

After creating an activity, click **OK**, and the Timer is ready for use.

Timing an activity

1. Click the **Start** button to begin timing (see Figure 25.9). Following is how you know your time is being tracked:

> **What is a Timer activity?**
>
> A Timer activity is a task that an employee or vendor performs on behalf of a customer. A Timer activity consists of an employee or vendor, a customer, a job related to that customer, and a date on which the activity in question is carried out on. A Timer activity correlates directly to the Enter Single Activity feature in QuickBooks.

FIGURE 25.9
The Timer button can start, stop, or resume timed activities.

- You see the digital readout begin to advance, one minute at a time. The colon between the two numbers (00:01) blinks to confirm that time is being tracked.

- Also, while time is elapsing, the activity displayed in the **Current Activity** line shows the word "Timing."

2. Stop the clock by clicking the **Stop** button. Resume again by clicking the same button, which shows the word **Resume**. To minimize the Timer so that it takes up less room on your computer screen, click the **Space Saver** button at the far right of the Timer (it shows two windows). You can also minimize the Timer by clicking the standard Windows **Minimize** button.

3. To edit an activity while you are working on it, click the **Edit Activity** button. While an activity is in progress, your

editing is limited to the memo area. At this time, you can alter the memo and type anything new you'd like to add. Time is still elapsing while you are editing.

4. When you are finally finished with this activity, there is no "saving the file" that has to be done. Close the Timer by selecting **Exit** from the **File** menu, or export the activity to QuickBooks.

Creating a New Timed Activity

At any time, you can start a new activity, perhaps a new job for the same customer, or another customer altogether.

Setting up a new activity

1. Click the **New Activity** button (see Figure 25.10), and the New Activity dialog box appears.

FIGURE 25.10

To create a totally new activity, using a new customer or job, click the **New Activity** button.

2. Fill out the fields as previously indicated in the "Timing an activity" section.

3. When you are done, click **OK**, and the Timer appears again.

4. As previously discussed, click the **Start** button to begin time tracking this activity.

5. Now, however, you can use the **Current Activity** drop-down menu to choose the activity you want to work on at the moment (see Figure 25.11).

FIGURE 25.11

Change to a new activity with the **Current Activity** drop-down menu.

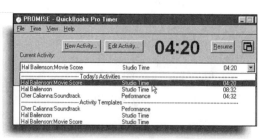

6. Switching between activities using the drop-down menu automatically starts the **New Activity** time tracking, and stops the previous activity.

7. Click **Stop** when you are finished with the tasks, and again, there are no files to save. Just exit the Timer when you are through, or prepare to export activities to QuickBooks for accounting, which is what we'll cover next.

Using an Activity Template

When you stop the clock on a Timer activity and begin a new one, that first activity remains available for you to make current and begin timing it again at any time, until you export it. However, the activity is also stored down below, near the bottom of the **Current Activity** list (see Figure 25.12), saved as an Activity Template.

How ironclad is the time data reported by the QuickBooks Timer?

If you are distributing the Timer to employees to obtain some sort of immutable record of time spent, the QuickBooks Timer doesn't really work that way. The Timer's digital time counter can be changed simply by clicking any activity in the **Current Activity** drop-down list, choosing **Edit Activity**, and typing a new number in the Duration window.

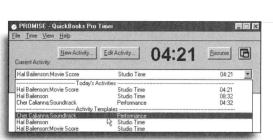

FIGURE 25.12

An Activities Template is found at the bottom of the **Current Activities** list.

An Activity Template saves everything about that current activity except the hours. It enables you to start from scratch with an activity identical to the one you are working on, but with the hours set to zero. Use the Activity Template to begin a new project that is similar to the first one, while changing perhaps only one or two items.

Exporting Timer Data to QuickBooks

When you export Timer data, you should create a new file by typing a name for it, and take care to note the folder you save that file in, so you can retrieve it quickly inside QuickBooks.

To simply export all timed activities, select **Export Time Activities** from the **File** menu, and do the following:

Exporting Timer data to QuickBooks

1. Click past the confirmation boxes, and the Create Export File dialog box appears (see Figure 25.13).

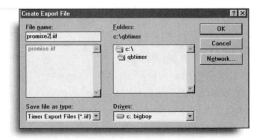

2. Make a note of the folder that you are saving your file into because after you open QuickBooks, you're going to have to locate this file again.

3. Type a name into the **File name** field, rather than choose an existing one. Make sure you use the .IIF file extension.

4. You see a confirmation that your file has been converted. The data is now available to be imported into QuickBooks.

How is this data retrieved in QuickBooks, and how is it used? Let's move on to the next section.

Opening Timer Data in QuickBooks

QuickBooks imports Timer data into payroll, the Enter Single Activity feature, the timesheet, and related reports. Here's how to import the data, and verify that it's where you want it to be.

When you created the .IIF file in the Timer, you made Timer data available for QuickBooks to import, but QuickBooks must still import the file itself before it can be used.

Importing and verifying data from the QuickBooks Timer

1. With QuickBooks open, choose **Timer Activities** from the **File** menu, and click **Import Activities from Timer**.

2. Click past the confirmation screen and an **Import** menu appears (see Figure 25.14). Chose the .IIF file you exported from your Timer, and click **Open**.

FIGURE 25.14
The Timer exports .IIF files, which QuickBooks can understand.

3. You hear a reassuring clang of the cash register, one for each activity that your faithful employees carried out, and see the QuickBooks Pro Timer Import Summary dialog box, as shown in Figure 25.15. The dialog box confirms the number of activities imported.

FIGURE 25.15
After importing from the Timer, you see a dialog box confirming the number of activities imported.

4. To learn more about your data, click **View Report**, and the Timer Import Detail report appears, as shown in Figure 25.16.

FIGURE 25.16

Immediately after importing Timer data, you can view a report on it.

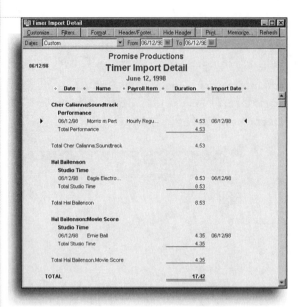

5. Each line of the report represents an activity carried out by an employee or vendor. Double-click one, and the same activity appears in the Enter Single Activity window (see Figure 25.17). You see all the fields filled in, except Payroll Item. (See Sidebar "QuickBooks Timer and payroll items.") Use the **Pre̲v** or **Next** arrow to view other activities carried out by this employee, or click the **Name** drop-down menu to view work done by a different employee or vendor.

FIGURE 25.17

Timer data activities import directly as QuickBooks single activities.

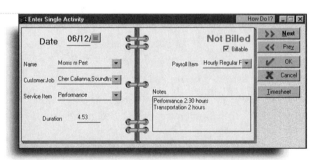

6. After you've viewed this line of the Timer data in the Enter Single Activity window, click the **Timesheet** button, and you see a whole week's worth of that employee's work displayed on the timesheet (see Figure 25.18), including the data you just imported from the Timer.

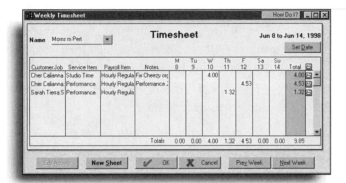

FIGURE 25.18
Data from the Timer is also available for the timesheet.

7. To see how the Timer data affected payroll, from the **Payroll and Time** tab of the Navigator, select **Create Paychecks**. The Select Employees to be Paid dialog box appears. You see all the hours reported by the Timer included in the list, for each employee.

8. If the jobs carried out on the Timer were done by subcontractors (vendors), select **Pay Bills** from the QuickBooks **Activities** menu, and you see all the time reported by the Timer on behalf of each vendor accounted for.

Creating Install Disks for the Timer

A huge question remains: How do you get the QuickBooks Timer to someone else's computer? Loan them your QuickBooks CD? That can be a bit cumbersome, especially when there are multiple users. Here's the solution: The QuickBooks Timer includes a program for creating install disks that you can distribute to the Timer users in your company. You can create one set of disks and pass them around, or create as many sets as you like.

QuickBooks Timer and payroll items

The first time a Timer activity is imported and appears in the Enter Single Activity window, you are prompted to associate that activity with a payroll item. That's because when your employee set up the Timer and carried out the tasks, she did not have access to payroll item data. The Timer does not deal with salary, wages, hourly rate, overtime rate, and so on. You have to add that here, after you import the Timer data back into QuickBooks.

Running the Timer Install disk program

1. Prepare three blank, high-density, floppy disks by labeling them Disk 1, Disk 2, and Disk 3.

2. Put Disk 1 into your floppy disk drive.

3. Make sure the QuickBooks CD is in your CD-ROM drive. Click **My Computer**, and right-click on the **QuickBooks CDRom** icon. Select **Open**, and locate the folder QB_tc.

4. Inside the QB_tc folder, click the **Create** icon, and follow the onscreen instructions.

5. Set aside those disks and give them to your employees or vendors who need to use the Timer.

Getting Your Employees Up to Speed with the Timer

Installing the Timer onto a computer from floppies is not a big chore. Simply have your employees put Disk 1 into their floppy drive and follow the onscreen directions. However, you can help them get started with the Timer by explaining to them a few points previously outlined, in the section "Getting started with the QuickBooks Timer." Specifically the following:

- Remember that you are providing them with data from QuickBooks, the **Customers: Jobs** list that they need to import before they can start time tracking. Point out that this data is in the form of an .IIF file, and direct them to install it in the same directory (or folder) as the QuickBooks Timer. The default Timer folder is C:\QBTIMER.

- Let them know that first they have to name and create a QuickBooks Timer file, just as soon as they start the program, before they do anything else.

- After the file is created, they have to import the .IIF file, as previously pointed out. Then they can start activities.

- Acquaint them with the drop-down menu system of setting up their own name, customer, and job, before actually clicking the **Start** button, to begin time tracking.

- After they've worked through all this, your employees and vendors may come to appreciate the convenience of using the QuickBooks Timer.

Backed Up and Condensed Timer Data

To facilitate faster transport and diminish transmission problems, the QuickBooks Timer enables you to condense and back up your data in one step. When you condense Timer data, the program automatically creates a backup of your file as well. After condensing a QuickBooks Timer file, it takes up less room on a floppy disk.

Condensing and Backing Up Timer Data

In this section, we discuss how to condense and back up Timer data. If you simply want to make a backup of Timer data, select **Back Up Timer File** from the **File** menu, and you are prompted to provide a filename for your backed up data. The following are three points to remember about backed up Timer files:

- After performing a backup, your original Timer data is untouched.

- Timer backup files have a .BDB file extension, whereas Timer files are .TDB.

- Backed up Timer files must be restored with the Timer's Restore feature before they can be used.

Condensing QuickBooks Timer data

1. With the Timer open, select **Condense Timer File** from the **File** menu (see Figure 25.19).

FIGURE 25.19

Condensing a file does not affect its usability.

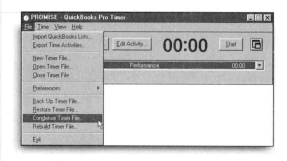

2. You are informed that the Timer performs a backup as well. Click **OK**.

3. The name of the backup file is selected for you. It is the same as your Timer file, except the file extension is .BDB, rather than .TDB. Click **OK** to confirm.

4. You receive no more messages. Your original QuickBooks Timer file is now condensed and has not been renamed. You also now have a new backup file, as explained in step 4.

5. As a result, your condensed file takes up a bit less room and is as usable as ever. There is no notable performance degradation.

Restoring Backed Up Timer Data

When you restore Timer data, you are asked to create a new file to restore to. That means you'll end up with a new Timer data file on your hard drive, at the end of the process. The program will not let you overwrite the old one. This is kind of nice from the viewpoint of protecting your data, but you can end up with "file clutter" if you carry out this process more than once or twice.

Restoring Timer data

1. From the **File** menu, select **Restore Timer File**.

2. You are prompted to select which file to restore from. Select it from the list provided.

When do you need to condense?

Because any type of file compression can potentially lead to problems, make sure you really need to condense your file, before doing so. For example, if your Timer data is far less than the capacity of a floppy disk, then there's really no need to condense it. However, if the Timer file is getting up around 900K or so, condensing is a good idea, because floppies do fail and are more apt to fail the more data you put on them.

3. You are then asked to type a name for your new Timer file. This is a bit confusing, because the directions say "Select A file to Restore TO." Well, you are not really selecting an existing file. You're creating a new one. So just type a name.

4. After a moment, your New Timer data file is created, and becomes the currently open Timer file.

Viewing and Editing Timer Data in Detail

To view a list of all Timer activities, even ones that have been exported, select **Time Activity Log** from the **View** menu. Click the **Date** drop-down menu at the upper left to select a date range. You'll see a list as shown in Figure 25.20. What can you view here that you can't view just by clicking the **Current Activities** list on the Timer? Following are some special features of this list:

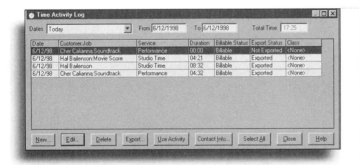

FIGURE 25.20
You have more control over managing activities in the Time Activities Log.

- You can see whether an activity has been exported yet.
- You can choose a date range for this list. If you want to see all the activities you did a week ago, or over a span of two or three days, use the **Dates**, **From** and **To** windows to create a custom date range for viewing activities.
- Double-click any activity in the list to edit it.
- To turn any activity into a template, click it once and select **Use Activity**.

- View any customer's contact info by clicking the **Contact Info** button at the bottom of the screen. (Contact info must have been provided from QuickBooks, you cannot add customer contact info in the Timer program.)

- Use the **Control** key and the mouse to select any combination of activities you want, and then export only those you selected, using the **Export** button

Budgeting

Use prior-year amounts as a starting point for creating a budget

Create budget reports that let you know how you are performing compared to your budget plan

Few things are as important—and as overlooked—as budgeting. Many businesses either don't take the time to make a budget, or after they create a budget, they stick it in a file folder and forget to look at it again.

Creating a working budget helps you keep an eye on the performance of your business and its relationship to your expectations. Using a budget helps you plan for the future, not just do business today.

QuickBooks provides you with everything you need to create a budget. It's up to you to take advantage of this powerful tool and make it work for you.

What Is a Budget?

A *budget* is a financial plan. It looks like a financial statement—just like the ones you produce for your company—but the numbers on the budget are based on goals, past performance, and consideration of future trends, rather than the actual transactions that make up your standard financial statements.

Often, you will use the income and expense numbers of the prior year as the starting point for a budget. Then you must consider your knowledge of the future expectations and anticipated trends of your industry and adjust the budget numbers to embrace those trends. In addition, you'll want to throw in a dose of your personal experience with the way your business operates and the way you expect it to operate, so that you can build a budget that accurately reflects your goals and reasonable expectations for the year or years ahead.

If you are in the new home construction industry and you know the new factory in town will bring hundreds of new employees, you may be able to reasonably expect your business to increase next year. Or, if your landlord has been raising the rent on other buildings he owns and your lease is due for renewal, you can safely expect your rent expense will increase in the near future.

Creating a Budget

The QuickBooks budgeting feature enables you to set up a budget amount for each income and expense account in your chart of accounts.

Traditionally, a budget is created for an entire year at a time, with amounts shown for each month of the year. The monthly amounts are often the same—using an average of annual amounts from the prior year as a starting point.

You enter the monthly amount you expect to earn or spend in the next year, and QuickBooks will automatically extend that amount to each month of the coming year. You can then revise individual budgeted amounts.

Alternatively, you can enter different amounts for each month of the budgeted year, or enter an initial monthly amount and ask QuickBooks to increase or decrease that amount each month by a particular percentage.

Before you begin the budget process in QuickBooks, you should print a copy of your prior year's (or several prior years') Profit and Loss Statement. This statement will be a guide for you as you create the budget. You may also want to schedule a session with other members of your company to discuss plans and expectations for the future and rough out a budget on paper before committing it to QuickBooks.

The First Year of Business

Sometimes it's difficult to know where to begin in creating a budget when you have no prior experience on which to draw. That doesn't preclude you from creating a budget, however. Some suggestions for resources when trying to project your first year of business are

- Contact financial advisors in the community who work with businesses of your type—accountants and bankers, for example—who might have some insight into what you can expect your first year.

- Try to meet with other members of your profession, either through professional societies, local business clubs, or direct contact with owners of similar companies, and explain that you are looking for guidance and helpful hints about determining the financial expectations of a company such as yours.

- Use the library and the Internet to research your field. You may be able to locate an Internet group of people in the same field as you who can lend advice and insight.

- Draw on your own understanding of the industry or profession. Your company may be new, but you have knowledge of the business. Sometimes a gut feeling based on experience and wisdom provides the best guidance.

Creating a budget in QuickBooks

1. Choose <u>A</u>ctivities, **Set Up Budgets**. The Set Up Budgets window will appear (see Figure 26.1).

FIGURE 26.1

Create a budget in this window by choosing the individual accounts, then designating budgeted amounts for the coming year.

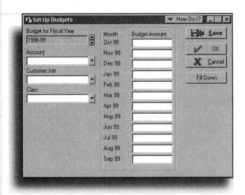

2. Determine the year for which you want to set up a budget. By default, QuickBooks assumes you want to create a budget for the next fiscal year. You can choose a year beyond the next fiscal year, or to view budgets you have created previously, you can choose a prior year and the prior budget information will appear.

3. Choose the account for which you want to enter a budgeted amount. Budgeting in QuickBooks is an account-by-account task. The drop-down arrow in the **Account** field provides you with a complete list of your entire chart of accounts. Typically, you will choose to budget for income and expense accounts only.

4. If applicable, choose either a **Customer:Job** or a **Class** for this budgeted amount.

5. QuickBooks will automatically fill in budget amounts based on an average of your prior year's activity, rounded to the nearest $100. You can accept these amounts and go on to the next account or enter your own budgeted amounts in each monthly block.

6. To enter your own budgeted amounts, in the first block of the Budget Amount column enter the amount you want to budget for the account you have selected.

7. To copy this amount down through the rest of the monthly blocks, click the **Fill Down** button. After you click this button, QuickBooks asks you to specify a percentage or an amount by which you want this amount to increase each month throughout the budgeted year (see Figure 26.2). You can enter **0**, which will provide you with the same budgeted amount for each month of the year, or you can enter a positive or negative number to cause QuickBooks to increase or decrease the number on a monthly basis. If my monthly budgeted amount for a particular account is $1,000, for example, and I enter a 4% increase, the budget will show $1,000 for the first month, $1,040 for the second month, $1,081.60 for the third month, $1,124.86 for the fourth month, and so on.

8. Repeat steps 3-7 for each account in your budget.

FIGURE 26.2

Indicate an amount or percentage by which the budgeted amount will increase or decrease each month.

Changing your budget

Although it is important to revise budgets when changes occur in the economic climate or when unexpected situations occur that affect your plans, it is just as important to keep your budget intact as much as possible. One of the main reasons to have a budget is to compare budgeted performance with actual performance so that you can better understand areas of your business that are not performing as planned.

9. After you have finished entering all your budget information, be sure to click the **Save** button. Your budget will not be saved if you don't click this button!

10. Click **OK** to close the budget window.

You can go back to the budget at any time and revise budget amounts. Choose **Activities**, **Set Up Budgets** to access your budget and make revisions.

Creating Budget Reports

You can choose from several budget reports. You can view the actual budget, see a comparison between the budget and actual performance, prepare budget reports based on your various jobs, or create a budget report for balance sheet accounts.

The Budget Overview Report

Take a look at your finished budget by preparing a Budget Overview report. This report, presented in the form of a profit and loss statement, shows all amounts budgeted for all accounts, with one column for each month of the year.

Print a copy of this handy report at the beginning of the year and keep it close, using it as a reference as you plan your expenditures and record your income.

Preparing the Budget Overview report

1. Choose **Reports**, **Budget Reports**. The Budget side menu will appear.

2. Choose **Budget Overview**. The Budget Overview report will appear.

3. Change the **Dates** if you wish to display a report for a time period other than the current fiscal year (the default report).

4. Choose how you want the **Columns** displayed on the report. By default the report appears with one column for each month. If you prefer to have quarterly, weekly, or some other calculation of budgeted amounts, click the **Columns** indicator and choose from the drop-down list.

The Budget Versus Actual Report

After you have created a budget and have begun entering transactions for the period covered by the budget, you can produce a report that shows you how you are performing in comparison with your plans. The Budget vs. Actual report displays all your income and expense accounts for a selected time period and shows you

- The actual total of transactions in those accounts
- The budgeted amount for the same time period
- The dollar amount over or under budget
- The percent over or under budget

Figure 26.3 shows a sample of the Actual vs. Budget report.

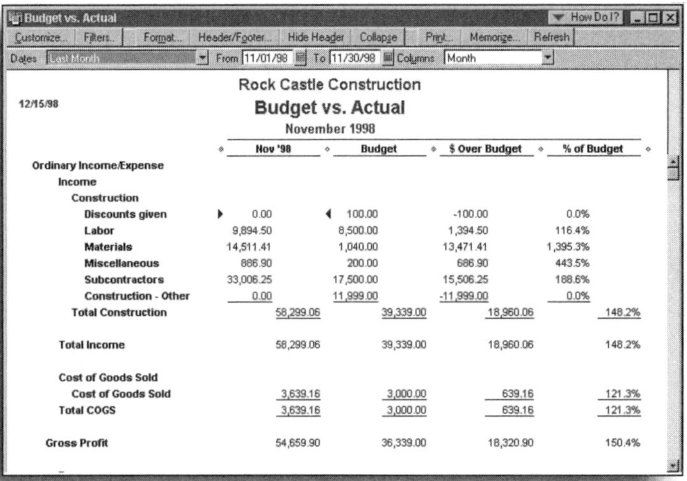

FIGURE 26.3

The Budget vs. Actual report shows you how your company is performing compared to the budget expectations.

Creating a Budget versus Actual report

1. Choose **Reports**, **Budget Reports**. The Budget side menu will appear.

2. Choose **Budget vs. Actual**. The report will appear.

3. Select dates to indicate the time period for which you want to display this report. By default, the report shows each month of your current year, with four columns for each

month, as described in the previous bulleted points. If the dates you choose include a partial month (such as the current month to date), QuickBooks will prorate the monthly budget amounts for the number of days in the month.

4. Alternatively, you can choose a method other than monthly for reporting your budget, by clicking the **Columns** drop-down list and selecting a budget; for example, **by Quarter**, **by Customer:Job**, or **by Class**.

Note that you can also select customizing and filtering options to deviate from the standard report format. You learned about these options in Chapter 21, "QuickBooks' Reports and Graphs."

The Budget by Job Overview Report

If you track income and expenses by jobs, and you have prepared a budget based on anticipated job activity, the Budget by Job reports will be useful to you. The Budget by Job Overview report displays all budgeted amounts, in a profit and loss statement format, with one column for each job.

Preparing the Budget by Job Overview report

1. Choose **Reports**, **Budget Reports**. The Budget side menu will appear.

2. Choose **By Job Overview**. The report will appear.

3. Change the **Dates** if you want to display a report for a time period other than the current fiscal year (the default report).

4. If you prefer to see this report broken out by a particular time period instead of by job, click the **Columns** button and choose from weekly, monthly, quarterly, and several other time periods. You can also choose to display this report **by Class**, if you use class tracking.

The Budget by Job Comparison Report

The Budget by Job Comparison report compares actual job performance to budgeted amounts. Each job occupies four columns: the actual activity, the budgeted amount, the amount over or under budget, and the percentage over or under budget.

Preparing the Budget by Job Comparison report

1. Choose **Reports**, **Budget Reports**. The Budget side menu will appear.

2. Choose **By Job Comparison**. The report will appear.

3. Change the **Dates** if you want to display a report for a time period other than the current fiscal year (the default report).

4. If you prefer to see this report broken out by a particular time period instead of by job, click the **Columns** button and choose from weekly, monthly, quarterly, and several other time periods. You can also choose to display this report **by Class**, if you use class tracking.

The Balance Sheet Overview Budget Report

Many companies don't budget for balance sheet items, only for income and expense items, thinking that they only have control over these revenue-producing accounts. A balance sheet budget can be particularly useful if you plan major asset or liability changes during the year, such as equipment purchases or large loans. Remember, it is your balance sheet that tells you how much your company is worth. Budgeting for changes in assets and liabilities will ultimately tell you how the expected value of your company will change.

The Balance Sheet Overview report shows the amounts that have been budgeted for balance sheet accounts.

Preparing the Balance Sheet Overview Budget report

1. Choose **Reports**, **Budget Reports**. The Budget side menu will appear.

2. Choose **Balance Sheet Overview**. The report will appear.

3. Change the **Dates** if you want to display a report for a time period other than the current fiscal year (the default report).

4. The report shows budgeted amounts by month. If you prefer to view budgeted amounts by some other time period (such as weekly or quarterly), click the **Columns** button and select a different time period.

The Balance Sheet Comparison Budget Report

The Balance Sheet Overview report shows the actual balance sheet amounts for each month of the current year, the amounts that have been budgeted for balance sheet accounts, the amount over or under budget, and the percentage over or under budget.

Preparing the Balance Sheet Comparison Budget report

1. Choose **Reports**, **Budget Reports**. The Budget side menu will appear.

2. Choose **Balance Sheet Comparison**. The report will appear.

3. Change the **Dates** if you want to display a report for a time period other than the current fiscal year (the default report).

4. The report shows budgeted amounts by month. If you prefer to view budgeted amounts by some other time period (such as weekly or quarterly), click the **Columns** button and select a different time period.

Forecasting Your Financial Future with QuickBooks

A sales forecast projects your company's future earnings

A cash receipt forecast projects what portion of your earnings will actually be received, and when

A cash outflow for inventory forecast projects the cost of inventory necessary to meet the sales projection

A cash outflow forecast projects your total company expenditures for a specified time in the future

Use a cash flow forecast to help you anticipate times when cash levels may be low so that you can always plan to have enough on hand to meet your company's needs

No successful business operates in the dark. You never want to get into a position where your company's available cash is not adequate enough to meet required expenditures.

In order to grow, there must be plans for the future and expectations of how those plans will be implemented. Forecasting techniques enable you to meet your short-term needs as well as prepare for the future.

You can use QuickBooks to help you prepare financial forecasts and thus project your business profitability into the years ahead.

Understanding the Types of Forecasting

There are several areas of your business in which forecasting can be useful. Try to envision how knowledge of the future would help you plan for the years ahead as you read through this list:

- *Sales Forecast.* Project future sales for your company, taking into consideration inflation, competition, and the economy as a whole.

- *Cash Receipts Forecast.* An offshoot of the sales forecast, this forecast includes expected receipts from all sources.

- *Cash Outflow for Inventory Forecast.* How much inventory will you need to supply the sales you predict in your sales forecast, and what will it cost?

- *Cash Outflow Forecast.* Starting with the cash outflow for inventory forecast, Cash Flow Forecast projects all other anticipated outflows.

- *Cash Flow Forecast.* Both as a monthly report and a glimpse into the long-range future, predicting your cash flow is a must for determining your ability to meet your business's obligations.

The cash flow forecast is a standard report in QuickBooks. The others are not. The following sections describe how you can create the various forecasting reports, so you can look to the future with some expectation of what to expect from your business.

Utilizing a Sales Forecast

A forecast of your company's sales provides you with a sense of what kind of revenue can be expected in the future. By predicting revenue, you can then determine several important factors, including:

- The quantity of inventory you need to meet the revenue demands
- The excess of revenue over cost of inventory to meet other expenses
- The availability of excess revenue to fund future expansion
- The need for additional sources of revenue

Preparing a Sales Forecast

To prepare a sales forecast, start with your current sales. In addition, you want to look at some other past activity. The farther into the future you want to predict, the deeper into the past you want to explore.

For example, if you are trying to forecast sales for next month, you want to examine last month's sales as well as last year's sales for the same time period.

Preparing a sales report

1. Choose **Reports**, **Custom Report**. The Customize Report window appears (see Figure 27.1).

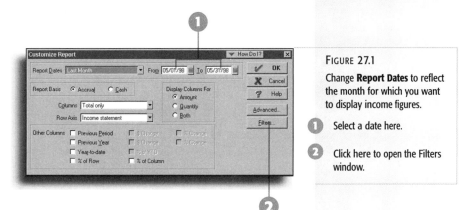

FIGURE 27.1

Change **Report Dates** to reflect the month for which you want to display income figures.

1. Select a date here.

2. Click here to open the Filters window.

2. Change **Report Dates** to **Last Month**. This causes your income report to show the activity for the prior month.

3. Click the **Filters** button. The Report Filters window appears (see Figure 27.2).

FIGURE 27.2

Filter out all accounts except for income by choosing **Account** in the **Filter** column, and then choosing **All ordinary income accounts** in the **Account** field.

4. Set the **Account** filter to **All ordinary income accounts**. This cause your report to show only your company's income accounts.

5. Click **OK** to close each window. The custom report showing your co ny's income for last month appears. Change the heading by clicking **Header/Footer** button at the top of the report and entering a new **Report Title**.

Printing a Sales Report

You can print a hard copy of this report by clicking the Print button at th of the report. Alternatively, you can transfer this report to a spreadsheet other program by printing the report to a file.

Printing to a file

1. Click the **Print** button, or choose **File**, **Print Report**. The Print Re window appears.

2. Indicate that you want to print to a file by clicking the **File** option but

3. Click the drop-down arrow across from File to display your choices: **ASCII text file**, **Excel/Lotus 123 spreadsheet**, or **Tab delimited f** (see Figure 27.3). Make a choice from among these three, depending the program in which you open this file. If you're not certain which choose, see the sidenote "Printing to a File."

4. Click **OK** to save your report to a file.

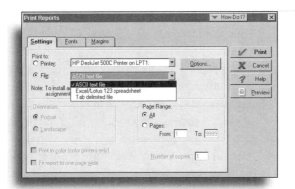

FIGURE 27.3
Choose the type of file to which you want to print.

You can change the appearance of the report in another program and create a new column for projected income for the future period for which you are forecasting. Open the program in which you want to view the report, and open the report.

If you would like to examine a report of sales for another period (such as last year's sales for the month you are forecasting), follow the same steps, indicating a time period different from **Last Month**.

Preparing Forecasts

After you have gathered information from which you can make a forecast, consider trends of your business, the business environment as a whole, and economic conditions that may affect your sales, when preparing a forecast of future sales.

Cash Receipts Forecast

A cash receipts forecast is somewhat different from a sales forecast, unless your business operates on a *cash basis*. A cash basis business is one in which all revenue is reported as income only when it is received, and all expenses are reported only when the bills are actually paid. A retail store, where income is recorded as it is received in the cash register, is an example of a cash basis business.

Printing to a file

QuickBooks provides three types of files to which you can print. Use these descriptions for guidance, but you may find you need to experiment with your own software to see which choice is best for you.

- *ASCII text file*. Use this type of file if you plan to open your report in a word processing program. Spaces appear between the columns when you open the file, so you may have to work with the appearance to make it look the way you want it to.

- *Excel/Lotus 123 spreadsheet*. Use this type of file if you plan to open your report in a spreadsheet program. When I open this type of file in Excel, I receive a message that this is a delimited file, meaning a character takes the place of tabs. In this case, the character is a comma. You should see a window in which you can indicate the delimiting character, then the program separates the information into columns, breaking it at the delimiting character. In other words, for every comma, a new column starts.

- *Tab delimited file*. This type of file can be opened in either a spreadsheet program or a word processing program. Tab characters appear between the columns of text.

The alternative is an *accrual basis* business, one in which revenue is reported when it is earned and expenses when they are incurred, regardless of the actual dates on which money is received or payments are made. When revenue is earned, an accounts receivable is recorded. The accounts receivable is reduced on the day that cash is actually received, but the income was reported back on the day when it was originally earned. Expenses are recorded when you receive a bill and an accounts payable is recorded. When the bill is actually paid, the accounts payable is reduced, but the expense was reported on the day when the bill was originally received.

Many small businesses operate on a cash basis, simply because it is easier and involves fewer steps. Taxable corporations and many S corporations and partnerships use accrual basis accounting because it is considered a truer representation of a business's financial position.

If yours is a cash basis business, you don't need to read about a cash receipts forecast, because your sales forecast accomplishes the same thing. For an accrual basis business, a cash receipts forecast provides a projection of when cash is actually received.

For example, your business may earn money evenly throughout the year, but perhaps it only sends bills to customers on a quarterly basis. Cash receipts, therefore, tend to bunch up around the months when bills are received by customers, and generally dwindle as the quarter cycle comes to an end.

Creating a cash receipts report in QuickBooks, if yours is an accrual basis business, is a bit tricky, but can be done. Here's one way to create a cash receipts report. This one is for the prior month, but you can choose any time period that helps with your forecasting.

Creating a previous month cash receipts report

1. Choose **Reports**, **Custom Report**. The Custom Report window appears.
2. Select **Last Month** for the **Report Dates**. This causes your report to show activity only for last month.
3. Select **Cash** for the report basis.

4. Click the **Filters** button. The Report Filters window appears.

5. With **Account** selected as the first filter, click the arrow in the **Account** field to the right of the **Filter** list, and choose **Selected Accounts**. A window appears showing all your company's accounts. Click each bank account (**Checking**, **Payroll**, and **Savings**, for example) and a check mark appears next to the account name. Click **OK** when you have selected all bank accounts.

6. Click **Amount** in the **Filter** list. In the **Amount** field, which appears to the right of the **Filter** list, indicate that amounts should be greater than zero (see Figure 27.4). This ensures that only deposits to your bank accounts are included in this report.

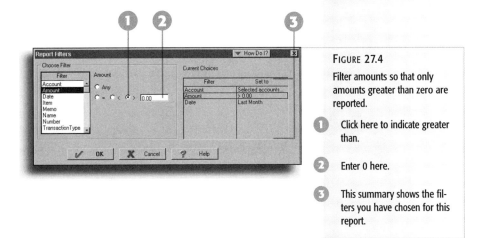

FIGURE 27.4

Filter amounts so that only amounts greater than zero are reported.

① Click here to indicate greater than.

② Enter 0 here.

③ This summary shows the filters you have chosen for this report.

7. Click **OK** to close the Report Filters window, and **OK** to close the Customize Report window. Your custom report appears onscreen.

You can choose to print a hard copy of this report, or print it to a file and open it in another program, as discussed in the previous section.

When determining a forecast for future cash receipts, consider factors such as your company's collection pattern for receiving payments from customers, your sales forecast (which you determined earlier), prior payment record of the customers who currently owe you money, time of the year, and any other factors that might influence the timing of payments.

You may find it useful to print out a copy of your current accounts receivable report (choose **Reports**, **A/R Reports**, **Customer Balance Detail**)—or any other report that would be helpful—when projecting future cash receipts.

Cash Outflow for Inventory Forecast

If your business is a service business, such as a law firm or a consulting business, you may have only very little or no inventory. The cash outflow for inventory forecast may be completely inapplicable in helping you determine the future performance of your business.

If, however, you do maintain an inventory, this forecast will be useful to you in helping determine what is probably the single largest expense item of your business.

The best way to determine a forecast for the cost of inventory is to start with the sales forecast that you determined in the section "Preparing a Sales Forcast." In order to meet the sales you have predicted, you need to produce or acquire a corresponding amount of inventory to fulfill those projected sales obligations.

Using your sales figures and cost of inventory figures for prior time periods, express your cost of goods sold as a percentage of your sales. Then use this percentage as a starting point for projecting future inventory costs.

Keep in mind fluctuations in the marketplace for the inventory or parts that you must purchase. Also consider the cost and quantity of goods you have on hand.

Cash Outflow Forecast

How much does your business spend? How much can you expect your business to spend in the future? Knowing how much you can expect to spend helps you determine whether or not the projected income and cash receipts will be enough to meet those expenditures. Determining this information early can help you plan and make adjustments, if necessary, in your business performance.

Cash outflow includes payments for all business-related purposes, including cost of inventory (as projected earlier), cost of maintaining the business (utilities, rent, repairs, and so on), payroll, expenditures for loan payments, and tax payments. Also consider anticipated purchases of equipment and other large payments that occur infrequently.

Prepare the QuickBooks report that helps you calculate a cash outflow forecast in exactly the same way you prepared the report for your cash receipts forecast, with one exception. When filtering the Amount information from your bank account, click the "less than" button ("<")—the second button rather than the third button (see Figure 27.4 where the third button has been selected). Leave the amount at zero.

Changing from "**greater than zero**" to "**less than zero**" results in a report that displays all cash outlays from your bank account(s) for the selected period, rather than all cash deposits.

From there, you can print the report or open it in another program, and make your cash outflow forecast using these amounts as a starting point.

Cash Flow Forecast

A cash flow forecast puts all the other reports together into one scenario—a prediction of when your business will receive and disburse cash, and what the cash balances will be at certain points in time.

There are many advantages to creating a cash flow forecast, some of which are itemized here:

- The forecast helps predict whether there will be enough cash throughout the projected period to meet the financial needs of the company.
- The forecast helps you determine how much cash will be available, and how much you may need to borrow in order to realize the plans of the company.
- A cash flow forecast that is well thought out and thorough attracts investors because it creates a favorable impression of your management capabilities.

You've already done all the work necessary to produce this report yourself, and using the reports you have worked up earlier in this chapter, your report will probably be much more accurate than anything QuickBooks can create for you.

However, a cash flow forecast report is included in QuickBooks, one of the standard reports on the **Reports** menu. Keep in mind that no thought goes into the preparation of this standard report—it is based solely on the past performance of your company. Therefore, no outside factors, such as the ones you probably considered when making your own reports, are taken into consideration.

I recommend printing a copy of the QuickBooks cash flow forecast and analyzing it. If your business is steady and totally predictable, this report will probably be a fairly accurate rendition of what you have to expect in the future.

If your business is subject to market trends, changes in the weather, seasonal buying habits, drastic changes in inventory costs, or other variations from any outside sources, this report will be minimally helpful. It may provide you with a steady path to follow, but it won't take into account any obstacles that may fall in your way.

To view and print the cash flow forecast report as produced by QuickBooks, choose **Reports**, **Other Reports**, and **Cash Flow Forecast**. Select any time period for which you want the report

to be prepared. By default, the report projects cash flow on a
weekly basis (see Figure 27.5). If you would prefer to see the
cash flow reported on some other basis (daily, monthly, or
another choice), click the **Customize** button and change the
Reporting Periods to the period that is most useful to you.

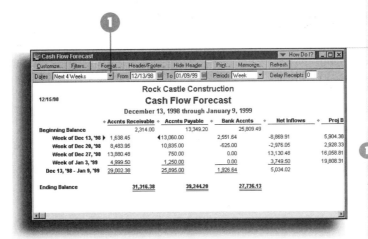

FIGURE 27.5

The QuickBooks standard cash
flow forecast report—an interesting starting point for analyzing the future based on past
transactions.

① Click here to change the time
period of this report.

Click the **Print** button and you can print a hard copy of this
report, or choose to print it to a file whereby you can open it in
another program as discussed earlier in this chapter.

Security

Never underestimate the power of backing up your company files

Protect important information with passwords

Close out your year and protect the prior year's numbers from an inadvertent (or even intentional) change

You don't need to be reminded how sensitive and confidential your financial data is. Not only could your company be crippled by the loss of financial information, but much of this information is not intended for the eyes of the casual observer.

You may not want your competition knowing how your business is doing, and you may not want some of your employees to know either. Also, your customers don't need to know the details of your business performance.

This chapter addresses many ways that you can protect your QuickBooks data and make sensitive information available only to those who have a right to see it.

Backing Up Your Company Files

The first issue of security is making backup copies of your QuickBooks data.

SEE ALSO

➤ *For detailed information about backing up data, see page 8*

There is no excuse for not backing up your company QuickBooks file. The amount of work you put into setting up the file alone is work that you don't want to have to repeat, and the quantity of data you could lose, after you've been using QuickBooks for awhile, can be staggering.

Additionally, I have found that after a company begins using QuickBooks to record all its financial transactions, the amount of paper and documents once stored may be reduced because it can create reports for any time period so easily using QuickBooks. The potential downside of this trend toward a "paperless office" is that a computer crash or the loss of data on a disk can wipe out months and even years of work with no easy way of reconstruction.

Working with Passwords and User Access

If more than one person uses the computer on which your company data is stored, you may want to use passwords to prevent unauthorized access to your data and to restrict users to performing certain activities with your company file.

When you use the passwords feature in QuickBooks, the person who opens QuickBooks is asked to enter a password before the company file ever opens (see Figure 28.1). QuickBooks provides different levels of password protection, so each user of your company file can have access to different areas of the program.

FIGURE **28.1**

Type an assigned password to gain access to company files.

If you choose to activate the password feature in QuickBooks, one person has unlimited access to the entire QuickBooks company file, and this person is known to QuickBooks as the administrator (although, technically, more than one person could know the password and access the program as the administrator). The administrator has the right to change how much of the program to which other users have access, import data from other financial software programs, export data to other software programs, and change information about the company, such as the name and address or the fiscal year. The administrator is also the only person with access to the EasyStep Interview.

Setting Up the Administrator First

After you have set up the administrator, you can establish other users and passwords so that you can control the access that other people have to the file. Only the person designated as the administrator can set up new users and establish how much of the program to which these users have access.

Optional passwords

Using passwords in QuickBooks is entirely optional. If you don't need this level of protection, you can skip this part of the book.

Setting up the administrator

1. Choose **F**ile, **Set up Users and Pass**w**ords**, **Set up Users**. The Set up QuickBooks Administrator dialog box appears (see Figure 28.2).

FIGURE 28.2

Enter the name you plan to use for the administrator, and then enter your choice of a password on each of the password lines.

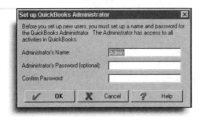

Don't forget your password!

When deciding what to use as your password, try to think of something that is easy for you to remember (but not so easy that others figure it out)—and then remember it! If you've given up all hope of remembering your password, and you are not the administrator, the administrator can assign a new username and rights for you. If you are the administrator, you're out of luck. You can start your company file all over again (ouch!), or call Intuit at 888-320-7276 and they can help you, for a fee. Obviously, the best remedy is to remember your password!

2. QuickBooks supplies a suggested name for your administrator, "Admin," in the Administrator's Name field. You can use this, or enter another name here.

3. Enter the password you want to use for the administrator. You have the option of not using a password at all (in which case anyone could sign on as the administrator), or entering any combination of letters, spaces, and numerals, from 1 to 16 characters. The password is not case sensitive, so it doesn't matter if you type upper or lowercase.

4. Enter your password again on the **Confirm Password** line.

5. Click the **OK** button.

6. A Set Up User List box appears (see Figure 28.3), from which you can choose to change your password, add new users, edit information for existing users, remove users (except the administrator), view the rights issued to any user, and set a closing date. All these options are explained in this chapter. Note that the administrator is the only person with access to this window.

7. Click **Close** when you have finished with this window.

From now on, each time anyone tries to open your company's QuickBooks file, the person accessing the program is asked to log in by entering the correct **U**sername and **P**assword (as depicted earlier in this chapter, in Figure 28.1).

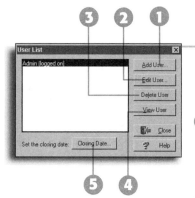

FIGURE 28.3

The administrator can perform a variety of security tasks from the User List window.

1. When you choose this option, you are be asked to identify to which areas of the company file this user has access.

2. Click the name of the user in the list at left, and then click this button to change a password or edit the areas of the company file to which this user is restricted.

3. Click the name of the user you want to delete, and then click this button.

4. Click a user's name at the left, and then take a look at the rights that have been issued to this user.

5. Click here to enter a closing date for this company.

Setting Up Access for Other Users

After your company administrator has been set up, you can begin setting up access for other users of the company's QuickBooks file. Part of the setup process includes determining to which areas of the company file the users should have access (and to which areas they should be prohibited access).

Setting up a new user

1. Choose **File**, **Set up Users and Passwords**, **Set up Users**. The User List appears.

2. Click **Add User**. The Set up user password and access box appears (see Figure 28.4).

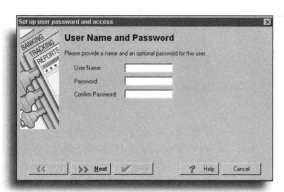

FIGURE 28.4

Enter the name and password for the new user. The password is optional.

3. Enter the username with which this user will log in. The name must be no longer than 29 characters and can include any combination of letters, spaces, and numerals. Case does not matter.

4. Enter a password (optional) for this user. You may want to have the user sit down at the terminal and enter the password, which appears on the screen as asterisks. The password is limited to 16 characters and can include any combination of letters, spaces, and numerals. Case does not matter. Enter the password a second time to confirm.

5. Click **Next** to proceed to the next screen. You are given the choice of assigning access for this user to **All areas** of QuickBooks or **Selected areas**. **All areas** of QuickBooks includes all areas except those specifically mentioned previously that are restricted to just the administrator. Click **Next** to continue. You are asked to confirm this selection, if you choose **All areas**.

6. If you choose **Selected areas** and click **Next**, you are given a chance to designate to which areas the user has access. See the following section regarding access to different areas of QuickBooks before making choices on the screens that follow.

Assigning Access to Areas of QuickBooks

When you set up a new user with selected access to QuickBooks, you are given a choice to issue **Full**, **Selective**, or **No access** to the areas of the company's QuickBooks file. For each area, if you choose **Selective access**, you then must choose either the capability to create transactions only, create and print transactions, or create transactions and print reports. The areas are as follows:

- **Sales and Accounts Receivable**: Provides the right to enter and print information regarding company income to bill customers; to create and edit customer, job; payment method, and ship via lists; and to customize sales forms. This area also includes the capability to create and print reports regarding sales, accounts receivable, and customers.

- **Purchases and Accounts Payable**: Provides the right to enter and print information regarding company purchase orders, bills, credit card charges, to enter payment for bills and sales tax, and to customize sales and purchase forms. Also includes the capability to create and print reports regarding purchases, accounts payable, and vendors.

- **Checking and Credit Cards**: Provides the right to write and void checks for expenses, make deposits, edit credit memos, enter credit card charges, print checks and deposit slips.

- **Inventory**: Provides the right to write and print purchase orders, enter receipts of inventory, adjust inventory totals, edit items on inventory list, enter bills, and create and print inventory, purchase, and vendor reports.

- **Payroll**: Provides the right to write and print paychecks and payroll tax forms, pay payroll taxes, enter year-to-date payroll amounts for employees, edit the employee and payroll lists, create and print payroll reports.

- **Time Tracking**: (If your company uses time tracking in QuickBooks Pro) Provides the right to prepare and print timesheets, enter time, import and export data to the Timer program, create and print timesheets and time reports.

- **Sensitive Accounting Areas**: Provides the right to use online banking, edit the chart of accounts, enter transactions in the register of any asset, liability, or equity account, reconcile accounts, create budgets, make general journal entries, use the Accountant's Review, and print registers.

- **Sensitive Financial Reporting**: Provides the right to create and print reports and graphs for all areas of QuickBooks except inventory and payroll.

- **Changing or Deleting Transactions**: Provides the right to edit and delete transactions in any areas in which the user has rights, as previously described. Includes a special provision to enable the user to edit or delete transactions prior to the closing date.

After choosing the areas of access, you see a screen like the one depicted in Figure 28.5. Click **Prev** to go back to any screen and make a change. Click **Finish** to accept your entries and close the window. Your new user is added to the User List. Click **Close** to close the User List box.

FIGURE 28.5

Look over this screen to make sure you have assigned rights to all appropriate areas for this user. Click Pre_v_ if you need to go to a previous screen to make changes.

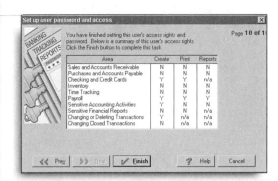

Protection from prying eyes

Protecting sensitive company information doesn't end with employee passwords. Customers can be nosy too. If your computer sits on a counter in your place of business, consider acquiring a glare screen that keeps all but the person directly in front of the monitor from seeing what is being displayed.

Year-End Protection: Closing Your Books

With many accounting programs, you are required to "close the books" as of the last day of each year. After this closing process has been completed, there can be no changes made to transactions prior to the date of closing.

Not so with QuickBooks. The transactions in your QuickBooks file go on and on and can be changed even years after they occurred. Accountants cringe at the idea of their clients being able to go back to the prior year and change the numbers after the year has closed. For better or worse, it can be done, unless you protect the prior year.

The administrator always has the right to go back to a prior year and change something. No other users have that right unless it is assigned.

Any user who has been given full access to the company files has the right to go back to a prior year and change information.

Preventing a user from changing prior-year information

1. Set a closing date by going to the User List.

2. Click the **Closing Date** button.

3. Enter a date.

4. Edit a user's profile (click the username, and then click **Edit User**) and choose the user's post-year-end access to company records on the Changing and Deleting Transactions screen (see Figure 28.6).

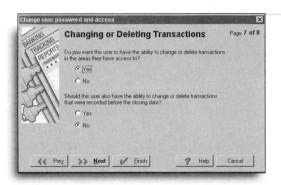

FIGURE 28.6

Click Next to get through each of the Change user password and access screens until you reach this one. Then choose Yes or No in the bottom half of the screen to enable or prevent user access to last year's company records.

Income Taxes

Rules and due dates for corporations are different from those of individuals

Prepare a variety of useful tax reports that aid in preparation of your business income tax return

QuickBooks offers three tax reports of varying detail for use in tax return preparation

Export data directly from QuickBooks to TurboTax if you use that program to prepare your business income tax return

As a user of QuickBooks, you will find that your income tax return preparation time is shortened considerably and made substantially easier. Although QuickBooks doesn't actually prepare income returns for you, you can prepare tax reports that give you all the information you need to prepare the tax returns yourself.

In addition, QuickBooks communicates with TurboTax, Intuit's tax software program, so if you are a TurboTax user, you can export your QuickBooks company file to TurboTax and create a tax return right on your computer screen (see "Tax Software Programs" later in the chapter for instructions on how to communicate with TurboTax).

Preparing Quarterly Estimated Taxes

If your business is a taxable corporation, or if you are the owner of the business and the business income is reported on your personal income tax return, a responsibility exists to estimate and pay quarterly income taxes.

The IRS requires quarterly payments as an alternative to withholding. Penalties are imposed if quarterly tax obligations are not met, so don't discount the importance of these payments, thinking you can catch up at the end of the year.

Depending on whether your business is a corporation, or you are paying taxes individually, the dates that quarterly payments are due and rules for calculating those payments vary.

Estimated Payments for Corporations

If your business is a taxable corporation (as opposed to an S corporation that passes its income through to its shareholders), the business itself is required to make quarterly payments if its income tax for the year is expected to exceed $500.

SEE ALSO

➤ *For a description of various types of corporate and business structures, see page 121*

Each quarterly payment should equal at least 25% of the lesser of 100% of the estimated income tax for the current year or

100% of the tax shown on the corporation's tax return for the preceding year (unless no tax return was filed in the preceding year, or that tax return was for fewer than 12 months).

Use form 8109, available from the IRS, to make payments on or before the following dates:

1st Quarter	April 15
2nd Quarter	June 15
3rd Quarter	September 15
4th Quarter	December 15

If the 15th of the month in which a tax payment is due falls on a Saturday, Sunday, or federal holiday, the tax payment is due on the first following business day.

Estimated Payments for Individuals

Individuals are required to make quarterly estimated payments when the income tax they expect to owe for the year (after any withholding) exceeds $1,000.

Each quarterly payment should equal at least 90% of the tax for the current year or 100% of the tax shown on the prior year's tax return (110% if the taxpayer's adjusted gross income for the previous year exceeds $150,000).

Use Form 1040-EasyStep Interview (available from the IRS), to make payments on or before the following dates:

1st Quarter	April 15
2nd Quarter	June 15
3rd Quarter	September 15
4th Quarter	January 15

If the 15th of the month in which a tax payment is due falls on a Saturday, Sunday, or federal holiday, the tax payment is due on the first following business day.

SEE ALSO

➤ *For information about downloading tax forms directly from the IRS, see page 477*

Assigning Tax Lines

If you plan to use QuickBooks to help create your income tax return, you want to assign tax lines to each of your company's accounts. When you assign tax lines, you enable QuickBooks to print tax reports for you that summarize how all your company's financial activity should appear on your tax return.

SEE ALSO

➤ *For information about setting up new accounts, see page 124 and various sections on setting up different types of new accounts in Chapter 5*

Assigning a tax line to an existing account

1. Choose **Lists**, **Chart of Accounts**. The Chart of Accounts window appears.

2. Click the name of the account to which you want to assign a tax line.

3. Click the **Account** button, and then click **Edit**. The Edit Account window appears.

4. Click the arrow to the right of the Tax Line area (see Figure 29.1). A list of possible tax lines appears. The tax lines that are displayed on this list are a result of the tax return you selected for this business when the business was set up.

Last year's tax return

You will find that it is extremely helpful if you have a copy of your company's prior year tax return by your side while assigning tax lines (or your prior year personal tax return, if the income and expenses of this company flow through to your personal tax return). If this is the first year this company has been in business and there is no tax return from last year to which you can refer, get a blank tax return and use it as a guide.

FIGURE 29.1

Choose a tax line from this pop-up list.

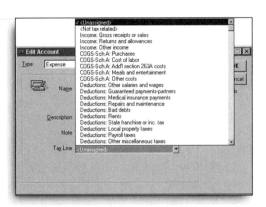

5. Scroll through the list until you find the tax line that is appropriate for this account, click that tax line, and the line

you have chosen appears in the **Tax Line** area of the Edit Account screen.

6. Click **OK** to save the tax line assignment for this account.

Tax Reports

Three income tax reports can be produced with QuickBooks: the Income Tax Preparation Report, the Income Tax Summary Report, and the Income Tax Detail Report. Each of these reports provides you with a different type of information that can be useful in the preparation of your tax return.

Income Tax Preparation Report

The income tax preparation report lists every account and the tax line to which it has been assigned.

If you need to know if and where your company's accounts have been assigned to tax lines, view or print this report and you can see at a glance the tax line location of every account, rather than looking up each account individually.

To view the Income Tax Preparation Report, choose **Reports** from the menu bar at the top of the screen, **List Reports**, **Accounts**, **Income Tax Preparation**. The Income Tax Preparation Report appears (see Figure 29.2).

You can print this report by clicking the Print button at the top of the report.

Income Tax Summary Report

Use the Income Tax Summary Report to gain an overview of your company's taxable income at any point in time. This report is excellent to use as a planning tool for preparing quarterly estimated payments.

All income and expense accounts that have been assigned to tax lines are summarized on this short report. The net income—the amount on which you pay income tax—is shown at the bottom of the report on a somewhat vaguely-described line: **Tax Line Unassigned (balance sheet)**.

FIGURE 29.2

Each of your company's accounts is listed at the left and the tax line (if one has been assigned) appears at the right.

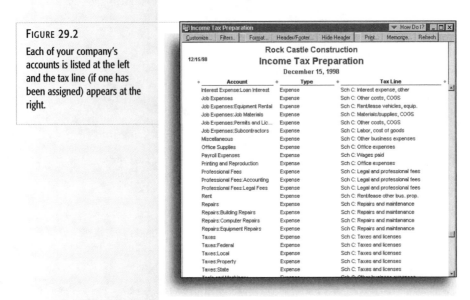

To prepare an Income Tax Summary report, choose **Reports**, **Other Reports**, **Income Tax Summary**. The report appears onscreen (see Figure 29.3), and you can click the Print button at the top of the report if you need a hard copy of this report.

FIGURE 29.3

Double-click any number on this report to see the detail of transactions that add up to the summary number.

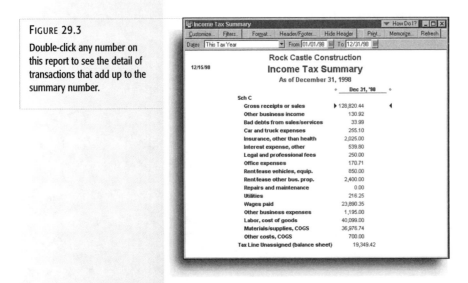

To see the detail of transactions and subaccounts that make up any of the amounts on this report, double click the amount for which you want detail. A report showing all the transactions that make up the number on which you clicked appears.

The dates at the top of the report indicate the time period being covered by this report. If you are interested in an income tax summary for a particular time period (the first three months of the year, for example), change the dates, then click the **Refresh** button to rewrite the report to the new dates.

You can close this report by clicking the "**X**" button in the upper-right corner of the report window.

Income Tax Detail Report

The largest and most thorough of all the tax reports, the Income Tax Detail Report, gives you comprehensive detail of all transactions for the selected time period, listed in order of tax lines.

You should always print a copy of the Income Tax Detail report before preparing an annual income tax return. Prepare to set aside some time to analyze this report, considering all the transactions for the year and where they fall in your tax return.

To create the Income Tax Detail Report, choose **Reports**, **Other Reports**, **Income** **T**ax **Detail**. Print a copy of the report by clicking the Print button at the top of the window.

With the Income Tax Detail Report onscreen (see Figure 29.4), you can double-click any transaction shown on the report and pull up the original document that created the transaction.

The dates at the top of the report indicate the time period being covered by this report. If you want to see an income tax report for a particular time period (for example, the first six months of the year or last year's report), change the dates, and then click the **Refresh** button to rewrite the report to the new dates.

> **The click that refreshes!**
>
> Don't forget to click the **Refresh** button whenever you make a change in the dates of a report. Otherwise, the dates at the top change but the numbers on the report do not!

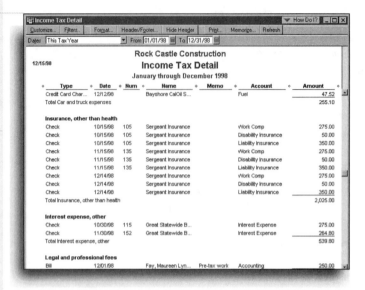

FIGURE 29.4

Double-click any number on this report and you are transported to the original document (for example, invoice, check, bill) where this transaction was created.

Tax Forms

Depending on the type of business that was indicated at the setup, your company files its annual income tax return on one of a variety of tax forms (such as 1120, 1120S, 1040, and so on). For a complete breakdown of various types of business income tax returns, see "Choose a Tax Return" in Chapter 4.

Tax forms are available from a variety of sources. If your company has filed a tax return in the past, you will probably receive a tax return form in the mail. If you don't, or if you can't find the one you received, here is a checklist of various places where you can seek out tax forms and instructions:

- *The IRS.* This may seem like an obvious place to start, but you'd be surprised at how many people are reluctant to set foot in an IRS office. You can, however, reach the IRS by phone at 1-800-TAX-FORM, and you can download tax forms from their Web site on the Internet:

    www.irs.ustreas.gov/prod/forms_pubs/forms.html

- *Public Library.* Generally a better place to look for individual tax forms instead of business tax forms, the library can be a lifesaver if it's the day before the filing deadline and you still don't have any forms.

- *Post Office.* Post offices are notorious hangouts for tax forms.

- *Law Library.* If you live near a law library, you can probably persuade a friendly librarian to lead you to the tax form books and point you in the direction of a copy machine.

- *CPAs and Lawyers.* They're not just for hiring. If you know a friendly CPA or lawyer, you may be able to persuade him or her to bring home a few tax forms for you.

Don't forget to pick up state forms as well. Your state revenue department can supply you with forms, and the preceding sources probably have state forms too. All states are now making tax forms available over the Internet.

SEE ALSO

➢ *For more information on state tax forms, see page 477*

Tax Software Programs

A handful of tax software programs are on the market that can greatly simplify the process of preparing your tax return. Intuit, the maker of QuickBooks, is also the maker of TurboTax. One advantage to using TurboTax for tax return preparation is that you can directly import your QuickBooks data into the TurboTax program.

To send information to TurboTax, you must first assign tax lines to every account that will ultimately provide a number for your tax return.

Start your TurboTax program. As soon as the program begins you are asked if you want to import information from QuickBooks. When you answer positively, you are taken to a screen (see Figure 29.5) on which you can review and revise tax lines (by clicking the **Change Links** button), and then click the **Import** button to perform the transfer of information.

QuickBooks data can be imported into TurboTax, TurboTax for Business, and TurboTax Pro Series, so no matter which version of TurboTax you own, the communication exists with QuickBooks.

FIGURE 29.5

The TaxLink screen appears
when you begin importing
QuickBooks data into
TurboTax.

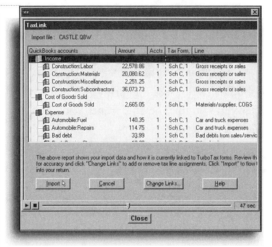

Non-Tax-Related Transactions

Some transactions occur, from time to time, in your business
that have no business on your tax return. Here is a checklist of
typical business transactions that you do not include as income
or deductions on your tax return:

- *Penalties you pay the IRS and state revenue agencies.* If you
  make a late tax payment, the interest portion is deductible,
  but not the penalty.

- *Costs of tickets for traffic violations.* The cost of breaking the
  law is not deductible.

- *Start-up costs of beginning a new business.* The legal fees, corporate filing fees, research costs, market surveys, and other
  expenses you incur that help you get your business rolling,
  can be amortized over a period of five years, but not deducted all in the first year.

- *Charitable contributions.* Unless you are incorporated, charitable contributions belong on a business-owner's Schedule A
  with other itemized deductions, even if the business paid the
  contribution.

- *Lobbying costs.* Even lobbying results in a direct benefit to
  your business, the costs are not deductible.

- *Dues to entertainment facilities.* The cost of specific entertainment events can qualify as a business deduction, but the country club dues won't fly.

- *Appreciation in property.* Assets your company owns may increase in value over the years, but you are not taxed on that increase (at least not until you sell the assets for a profit).

Hiring a Pro

If you are considering hiring a professional to help with your tax return preparation or to advise on tax issues, you should be aware of both the benefits and consequences. This can be a money-saving expenditure, if the professional helps you cut your taxes. It can cost you more in the long run, however, if the "professional" steers you the wrong way. Here are some points to keep in mind when looking for professional help:

- How long has the professional worked in the tax field?

- What is the education and experience of the professional?

- Will the professional provide you with referrals?

- How much experience has the professional had at representing clients before the IRS?

- Has the professional ever been fined or penalized with respect to tax work performed?

- Does this professional plan to be in the same line of business five years from now?

- What is the fee and how is it determined?

- What is the cost to you for representation if your tax return is audited?

Installation of QuickBooks

You need to install QuickBooks on your hard drive to use the program. This appendix gives you the information you need to perform that installation.

Hardware and Software Requirements

QuickBooks installs on most computers without any problem. If you have an older machine, however, or if you are concerned that there might be problems with installation, review the requirements listed in the following sections to make sure you can use this program.

The following hardware items are required for you to properly install QuickBooks version 6.0:

- IBM 486/66 (or higher) or compatible computer. Pentium is recommended.
- 16MB RAM. 32MB is recommended.
- Hard disk with at least 35MB available space for QuickBooks, 45MB available space for QuickBooks Pro. Add an additional 9MB available space if you are installing the QuickBooks Timer.
- CD-ROM drive (however, you can request disks from Intuit if you don't have a CD-ROM drive).

Monitor resolution

You might have to adjust the resolution of your monitor if you find some QuickBooks screens do not fit on the screen. Click the **Start** button at the bottom of your screen, choose **Settings**, **Control Panel**, double-click the Display icon, click on the **Settings** tab, and adjust the desktop resolution.

- 8-bit or 16-bit sound card if you are using the CD-ROM version and want to use the program's sound features.

- A monitor capable of displaying at least 256 colors.

- A printer, if you plan to print reports, forms, lists, or mailing labels.

Obviously, you must own a copy of QuickBooks or QuickBooks Pro. In addition, you need to have Windows 95 or higher, or Windows NT 4.0 or higher with Service Pack 3.

Performing the Installation

Installing QuickBooks

1. Close all programs currently running on your computer.

Installation doesn't begin automatically

If the installation doesn't begin automatically, click the **Start** button, choose **Run**, enter D:\Autorun.exe, and click **OK**, where D: is the CD-ROM drive.

2. If you are installing from the CD-ROM, insert the CD-ROM in your computer's CD-ROM drive. The installation starts automatically, and you see the screen pictured in Figure A.1.

FIGURE A.1

Click on the Install button to install QuickBooks onto your hard drive.

3. Follow the prompts onscreen to proceed to the next screen, agree to the license agreement, and enter the key registration code for your copy of the software. The key registration code appears on an orange sticker on your CD case.

4. In the Choose Destination Location window, verify the correct location of where you want QuickBooks to reside on your hard drive. Then click **Next**.

5. On the Accept Program Group screen, you are asked if you want to add the QuickBooks programs to your **Start** menu. Click **Next** to accept this option and proceed.

6. Look over the choices you've made. If you need to make any changes, click **Back** to return to previous screens. Otherwise, click **Next** to proceed.

7. You will see a message asking if you want to add a QuickBooks shortcut to your screen. Clicking **Yes** adds an icon for your QuickBooks program to your main Windows desktop.

8. Click the **Finish** button and you have completed the QuickBooks installation.

9. You are then asked if you want to upgrade to the Internet Explorer version 4.0. Click **Yes** if you need to add this browser to your computer. If you already have an Internet browser installed, you can use your own Internet browser for connecting to the QuickBooks site.

10. If you choose **Yes**, to install the Internet Explorer, follow the onscreen instructions for installation.

11. If you are installing QuickBooks Pro, you are given an option to install the Timer, a time-tracking program (for more information about this program, see Chapter 25, "QuickBooks and Time Tracking"). If you want to install this program, click **Next** through the three installation screens. Before you use the Timer, you are told that you must restart your computer. Choose whether or not you want to restart at this time and then click **Finish**.

The installation process is completed! When you have finished installing QuickBooks, put your CD-ROM or disks in a safe place.

Installing from Floppy Disks

If you are installing from disks, insert Disk 1 in your computer's disk drive, click on the **Start** button, choose **Control Panel**, and double-click on **Add/Remove Programs**. Click the **Install** button, click **Next**, and you should see the Run Installation Program window as depicted in Figure A.2. If you don't see this window, make sure the disk is seated properly in the disk drive and try again.

FIGURE A.2

Click on Finish, then follow the onscreen prompts to complete the installation of QuickBooks onto your hard drive.

Sharing QuickBooks on a Network

If you use QuickBooks Pro, you have the option of installing the program on a network and having up to five simultaneous users. Without the Pro version of QuickBooks, you can use QuickBooks on a network, but only one person can have access to the company file at a time.

This appendix discusses the installation and use of QuickBooks Pro in a multiuser environment.

Network Requirements

Before installing your software, make sure the following items are in place:

- Windows NT 4.0 or NetWare Network File Server
- Peer-to-Peer File Server using Windows 95 or Windows NT 4.0 with Service Pack 3 file sharing
- A separate copy of the QuickBooks program for each user

Performing the Installation

The QuickBooks program needs to be installed separately on each computer. You must purchase separate QuickBooks programs for each user. You can purchase QuickBooks in a five-pack if you plan to have five users.

SEE ALSO
➤ *For more information on installation of QuickBooks, see page 557*

The company file, which is shared by all users, resides on a shared network directory.

Setting Up Your Users

QuickBooks comes with a New User Setup Wizard that can guide you through the process of making your QuickBooks company file accessible to more than one user. While setting up user accessibility, you can indicate how much access each user is entitled to have. The access options are as follows:

- *Full access.* The user has access to all areas of the company file.

- *Selective access.* The user has access to certain parts of an area of the company file (for example, he may be able to produce reports but cannot write checks).

- *No access.* The user has no access to certain areas of the company file (for example, the payroll person may be the only one who has access to the payroll area).

Each user you set up has a unique username and password. When a user opens the program and identifies himself or herself, only the designated areas of the program are accessible.

To access the New User Setup Wizard, choose **File**, **Set up Users & Passwords**, **Set up Users**. The first user is the administrator ("Admin") (see Figure B.1) and this user sets up the priorities for all other users on the system. Remember that only a maximum of five people can be set up to use the company file at one time.

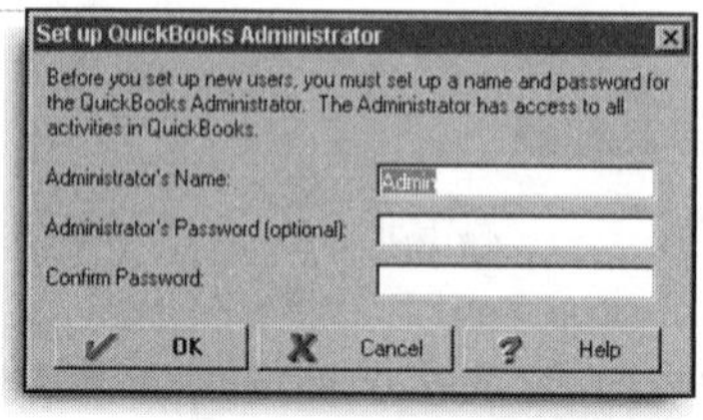

FIGURE B.1

Establish your administrator first and assign a password. Then you can set up more users.

For more information about setting up passwords and giving access to selected parts of the program to other users, see Chapter 28, "Security."

Multi-User and Single-User Mode

To make your QuickBooks program accessible to multiple users, you must place the program in multiuser mode. This is done by choosing **File**, **Switch to multiuser mode** (see Figure B.2). You will receive a message indicating that the file can be used by multiple users.

FIGURE B.2
A menu choice switches you between multi-user and single-user mode.

To go back to single-user mode, choose **File**, **Switch to single-user mode**.

Transferring Data Between QuickBooks and Other Applications

This appendix provides information for Quicken users who would like to transfer their Quicken data to QuickBooks rather than re-entering information in QuickBooks or losing valuable historical information.

This appendix also includes instructions for exporting information from QuickBooks to any spreadsheet, database, or word processing program. You are freed from some of the reporting limitations in QuickBooks when you can take the QuickBooks data and use it in another program.

Using QuickBooks with Quicken

If you have been a Quicken user, you will be pleased to know that QuickBooks communicates directly with Quicken. You can transfer files from Quicken into QuickBooks without having to re-enter information.

When you transfer information from Quicken into QuickBooks, your Quicken files remain intact so you can continue using Quicken while you make the complete transition into QuickBooks.

What version of Quicken do you use?

QuickBooks automatically converts files from Quicken for Windows and later versions of Quicken for DOS. If you're using Quicken for Macintosh or versions 1–4 of Quicken for DOS, you can call Intuit at 1-800-446-8846 to request free software that will enable you to perform the conversion.

In addition, if you've been using Quicken for a combination of personal and business finances, you can move the business portion of the file into QuickBooks and continue using Quicken for your personal finances.

Before you convert from Quicken to QuickBooks, you will want to perform a few tasks to get your Quicken files in order for the transition:

- Clear any to-do's that are pending in your Quicken file.
- Turn off the option for memorizing transactions in your Quicken file. With this option turned off, QuickBooks will convert all your existing memorized transactions.
- Delete any memorized transactions in Quicken that you don't want to convert to QuickBooks.

Converting Quicken files to QuickBooks

1. Close Quicken so the program is not running.

2. Open QuickBooks. From the **File** menu, choose **Convert From Quicken**. An Important Documentation window appears, giving you the option to view detailed information about converting from Quicken. This information is useful, and you should read it before you continue the conversion.

3. Click **OK** when you are ready to proceed with the conversion. The Convert a Quicken File window appears. Select a Quicken file to convert.

4. Click the **Open** button to open the Create a new QuickBooks for Windows file window. Enter the name you want to give to the new QuickBooks file.

5. Click the **Save** button. QuickBooks begins the process of setting up your new data file.

6. You are asked if there is an accounts receivable account in Quicken. If you answer Yes, you are asked to indicate which account is used for accounts receivable.

7. You will be told your data has been converted successfully. Click **OK** to leave this screen. One more screen appears, giving you the option to read industry data. Choose **Yes** if you want to read this material (also available from the Help

menu in the QuickBooks program), or click **No** to open your new QuickBooks file.

Using QuickBooks with Your Favorite Program

You can create reports in QuickBooks and transfer them to your favorite spreadsheet, word processing, or database program. You can also transfer lists and registers.

Transferring information to another program

1. Open the report, list, or register in QuickBooks.

2. From the **File** menu, choose **Print (Report, List, or Register)**. The Print window appears.

3. On the Settings tab, indicate that you want to print to a file.

4. For the type of file, choose **ASCII text file, Excel/Lotus 123 Spreadsheet**, or **Tab delimited file**. Note that the Excel/Lotus 123 Spreadsheet option seems to have been originally created only for Lotus spreadsheets. If you're exporting a file to Excel or Quattro Pro, see the special considerations noted in the next section.

SEE ALSO

➤ *To print a file to another program, see page 413*

5. Choose which pages of the report, list, or register you wish to print (the default is **All pages**).

6. Click the **Print** button, give a name to the file you are creating, and indicate the folder in which it should be stored. Click **OK** when you have entered the file name information. The file is saved and you are returned to the QuickBooks screen.

Exporting QuickBooks data to Quattro Pro

If you plan to export a QuickBooks file to Quattro Pro, save the file as a tab-delimited file. The file will open in Quattro Pro with the information separated properly into columns.

Exporting Data to Excel

Which file type you choose doesn't seem to matter when you're printing to a file you expect to open in Excel. The process in recent versions of Excel is the same as in previous versions.

Exporting QuickBooks data to Excel

1. From the **File** menu, choose **Open**. The Open window appears.

2. Change the Files of type option to **All files**.

3. Find the name of the file you wish to open and click on it. Then click the **Open** button. The Text Import Wizard appears.

4. Click **Next** in the Text Import Wizard and indicate that the file uses a Comma as the delimiter (unless you chose the option of saving the file as a tab-delimited file, in which case the delimiter is a Tab).

5. Click **Next** and then click **Finish**; the file appears onscreen in Excel. You might have to adjust column widths to view all of the data.

If you have an earlier version of Excel, check the program's instructions for opening delimited files, remembering that QuickBooks uses a comma as the delimiter unless you choose the tab-delimited file. A delimiter is a character that takes the place of column breaks. When you identify the delimiter to Excel, Excel separates the information into columns based on the positions of the delimiter character.

State Revenue Agencies

If you are interested in getting set up to collect and pay payroll taxes, sales taxes, or income taxes, you should contact your state revenue department. Below is a list of all state taxing agencies, with phone numbers, addresses, and Internet addresses.

Alabama—334-242-1000
Department of Revenue
Income Tax Forms
P.O. Box 327410
Montgomery, AL 36132-7410
www.ador.state.al.us/

Alaska—907-465-2320
Department of Revenue
State Office Building
P.O. Box 110420
Juneau, AK 99811-0420
www.revenue.state.ak.us

Arizona—602-542-4260
Department of Revenue
Attention: Forms
1600 W. Monroe St.
Phoenix, AZ 85007-2650
www.revenue.state.az.us/

Arkansas—501-682-1100
Department of Finance &
Administration—Revenue Division
P.O. Box 8055
Little Rock, AR 72203
www.state.ar.us/revenue/rev1.html

California—800-852-5711
Franchise Tax Board
Tax Forms Request
P.O. Box 942840
Sacramento, CA 94140-0070
www.ftb.ca.gov

Colorado—303-232-2416
Department of Revenue
1375 Sherman St.
Denver, CO 80261
www.state.co.us

Connecticut—203-297-4753
Department of Revenue Services
State Tax Department
25 Sigourney St.
Hartford, CT 06106
www.state.ct.us/drs/

Delaware—302-577-3300
Department of Finance
Division of Revenue
Delaware State Building
820 N. French St.
Wilmington, DE 19801
www.state.de.us/govern/agencies/revenue/revenue.htm

District of Columbia—202-727-6170
Department of Finance & Revenue
Room 1046
300 Indiana Ave., N.W.
Washington, D.C. 20001
http://www.dccfo.com/taxpmain.html

Florida—904-922-9645
Department of Revenue
Supply Department
168-A Blounstown Highway
Tallahassee, FL 32304
http://sun6.dms.state.fl.us/dor/

Georgia—404-656-4293
Department of Revenue
Income Tax Unit
P.O. Box 38007
Atlanta, GA 30334
www2.state.ga.us/departments/dor

Hawaii—800-222-3229
First Taxation District
830 Punchbowl St.
P.O. Box 259
Honolulu, HI 96809
www.hawaii.gov/icsd/tax/tax.htm

Idaho—208-334-7789
State Tax Commission
P.O. Box 36
Boise, ID 83722
www.idwr.state.id.us/apa/idapa35/taxindex.htm

Illinois—800-356-6302
Department of Revenue
101 W. Jefferson
Springfield, IL 26794
www.revenue.state.il.us

Indiana—317-232-2240
Department of Revenue
100 North Senate Avenue
Room N105
Indianapolis, IN 46204
www.ai.org/dor/

Iowa—515-281-3114
Department of Revenue & Finance
Taxpayer Services Section
P.O. Box 10457
Des Moines, IA 50306
www.state.ia.us/government/drf/index.html

Kansas—913-296-4937
Department of Revenue
Division of Taxation
Taxpayer Assistance Bureau
P.O. Box 12001
Topeka, KS 66612-2001
www.ink.org/public/kdor

Kentucky—502-564-3658
Revenue Cabinet
Property and Mail Service
200 Fair Oaks Lane, Bldg. 2
Frankfort, KY 40602
Revweb@mail.state.ky.us

Louisiana—504-925-7532
Department of Revenue
P.O. Box 201
Baton Rouge, LA 70821
www.rev.state.la.us

Maine—207-624-7894
Bureau of Taxation
Income Tax Section
State Office Bldg., Station 24
Augusta, ME 04332
www.state.me.us/taxation

Maryland—410-974-3951
Comptroller of the Treasury
Revenue Administration
110 Carroll St.
Annapolis, MD 21411
www.comp.state.md.us

Massachusetts—617-887-6367
Department of Revenue
Customer Service Bureau
P.O. Box 7010
Boston, MA 02204
www.magnet.state.ma.us/dor/dorpg.htm

Michigan—800-367-6263
Department of the Treasury
Revenue Administrative Services
The Treasury Building
430 W. Allegan St.
Lansing, MI 48922
http://www.treas.state.mi.us/

Minnesota—800-652-9094
Department of Revenue
Mail Station 4450
St. Paul, MN 55146-4450
www.taxes.state.mn.us

Mississippi—601-354-6247
State Tax Commission
750 South Galatin
Jackson, MS 39204
http://www.treasury.state.ms.us/

Missouri—800-877-6881
Department of Revenue
P.O. Box 3022
Jefferson City, MO 65105-3022
www.state.mo.us/dor/tax

Montana—406-444-2837
Department of Revenue
Income Tax Division
P.O. Box 5805
Helena, MT 59604
www.mt.gov/revenue/rev.htm

Nebraska—800-747-8177
Department of Revenue
P.O. Box 94818
Lincoln, NE 68509-4818
www.nol.org/revenue

Nevada—702-687-4892
Department of Taxation
Capitol Complex
Carson City, NV 89710-0003
www.state.nv.us/taxation/

New Hampshire—603-271-2191
Department of Revenue Administration
61 S. Spring St.
Concord, NH 03301
www.state.nh.us/

New Jersey—609-292-7613
Division of Taxation
CN 269
Trenton, NJ 08646
www.state.nj.us/treasury/taxation/

New Mexico—505-827-0700
Taxation and Revenue Department
P.O. Box 630
Santa Fe, NM 87504-0630
www.state.nm.us/tax

New York—800-462-8100
Department of Taxation & Finance
Taxpayer Service Bureau
W. Averell Harriman Campus
Albany, NY 12227
http://www.tax.state.ny.us/

North Carolina—919-715-0397
Department of Revenue
P.O. Box 25000
Raleigh, NC 27640
http://www.dor.state.nc.us/DOR/

North Dakota—701-328-3017
Office of State Tax Commissioner
State Capitol
600 E. Boulevard Ave.
Bismarck, ND 58505-0599
http://www.state.nd.us/taxdpt/

Ohio—614-433-7750
Department of Taxation
Income Tax Division
P.O. Box 2476
Columbus, OH 43266-0076
http://www.state.oh.us/tax/

Oklahoma—405-521-3108
Tax Commission—
Income Tax Division
2501 Lincoln Blvd.
Oklahoma City, OK 73194
http://www.oktax.state.ok.us/

Oregon—503-378-4988
Department of Revenue
955 Center St., N.E.
Salem, OR 97310
www.dor.state.or.us

Pennsylvania—717-787-8201
Department of Revenue
Strawberry Square
Harrisburg, PA 17128
www.revenue.state.pa.us

Rhode Island—401-277-3934
Division of Taxation
One Capitol Hill
Providence, RI 02908-5800
www.tax.state.ri.us

South Carolina—803-737-5000
Tax Commission
Individual Income Tax Division
P.O. Box 125
Columbia, SC 29214
www.state.sc.us/dor/dor.html

South Dakota—605-773-3311
Department of Revenue
700 Governors Dr.
Pierre, SD 57501
www.state.sd.us/state/executive/revenue/revenue.html

Tennessee—615-741-4465
Department of Revenue
Andrew Jackson State Office Bldg.
500 Deaderick St., 4th Floor
Nashville, TN 37242
www.state.tn.us/revenue

Texas—512-463-4600
Comptroller of Public Accounts
State of Texas
Starr Building
111 West 6th
Austin, TX 78701
www.window.state.tx.us

Utah—801-297-2200
State Tax Commission
210 North 1950 West
Salt Lake City, UT 84134
www.tax.ex.state.ut.us

Vermont—802-828-2515
Department of Taxes
109 State St.
Montpelier, VT 05609
http://www.state.vt.us/tax/

Virginia—804-367-8031
Department of Taxation
Taxpayers Assistance
P.O. Box 1880
Richmond, VA 23282-1880
Attn: Forms Division
www.state.va.us/tax/tax.html

Washington—360-786-6100
Department of Revenue
General Administration Bldg.
P.O. Box 47478
Olympia, WA 98504-7478
www.ga.gov/dor/wador.htm

West Virginia—304-558-3333
State Tax Department
Taxpayer Service Division
P.O. Box 3784
Charleston, WV 25337-3784
http://www.state.wv.us/taxrev/

Wisconsin—608-266-1961
Department of Revenue
Shipping and Mailing Section
P.O. Box 8903
Madison, WI 53708-8903
www.dor.state.wi.us

Wyoming—307-777-7378
The State of Wyoming
Revenue Department
Herschler Building
122 W. 25th
Cheyenne, WY 82002
www.state.wy.us

Glossary

account   A record for maintaining financial information. A separate record, or account, is used for each type of information, such as cash, sales revenue, repairs expense, and so on.

accounts payable   An account that tracks the amounts you owe for items or services you purchase.

accounts receivable   An account that keeps a running balance of the amounts that your customers owe you.

accrual basis   A system of accounting in which revenue is reported when it is earned and expenses are reported when they are incurred, regardless of the actual dates on which money is received or payments are made.

accumulated depreciation   An account comprised of the total of depreciation expense deducted.

aging   The process of tracking due dates of unpaid bills.

amortization schedule   A report that shows the balance of the loan after each payment is made and a breakdown of the interest and principal portion of payments on the loan.

asset   Rights and resources that belong to your company and have future value.

balance sheet   A report showing the value of a business based on assets (items and resources owned), liabilities (amounts owed), and equity (the difference between assets and liabilities).

base pay rate   The rate for working standard hours, as distinct from a rate for overtime or holiday hours.

book value   Add the value of the company's assets (items that the company owns), subtract what the company owes (amounts due to others), and the resulting amount is the *book value* of the company, or equity.

budget   A financial plan with numbers based on goals, past performance, and consideration of future trends, rather than the actual transactions that make up your standard financial statements.

capital   Amounts invested in a company by its owners.

cash basis   Revenue is reported as income only when it is received, and expenses are reported only when the bills are actually paid. A retail store, where income is recorded as it is received in the cash register, is an example of a *cash basis* business.

chart of accounts   A group of categories into which you will categorize your company's income, expenses, debts, and assets so that you can make sense of all your business transactions in the form of professional-looking financial statements.

contra asset   The accumulated depreciation account is a type of asset account, but because its purpose is to offset the value of the assets by amount of the accumulating depreciation, it is referred to as a *contra asset* account.

cost of goods sold   The cost of goods held in inventory and then sold.

credit   Depending on the type of account, a credit is either an increase or a decrease to the balance of the account. Liability, equity, and income accounts are increased with credits. Asset and expense accounts are decreased with credits.

credit memo   A statement that reduces the balance due on a purchase. It is usually a result of a return of merchandise or a defect in merchandise.

customer type   If you sell merchandise, you might have different terms for wholesale, commercial, and retail customers. QuickBooks can account for these as *Customer Types*.

daily activities   QuickBooks activities that should be performed daily, such as entering bills, checks, deposits, sales, and employee time.

debit   Depending on the type of account, a debit is either an increase or a decrease to the balance of the account. Liability, equity, and income accounts are decreased with debits. Asset and expense accounts are increased with debits.

equity   The net worth of the company, or the total assets reduced by the total liabilities.

equity account   In describing different types of accounts, the term *net worth* is often applied to the sum of a company's *equity* accounts. If you add the value of the company's assets (items that the company owns), subtract what the company owes (amounts due to others), the resulting amount is the *book value* of the company, or equity.

estimate   A preliminary listing of the costs and time you anticipate will be associated with a particular job.

expenses   Costs incurred in an attempt to obtain revenue.

expense accounts   Accounts into which you categorize the expenses paid that keep your business running.

fiscal year   One complete 12 month cycle. The 12-month period you use for reporting your business activity on yearly financial statements.

FOB   Free On Board. The phrase applies to the transfer of ownership of merchandise from seller to buyer and is based on where the merchandise is in the shipping process.

general journal entry Adjustments that are made to the balances in your accounts without the use of forms, such as invoices, bills, and checks. A general journal entry must always have two sides—a debit and a credit.

income The excess of revenues over expenses.

income accounts Accounts that reflect the earnings of your company.

inventory The items you sell to earn money in your business. You may sell machine parts, books, or groceries that you purchase somewhere and offer for sale to others. Or you may produce your own inventory, such as clothing that you make, ships that you build, or pottery that you create.

item The QuickBooks way of describing any piece of information that has an amount associated with it and that can appear on a form.

job As a contractor, you may agree to build three different homes. Each home would be considered a job, and QuickBooks can track the income and expenses for each home separately.

job type As a wedding photographer, you might offer a standard and a deluxe picture package. Each service could be identified in QuickBooks as a *Job Type*, under the main *Job* Photography.

liability Obligations that you must satisfy by the disbursement of assets (such as payment of cash) or by the performance of services.

line of credit A type of loan, usually a bank loan, from which you can draw money when needed and pay it back on a predetermined schedule.

maintenance releases Intuit updates QuickBooks from time to time by issuing *maintenance releases* that you can download from its Web site (www. intuit.com). Between full, new versions of its products, Intuit may offer several maintenance releases to fix small problems and offer the latest information to its customers.

merge To transfer all the transactions from your original account into your new account, thus making it appear that there have never been transactions in your original account.

net income The result when total expenses are deducted from total income.

net worth The term applied to the sum of a company's *equity* accounts. If you add the value of the company's assets (items that the company owns)and subtract what the company owes (amounts due to others), the resulting amount is the *book value* of the company, or equity.

parent account In QuickBooks, the major category of an account. You can provide more detail of the components of a parent account by creating subaccounts. The total value of all the subaccounts of one parent make up the total amount in the parent account.

principal The face value of a loan.

profit and loss statement   A statement covering a specific time period and listing income earned for the period and expenses incurred during the period.

service items   A job you perform for which you charge a customer.

start date   The date on which you want to begin tracking information in QuickBooks. When you set up a company in QuickBooks, you will need to enter all transactions that have occurred in the company from the start date to today.

subaccount   In QuickBooks, the subsidiary category of an account. You can provide more detail of the components of a parent account by creating subaccounts. The total value of the subaccounts of one parent make up the total amount in the parent account.

type lists   In a submenu of the Lists menu, you'll find Other Lists. Of particular interest here are the *Type Lists*. Types allow you to further break down your lists into subgroups that make sense for your business.

vendor type   As a restaurateur, perhaps you purchase consultation and marketing services to come up with plans to bring in more customers. You would not group these transactions in the same expense category with ordering paper cups and food inventory. In this case, you'd set up two *Vendor Types*.

weighted average   A method of valuing your inventory on hand. As each new item is added to the total inventory, the cost of the new item is added to the cost of all pieces of the same item on hand to provide a total. When an item is sold, the total cost of all inventory items is divided by the number of pieces on hand to determine an average cost. This cost is reflected at the time of sale as the cost of sales for the item sold.

Index